1001 THINGS EVERYONE SHOULD KNOW ABOUT WORLD WAR II

To Kilroy

BROADWAY BOOKS   NEW YORK

1001 THINGS EVERYONE SHOULD KNOW ABOUT WORLD WAR II

FRANK E. VANDIVER

BROADWAY

A hardcover edition of this book was published in 2002 by Broadway Books.

PRINTED IN THE UNITED STATES OF AMERICA

BROADWAY BOOKS and its logo, a letter B bisected on the diagonal,
are trademarks of Random House, Inc.

Visit our website at www.broadwaybooks.com

First trade paperback edition published October 2003

Book design by Lisa Sloane

The Library of Congress has cataloged the Broadway hardcover edition as follows:
Vandiver, Frank Everson, 1925–
1001 things everyone should know about World War II / by Frank E.
Vandiver.—1st ed.
p.   cm.
Includes index.
1. World War, 1939–1945.   I. Title: One thousand and one things everyone should know about
World War II.   II. Title.
D743 .V36 2002
940.53—dc21
2001043422

ISBN 0-7679-0584-9

1   3   5   7   9   10   8   6   4   2

PREFACE

No selection of 1001 entries could encompass the size, sweep, carnage, cost, heroism, and anguish of World War II. Much more truly a world war than the Great War of 1914–18, the second global conflict raged through Europe, Asia, Africa, the Middle East, and across most oceans. Somewhere between fifty million and seventy million people perished in it or because of it, and the wounded defy statistics. A new style of war emerged, a combination of air-sea-land actions orchestrated into strategies of movement in which logistics played the most vital role. War leaders, civilian and military, garnered such fame as to make them nearly the dominant figures of the twentieth century. All important national leaders have biographical sketches in this book save Franklin D. Roosevelt, who is so central to the war that it is a surrogate sketch in itself. Obviously, the choices are not Everyman's; some readers will be irked by what's in, others by what's out, still others angered by imbalances. I offer not a comprehensive history of World War II but, rather, my personal selection of important things that shaped it or were shaped by it; some things the war caused or modified; some people important to it or in it; some unusual things that happened; people who ran it, suffered it, and survived with an overwhelming awareness of the price of peace.

Two caveats: First, there are varied versions of some of my selections—if mine is not the one you know, remember these are my highly personal choices and probably not the same ones I would make if I did the book again. Second, repetitions in the book stem from a desire to offer a straightforward narrative while permitting subtopics to be followed chronologically.

My gratitude goes to many for help that made the collection and composition possible. Dr. Scott Bowden, University of Texas at Arlington, unscrambled the timing of the launch of Operation Barbarossa with typical courtesy. William B. Schell gave me an important collection of Nazi photographs. Edith Anderson Wakefield, College Station, my incomparable research assistant, did her customary splendid work in suggesting topics, in checking facts and numbers,

in selecting pictures and fashioning captions. Ms. Shannon Maxwell, my administrative assistant at Texas A&M University, suffered through various drafts of the manuscript with customary good humor and skill. Gerald Howard, my splendid editor at Broadway Books and student of World War II, kept me focused on the facts; his splendid assistant, Jay Crosby, pushed things along to deadlines. I am permanently indebted to them both. My thanks to my agent, John Hawkins, who smoothed the way with customary wit and toleration. I am in endless debt to the staff of the Sterling C. Evans Library of Texas A&M University for letting me check out books far too long and for patience beyond the ordinary in facilitating interlibrary loans.

My wife, Renée, lent her artist's eye to picture selection and her acute critical ear to the book during composition, endured long reaches of isolation, and remains my severest critic and dearest friend.

A comprehensive World War II bibliography would require volumes. For brief and stimulating overviews, I recommend the encyclopedic I. C. B. Dear and M. R. D. Foot, editors, *Oxford Companion to World War II* (1995, and unfortunately already out-of-print), and the more popularly written C. L. Sulzberger and Stephen E. Ambrose, *American Heritage New History of World War II* (1997). This work is deeply indebted to the many contributors to the *Oxford Companion* as well as to C. L. Sulzberger, and the editors of American Heritage, *American Heritage Picture History of World War II* (1966), Louis L. Snyder, *Louis L. Snyder's Historical Guide to World War II* (1982), Jonathan Heller, ed., *War and Conflict—Selected Images from the National Archives, 1765–1970* (1990), Vincent J. Esposito, ed., *The West Point Atlas of American Wars, Vol. II, 1900–1953* (1959), and Richard Holmes, *World War II in Photographs* (2000).

Frank E. Vandiver
College Station, Texas
January 2002

CONTENTS

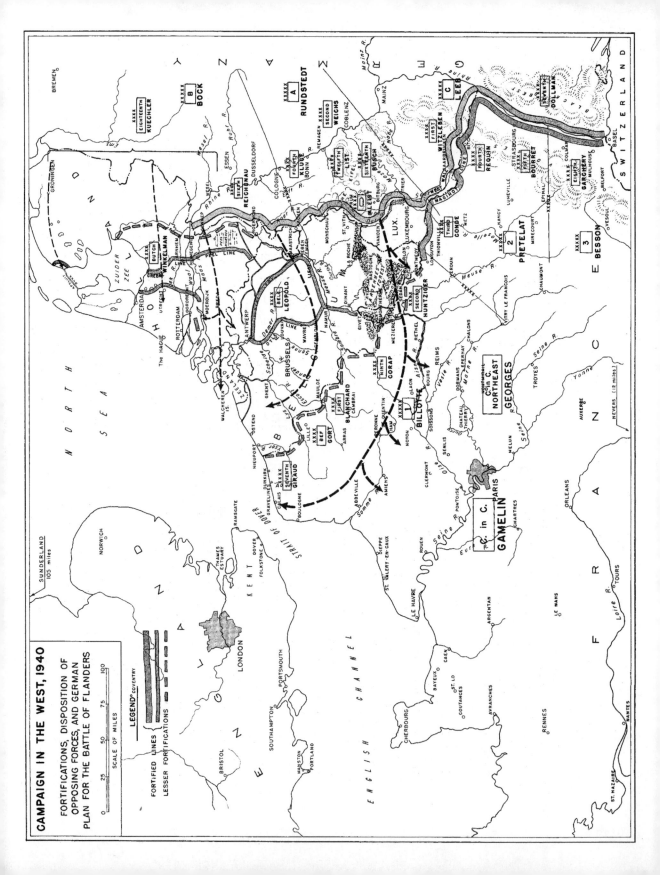

CAMPAIGN IN THE WEST, 1940

FORTIFICATIONS, DISPOSITION OF
OPPOSING FORCES, AND GERMAN
PLAN FOR THE BATTLE OF FLANDERS

1939–40
THE FIRST YEAR
OF THE WAR

"DEADLY PERIL"

—*Haile Selassie I of Ethiopia*

1 Adolf Hitler sent five armies into Poland on September 1, 1939, in a surprise attack. Of Poland's two million first-line troops, only a third were in the field. Poland's cavalry was chopped up by German armor, and its few planes were smashed on the ground in a massive sweep by the Luftwaffe (the German air force). Poland fought bravely, hoping for British and French help, but was stabbed in the back by Russia on September 17, 1939. (Stalin's armies took most of eastern Poland but blocked Germany's route to Galicia's oil and to Romania.) Warsaw held out until September 27—the blitzkrieg had triumphed in one month.

2 Great Britain and France, Poland's pledged allies, still squirmed to negotiate but finally, on September 3, 1939, both declared war on Germany. British prime minister Neville Chamberlain's dream of peace died with the blitzkrieg, but neither he nor Premier Edouard Daladier, France's virtual dictator, had strong public backing for war. Support came with the invasion of Poland.

3 The Allies (they quickly were known by that old term) expected Hitler to turn on them swiftly. He fooled them and the world by keeping a garrison behind the facade of the Siegfried Line (q.v.) facing France's vaunted Maginot Line (q.v.) during the winter of 1939–40. France's sprawling concrete warrens and tank barriers were new engineering marvels devised to prevent the appalling trench warfare of World War I. French troops, convinced of Maginot's impreg-

nability, huddled in confidence despite their failure to connect with Belgian defenses. British soldiers, happy with the winter *Sitzkrieg*, or "phony war," enshrined it in song:

> *We're gonna hang out the washing on the*
> *Siegfried Line,*
> *Have you any washing, Mother dear?*
> *We're gonna hang out the washing on the*
> *Siegfried Line,*
> *'A cos the washing day is here.*
> *Whether the weather may be wet or fine,*
> *We'll just rub along without a care,*
> *We're gonna hang out the washing on the*
> *Siegfried Line,*
> *If the Siegfried Line's still there.*

Hitler correctly gambled that the French would not venture out of their forts and moved to deal with other parts of Europe, while his newly resurgent navy threatened Britain's sea power.

4 While Stalin made peace with Finland in March 1940, ending the "Winter War" that so embarrassed the USSR for two years, Hitler concentrated on securing his flanks and acquiring bounteous strategic supplies. Petroleum products and steel were essentials. Hitler needed access to the Atlantic for petroleum and looked to Sweden for iron ore. **5** German tanks and troops swarmed into Denmark at 5:00 A.M., April 9, 1940, and into Norway late that afternoon—the pretext was "indisputable evidence" that the Allies were about to end Scandinavian neutrality.

British Expeditionary Force (BEF) arriving in France, September 1939.

Finnish ski troops, December 1939. Nicknamed the "White Death," they inflicted heavy casualties (two hundred thousand Red Army dead) during the Finnish-Soviet "Winter War."

6 Norwegian resistance was disorganized but bitter. In Oslo Fjord the Norwegians sank the Nazi armored cruiser *Blücher* using artillery and torpedoes; a thousand men were lost. The pocket battleship (q.v.) *Lützow* (formerly known as *Deutschland*) and light cruiser *Emden* were damaged as well.

7 Half of Norway's population fled northward; King Haakon VII (q.v.) fled to England to create a government in exile.

8 On the afternoon of April 9, the occupiers announced that Maj. Vidkun Quisling (q.v.) was running the country. By day's end, Germany had triumphed.

Norwegian underground opposition began quickly.

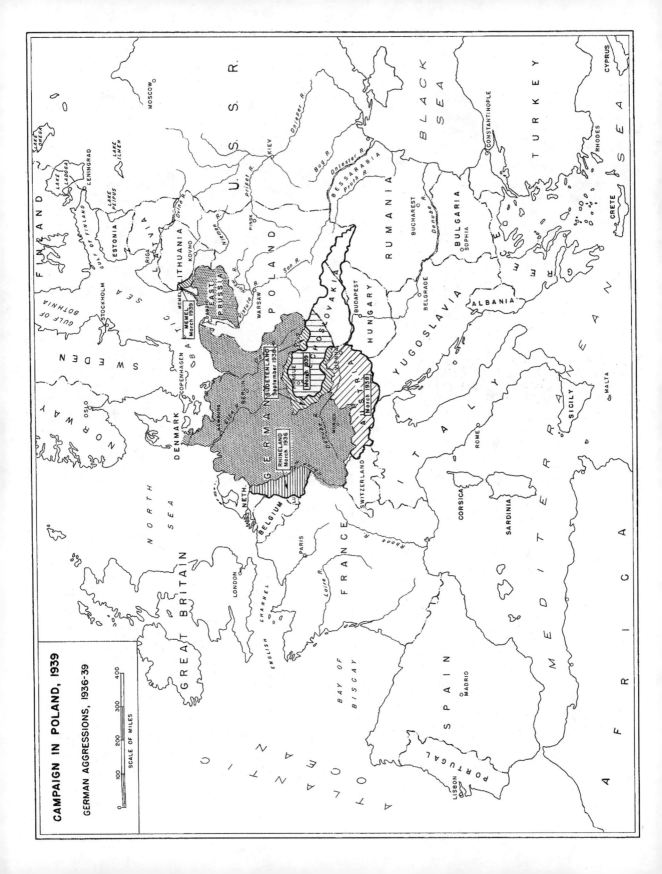

CAMPAIGN IN POLAND, 1939

GERMAN AGGRESSIONS, 1936-39

SCALE OF MILES

0   100   200   300   400

On May 14, 1940, the Luftwaffe dropped one hundred tons of high explosives on Rotterdam, reducing the city center to rubble and horrifying the world (initial casualty estimates were thirty thousand).

9 **Completely surprised by the Scandinavian attacks, Britain and France fumbled a desperate retaliation.** They gathered some thirteen thousand British and French troops for a hasty landing at Namsos and Andalsnes, Norway, in mid-April. These green troops, without proper clothing, artillery, or air cover, were outnumbered, outmaneuvered, and, by early June, beaten and withdrawn. "Britain's finest troops," said Winston Churchill, "have been baffled by the vigor, enterprise, and training of Hitler's young men."

10 **Scarcely pausing to digest his Scandinavian conquests, Hitler pressed on into the Low Countries.** Before dawn on May 10, 1940—one of the Allies' greatest days (Churchill took power), one of the worst for Belgium, Holland, and Luxembourg—Nazi propaganda asserted that German troops were coming to protect the three small nations against a French and British invasion. German invaders arrived before their excuse.

Airborne troops seized bridges, held roads, and largely bypassed Dutch water defenses. Fighting flared fiercely. **11** **A German attempt to capture Queen Wilhelmina (q.v.) and her government stalled at The** Hague's airfields. Furious resistance at Rotterdam drove Hitler to order a brutally spiteful bombing of the city with hideously screaming Stuka dive bombers that killed more than eight hundred and wounded thousands. The world was shocked.

12 **Belgium fell quickly—even supposedly impregnable Fort Eben Emael yielded to an eighty-man German com-**

German ships bringing in troops, Narvik, Norway, April 9, 1940. Within two months the Germans had occupied the whole country.

Belgian refugees, 1940.

mando force in thirty hours. King Leopold III, against advice, surrendered, delayed informing the French and British, exposed their flank, and exiled himself in a castle.

13 **Winston Churchill (q.v.) became England's prime minister on the day Hitler's troops swamped the Low Countries.** Prime Minister Neville Chamberlain (q.v.) resigned under angry parliamentary attack because of blunders like the Norwegian expedition. Clement Attlee (q.v.), Labour's leader, told the House that "we cannot . . . leave our destinies in the hands of failures," and retired Fleet Admiral Sir Roger Keyes pronounced the Norwegian debacle "a shocking story of ineptitude which . . . ought never to have happened." Another member damned Chamberlain with Cromwell's exhortation, "You have sat too long here. . . . In the name of God, go!" Venerable David Lloyd George, rising like a conscience from the past, urged a new PM. "Mr. Churchill," he said in that piping voice, "will not allow himself to be converted into an air-raid shelter to keep the splinters from hitting his colleagues." When Chamberlain resigned on May 10, Churchill formed a coalition government and purposed to make war, while offering only "blood, toil, tears and sweat."

14 **Hitler gave no respite. On May 12 the blitzkrieg swept into France.** Large French and British reinforcements went to help Belgium but were outflanked, and on the sixteenth a strong French line broke at Sedan. Then German armor surprised everyone by driving through the supposedly impassable Ardennes Forest (a strategy formulated by Gen. Erich von Manstein [q.v.]) and threatened to trap a huge Allied force against the Channel coast.

15 **German flanking movements confused Allied responses; the Ardennes surprise virtually broke the French army.**

16 **Amid the wreckage of a terrible defeat, the Allies fashioned an inspiring moment of salvation.** Nothing like it had ever happened. Almost 340,000 isolated British, French, and Belgian troops huddled in northern France near the Strait of Dover entrance at Dunkirk. They should have been disorganized (they

Admiral Sir Bertram Ramsay, who coordinated the Dunkirk evacuation (Dynamo) and served as Allied naval C-in-C for the Normandy landings of June 1944 (Overlord).

were), they should have been demoralized (they were), they should have been killed by the Luftwaffe (many were), they should have surrendered (they did not). They waited in a kind of dolorous patience.

17 Radio calls from the Admiralty summoned all Britons who had propeller-driven boats between thirty and one hundred feet long to gather by the Channel to help evacuate Dunkirk's stranded troops. On May 26, 1940, a military and civilian armada of British, French, Dutch, and Belgian craft swarmed Dunkirk. Boatmen of all hues and jobs manned them (a group celebrated in the novel and movie *Mrs. Miniver* [1940]) with a heroism matched by the patient lines of men they saved. It was a comical, unsightly, unmilitary, undisciplined conglomerate of boats aimed at a glorious, unrehearsed, unbelievable rescue that succeeded beyond any predictions.

A nine-day miracle, some called "the extraction." **18** General von Rundstedt (q.v.) contributed to it by halting his tanks outside the port and leaving Allied extinction to the Luftwaffe, not anticipating Britain's heavily outnumbered Royal Air Force to maintain near control of the air over the beaches.

19 A day after the last Allied soldier left Dunkirk, an air raid hit Paris; two days later, on June 5, 1940, 120 German divisions struck at four vital points in French defenses. General Maxime Weygand (q.v.), newly commanding France's forces, tried to fix a line south of the Somme—but his best troops had been lost in Belgium and his line, along with the Maginot Line, was flanked as German tanks rumbled through the countryside. Retreat became a rout that added to the awful confusion of refugees streaming south from Paris. Strafed by the Luftwaffe, threatened by tanks, demoralized French troops bolted across the Marne. **20** Declaring Paris an open city, a crumbling French government raced to Tours, then Bordeaux, as the army and the country (riddled by enemy agents—the fifth column) disintegrated.

While operation Dynamo successfully evacuated over three hundred and thirty thousand men, heavy equipment and transport had to be sacrificed and some men were captured. This German photo shows a line of British prisoners.

21 Jealous of Hitler's successes, Italian dictator Benito Mussolini (q.v.), without telling Hitler, declared war on "the plutocratic and reactionary democracies" on June 10, 1940, and threw four hundred thousand Italian soldiers into southeastern France on the twenty-first. **22** President Roosevelt aptly described this perfidy: "The hand that held the dagger has struck it into the back of its neighbor."

23 Hoping to brace the French into honoring their pledge of making no separate peace, Churchill on June 12 suggested England and France unite into a new nation. France refused and turned to aging World War I hero Marshal Henri Pétain (q.v.) to head the hapless gov-

Compiègne, France; correspondent William Shirer (center) typing up an account of the Franco-German armistice signed here on June 22, 1940. In the background is the hall in which the French housed the railway carriage used for the World War I armistice ceremony as well as the signing. Taken to Germany, the carriage was destroyed in an air raid.

ernment. Pétain asked for an armistice, and Hitler exacted vengeance as French representatives were forced to capitulate, on June 22, 1940, at Compiègne in the same railroad car used for the signing of the German surrender in 1918.

24 Hitler had won a stupendous victory against the vaunted French army at a small cost. His troops occupied more than half of France, while Italy—agreeing to an armistice on June 24—garnered the few hundred yards taken by an inept invasion.

Pétain headed a government at Vichy and tried fervently to appease Hitler, who let him run his piece of France as a dictatorship for a time.

25 France's defeat confounded Churchill. Vichy held sway over French colonial areas in North Africa and controlled large naval forces. French warships in Portsmouth and Plymouth were quickly seized by the British, while those in North Africa (possibly allied with Italian ships) posed serious threats to Allied control of the Mediterranean. Aware that these threats must be eliminated, Churchill offered various amnesties to French naval commanders in Oran. **26 After refusal by these officers, on July 3, 1940, the prime minister initiated Operation Catapult there—a devastating ten-minute British bombardment and heavy air attack.** As a result, most French ships at Oran were sunk or damaged, to Churchill's rueful satisfaction.

German propaganda fanned latent French anti-British feelings and urged an alliance against "perfidious Albion." French reactions varied from understanding to enmity.

27 England stood alone now and expected a swift battle for survival. Churchill gripped the challenge in his island's standing "as the sole champions now in arms to defend the world cause. . . . We shall do our best to be worthy of that honor." Hitler had always felt a

Photo from the collection of Heinrich Hoffmann (Hitler's personal photographer) showing the Führer in Paris (Eiffel Tower in the background), June 23, 1940.

French fleet at anchor, the port of Mers-el-Kébir, Algeria. On July 3, 1940, when Adm. Marcel Gensoul refused to comply with British demands, Vice Adm. James F. Somerville's Force H opened fire on the port. 1,297 French sailors were killed, and the Vichy government broke off diplomatic relations with Britain.

kind of ambivalence toward Britain—he hated the British but respected them, held them in a kind of hostile awe. Even though he had conquered western Europe, he knew he would have to deal with Britain.

28 Secretly issuing War Directive No. 16 on July 16, 1940, Hitler schemed to eliminate the Home Islands as a base against him, even expected to occupy the whole of England as a result of Operation Sea Lion, the invasion of Britain. Some of his generals warned against the invasion, and Hitler himself may have hoped that visible cross-Channel preparations would tempt the British to start negotiations.

29 On July 19, Hitler addressed the Reichstag in disingenuous terms. "I am not the vanquished seeking favors, but the victor speaking in the name of reason." Peace could come quickly if Britain recognized German conquests in Europe and rights to a lost colonial empire. No answer came. Subsequent German bombing of Britain's coastal airfields and radar (q.v.) sites began the Battle of Britain.

30 *Reichsmarschall* Hermann Göring (q.v.), aviation hero of World War I and close confidant of the Führer, commanded the Luftwaffe and the air blitzkrieg against Britain. He had every reason to feel confident. The odds were with the Germans—they had nearly 600 bombers, more than 700 single-seat fighters, 140 reconnaissance craft, and could use an air fleet from Norway. Against them Britain boasted only 700 fighters. What Göring had not counted on was that the British planes were fast and rugged and supported by radar as well as other scientific surprises.

31 August 1940 brought the heaviest German raids—on the thirteenth nearly 500 bomber and 1,000 fighter sorties rained bombs. On the fifteenth over 1,200 Luftwaffe planes filled English skies. In two weeks more than 600 German planes went down against only 260 British. Still, the odds were chilling. Göring guessed by early September that the RAF had lost a quarter of its pilots—he was nearly right. Fortunately, however, he lacked a coherent strategy for success; for instance, the Luftwaffe did not concentrate on vital British radar sites.

32 **Hitler, ever susceptible to goading, fumed over a British air raid on Berlin and retaliated by shifting Göring's target to London on September 7.** For twenty-three days German bombers struck London—terrible fires were started, swaths of buildings vanished, thousands of civilians were killed or wounded, and many people lived their nights in the underground tunnels of the city's extensive "tube" (subway) system. Despite this, they worked on in factories, offices, fought fires, and tended wounded, all in good spirits. And they loved Churchill for walking with them through the rubble and waving his famous "V for victory" sign. Terror bombing of London did not break British morale, and the RAF continued flying and shooting down the Luftwaffe.

Hitler shifted his aim again to bomb other parts of England. **33** **The Coventry raid, November 14, 1940,**

Heinkel He-111 over Wapping, London, on "Black Saturday," September 7, 1940.

was probably the most destructive. It wrecked a good part of Lady Godiva's city, including magnificent fourteenth-century St. Michael's Cathedral, smashed many war industries, killed nearly four hundred people, wounded nearly nine hundred more, and left a terrible bitterness behind.

A disturbing rumor compounded this bitterness. After the war, whispers hinted that four hours before the raid began, Churchill had learned via ULTRA (q.v.) (British Intelligence's secret code-breaking operation) that Coventry would be bombed that night, but permitted only a few people to be notified in order to protect the ULTRA secret. RAF Fighter Command *was* notified, but the electronic countermeasures instituted failed to work (the jammers were incorrectly set); and 449 of the 509 German planes dispatched reached their Coventry target with disastrous results. The myth that Coventry was sacrificed to protect ULTRA persists.

34 **By mid-September, Göring's vaunted Luftwaffe had lost the Battle of Britain.** Hitler postponed Sea Lion indefinitely. It was a more momentous defeat than anyone guessed. Costs were high for both sides.

35 **Enemy bombing from 1940 to 1945 would kill some 30,000 Londoners (more than 13,000 of these deaths occurred in 1940); another 120,000 would be wounded.** Battle of Britain losses for the RAF are estimated at some 800 fighters; German losses are guessed at about 1,300 planes. **36** **Churchill summed it up best: "Never in the field of human conflict was so much owed by so many to so few."**

37 **On September 27, 1940, Germany and Italy expanded their 1939 Pact of Steel to include Japan.** This new Tripartite Pact recognized and confirmed spheres of influence—Japan in Greater East Asia; Germany and Italy in Europe. By extending the Rome-Berlin Axis to include Tokyo, Hitler hoped to keep the United States out of the war. Americans were unimpressed. The Axis members pledged mu-

Photo of Tower Bridge taken during the first mass air raid on London, September 7, 1940. Some two thousand civilians were killed or seriously injured.

London rail station, 1940, troops arriving and children departing. The British government evacuated some four million children and adults from large cities; another two million left privately. The first evacuees left September 1, 1939; the "phony war" ensued; and by early 1940, 80 percent had returned to their homes.

tual aid should one be "attacked by a power at present not involved in the European war or in the Chinese-Japanese conflict." Satellite nations joined the Axis later—Hungary, Romania, Slovakia, Bulgaria, Croatia. Yugoslavia tried to join under stipulations but political upheaval stopped ratification.

38 Increasingly jealous of Hitler's successes and convinced of Britain's imminent defeat, Mussolini attacked British possessions protecting Egypt. British Somaliland fell in August 1940, and in September, Marshal Rodolfo Graziani (q.v.) led a huge Italian and native force from Libya into Egypt. After a short march to Sidi Barrani, just inside Egypt, the invaders stopped for supplies and reinforcements.

39 At this critical moment Churchill made perhaps his most important war decision. As Britain stood exposed, he took a fearsome gamble and dispatched troops from England, India, Australia, and New Zealand to North Africa and sent some RAF bombers against Italian airfields. It was a desperate thing to do and it was right—protecting North Africa—especially the Suez Canal—was vital.

40 In December 1940, Gen. Sir Archibald Wavell (q.v.) unleashed Lt. Gen. Richard O'Connor's British Western Desert Force (36,000 troops) in a counterattack that pushed from Sidi Barrani to El Agheila in two months and took 138,000 prisoners and sprawls of supplies at a cost of only 624 casualties. Wavell's offensive quickly captured Tobruk and Benghazi and, for the nonce, saved Egypt. Wavell hoped to clear Eritrea and Ethiopia but was thwarted by the Churchillian strategy for Greece.

41 Mussolini's embarrassments in Egypt were compounded by his humiliation in Greece. In another try for spoils and glory, Mussolini launched an invasion of Greece from occupied Albania on October 28, 1940—again without telling Hitler. The whole thing went wrong from the start. Poor intelligence, muddled leadership, inferior equipment, and an unexpectedly defiant enemy stalled the Italian advance.

42 Evzones, Greece's highly trained and motivated mountain soldiers, halted the invasion and soon counter-attacked into Albania. They attacked from mountain ridges, plastered valley-bound Italian infantry with outmoded mountain guns, demoralized them in close encounters with knives and teeth—biting wounds were common. By the end of the year, Greeks held a fourth of Albania.

43 Churchill wanted to help the Greeks but did not want another Norway. Dispatching Sir Anthony Eden (q.v.) and Gen. Sir John Dill (q.v.) to the new war zone, he asked them to assess the potential of opening an Allied front on the north side of the Mediterranean—and they reported favorably. Recklessly taking men from Wavell and other embattled areas and scraping together modest air support, Churchill sent in fifty-five thousand men.

Mines were used widely in the Western Desert campaigns. This October 1940 photo shows British soldiers laying antitank mines (one per yard) in a position running toward the Mediterranean.

44 Hitler realized that, like it or not (he did not), he would have to help Mussolini. As he had been planning a Russian invasion for some months, he could not risk the possibility of a strong British threat on his Mediterranean flank.

ACTION AT SEA, 1939–40

45 Despite being a great sprawling conflict of armies and air armadas, World War II was, more than anything else, an ocean war. Unprecedented masses of men and supplies were moved around the globe on merchantmen stalked by warships and submarines and aircraft carriers. And in the long run those merchantmen made the difference. Warships fought blazing battles to keep supply lines open.

46 At the outset Britain appeared to command the seas. Appearances were deceiving. The Royal Navy's tradition-bound, caste-ridden ossification after World War I had maintained a fleet lashed to old tactics and old technology, charged with duties from the Atlantic to the Mediterranean, the Indian Ocean, and the Pacific. As for Germany, Hitler had concentrated on modernizing land and air forces while naval improvements languished into the late 1930s. German naval chief Adm. Erich Raeder (q.v.) expected to have, by 1942, thirteen battleships, four aircraft carriers, and 250 submarines. Raeder abandoned his surface ship program when war came and concentrated on producing submarines. This restriction of force made the French and Italian fleets especially important.

47 That importance led to another British strike in the Mediterranean. Mussolini boasted that an overburdened British fleet could not control *mare nostrum* ("our sea"), and Britain's supply lines from Gibraltar to Malta and on to Suez were continually threatened by the strong and fast Italian fleet based at Taranto on Italy's boot heel. Allied supply routes

had to be protected, and a British flotilla commanded by Adm. Andrew Browne Cunningham (q.v.) skirmished with Italian warships. **48 On Monday evening, November 11, 1940, British ships took position in Taranto Bay.** From the aircraft carrier *Illustrious*, a first raid of twelve Swordfish, the eldest serving British planes, skimmed the water in the dark to launch torpedoes into the huddled Italian ships. A second raid of nine planes followed shortly. These devastating first-of-their-kind torpedo runs set the harbor afire and crippled three battleships, two destroyers, and two other vessels. Cunningham lost two Swordfish and counted one officer killed and three men missing.

Mussolini, man of bombast who saw any defeats as disasters, pulled his remaining fleet to Naples. Britain's supply routes were open.

49 Hitler's navy avoided being completely bottled up when Denmark and Norway were occupied. But even before the war began, three of Hitler's newest vessels cruised the Atlantic—*Admiral Graf Spee*, *Admiral Scheer*, and *Deutschland* (later renamed *Lützow*). **50 These feared "pocket battleships," constructed to evade treaty limits on German tonnage, were speedy (twenty-eight knots), heavily armed (six eleven-inch, eight 5.9-inch guns) and armored, and supposedly able to outrun any ship they could not sink.**

51 *Graf Spee* **did the most damage.** Slipping into the Atlantic about a week before war began, she sailed south and, on September 30, 1939, sank a British ship off Brazil. Suddenly aware of the threat, the Admiralty mustered twenty-three ships to find *Graf Spee* and *Lützow*. Between the end of September and early December, *Graf Spee* sank nine British ships. Captain Hans Langsdorff mystified opponents with his appear-attack-vanish tactics and surprised many by his care for survivors.

52 Langsdorff intended to cripple British trade with South America. In an effort to foil him, Commodore

Pocket battleship *Graf Spee,* scuttled on the orders of her captain, Hans Langsdorff, December 17, 1939, the River Plate, off Montevideo, Uruguay.

Henry Harwood, commanding three cruisers, *Achilles, Ajax, Exeter,* and a few smaller vessels, set a trap off the mouth of the River Plate. When *Graf Spee* appeared on December 13, 1939, Harwood attacked from three directions, temporarily confusing Langsdorff, but soon *Exeter* was out of action, and, though hit several times, *Graf Spee* had the best of the fight. Nevertheless, Langsdorff guessed more enemy ships were on the way and turned into Uruguay's Montevideo harbor and asked for repairs and supplies. Ordered out in two days, Langsdorff reported his plight to Berlin. **53 Hitler personally presided over a meeting that ordered the captain to refuse Uruguayan internment, to try to get to Buenos Aires, and, if necessary, scuttle the ship.**

54 Fooled by furious British radio traffic about shadow fleets coming, Langsdorff on December 17 took *Graf Spee*—watched by thousands—out toward sea and blew her up. After being interned with his crew in Argentina, Langsdorff, wrapped in an Imperial Navy flag, shot himself. Britain rejoiced, Germany sulked.

Churchill called the German captain "a high-class naval person."

Pocket battleships were not through yet. *Admiral Scheer,* on November 5, 1940, sank six merchant ships and the escort of an Allied convoy (the *Jervis Bay*) in the North Atlantic and continued raiding.

55 Submarine warfare began almost before the war. On September 3, 1939, German submarine U-30, Senior Lt. Fritz-Julius Lemp commanding, sank the unarmed British liner *Athenia,* carrying 1,417 passengers bound for Montreal; 112 lives were lost, including 28 Americans. Lemp's excuse was that he thought the ship was armed. Hitler's propaganda chief, Dr. Paul Joseph Goebbels (q.v.), explained the whole thing away by saying that Churchill had ordered a bomb put on the ship to inflame world opinion against Germany!

56 Captain-Lieutenant Günther Prien and the crew of U-47 pulled off the most daring German submarine deed of the war. Early in the morning of October 14, 1939, the U-boat had wormed its way into the great British naval base at Scapa Flow in the Orkney Islands. Several torpedoes missed or misfired, but the 30,000-ton battleship HMS *Royal Oak* finally was hit and sank in fifteen minutes. Confusion and chaos aided U-47's escape. Hitler personally gave Prien the Iron Cross (First Class).

THE UNITED STATES, 1939–40

57 **Franklin Delano Roosevelt set his own style.** He had a deep sense of democracy that brought him, despite an aristocratic New York upbringing, close to the American people. Heartiness helped him, and it showed in folksy radio "fireside chats" that took him into living rooms across America. The things he said helped, strong words to encourage a Depression-battered nation, words about not having to fear anything but "fear itself." And then there were the programs he proposed that rekindled hope in a country drifting from its early promise. His first hundred days in office produced an avalanche of new programs and ideas that struck old-line conservatives as a socialistic reign of terror—but he was doing something. If some of the ideas failed, at least he tried—and a lot of his New Deal innovations did work. So, as his neighborly messages wafted through the land, Americans listened to this calm, sensible man who believed in them. He "chatted" with them on the evening of September 4, 1939, the day after Great Britain and France declared war.

58 **"My fellow Americans and my friends," came the familiar beginning, "tonight my simple duty is to speak to the whole of America."** He went on to talk of the war, of Poland's agony, and of America's devotion to peacemaking. He said, too, that America would be neutral according to law, that a neutrality proclamation was coming, but he was a realist: "I cannot ask that every American remain neutral in thought as well. . . . Even a neutral cannot be asked to close his mind or conscience."

59 **FDR felt that America would get into the war, and his own sympathies were with the Allies.** But he had to play a close game in an election year; he would listen, cajole, and nudge public opinion and hope the Allies could hold out.

60 **Slowly, FDR's program became America's.** Much of what he wanted to do and did stemmed from his close relationship with Prime Minister Churchill. They had begun an open correspondence when Churchill was first lord of the Admiralty, and it had grown in familiarity and friendship. As prime minister, Churchill kept the president informed of Britain's problems and needs, and the president used this information to tweak America's conscience.

61 **Roosevelt got ahead of the country when, in a speech at Charlottesville, Virginia, on June 10, 1940, he spoke of Mussolini's backstabbing and pronounced that America could ill afford to be "a lone island in a world dominated by the philosophy of force."** He promised to "extend to the opponents of force the material resources of this nation." **62** **Isolationists fumed, and lots of them were prominent, their voices loud: Charles A. Lindbergh, Sen. Gerald P. Nye, the rogue priest Father Charles Coughlin, for instance.** Many in Congress shared the idea that foreign wars should remain foreign. So FDR shifted to more devious ways of getting his way; he began doing things without asking permission. **63** **In November 1939 he had signed a Neutrality Act that repealed an arms embargo and allowed "cash and carry" sales to belligerents.** After Dunkirk, Roosevelt ignored that law and began sending old arms and ammunition to Britain—a risky decision he made entirely on his own.

Acutely aware of Hitler's threat, fearful that England might not hold on, Roosevelt pushed hard for American preparedness. **64** **The U.S. Army was pitifully small, its command structure thin but professional.** If

America went to war, the heaviest burden would fall on the army's chief of staff. **65 Carefully considering candidates to fill this spot in September 1939, Roosevelt listened to various advisers (including World War I hero General of the Armies John J. Pershing), and picked Lt. Gen. George Catlett Marshall—surely the best appointment of Roosevelt's career.** Unlike, the two got along remarkably well, and the jaunty, self-confident commander in chief invited the closed, taciturn general's constant candor. **66 Marshall wholeheartedly supported conscription and, in September 1940, Congress allowed the first peacetime draft in American history.**

Churchill's messages stiffened FDR's resolve. **67 In a July 1940 cable, Churchill announced the loss of eleven British destroyers in ten days; Britain needed help.** FDR promptly moved to transfer fifty obsolete destroyers to England—in return for ninety-nine-year leases on bases in the Caribbean and western Atlantic. Even Churchill conceded that this act would have justified a German war declaration.

68 But it was a December 1940 cable from the prime minister that pushed FDR to a historic commitment. It arrived by pouch mail while the president was vacationing in the Caribbean.

London
December 7th, 1940
My Dear Mr. President:
As we reach the end of this year I feel that you expect me to lay before you the prospects for 1941. I do so strongly and confidently because it seems to me that the vast majority of American citizens have recorded their conviction that the safety of the United States as well as the future of our two democracies and the kind of civilisation for which they stand are bound up with the survival and independence of the British Commonwealth of Nations. . . .

69 Churchill wrote of industrial mobilization, of how to meet overwhelming land force with naval power, of the insidious erosion of merchant tonnage by submarines, of **Vichy's threats, of Japan's foreboding thrusts southward in the Pacific.** In the upcoming year, necessity compelled attention to needs: aircraft, increased freight tonnage, to the possibility of "the gift, loan or supply of a large number of American vessels of war, above all destroyers already in the Atlantic."

70 Finally, the prime minister talked about bankruptcy. A nearly empty royal treasury indicated that "the moment approaches when we shall no longer be able to pay cash for shipping and other supplies. . . ." Britain, Churchill promised, was amply willing to bleed for the cause, but it desperately needed aid.

71 FDR grasped what had to be done, but how could he do it? One of the prime minister's phrases gave the answer: "gift, loan or supply." **72 In one of his humorously oblique press conferences, on December 17, 1940, the president said there was no particular news—skeptical chuckles—but he did have a startling opinion. "There is absolutely no doubt in the mind of a very overwhelming number of Americans that the best immediate defense of the United States is the success of Britain in defending herself."** Some people, he said humorously, wanted to give things to Britain, some wanted to lend it money to buy American arms and ships. He offered a middle course. "I am trying to . . . eliminate the dollar sign. That is something brand new in the thoughts of everybody. . . . get rid of the silly, foolish, old dollar sign." **73 Following the surprised laughter, FDR compared his plan to lending a neighbor a hose to fight a house fire—the hose would be returned or replaced.** Robert E. Sherwood, playwright, presidential speechwriter, Roosevelt biographer, put the story in perspective. "I believe . . . that with that neighborly analogy, Roosevelt won the fight for Lend Lease." Hard debates would follow, but most Americans caught the president's meaning, and agreed.

74 Roosevelt defeated battling Republican Wendell Willkie in the 1940 election. It was a tough race for Willkie, who shared most of his opponent's views on the

war. Reelection unshackled the president. He openly railed at Nazism, attacked appeasers, and wrapped his whole yearlong crusade for the Allies in his best fireside chat, on December 29, 1940. **75 "We must be the great arsenal of democracy," he proclaimed, and much had been done to make that happen.** He went on to denounce anyone who would negotiate peace with such fiendish enemies as Hitler and Mussolini. He aimed a special thrust at isolationists—"We cannot escape danger, or the fear of danger, by crawling into bed and pulling the covers over our heads." At the end of that first war year, FDR saw the future, and it was America's to make.

HEADS OF STATE

76 It may be true that some people become what they were. Certainly that's true of Adolf Hitler (1889–1945). He did things of dark genius, challenged the world, and nearly made it his own, won and lost empires, and in the end remained what he had been—failed artist, vagabond rabble-rouser, army corporal with delusions of grandeur.

Hitler's childhood years in Austria, his bad relationship with an overbearing father, Alois Hitler, and his affection for an apparently indulgent mother, Klara, have fascinated prides of psychoanalysts.

There seems scant evidence, though, that young Adolf suffered overmuch; he dropped out of school in September 1900, and his mother let her "moonstruck" son spend his days at the Linz library reading German history and mythology. Steeped in German romanticism, Hitler nursed artistic ambitions. Both ambitions and ego were shattered when he was refused admission to Austria's Academy of Fine Arts; despairing, he blamed "the system" and the rebuff festered.

Vienna itself offered some compensation. Hitler loved its ambience, its Wagnerian music; he became a drifter, eked out pittances drawing postcards and posters, lived finally on an orphan's niggling pension and on a tiny inheritance from his mother's family. It was at this time that the bubbling politics of Austria's capital began to energize the short, puffy-faced, bug-eyed youth, whose dark, drooping lock of hair and short moustache picked him out in anti-Semitic and anticommunist gatherings. A move to Munich in 1913 introduced him to a gay, exciting city, filled with beer halls, women, and politics. **77 Here, too, he succeeded in shiftlessness until, in August 1914, he enlisted in the 16th Bavarian Reserve Regiment and found himself among a class he had always wanted to join—students, young professionals, obvious future leaders.**

78 Good soldier Hitler served at or near the front for four years as a messenger, fought in forty-seven battles, and earned the Iron Cross (First and Second Class), along with the rank of lance corporal. From the awful cauldron of the Western Front, Hitler took lessons in violence and terror and their uses. From the horror of German humiliation, Hitler conjured a vision of Germany redivivus.

A brief period as an army instructor in antileftist courses introduced Corporal Hitler to public speaking, and he had a gift for it. In Munich's beer halls of the twenties Hitler honed his speaking skills into a mesmeric, demagogic style that entranced glory-hungry audiences. He spoke of shame and the weakness of the Fatherland under the Weimar regime; he talked of Germany's destiny of greatness, of revival soon to come. A little fame inflamed Hitler's ambition. He joined the tiny German Workers' Party in 1920, reshaped it into the National Socialist German Workers' Party, made himself its head, and garnered members and greater fame.

79 Expecting momentary collapse of the Weimar government, Hitler led the abortive Munich Beer Hall Putsch, November 8–9, 1923; arrested, he dramatized his trial and made his name across Germany. **80 Comfortably imprisoned in Landsberg fortress for a year, he dictated volume one of his autobiography to Rudolf Hess and others—he wanted to title it** *Four and a Half*

December 2, 1914, photo of Hitler (see inset) in the crowd at the Odeonplatz, Munich.

Years of Struggle against Lies, Stupidity, and Cowardice, but the publisher suggested *Mein Kampf (My Struggle, 1925)*. A harangue against internationalism, socialism, flabby liberalism, and Jews, the book presented a twisted neo-Nietzschean appeal to strength through will. As a blueprint for racial purity, economic autarky, and military power, it sold well in Germany and surprisingly well in general. Various critics dismissed it as a diatribe against the Versailles Treaty, but a few read it as a road map to horror.

Hitler revived his party in 1925—it was widely called the Nazi Party—and consolidated his personal control with brown-shirted storm troopers, intimidation, and brutality. **81 By 1932 the Nazis were the largest party in the Reichstag, and aging president Paul von Hindenburg made Hitler Germany's chancellor in January 1933.** When the Reichstag burned later that year, the Nazis outlawed the Communist Party and

Hitler won dictatorial powers. He controlled Germany, and on Hindenburg's death in 1934 he took the presidency.

82 So began his new order in Europe. In two years he denounced the disarmament clauses of the Versailles Treaty; created new high commands for a quickly expanding army, navy, and air force; took Germany out of the League of Nations; signed a nonaggression pact with much-hated Poland; and, in one of his greatest diplomatic coups, guessed the old Allies too flabby to halt his "bluffkrieg" when he rearmed the Rhineland.

83 Wanting to protect his flanks when he warred with France, he riddled Austria with "tourists" and arranged a coup there in March 1938. Next he sought Czechoslovakia's frontier Sudetenland, a narrow strip of bor-

Der Führer spricht. Hitler speaks.

some scholars defend it yet as buying time to prepare for war. Critics denounce it as a cowardly sellout of an ally and a pusillanimous encouragement to Hitler.

Convinced he had cowed the western Allies, Hitler shored up his eastern flank with another diplomatic coup, the Russo-German Pact of August 1939, and invaded Poland on September 1. To his surprise, Britain and France declared war.

Some of his generals doubted his military wisdom and sneered at his assumption of army command. But swift success in Poland, deft campaigns in Scandinavia, the Low Countries, and France, and Field Marshal Erwin Rommel's (q.v.) successes in North Africa converted the doubters. Although untrained in high command, Hitler had luck—Napoleon looked for it in all his generals—plus a gambler's nerve and apparently flawless intuition.

85 **Benito Amilcare Andrea Mussolini, 1883–1945, was, in some ways, his own caricature.** Born in Dovia in the lower Po Valley on July 29, 1883, the son of a schoolteacher mother and a blacksmith/labor leader father, Mussolini was named after Mexican revolutionary Benito Juarez. A rowdy and indifferent student, Mussolini nonetheless was well educated and became a teacher at eighteen, although he hated both the work and his students. He dodged the draft for two years in Switzerland, where he became a political activist. Back in Italy in 1904, he did his army service, then returned to teaching but found revolutionary rabble-rousing more stimulating, which led to his first jail stint in 1908.

86 **Aware of the power of the press, Mussolini edited several newspapers, especially the Italian Socialist Party's** *Avanti.* More nationalist than his socialist colleagues, Mussolini left the party in 1914 along with the fiercely nationalistic poet Gabriele D'Annunzio, and started his own paper, *Popolo d'Italia.* Called up in 1915, the short, ragged Mussolini served honorably. **87** **Wounded out of service, he returned to his paper and in 1919 began organizing the Fascist Party, for**

der country filled with Germans who, he claimed, needed the Fatherland's protection—and filled, too, with Czechoslovakia's most formidable fortifications.

84 **The Führer risked war but had peace forced upon him by Czechoslovakia's timid allies.** Prime Minister Neville Chamberlain (q.v.) and Premier Edouard Daladier (q.v.) chose appeasement rather than a war their countries were too weak to fight. Their public abasement at Munich, September 30, 1938, revolted many who heard them on the radio and watched them on Movietone News as Hitler, joined by Mussolini, signed an agreement giving him all he had asked. Forgetting his promises, Hitler swallowed the rest of Czechoslovakia in six months.

Was appeasement the right policy? Majorities in France, Britain, even the United States, supported it;

which he devised such neo-Roman symbolism as the fasces, heroic architecture, nearly endless parades, intimidating black-shirted storm troopers, and a monotheistic command chain with himself as *Il Duce* ("the leader"). All these actions were watched closely by an admiring Adolf Hitler.

88 In October 1922, King Victor Emmanuel III asked Mussolini to form a government, and so began an orgy of opera buffa empire building. Charmed with the idea of a Roman revival, *Il Duce* first set his Italian house in order, raised national morale by efficient administration, "made the trains run on time," and cleaned up the country. Then he turned outward to give Rome once more its grand dominion.

89 Looking to assuage old wounds, *Il Duce* invaded Ethiopia in 1935 in reprisal for a humiliating defeat there in 1896—and nearly suffered it again as poorly armed Ethiopian warriors showed the woeful weakness of the "modern" Italian army. But this Ethiopian adventure chilled Italy's relations with the West and drove the Duce closer to Hitler, who had watched with interest the failure of the League of Nations, and of France and Britain to halt the Duce. **90** Mussolini collaborated in the Austrian takeover and in the Munich debacle, earned Hitler's gratitude, and joined him in the Pact of Steel that created the Rome-Berlin Axis in May 1939.

91 Edouard Daladier, 1884–1970, a politician who held various cabinet posts and the premiership several times, is sometimes blamed for France's unpreparedness in 1939. Born in the Vaucluse on June 18, 1884, Daladier's excellent education and wit won him powerful friends who urged him into politics. He took special interest in defense and served as war minister in the 1930s, minister of national defense late in that decade, and as premier twice in the

early 30s and 1938–40. His dilatory rearmament policies weakened his country, and that very weakness led him to the humiliation of signing the Munich Agreement with Hitler (q.v.).

92 Forced out of government in March 1940, Daladier rejected the Vichyites, fled to North Africa, but was returned to France and imprisoned. Turned over to the Germans in 1943, he was liberated May 4, 1945, along with several other important French detainees (including the former prime minister of France, Paul Reynaud, Generals Gamelin and Weygand, and de Gaulle's sister, Mme. Cailliau). Unlike most prewar French leaders, Daladier returned to politics and retained some influence. His *Prison Journal, 1940–1945*, is an important historical source. Daladier died in 1970.

93 Henri Philippe Omer Pétain, marshal of France, 1856–1951. Born in northwestern France and a graduate of St. Cyr military academy, Pétain became a great hero because of his valiant defense of Verdun

Hitler and Mussolini in an open car, Munich, June 1940.

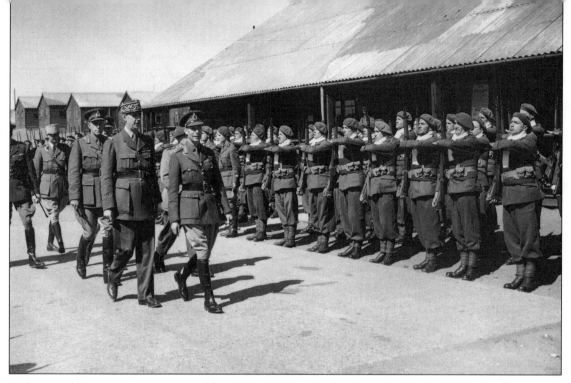

Charles de Gaulle accompanying George VI on an inspection of Free French troops, summer 1940.

in 1916. Added luster came when he competently quelled a major army mutiny in 1917. Made a marshal of France in 1918, he then became a military adviser and diplomat. As France collapsed in 1940, Pétain, at age eighty-four, became premier and sought an armistice with Germany.

94 **As head of state of what was left of France, he had his capital at Vichy.** Accused of collaborating with Hitler, Pétain and his government were hated by many Frenchmen, including de Gaulle. The aged general argued that he had preserved something of France, that the armistice was an act of national salvation. At various times he apparently flirted with the West. He lost most supporters when he permitted thousands of Frenchmen to be sent as laborers to Germany.

95 **Hitler occupied all of France in November 1942, and Pétain was taken to Germany but finally opted to return to France.** After the war he was arrested for treason. Much controversy surrounded the trial of the aged

hero, but he was convicted. Imprisoned, he died in 1951, at the age of ninety-five.

96 **Charles André Joseph Marie de Gaulle, 1890–1970, was a French general whose wartime career proved the admirable power in a man who would not truckle.** Well born in Lille, France, November 22, 1890, de Gaulle was a gifted student at St. Cyr and opted for assignment to the infantry regiment of one of his favorite teachers, Col. Philippe Pétain—their relationship waxed and waned.

97 **De Gaulle expected war and had, more than any other French officer, studied the Great War, from which he deduced that tanks would dominate the next battlefields.** Speaking and writing (*The Philosophy of Command*, 1932; *The Army of the Future*, 1941) heretical ideas about a professional mechanized army damaged his career, and when war came in 1939 he ranked as probably the most obscure of France's *generals de brigade*. The success of the blitzkrieg finally brought him command of the 4th Armored Division, and in a series of counterattacks (sans air support) he forced the only German withdrawals in the Battle of France.

98 Lured briefly into the role of war minister, he fled the country when Pétain took the presidency and sought an armistice. From England on June 18, 1940, he spoke to France by radio. "Moi, le général de Gaulle," he began and then talked emotionally of France's plight and of the need to fight on for honor; France had lost a battle but not the war. Unknown he was when he started; by the end of his remarks he had a thin but hopeful following among the French in England, the colonies, and in France itself.

99 A good many powers ran against him—Pétain had him stripped of French citizenship and condemned to death, many appeasers laughed at the brashness of a nobody, and the United States backed the shoddy Vichy pretenders. He had allies, though, chief among them Winston Churchill, who wanted some way to harness French help at home and in the colonies. In June 1940 the prime minister anointed the irksomely pushy de Gaulle as "chief of the Free French." The general adopted the cross of Lorraine as a national symbol and soon organized the Fighting French National Committee as a kind of provisional government.

At first de Gaulle held sway over a small group in England and some uncounted few in France; the colonial empire remained hesitantly loyal to Vichy. **100** But Free French power slowly swelled as followers posted victories in Gabon and de Gaulle issued the Brazzaville declarations in October 1940, damning the Vichy regime as a toadying puppet of Germany.

101 Troubles were inevitable between Britain and Free France. Churchill, trying to win help from all comers, would use some Vichy French officials in North Africa, some anti-Gaullists among the Free French, and sometimes simply excluded the tall, arrogant, difficult general from important conferences and decisions. De Gaulle protested when he could, met slights with scorn, and worked steadily for recognition as France's real leader. Clumsy Allied efforts to merge de Gaulle's efforts with those of Gen. Henri Honoré Giraud failed, only to show that Gallic emotionalism remained stronger than reason. Exclusion from Allied planning for the North African landings infuriated de Gaulle, and he carried a long grudge.

Agreeing to a contrived alliance with Giraud (who finally faded from prominence if not from mischief), de Gaulle solidified his power, even against the steady dislike of President Roosevelt.

102 Reinforcing his authority, the general founded the French Committee of National Liberation (FCNL) in June 1943, and it functioned effectively as a government in exile amid much Allied trepidation.

103 In what must rank as his beau geste supreme, he transformed FCNL into the Provisional Government of the French Republic—two days before D-day—and, at long last, the United States recognized the FCNL as "qualified to exercise the administration of France."

Haughtily mindful of his role as a male Joan of Arc, de Gaulle demanded to lead the invasion of France in 1944. Harshly refused that honor by Churchill, Roosevelt, and General Eisenhower (q.v.), and irked to hear that the Allies intended to bypass Paris, the general demanded that a French force occupy the capital.

104 He contrived to arrive just behind the French 2nd Armored Division on August 25, 1944. There were quibbles still. "Le Grand Charles" fumed at being left out of the Yalta and Potsdam conferences (Stalin [q.v.] opposed), and argued about postwar arrangements, but did a vital service in disbanding the resistance groups without trouble.

After the war, he organized a new political party, served as president of the Republic, presided over the devolution of the colonies, and, as France grew bored with progress, survived five assassination tries. He wrote several important volumes of memoirs and died at his home in Colombey-les-Deux-Eglises on November 9, 1970.

105 Vidkun Abraham Lauritz Jonsson Quisling, 1887–1945, was a Norwegian army officer who collaborated with Germany. Serving as military attaché in Russia, Quisling worked on disaster relief projects with the great explorer Fridtjof Nansen and with the League of Nations. Resigning as Norway's defense minister in 1933, Quisling formed the feckless National Union party, and, with its failure, he turned to Hitler for help, urging an invasion of Norway. Hitler had little regard for Quisling but did like his idea of invading Norway. The Germans arrived in April 1940 without warning Quisling. Undaunted, he declared himself head of the government—a boast denied by the king—and his attempted coup fizzled in a week. Appointed minister-president under German control in February 1942, he was loathed by Norwegians for collaborating with the Nazis and for sending Jews to Germany; even his puppeteers mocked him.

106 Quisling was executed October 1945—his name becoming a lasting synonym for "traitor."

107 Arthur Neville Chamberlain's strange career shows that some leaders can succeed in self-delusion and fail in disillusion. Born into an important business family in Birmingham, March 18, 1869, Chamberlain became the city's lord mayor and entered Parliament as a Conservative in 1918. As director general of labor recruiting during WWI, he learned much about Britain in war and about the general strength of the empire. Those lessons, he felt, qualified him to understand global problems.

British and French public opinion did not favor war in 1938 or early 1939, and Chamberlain's options were severely limited. **108** Chamberlain saw his journey to Munich in roseate perspective as he waved a copy of the agreement with Hitler before London crowds on September 30, 1938. "I believe it is peace in our time."

Optimistic but concerned about preparedness, Chamberlain finally opened the coffers he so jealously guarded and urged rapid rearmament. A year proved how wrong he had been about Hitler—the worthlessness of whose word could be guessed from *Mein Kampf.* **109** On September 3, 1939, after two ultimatums to Germany went unanswered, Chamberlain's great desire to be one of history's peacemakers collapsed and he took England into war. "This is a sad day for all of us," he told the House of Commons, "and to none is it sadder than to me. Everything that I have worked for, everything that I have ever hoped for, everything that I believed in during my public life, has crashed into ruins." True enough, and the denouement came from hubris and iron conviction of his international acumen. Soviet ambassador Ivan Maisky assessed that acumen in cruel candor: "Insofar as foreign affairs were concerned Chamberlain produced the impression of innocence bordering on idiocy." Churchill characterized Chamberlain as a penny-pinching egotist.

British prime minister Neville Chamberlain arriving at Heston airport, after the Munich Conference, September 1938.

There came a sad trailer to the Chamberlain administration. He hung on until the Norwegian venture failed and then yielded to Winston Churchill (q.v.), the man whose voice had echoed for years from Parliament's back benches calling on England to drop its blinders and see the evil lurking in Hitler's madness.

A loyal follower of Churchill's policies, Chamberlain served in the Cabinet until October and died November 9, 1940, a brokenhearted man.

110 **Winston Leonard Spencer Churchill, 1874–1965, prime minister of Great Britain, was a man whose egregious conceits were exceeded only by his talents.** It is fitting to misquote one of his greatest lines and turn it on him: Never has one man done so much for so many. His life and derring-do fill hundreds of volumes, and he bulks in history as much a symbol as a person. What to say? Rhetorician: by nature; litterateur: by avocation; bon vivant: certainly; raconteur: verily; adventurer: gleefully; statesman: by design; warrior: by blood—and yet there is more, an amalgam of wants and deeds and hopes and fears, of romance and disaster enough to challenge Shakespeare's imagery.

Young Winston was somewhat overawed by the history swamping him from the start. Born at Blenheim Palace, seat of conqueror Marlborough himself, son of famously eccentric Lord Randolph Churchill and the beautiful heiress Jeanette "Jennie" Jerome of New York, young Churchill had a lonely, insecure childhood, but in an inner life of reading, listening, and yearning he forged the heart and strength to sustain his sense of destiny.

111 **Commissioned in the 4th Queen's Own Hussars in 1895, after being graduated from Harrow and Sandhurst, Churchill virtually turned the army to his whims.** When trouble erupted in Cuba, he got himself detached there as a correspondent. His war dispatches were popular, and he returned to England with a writer's modest reputation and a love for Havana cigars.

He starred at polo for his regiment in southern India, but galloped off as soon as he heard of a British expedition against the Pathans on the Northwest Frontier. Two newspapers commissioned him to cover the fighting. Happily he rode to the front and into hand-to-hand combat, an experience that produced the first of his many best-sellers, *The Story of the Malakand Field Force* (1898). Ignited by a flicker of fame, Churchill looked for other fields to bring him more excitement and money. Rumors of trouble in the Sudan, of the great general "Chinese" Gordon besieged in Khartoum, pointed to the place; his mother persuaded the prime minister to arrange her son's transfer to Lord Kitchener's army marching to save Gordon.

A great canvas of war spread before him now: rafts of dhows, feluccas, transports, gunboats; huge dumps of munitions, rations, fodder; sprawling corrals of horses, camels; vast cannon parks; rank on rank of khaki-clad "Tommies" in pith helmets, thousands of native levies, laborers, all toiling along the railroad that hugged the Nile south from Cairo. As he looked on and felt the massive energy, he grasped the importance of the Anglo-Egyptian desert, the Nile, and the need to control the Suez Canal.

Kitchener's army arrived too late to save Gordon from the hordes of the Khalifa, who proclaimed himself the long awaited Mahdi. Kitchener brought the Mahdi's huge army of dervishes to battle at Omdurman on September 2, 1898, and Churchill found himself with the 21st Lancers in one of the last great cavalry charges. It was a close fight, and Churchill's account in *The River War* (1899) won a wide audience.

Back in England, riding the crest of the book's popularity, Churchill resigned from the army and flung himself with gusto into Conservative politics, standing for Parliament from Oldham, a largely Liberal district. Defeated, not daunted, he turned to the Boer War in South Africa. The *Morning Post* hired him to report from there and he happily sailed to one of his defining adventures. Captured by the Boers, he climbed a prison wall, escaped, and became something of a world hero. Oldham now sent him to Parliament.

Churchill made a good parliamentary reputation which he nearly ruined by joining the Liberal Party in 1903, but was reelected under that banner in 1906 and soon began a steady move to power. **112 As First Lord of the Admiralty in 1911, he reorganized the ossified naval hierarchy, modernized the Royal Navy, pushed antisubmarine warfare, and instituted a fleet air arm.** He had watched the growth of German military might and expected war.

When war came in 1914 the fleet was ready, but Churchill yearned to get into action himself. Ignoring his ministerial duties, he ineptly dabbled in personal command. Aware of arguments between "Western Front" advocates and those who sought softer places to hit the Central Powers, Churchill, in 1915, conceived the disastrous Dardanelles-Gallipoli campaign.

Out of the government, nearly the scapegoat for Gallipoli, Churchill went to the Western Front in November 1915; finally in January 1916, Lieutenant Colonel Churchill took charge of the 6th Battalion, Royal Scots Fusiliers. In his element, he proved a fearless, effective, and well-liked commander. **113 He returned home in May 1916, and in July 1917, Prime Minister David Lloyd George made the mercurial Churchill minister of munitions. Always innovative, Churchill had supported tank development and now increased their production; he visited battlefields often to judge arms and munitions, and alleviated the serious Allied shell shortage.** Again colonial secretary in 1921, he lost his parliamentary seat in 1922, but was returned to Parliament in 1924 as a Conservative and became chancellor of the exchequer. With the Conservatives out in 1929, Churchill lost that office but remained in the House. Occupied with writing, he published his four-volume history of the Great War, *The World Crisis* (1923–29) and from 1933 to 1938 he wrote a monumental biography of his ancestor, *Marlborough, His Life and Times.*

114 None of these massive efforts distracted Churchill from world events, and he watched Hitler in ever-rising alarm. He sat in the House "like the conscience of England," his cadenced voice warning of German rearmament and of Hitler's evil designs on Europe. But backbench warnings were background noise, and Churchill's calls for more guns and planes branded him a warmonger.

115 When war came, Churchill returned as first lord of the Admiralty with a short word to the fleet: "Winston is back." Still with the defects of his virtues, he threw himself not only into perfecting fleet readiness but again into personal command. Supporting the dismal Norwegian venture, he slipped the blame and assumed Chamberlain's place as prime minister on May 10, 1940, in the fallout following the disaster. Did he have qualms? "I felt as if I were walking with destiny, and that all my past life had been a preparation for this hour and for this trial."

Crisis sharpened Churchill's focus, and first he put his stamp on England. He formed a coalition government, then won a vote of confidence on May 13, 1940, after he told the House candidly that he had "nothing to offer but blood, toil, tears and sweat," and announced that Britain's policy "is to wage war, by sea, land, and air, with all our might and with all the strength that God can give us: to wage war against a monstrous tyranny, never surpassed in the dark, lamentable catalogue of human crime."

Soon the whole anger of Germany rolled to the Channel and hovered over Britain. Churchill spoke again: "Hitler knows that he will have to break us in this island or lose the war. If we can stand up to him all Europe may be free and the life of the world may move forward into broad, sunlit uplands," while failure would bring "the abyss of a new dark age. . . . Let us, therefore, brace ourselves to our duty and so bear ourselves that if the British Commonwealth and Empire lasts for a thousand years men will still say, 'This was their finest hour.' "

116 Working to prepare England for invasion, deploying installations of the new scientific weapon, radar, the prime minister looked ahead and knew in his heart that victory, perhaps even survival, depended on getting the United States into the war. Correspondence with President Roosevelt had continued since late 1939; now Churchill assumed it as tool of war and over a thousand messages were exchanged. Those messages alerted Roosevelt to Britain's determination, exposed its growing financial weakness, and led to spare arms for Dunkirk's survivors, to the fifty destroyer deal, and the Lend-Lease program, which probably insured victory.

Everything seemed worse for the Allies on June 22, 1941, as Hitler invaded Russia and the blitzkrieg rolled over weak opposition in a steel tsunami of success. **117** More certain than ever of what must be done, Churchill achieved one of his greatest diplomatic coups by meeting President Roosevelt at Placentia Bay, off Newfoundland.

118 Enmeshed in the dailiness of war, Churchill often meddled too much in his generals' decisions (the Greek venture is a striking example), often proposing strategies beyond resources, but as a morale builder he was magnificent—not only by speaking but also by trekking the rubble of London and other cities, visiting various theaters of war, always full of enthusiasm, brandishing a hallmark Havana and his two-fingered "V for victory" sign.

119 Japan's attack on Pearl Harbor, December 7, 1941, convinced him of Allied victory. A quick visit to Washington welded a Combined Chiefs of Staff organization that worked well through the war. Though he often disagreed with Roosevelt (he favored a North African invasion before a cross-Channel attack, while FDR was dubious; Churchill worked with the Russians but distrusted them, while Roosevelt felt he could deal with "Uncle Joe" Stalin), often quibbled about resources, and sometimes about commanders, their relationship warmed to friendship

which was rekindled at each of more than a dozen Allied conferences.

Churchill tried to accept gracefully America's growing power that brought it a louder voice in war matters. But he did prevail in his North African strategy, in dominating the Mediterranean, and in invading Sicily and Italy. The prime minister accepted Gen. Dwight D. Eisenhower (q.v.) as Supreme Allied Commander for the big invasion effort in 1944, but fell out with FDR over action once the landings were made. Loyal to his generals, Churchill supported Field Marshal Bernard Law Montgomery's (q.v.) notion to drive a thin but powerful wedge from the Low Countries into Berlin—even though this would violate an agreement with Stalin. Montgomery thought Eisenhower's broad front plan would give German forces too much reaction time and waste men and matériel. FDR supported Eisenhower, so the Allies advanced on a broad front toward the Elbe—and historians still argue about which strategy was right.

120 Churchill seemed at his best in conferences, often reconciling sharply differing views and reducing irks to laughter. Worried about postwar Europe, he sought at the Yalta and Potsdam gatherings to limit Stalin's options, but received scant help from FDR or his successor, Harry Truman. Still, not all of Europe was lost; Britain, France, Russia, and the United States shared governance in Berlin, and a wrecked, bisected Germany still survived.

121 When it was over, Churchill was shuffled off the political stage with some indecency, even before the Potsdam Conference ended. It hurt him, of course, but the British people did not reject him; they were rejecting too many years of hardship and hoping to make things easier. He became prime minister again in 1951 and worried increasingly about what he called the "iron curtain" that Stalin had draped across Central Europe. That worry spurred his staunch efforts to weld the two great Anglo-Saxon nations together for the cause of peace, a peace he had done so much to win.

He died on January 24, 1965, in his well-loved London, the city he had saved.

122 Haakon VII, 1872–1957, king of Norway. Refusing Hitler's demand for surrender of his country, the king continued resistance from Trondheim. Upon the Allied withdrawal from Norway, the king led a government-in-exile from London. Keeping contacts with resistance elements, Haakon, in late 1944, helped in a Russian attack on German positions through Finland.

123 Helena Paulina Maria Wilhelmina, queen of the Netherlands, 1880–1962, actively resisted the German invasion in May 1940. In London she organized a government-in-exile that cooperated with Dutch resistance forces. She addressed a joint session of the U.S. Congress in 1942. The queen abdicated in 1948 in favor of her daughter Juliana.

ALLIED MILITARY LEADERS, 1939–40

124 Andrew Browne Cunningham ("ABC"), British admiral and first sea lord, 1883–1963. Dublin born, January 7, 1883, into a prominent Scottish family, Cunningham attended a Royal Navy preparatory school, and served an eighteen-month sea tour. Voluntary duty with the Naval Brigade in the Boer War launched ABC's career. A destroyer commander from 1911 to 1918, he overawed his men with his superb seamanship and charmed them by displaying a generous spirit and a sailor's mien.

125 Aggressive, action oriented, ABC reached flag rank in 1932 and vice admiral in 1936, put in some London staff planning time, and became commander in chief of the Mediterranean in 1939 as acting full admiral. With Italy in the war, June 10, 1940, and France out a few days later, ABC's tasks were to win over or neutralize French navy units and protect British communications in the Mediterranean. Again he did well, finally crippling the Italian fleet by launching a daring attack at Taranto (q.v.) in November 1940.

126 ABC's depleted and antiquated flotilla did heroic duty supporting Churchill's ill-starred Greek venture. Despite losing two of four battleships, a lone aircraft carrier, five cruisers, and eight destroyers, ABC kept supplies running through Gibraltar to embattled Malta and Tobruk. Superior service took him to the Combined Chiefs of Staff in London, but luck switched him to command the navy in the North African landings, and he supported Allied landings in Sicily and Italy.

After facing in the Mediterranean what one authority says were the "heaviest odds in British naval history," ABC became first sea lord in October 1943, held the post until 1946, and died in London in June 1963—one of the true heroes of the Royal Navy.

127 Harold Rupert Alexander (Alex), British field marshal, 1891–1969, one of the most prominent Allied commanders, was born in London, December 10, 1891, into an aristocratic family. Educated at Harrow and Sandhurst, he joined the Irish Guards, served four years on the Western Front in World War I, later in Poland and Turkey, attended the staff college, fought on India's Northwest Frontier, and became a major general in 1937. **128** He took command of the BEF during the evacuation from Dunkirk, May–June 1940. Promoted to lieutenant general in December, he went to Burma at a critical moment and launched a spoiling counterattack against Japanese forces but finally had to abandon Burma to vastly superior enemy numbers.

After serving briefly as Eisenhower's (q.v.) deputy in North Africa, Alex took over the new Near East Command in Cairo on August 9, 1942. He got along extremely well with General Montgomery (q.v.), newly in charge of the British Eighth Army, and did much to organize the important victory at El

Alamein in November; Alex headed the main British advance westward and again became Eisenhower's deputy through the end of the Tunisian campaign. Alex also led the Fifteenth Army Group in Sicily and Italy.

129 **Promoted to field marshal after Rome fell, he was appointed Supreme Allied Commander, Mediterranean, and did outstandingly well in this role.**

As the last and one of the most popular governors-general of Canada, he served from 1946 to 1952. The First Earl of Tunis died near Windsor on June 16, 1969.

130 **John Greer Dill, British field marshal, 1881–1944, an outstanding strategist, was commissioned from Sandhurst and served in the Boer War and in the Middle East.** Promoted to full general in 1937, Sir John commanded a corps in France, but was called to be vice chief of the Imperial General Staff in April 1940, succeeding to the chief's job in May; Dill became a field marshal in November 1941. Overstressed by early disasters and from working with the indefatigable Churchill (q.v.), Dill was posted to Washington as senior British military representative on the Combined Chiefs of Staff. **131** **Immensely popular, Dill was cherished by FDR and George Marshall as a trusted confidant.**

Sir John's strategic advice was eagerly sought for all Allied operations. He became ill in 1944 but stuck to his post. **132** **When he died in November 1944, General Marshall arranged for him to be the first foreigner buried in Arlington Cemetery.**

133 **John Standish Surtees Prendergast Vereker Gort, 1886–1946, British field marshal, who led the British Expeditionary Force to France in September 1939.** Son of an Irish peer, Lord Gort joined the Grenadier Guards in 1905. He commanded the 1st and 4th Battalions of the Guards in 1917–18, won the Victoria Cross, the Military Cross, and two Distinguished Service Crosses, became commandant at Camberley, and was

jumped over several senior officers to become chief of the Imperial General Staff in 1937.

When war came, Gort was made commander in chief of the BEF. Regarded by some as unimaginative and uninspiring, Gort's steadiness and tactical sense saved the BEF when its flanks were exposed by collapsing Belgian and French armies. Directing a skillful delaying action, he led his force, along with many Allied troops, to Dunkirk. Turning over command to General Alexander (q.v.), Gort was evacuated to London on May 31, 1940.

Service as inspector general of the forces for training in 1940–41 was followed by assignment as governor of Gibraltar. **134** **Gort, as governor-general and commander in chief, Malta, 1942–44, did heroic duty holding that embattled island and was promoted to field marshal in 1943.** He later served in the Middle Eastern theater. Lord Gort died in London.

135 **Edward Smigly ("Lightning")-Rydz, 1886–1943(?), Polish commander in chief, is sometimes blamed for his country's ill-advised reliance on cavalry in 1939.** Escaping to Romania, he returned to fight with the Polish resistance and probably was killed in 1943. A controversy arose about his grave; Poles are alleged to have hidden it from the Germans in order to save a hero's body.

136 **Archibald Percival Wavell, 1883–1950, was an important British general.** The son and grandson of generals, Wavell did the expected and was graduated at the head of his Sandhurst class in 1901 and commissioned into the Black Watch. A gifted writer, Wavell achieved the highest marks in the staff college and served on the Western Front in World War I. Losing his left eye at Ypres, he won the Military Cross, did a tour with the Russians in the Caucasus, and then worked closely with Sir Edmund Allenby (whose biography Wavell published in 1940) in the Middle East.

137 A stocky, phlegmatic sort, Wavell earned admiration for his perceptive unconventionality. Posted to command the Middle East in July 1939, Wavell had few men and fewer supplies. Still, in a series of remarkable actions, he fought for the British and Italian Somalilands (and strongly against Churchill's [q.v.] meddling), stopped an Italian advance from Libya toward Egypt, and counterattacked in December 1940 with some 36,000 troops. British success was phenomenal—140,000 prisoners taken in two months and Cyrenaica cleared of the enemy.

Unhappy with Churchill's decision to aid Greece against Hitler, Wavell might have persuaded the prime minister against the venture but acquiesced. Disaster resulted and dimmed Churchill's already poor opinion of Wavell, whom he thought dull and argumentative. The general, though, did remarkably well in clearing East Africa of Italian troops and, despite being surprised, held up Gen. Erwin Rommel's (q.v.) March-May 1941 offensive toward Egypt by holding the port of Tobruk, thus creating a flanking threat that forced a German halt just inside Egypt. Subsequent attempts to relieve Tobruk failed, and Wavell was shunted to the apparently benign command of India. War with Japan soon involved Wavell in various attempts to shore up Britain's overextended and poorly organized Far Eastern positions. Forced to fight for Singapore, Wavell lost it, tried to hold Burma and lost it, too.

138 Promoted to field marshal in January 1943, Wavell tried to regain Burma, but his main attempt, under Gen. William Slim (q.v.) failed. As viceroy of India in June 1943, Wavell's duties were mainly political and he did extremely well.

Although denigrated by Churchill, Wavell retained the respect of his military contemporaries and deserves high praise for holding the Middle East at critical junctures.

AXIS MILITARY LEADERS, 1939–40

139 Günther Blumentritt, 1896–1967, was a German general of marked staff and combat ability. Blumentritt served on the Eastern Front in WWI, remained in the army, and then spent time in various staff positions early in WWII. **140** Blumentritt was Field Marshal Gerd von Rundstedt's (q.v.) chief of operations in France and helped implement the Manstein Plan for a panzer attack through the Ardennes. After a stint in Russia as chief of staff of the Fourth Army, Blumentritt, now a *Generalleutnant* (equivalent to a U.S. major general), became chief of operations at army headquarters early in 1942.

Although not really part of the plot to kill Hitler in 1944, Blumentritt feared guilt by association—as he knew many of the conspirators. Hitler, though, gave him a command assignment in the west, where he briefly opposed Montgomery's (q.v.) forces in the Low Countries. Promoted to SS (q.v.) general in September 1944, Blumentritt directed operations against other Allied forces in northwest Germany until war's end.

Taking up writing after the war, he published a life of his friend Field Marshal von Rundstedt in 1952.

141 (Moritz Albert Friedrich) Fedor von Bock, 1880–1945, German field marshal and panzer leader. An old-line Prussian, Bock served with distinction in WWI and led German forces in Austria and the Sudetenland. *Generaloberst* Bock commanded an army group brilliantly in Poland, but he did not stop mass murders of Jews. After France's fall, Bock became a field marshal. Heading the main Russian thrust, Bock pushed Army Group Center toward Moscow and by July 1, 1941, had taken 300,000 prisoners. Within a month Bock reached Smolensk, only 225 miles from Moscow. Bock's drive stalled when Hitler siphoned men to other ventures, but revived in October and nearly reached Russia's capital. Mud and stiff resistance at last stopped Bock. Illness forced his relief but he returned to the field within a month as commander of Army Group South.

Assaulted on both flanks, Bock evaded disaster by attacking and inflicting 250,000 casualties on the enemy. Despite his efforts, Hitler was displeased. Sensing this, Bock retired in July 1942, ostensibly for health reasons. He did not join the plot against the Führer in 1944. Bock died in an air raid May 4, 1945.

142 Wilhelm Joseph Franz Ritter von Leeb, 1876–1956, a textbook Prussian, was among the "uncooperative" German generals retired by Hitler in 1938, but was returned to command in August 1939. A highly regarded expert on defense, Ritter (hereditary knighthood) von Leeb's attacks in France were effective, and he was made a field marshal in July 1940.

Heading Army Group North in the Russian invasion with the task of holding the coastal flank in the drive toward Moscow, Leeb advanced rapidly over tough terrain. Hitler switched objectives in July 1941, however, and Leeb's reinforced army group swerved for a quick capture of Leningrad. The Finns did not advance from the north in support, but Leeb might have taken the city had Hitler not changed his mind again and decided on a siege there.

As the Russian campaign failed, Leeb urged a withdrawal and regrouping of German armies—which Hitler rejected. Pleading ill health, Leeb asked to be relieved in January 1942.

An anti-Nazi, Leeb tried to organize opposition to Hitler but found few supporters. He died in April 1956. His revealing diaries were published some twenty years after his death.

143 Galeazzo Ciano, 1903–44, Italian aviator and diplomat, was Mussolini's son-in-law and an opponent of Italy's joining the war. A bomber pilot in Mussolini's Ethiopian venture, Ciano commanded a bomber squadron for a short time after Italy's entry

into WWII. His father-in-law made him Italy's foreign minister, but after violent arguments about the war Ciano became Italy's ambassador to the Vatican.

144 Ciano voted against Mussolini at the critical Fascist Grand Council meeting in 1943 that ousted *Il Duce.* Ciano became a prisoner of the Germans. After Hitler restored Mussolini as a puppet state leader, Ciano was returned to Italy and shot in Verona on January 11, 1944.

Ciano's diaries were widely sought by Axis minions since they contained brutally revealing insights into Nazi and Fascist affairs. Some papers were retrieved, Ciano's loyal wife, Edda, got his diaries out and had them published. They remain an important historical source on the wartime Axis.

145 Hermann Wilhelm Göring, 1893–1946, aviator and high Nazi official, headed the Luftwaffe and was Germany's only *Reichsmarschall.* After a lonely early childhood, Göring entered the army, was accepted for flight training in 1915, and, after shooting down twenty-two enemy planes, won the Pour le Mérite. A wanderer after WWI, Göring married a Swedish baroness, who persuaded him to work for Germany's revival. Hitler mesmerized them both and Göring became an active Nazi. Captain Göring participated in Hitler's Beer Hall Putsch, 1923, where he was painfully wounded, and became an obese hypochondriac addicted to morphine. Recovered, he returned to Germany in 1927 and was elected to the Reichstag the next year.

146 Göring's fortunes soared when Hitler took over Germany in January 1933. The new chancellor put Göring in the cabinet, made him air commissioner, and loaded other rich sinecures on his willing friend. Göring used his new power to create a political police force, the dreaded Gestapo (*Geheime Staatspolizei*) [q.v.]. He cooperated in the Blood Purge of 1934. Hitler made Göring a field marshal in 1938 and announced him as deputy and legal successor in 1939.

147 As head of the Luftwaffe, Göring did well—Hitler made him *Reichsmarschall* on July 19, 1940 with wide if imprecise powers—but his fortunes declined abruptly after failing to win the Battle of Britain. Again a morphine addict, the huge libertine turned to amassing money and stealing art treasures all over Europe.

148 As Russian troops neared Berlin in 1945, Göring tried to carry out provisions of the succession act, infuriated Hitler, and narrowly escaped assassination.

Convicted at Nuremberg of war crimes and sentenced to death, Göring took poison and died on October 15, 1946, not long before he was to be hanged.

149 Rodolfo Graziani, 1882–1955, Italian marshal who suffered one of the worst defeats of the war, was born near Rome. Wounded in WWI, Graziani in the 1930s brutally subdued Libya and Abyssinia and was promoted to marshal of Italy. As head of the Italian army in 1939, he led the abortive attack on southern France in June 1940. Back in Libya later that year, he launched an attack toward Egypt with a nearly disorganized rabble of some 250,000 men. Stopping at Sidi Barrani, Graziani dug in, only to be disastrously routed by General Wavell's (q.v.) 36,000 troops. In the rout more than 130,000 Italian soldiers were captured along with huge depots of supplies.

150 Graziani resigned from the army in March 1941 but, in September 1943, became defense minister in Mussolini's puppet government. After surrendering, he was sentenced to prison but soon released.

151 Erich Fritz (von Lewinksi) von Manstein, 1887–1973, one of the ablest German blitzkrieg commanders, was born into an army family in Berlin; his uncle was Paul von Hindenburg. During WWI, Manstein served on various fronts but fought mostly in France.

Posted to Poland at the opening of WWII,

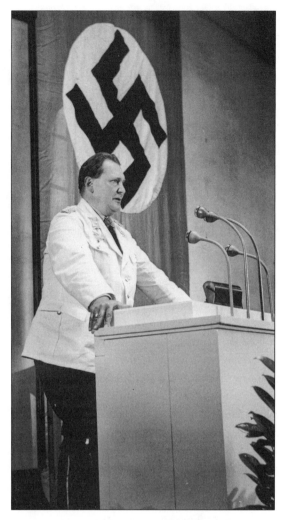

Hermann Göring addressing the Reichstag. The banner behind him displays the swastika (*Hakenkreuz*), the symbol adopted by the Nazi Party and incorporated into the German flag in 1935.

Manstein became General von Rundstedt's (q.v.) chief of staff in Poland and in France. He did not reap the rewards deserved for his brilliant plan for a panzer strike through the Ardennes because Hitler resented Manstein's doubts about an expanded war.

152 A panzer corps commander during the Russian invasion, Manstein's abilities in field command brought him promotion to *Generalleutnant* early in 1941 and *Generaloberst* on January 1, 1942. Commanding the 11th Army, Manstein drove into the Crimea, stymied a Russian counterattack, was made a field marshal on July 1, 1942, and took Sevastopol the next day. As commander of Army Group Don, Manstein was unable to relieve Stalingrad, though he performed outstandingly in covering retirements of various German forces.

Hitler apparently disliked him (retreaters were not the Führer's favorites) and almost relieved him, just before Manstein began one of his greatest ventures, in February 1943—breaking through enemy defenses, he retook Kharkov and Belgorod.

Manstein persisted in disagreeing with the Führer and finally, on March 30, 1944, he was shelved for the rest of the war.

Sentenced to eighteen years' imprisonment for war crimes in 1950, Manstein was freed in 1953 and was a military adviser to the Federal Republic of Germany. His memoirs, *Lost Victories* (1958), remain an important source. The field marshal died at age eighty-five.

153 Erich Raeder, 1876–1960, was the admiral commanding Germany's fleet until January 1943. After service in WWI, Raeder became an admiral and head of the navy in 1928, and Hitler kept him on in 1933 despite Raeder's antipathy to the Nazi party. Luckily for Raeder, Hitler had little interest in the navy and left its commander alone.

Promoted to grand admiral in 1936, Raeder resisted Hermann Göring (q.v.), whose bungling left naval air support in a shambles. The admiral expected to have a fleet ready to challenge Britain's in 1942—thirteen battleships, four aircraft carriers, numerous support craft, plus 250 U-boats. **154** War came too soon, forcing concentration on U-boat production. Nonetheless he cooperated, only asking that Norway be taken, which would give German ships easy access to the Atlantic.

Opposed to Hitler's Russian gamble, Raeder

nonetheless did what he could to support it in the Baltic. Loss of the *Bismarck* (q.v.) in May 1941 was a blow from which the grand admiral never fully recovered. Hitler, who tolerated Raeder from necessity, lost faith in him after *Lützow* and *Admiral Hipper* broke off action without permission against a large Atlantic convoy late in 1942. Raeder resigned in January 1943, was succeeded by Adm. Karl Dönitz (q.v.), and assumed the honorific position of admiral inspector of the navy.

Convicted of war crimes in Nuremberg and sentenced to life imprisonment, Raeder was released in 1955 and died at age eighty-four.

155 Karl Rudolf Gerd von Rundstedt, 1875–1953, one of the most complicated and ablest German generals, entered the elite Military Academy in 1902 and survived the three-year course that eliminated 75 percent of the students. He served mostly on the Eastern Front in WWI and remained in the army after that war. Although protesting various Nazi policies, Rundstedt tried to adhere to the idea that "a soldier cannot participate in political activities." **156** *Generaloberst* Rundstedt retired after the Munich crisis but was called back to duty

The Führer and Grand Admiral Raeder.

in August 1939 and led Army Group South into Poland. His brilliant campaigning won him another army group command in the west where his panzer and infantry divisions broke through the "impassable" Ardennes.

Accused by some of delaying a tank attack on the Allies stranded at Dunkirk because he wanted infantry in the lead, Rundstedt put the blame on Hitler.

A brilliant sweep southeastward behind the Maginot Line bagged numbers of French troops and trapped the French Army of the Alps. For these successes, Rundstedt received his field marshal's baton in July 1940 and became commander in chief–west, responsible for the coastal defense of occupied France and the Low Countries.

157 Involved late in planning for Operation Barbarossa (the Russian invasion) [q.v.], Rundstedt used his WWI Eastern Front experience in trying to convince Hitler of the difficulties ahead and argued that the main drive be toward Leningrad, where the Finns would help; next, Rundstedt advised a drive on Moscow before winter. This sound strategy would diminish Rundstedt's own role, since he commanded Army Group South, which would drive into the Ukraine. Hitler accepted only part of this strategy—a secondary role for the Ukraine offensive.

Rundstedt attacked on June 22, 1941, with fifty-seven divisions, a mixture of German, Hungarian, Italian, and Slovakian forces—his natural courtesy and diplomacy insuring effective melding of efforts. After destroying large Russian forces, Rundstedt pushed into the Crimea. He assisted in the encirclement of Kiev, which bagged 665,000 prisoners and almost ended Russian resistance. Continuing the Ukraine operations, Rundstedt moved on Kharkov and Rostov. Overworked, weary of Hitler's refusal to allow even small retreats, Rundstedt suffered a heart attack in November 1941, but kept command and pushed on to take Rostov on the Don. When it was lost, Hitler sacked him.

158 When the United States entered the war in December 1941, Hitler called the field marshal to be commander in chief–west and to exercise unified command of the Mediterranean and western coasts. From headquarters in Paris, Rundstedt rounded up reinforcements and equipment and argued with Field Marshal Rommel (q.v.) (sent to help) about defensive strategy—Rundstedt wanted a mobile defense to lure the Allies into traps, while Rommel urged holding the coastline. Personalities interfered with cooperation; Rundstedt commanded from headquarters through staff officers while Rommel went to the troops.

159 Diplomacy and politics intruded on Rundstedt, but his tactful talks with Marshal Pétain (q.v.) smoothed the full occupation of France in mid-November 1942. In September 1943 his tact also eased problems of transition when Italy joined the Allies.

Allied air strength during the June 1944 invasion negated both mobile and fixed defensive strategies, and both Rundstedt and Rommel thought the war lost. Rundstedt's strong views brought another sacking on July 2, 1944. Hitler still trusted him and in August 1944 gave him the unpleasant duty of heading a court of honor to dismiss from the *Wehrmacht* officers involved in the July 1944 plot to kill the Führer. Although Rundstedt knew that once removed from military rolls the plotters would be killed, he condoned weak evidence which the defendants were not allowed to refute.

160 Restored to the western command in September, Rundstedt—against his better judgment—agreed to Hitler's fantastic scheme of a great drive through the Ardennes in December 1944 (the Battle of the Bulge). A failure in a few days, the drive wasted vital men and equipment. After the Allies crossed the Rhine, Rundstedt was once again sacked, but with a kind of affection Hitler softened the blow: "I thank you for your loyalty."

Captured by Americans on May 1, 1945, and imprisoned, Rundstedt filled his time working with various historians of the war and was released in 1948.

Not the typical Prussian soldier, Rundstedt is difficult to see clearly. Trained in old army traditions, a patriot, usually apolitical, he cherished the respect of colleagues and although not arrogant, he held his honor high. Some puzzles cloud his reputation. In the Battle of France, for instance, he tried to blame Hitler for his own decision not to launch tanks against the Dunkirk beach. Although he loathed Nazi "final solution" actions, he did not oppose them strongly. Although he often loudly disagreed with Hitler about strategy, he, like most German generals, obeyed orders, and Rundstedt kept answering Hitler's calls to duty. At Nuremberg he said he never thought of participating in a coup: "For all time I should have been held up as a traitor to my country." It is difficult to avoid the conclusion that, in some matters of principle, Rundstedt lacked moral courage—be it said, though, that opposing Hitler was a dangerous game.

PEOPLE

161 Clement Richard Attlee, 1883–1967, British statesman, leader of the Labour Party and prime minister. London born and converted to socialism by work on the London docks, Attlee became a Labourite in 1908. A major in World War I, wounded several times at Gallipoli, Mesopotamia, and France, Attlee won a Limehouse seat in Parliament in 1922 and became leader of his party in 1935.

A war supporter, he joined Churchill's government, became deputy prime minister in February 1942, and smoothed many labor problems in England during the war. Attlee took over for Churchill when the prime minister was abroad.

With Anthony Eden (q.v.) he attended the San Francisco Conference on World Security in 1945; with Churchill, he went to the Potsdam Conference but returned to England for the election that made him prime minister. He then returned to Potsdam.

Vigorously changing Britain by nationalizing several industries, instituting the National Health Service, and giving independence to India and Burma, the colorless, underestimated Attlee showed much of Churchill's energy.

His predecessor could never take Attlee seriously, though, and made him the butt of classic Churchillian humor: "Did you see that empty taxi drive up and Attlee get out?" "Attlee is a sheep in sheep's clothing;" "Yes, Attlee is a modest man, with so much to be modest about."

162 (Robert) Anthony Eden, 1897–1977, British statesman and foreign secretary who helped forge the Grand Alliance. Born to wealth, Eden had the proper background at Eton, was commissioned in the King's Royal Rifle Corps, served two years on the Western Front, became adjutant of his battalion in 1917, won the Military Cross, and was the youngest (age twenty) brigade major in the British army by 1918.

Taking first class honors in Oriental languages at Oxford in 1922, Eden entered Parliament as a conservative in 1923. Much traveling and writing prepared him to be undersecretary for foreign affairs in the 1930s and foreign secretary in 1935. Arguments with Neville Chamberlain about Mussolini led to Eden's resignation in February 1938, but Chamberlain in 1939 tapped him for dominion secretary. Churchill gave him the war portfolio in May 1940 and made him foreign secretary that December. Wrong about the Norway invasion and support for the Greeks, Eden was right about de Gaulle, whom he supported. Churchill relied on him at all the Allied war conferences, and he headed the British delegation at the San Francisco conference that founded the United Nations.

Churchill called him to the same post again in 1951. Eden followed Churchill as prime minister in 1955. He died in Wiltshire on January 14, 1977.

163 Paul Joseph Goebbels, 1897–1945, Nazi propaganda chief, worked fervently to compensate for his small body, outsized head, clubfoot, and jug ears—disqualifying defects for a member of Germany's "super race." Goebbels hated such labels as "Little Joe" or "the cripple" and made action his best defense. Exempted from World War I service, he proved a good student and earned a Ph.D. in German philology from Heidelberg University in 1921. He became a Hitler fan and developed an effective, semihysteric rhetoric in urging Nazism.

Goebbels supported Hitler in a feud over Nazi leadership which cemented relations with the future Führer. In 1927 he founded a disreputable newspaper, *Der Angriff* (*The Attack*), which pushed Nazi ideas at any cost to honesty. He stage-managed the early party rallies that offered pageantry to a Gothic people. These rallies and their symbolism forged an almost mystical union between Hitler and his followers, enlarged as Goebbels popularized "Heil Hitler" and "Führer." **164 By 1933, as minister of public enlightenment and propaganda, Goebbels had patented his "big lie" theory—the bigger the lie, the louder and wider it is told, the more it is believed.**

165 When Germany's fortunes sagged at Stalingrad and in North Africa, Goebbels stepped into the leadership gap left by Hitler's preoccupation with military matters. In a February 1943 speech that called for total war, he urged everyone—especially industrialists and financiers—to commit everything for victory. Blending patriotism with fear, Goebbels revealed the mounting dangers to the nation and recalled Allied demands for unconditional surrender; offering hope, he suggested that the Allies shared an interest in halting Bolshevism.

166 It was his quick Berlin roundup of disloyal officers after the July 20, 1944, coup attempt that brought the crippled dynamo the job he wanted—Reich plenipotentiary for total war—but he realized it came too late.

Loyal to the last, he, his wife, and six children went with Hitler to the *Führerbunker*. There Goebbels worked his last wizardry. Only a Wagnerian end would preserve the Führer's legend, he said, a

"twilight of the gods." He and his wife witnessed Hitler's marriage to Eva Braun, their deaths, and then burned their bodies. The Goebbels then kept their troth to the Third Reich—they poisoned their children and killed themselves.

Goebbels probably did more to create the Nazi mystique than anyone else. From that mystique he built a myth that shrouded a reality of horrors.

167 Heinrich Himmler, 1900–45, became the second most powerful Nazi and the engineer of mass murder. A cherubic face softened by a moustache and glasses belied Himmler's unstable mind and ferocity. After serving in WWI he received an agricultural degree, played a minor part in Hitler's Beer Hall Putsch in 1923, joined the Nazi Party, and found an outlet for his ambition as head of Hitler's bodyguard in 1929.

168 In March 1933, Himmler opened one of Germany's first concentration camps at Dachau. Taking control of all German police agencies in 1934, he organized that year's Blood Purge and SS (q.v.) takeover of the concentration and detention camps run by the SA (*Sturmabteilung* or Storm Detachment).

169 Absorption of the SA camps was part of Hitler's destruction of the Brownshirt organization, whose leader, Ernst Röhm, had become too ambitious by far and threatened Hitler's control of the Nazi Party. As the war continued, Hitler increased Himmler's power. Charged with carrying out the "final solution," Himmler organized death camps across eastern Europe with fiendish efficiency: victims' hair was saved for mattresses, gold from their teeth for the treasury, their body fat for soap, and sometimes their tattooed skin for lampshades.

Power mad, Himmler sought to create an empire of his own, with an army (the *Waffen-SS*) and sizable economic/industrial interests. **170 The foiled July 1944 plot to kill Hitler gave *Reichsführer-SS* Himmler control of the reserve army, and he ordered a *levee en masse* of older men and boys—the *Volkssturm*.** As German fronts col-

Heinrich Himmler inspecting a POW camp (*Gefangenenlager*) in Russia, circa 1941.

lapsed on all sides, Hitler even gave his protégé command of two army groups, with sad results.

Overburdened and oppressed, Himmler's always delicate sanity wavered; psychosomatic illnesses plagued him and survival became an obsession. Unsuccessful attempts at peacemaking enraged Hitler, and Himmler escaped to the Allies, only to commit suicide on May 23, 1945.

171 Carl Gustav Emil, Baron von Mannerheim, **1867–1951, was born near Turku in present-day Finland, then part of European Russia.** A loyal tsarist cavalry officer, Mannerheim was a corps commander in 1917 and in 1918 successfully led the White Finns against the Reds and won Finland's independence. **172 He came out of retirement to lead Finnish resistance to Russia's invasion in 1939**—the Mannerheim Line stalled the Red Army across the Karelian Isthmus for thirteen weeks, but Russia finally annexed a large piece

of Finland. In 1941, Field Marshal Mannerheim led a corps cooperating with German forces, retook the Karelian Isthmus area, but declined to support the German attack on Leningrad (q.v.).

173 As president of Finland, Mannerheim signed a truce with Russia in September 1944 which again preserved his country's independence. He resigned in March 1946 and died in Lausanne. He remains Finland's national hero.

THINGS

174 Blitzkrieg, the highly mobile warfare launched by Germany in 1939. Profiting by losing the Great War, German military planners scrapped most of their old notions and looked for a different way to win. Tanks, introduced in WWI, had not dominated battles but had shown potential. **175 German general Hans von Seeckt expanded the mobile idea in the 1920s, and a young French officer, Charles de Gaulle, published *The Army of the Future* (1941) that outlined similar warfare— German officers read his book while French officers scorned it.**

German field marshal Rommel (q.v.) best explained the blitzkrieg. "The act of concentrating strength at one point, forcing a breakthrough, rolling up and securing the flanks on either side, and then penetrating like lightning, before the enemy has time to react, deep into his rear" (*Keil und Kessel*).

Perfected in Poland, these new tactics combining the use of tanks, airpower, and mechanized infantry soon changed the war.

176 Fifth column, a term describing secret infiltration of a country by enemy agents, was first used during the Spanish Civil War in the 1930s. A Fascist general announced that he was attacking Madrid with four columns, but had enough subversives inside the city to constitute a "fifth column." Germany dispersed "tourist" fifth columns widely before attacking in Europe.

177 Gestapo, acronym of *Geheime Staatspolizei* (secret state police), the dreaded state security force of Germany. Founded by Göring in 1933, the overwhelmingly Nazi Gestapo became part of the SS (*Schutzstaffeln*) [q.v.], Himmler's black-uniformed elite of German security. Virtually a rogue organization whose actions were unappealable, the Gestapo arrested thousands, most of whom vanished in concentration camps. Agents of this outlaw force followed the armies as part of the wide-ranging death squads. Bureaucracy alone restrained the Gestapo: German security organizations grew into an overlapping, Byzantine snare that sometimes stymied action.

178 The Maginot and Siegfried Lines were important defenses between France and Germany. French horror of WWI's trenches led to the building of the Maginot Line, a series of forts connected by heavy concrete tunnels running from Switzerland to the Belgian border. Built to survive the fiercest bombardments, this staggering engineering feat showed French military planners still obsessed with fixed fortifications. In a dismal demonstration of the "Maginot Line mentality," they consigned more than one hundred divisions to the concrete warrens while Germany struck Poland. A basic flaw ruined the Maginot concept— the line did not extend into Belgium.

179 Hitler's blitzkrieg in June 1940 flanked the Maginot Line and left it useless. Germany built the so-called Siegfried line (really a WWI name) from 1936 to 1939 in semiresponse to the Maginot effort. The three lines running from Switzerland to Luxembourg were lightly built Potemkin defenses, constructed for much show and little strength. These lines were of some value to retreating Germans in 1944–45, however.

180 SS (*Schutzstaffeln*), formed in 1925 as Hitler's small personal bodyguard, the SS numbered 250,000 men by 1939. Largely the fiefdom of Heinrich Himmler (q.v.), the SS grew into a conglomerate of police forces and business and manufacturing enterprises that retained responsibility for internal security and the relentless pogrom called the "final solution." The *Allgemeine-SS* (general SS) handled police, racial, and political matters, while the *Waffen-SS* (armed SS) guarded the Führer, managed the concentration and death camps, and deployed nearly forty divisions of elite, fanatical soldiers.

Drained of pity, bound to Hitler by the motto he gave them ("Thy Honor is Thy Loyalty"), the *Waffen* fanatics murdered and brutalized German civilians, Jews, "inferior" races, even prisoners of war, and left a legacy of shame.

181 Radar, acronym for *r*adio *d*etection *a*nd *r*anging, proved one of the most important scientific improvements to warfare. After Scottish physicist Robert Watson-

Watt produced a usable radar system in 1934–35, a scramble began to better his design. Ultrahigh frequency radio waves pulsed from a directional antenna; when intercepted by planes, tanks, ships, cannon, or formations, the reflected-back pulses displayed the objects on a radar screen even through fog and clouds. Most major industrial nations had perfected some form of radar by 1941, but Britain (after developing the cavity magnetron which produced microwave frequency power) and the U.S. (whose technicians refined radar for precise fire control) led in applications. Russian scientists produced various types in the 1930s. Germany, then far ahead of any other country, deployed ground radar for air defense and, in 1936, installed it on a pocket battleship—but German research suffered from hubris and dwindled after 1940.

182 **Victory in the Battle of Britain not only owed much to the RAF but also to radar—the antennae sweeping the Channel coast and across England helped maximize the force of inferior numbers.** As the air war intensified, radar improved apace and soon changed military tactics.

183 **ULTRA; first, the security classification for intelligence gained from German sources, including the sophisticated "Enigma" machine; then gradually, the name for the information itself.** Information from Polish sources convinced British authorities in 1939 that the Germans were working on a complicated code-writing machine. Again with Polish help, Britain received a machine. **184** **After code-breakers at Bletchley Park copied the machinery, they were able to decipher later German radio traffic.** This amazing intelligence coup shaped much Allied planning.

1941

THE SECOND YEAR OF THE WAR

SNEAK ATTACKS

A despised enemy has often maintained a sanguinary contest, and renowned states have been conquered by a very slight effort.

—Hannibal

THE UNITED STATES

As one year blended into another, nothing seemed different. War raged and German fortunes still soared. France was finished. Britain kept up a seemingly forlorn hope, while the United States lurched into a war economy and a growing awareness of Hitler's menace. British propaganda, shrewdly managed and not entirely honest, showed Germany to be the same beast of the "rape of Belgium" in 1914. Pictures, doctored documents, and varied testimonies all chipped effectively at American isolationism.

185 **An American destroyer, *Kearny*, was torpedoed in mid-October, and on October 31, another, *Reuben James*, became the first U.S. Navy vessel sunk, losing 115 men.** All of these things worked a masterful montage of mind-changing to achieve another American revolution.

186 **Though historically a warlike people, Americans are slow to fight.** That hesitancy hampered President Roosevelt's growing purpose to oppose Hitler. Some secrets he knew filled him with fear, secrets he dared not share with the public. **In October 1939 the president read an intriguing letter from the distinguished German exile, Albert Einstein, revealing that recent research in atomic energy made possible a new and terrible bomb and suggesting American reaction.** Roosevelt created a uranium advisory committee and supported a modest fund to buy uranium oxide.

187 **Late that summer the president had received from the War Department a gloomy summary of America's military situation.** This important memorandum displeased the president because it focused on strategic problems he did not want to consider—the possibility of Britain's defeat, the inadequacy of U.S. armed forces to meet dangers east and west, and a call for greatly increased war production. The memo's predictions resonated with Roosevelt's worries about a nearly bankrupt Britain's capacity to stay in the war. An October update about Britain's economy spread gloom over the White House; the attached request for equipment for at least ten divisions turned gloom to near panic sustained by Churchill's own words.

188 **Remembering Churchill's December 7, 1940, letter (see previous chapter) and his own call for America to be the arsenal of democracy, Roosevelt proposed a Lend-Lease program to Congress in his annual message to Congress, January 6, 1941.** "Let us say to the democracies: We Americans are vitally concerned in your defense of freedom. . . . We shall send you in ever increasing numbers, ships, planes, tanks, guns. . . ." In early March 1941, the Lend-Lease Act (q.v.) passed and conferred unprecedented powers on the president to lend, lease, sell, or trade war supplies to any country whose defense he thought vital to the safety of the United States. That act probably assured victory for the Allies. Churchill called it "the most unsordid act in history." Initially aimed at helping Great Britain, the program provided the British Empire more than thirty billion dollars worth of war goods by 1945.

189 In that same message Roosevelt went further and proclaimed that Four Freedoms were essential to the world: freedom of expression, freedom of worship, freedom from want, and freedom from fear.

Emboldened by America's reception of Lend-Lease and his increasingly pro-Allied rhetoric, Roosevelt declared an "unlimited national emergency" in May (which set a whole machinery of law in motion), froze German and Italian assets in the United States in June, and in August made his boldest move.

190 Roosevelt and Churchill met—each arriving by warship—at Placentia Bay, Newfoundland, August 9–12, 1941. They and their numerous staff aides discussed cooperation in war and peace. Looking hard at the crucial Battle of the Atlantic, they counted Allied shipping losses and assessed the rising U-boat menace. Reports from the new Russian front brought scant encouragement as the blitzkrieg engulfed entire Soviet armies. Japan's aggressiveness in the Pacific basin also hung doomlike over all discussions.

191 On August 12 came the Atlantic Charter, a "Joint Declaration by the President and the Prime Minister . . . to make known certain common principles in the national policies of their respective countries on which they base their hopes for a better future for the world." Some of its eight provisions echoed Wilsonian idealism—neither country had territorial ambitions; they would support territorial self-determination in any new or changed countries; they would support the right of all people to choose their government and wanted sovereignty and self-government restored to occupied countries; they would support freedom of commerce for all nations along with increased security and enhanced economies; they would support a post-Nazi peace that would enable all men everywhere to live in freedom from fear and want; they would support freedom of the seas; they would support disar-

mament and the creation of an international system of security.

192 Unofficial and nonbinding, the Atlantic Charter had immense moral power and boosted sagging Allied spirits everywhere. Quickly nine governments-in-exile and the Soviet Union endorsed the charter. **193** Its main long-range achievement would be an international peacekeeping organization—the United Nations. Short-term results were also important. Churchill got what he wanted—almost total commitment of the United States—and Roosevelt staked out America's claim to a large role in the future.

Back home the president basked in general approval of the charter, but he knew the fragility of declamations against the odds. And the odds were not running for the United States at the moment. Although still a nonbelligerent, the country faced danger from west and east.

194 Roosevelt watched anxiously as Japan's "Greater East Asia Co-Prosperity Sphere" expanded. A stage name, this "sphere" cloaked Nippon's grab of the resource-rich South Pacific area including the Philippines, Borneo, Java, Sumatra, Malaya, Thailand, Indochina, and Burma. By early 1941, Roosevelt hoped that Japan was facing serious strategic materials shortages caused by Allied fuel, financial, and other embargoes.

195 Recent Pacific history did not encourage President Roosevelt. He knew that Japan's incursions into China since 1937 had been both physical (including the infamous Rape of Nanking in December) and economic (cutting supply routes to Chiang Kai-shek's [q.v.] Nationalist China), that Japan had joined Germany and Italy in the Tripartite Pact, and in April 1941 had signed a nonaggression treaty with Russia that protected the Japanese empire's western and northern flanks, and pressed ahead with occupation of Indochina. Possibly missing the point that Japan's Pacific strategy in 1941 may have stemmed as much from American pressure as from imperial ambition, the president had turned up the heat when he froze Japan's American assets in July 1941.

196 **FDR's Far Eastern options were somewhat limited by a vital decision taken by the first American-British-Canadian combined staff talks (ABC-1) in January 1941:** if the U.S. got into the war, operations against Germany would have priority.

Japan's rising truculence toward the West obviously stemmed from Hitler's European triumphs and the resultant weakening of Britain's, France's, and Holland's Far Eastern colonial positions. Apparently, though, Japan still cherished some hope of keeping America at peace. **197** **In February 1941, Kichisaburo Nomura went from Tokyo as a new ambassador to Washington with the task of cooling relations.** Negotiations trundled along a discouraging path—neither Japan nor the U.S. would compromise.

198 **Although keeping a wary eye on Japanese actions, FDR focused mainly on his country and on Europe.** Happily he noted that the distinctly un-neutral actions he took were generally accepted. Congressional support of Lend-Lease, a bulging rearmament budget ($37 billion in 1941), and foreign orders for war matériel banished remnants of the Great Depression as unemployment dwindled, war production erupted, and wages ballooned. Nonetheless, he still moved carefully in molding the "arsenal of democracy."

199 **The slow shift to a war economy began America's acronymization.** Earlier, in 1940, the Office of Emergency Management (OEM) coordinated a series of new agencies. An Office of Civilian Defense (OCD) opened in May 1941 to arrange interstate cooperation in emergencies. Increasingly aware of science's obtrusion into war and stimulated by Einstein's concerns, Roosevelt sponsored the Office of Scientific Research and Development (OSRD) in June 1941 headed by Dr. Vannevar Bush, to replace the National Defense Research Committee; soon OSRD

reorganized atomic research. Within a month the Office of Coordinator of Inter-American Affairs (CIAA) appeared; Nelson Rockefeller's task was to coordinate U.S.–Latin American relations and minimize vigorous German incursions to the south. A changing economy spawned the Office of Price Administration (OPA) in August, and the changing industrial scene spawned the Office of Production Management (OPM) late in 1941. As supplies poured to the Allies, the Office of Lend-Lease (q.v.) Administration opened in October 1941 and struggled to manage an inchoate enterprise. This trickle of "alphabet agencies" became a torrent after Pearl Harbor.

200 **Americans took the social and economic changes of 1941 in a quickening stride.** A war production boom stimulated the economy, and consumer goods poured into stores as Christmas 1941 approached. With sudden prosperity, national morale soared. Conscription caused criticism, of course—the whole thing seemed highly un-American—but public crisis awareness muffled opposition. Congress, though, remained touchy about the draft and showed a growing desire not to extend it beyond one year. General Marshall campaigned to continue conscription and, in a historic vote, the House concurred with the Senate's approval by a vote of 203–2.

201 **Marshall's concern spread across the whole military spectrum. Although respecting FDR highly, the chief of staff chafed at the president's vacillation throughout most of 1941.** But FDR had made a political pledge that no American boys would go to war, and that burdened him as things grew worse for the Allies, so much worse that he had declared an unlimited national emergency in May and was shocked when Hitler attacked Russia in June. At first appearing to be a great British boon because it aimed Germany eastward, the invasion's swift success turned into a burgeoning Allied disaster. FDR reacted slowly—a fact never forgotten by the Soviet Union's brutal leader. **202** **Finally Harry Hopkins, FDR's trusted con-**

fidant, went to Moscow in July to talk about Russia's needs, Lend-Lease (q.v.), and other concerns. Stalin pulled no punches: enter the war. An October list of supplies began an account pegged at one billion dollars that escalated to more than eleven billion by war's end.

Marshall's concerns expanded. Hitler deployed more than 250 divisions in his Russian attack, a staggering number to an America which could hardly gather one in the middle 1930s. But Hitler's war forced drastic changes in the U.S. armed services. Men spilling in from the draft caused all kinds of astounding training and logistical problems. Camps had to be built, and food, munitions, clothing, transportation, medicines, all the "sinews of war," had to be manufactured, bought, and distributed—along with Allied needs. After temporary delays, U.S. production rose to the challenge and supplied both the Allies and "our boys"—an unprecedented expansion that boded ill for the Axis.

203 Still, with the regular army scattered and numbering some 1.6 million largely untrained, poorly equipped men (WWI rifles, ammunition, and artillery were still standard); with an acute plane shortage (despite FDR's call for fifty thousand); with a navy counting about fifteen hundred mostly elderly vessels, America had to rely on others to fight.

204 Everything changed for everybody on December 7, 1941, when Japan attacked Pearl Harbor. It happened at 7:50 A.M. on a lazy morning when only a few military folk were doing special Sunday duty. A lone radar operator reported a good many planes coming, but they were assumed to be an expected friendly squadron from the U.S. and no alert was sounded. **205** Once over Oahu,

183 Japanese planes divided; dive bombers headed for Hickam Airfield, Wheeler Field, and Ford Island, where they found American planes neatly lined up for them. Fifty bombers, forty torpedo aircraft, and forty-three zero fighters attacked the battleships anchored at Ford Island. In a matter of minutes, smoke, fires, and chaos covered the harbor. USS *Arizona* looked like scrap, *Oklahoma* had capsized, *California* and *West Virginia* sank, while *Nevada*, badly damaged, got up steam and started moving. *Maryland* and *Tennessee* were damaged but afloat.

206 After another attack wave came and went, the harbor resembled a burning junkyard. Within two hours at least nineteen warships—battleships, cruisers, destroyers, and support vessels—were smashed or hit. Navy and Marine Corps losses were nearly 2,120 killed, almost a thousand wounded, and another thousand missing. Army losses were lighter—226 killed and almost 400 wounded. Most American

Captured Japanese photograph taken during the attack on Pearl Harbor, December 7, 1941. Smoke rising in the distance over Hickam Field.

ABOVE: USS *Arizona* burning, Pearl Harbor, December 7, 1941. BELOW: USS *West Virginia* aflame; fireboats with water hoses.

LEFT: USS *Downes* (left) and USS *Cassin* (right) after the Japanese attack. In the rear is USS *Pennsylvania*, flagship of the Pacific Fleet, which suffered lighter damage. RIGHT: Burned B-17C at Hickam Field. BELOW: USS *Shaw* exploding, December 7, 1941.

planes were destroyed or damaged. Civilian losses were high.

Nearly destroying the Pacific Fleet had cost Japan fewer than a hundred men, twenty-nine planes, one regular and five midget submarines.

207 It might have been worse: three U.S. aircraft carriers and most heavy cruisers were absent that Sunday on support missions for Midway and Wake Islands, and, in a stupendous blunder, the Japanese did not destroy exposed tanks near the harbor holding 4.5 million barrels of oil.

208 District of Columbia traffic was light that Sunday and Washington's mood was good. People knew about troubles with Japan, but the presence of two emissaries from Tokyo who were in talks with Secretary of State Cordell Hull offered hopes for Pacific peace. And they were planning to talk again that day. When the Japanese arrived at 2:20 P.M. on December 7, Ambassador Nomura and special envoy Saburo Kurusu handed the secretary a long dispatch from Tokyo which essentially rehashed old arguments. The message should have been delivered at 1:00 P.M., which would have anticipated the Pearl Harbor attack by about half an hour—just the warning time prescribed by the emperor—but transcription ran slow and the emissaries waited.

209 So, by the time they arrived, Hull knew about the attack. Stiffly formal, he received their dispatch, read it, and seethed. Choking with anger, the tall Tennessean said, "In all my fifty years of public service I have never seen a document that was more crowded with infamous falsehoods and distortions . . . on a scale so huge that I never imagined until today that any government on this planet was capable of uttering them," and dismissed his visitors. Some sources record—though Hull denied it—that as they left, he mumbled "Scoundrels and pissants!" Apparently they had been kept in the dark about the attack.

210 Appearing before a joint session of Congress on December 8, a grimly determined President Roosevelt delivered a war message:

Yesterday, December 7, 1941—a date which will live in infamy—the United States of America was suddenly and deliberately attacked by the naval and air forces of the Empire of Japan.

The United States was at peace with that nation and, at the solicitation of Japan, was still in conversation with the government and its emperor looking toward the maintenance of peace in the Pacific.

Indeed, one hour after Japanese air squadrons had commenced bombing in Oahu, the Japanese ambassador to the United States and his colleagues delivered to the Secretary of State a formal reply to a recent American message. While this reply stated that it seemed useless to continue the existing diplomatic negotiations, it contained no threat or hint of war or armed attack.

It will be recorded that the distance of Hawaii from Japan makes it obvious that the attack was deliberately planned many days or even weeks ago. During the intervening time, the Japanese government has deliberately sought to deceive the United States by false statements and expressions of hope for continued peace.

The attack yesterday on the Hawaiian Islands has caused severe damage to American naval and military forces. Very many American lives have been lost. In addition, American ships have been reported torpedoed on the high seas between San Francisco and Honolulu.

Yesterday, the Japanese government also launched an attack against Malaya.

Last night, Japanese forces attacked Hong Kong.

Last night, Japanese forces attacked Guam.

Last night, Japanese forces attacked the Philippine Islands.

Last night, the Japanese forces attacked Wake Island.

This morning, the Japanese attacked Midway Island.

Japan has, therefore, undertaken a surprise offensive extending throughout the Pacific area. The facts of yesterday speak for themselves. The people of the United States have already formed their opinions and well understand the implications to the very life and safety of our nation.

As commander in chief of the Army and Navy, I have directed that all measures be taken for our defense.

Always will we remember the character of the onslaught against us.

No matter how long it may take us to overcome this premeditated invasion, the American people in their righteous might will win through to absolute victory.

I believe I interpret the will of the Congress and of the people when I assert that we will not only defend ourselves to the uttermost, but will make very certain that this form of treachery shall never endanger us again.

Hostilities exist. There is no blinking at the fact that our people, our territory and our interests are in grave danger.

With confidence in our armed forces—with the unbounding determination of our people—we will gain the inevitable triumph—so help us God.

I ask that the Congress declare that since the unprovoked and dastardly attack by Japan on Sunday, December 7, a state of war has existed between the United States and the Japanese Empire.

211 Senatorial approval was unanimous; the sole dissenting House vote came from pacifist Jeannette Rankin of Montana, who had also voted against war in 1917.

212 General Marshall, Adm. Harold R. Stark (q.v.), Chief of Naval Operations, and Congress pondered whether or not the Hawaiian Department's commander, Lt. Gen. Walter C. Short, and Adm. Husband E. Kimmel, CINCPAC, had failed in their duties. Historical opinion is

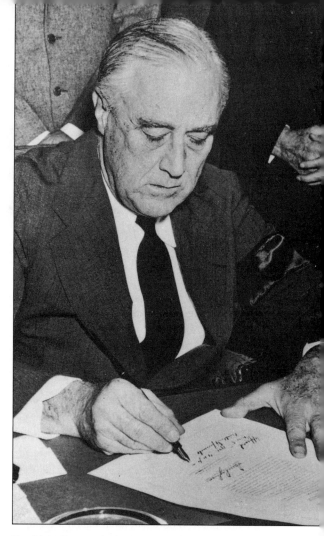

President Roosevelt signing the U.S. declaration of war against Japan, December 8, 1941.

running against them now. In any event, both were relieved of their commands, investigations were launched, and gradually blame spread to include Washington's higher echelons—not enough warning went to Honolulu, where interservice rivalry confused responses. **213** In addition, historians argue still about FDR's part in the Pearl Harbor mess, with some suggesting that he deliberately baited the Japanese into the attack, others that he was hardly so cynical.

214 Bad news swamped Washington and left scant time for looking back. Guam fell quickly. Wake Island,

Boeing B-17. General Henry H. "Hap" Arnold, wartime commander of the U.S. Army Air Forces, called the B-17 the "backbone of our worldwide aerial offensive." B-17s served in all theaters, and the B-17F dropped more tons of bombs than any other American plane in World War II.

after fighting off the first enemy landing, surrendered late in December while the Philippines were invaded. General Douglas MacArthur (q.v.), commanding the Philippine Department and United States Army Forces Far East (USAFFE), although well warned of war by December 8, did not disperse his B-17 (q.v.) bombers or modern fighters and lost almost half of them on the ground to raiders from Formosa. The small U.S. Asiatic Fleet fled southward as Luzon was invaded on December 10–12.

MacArthur's 80,000-man force waged a remarkably skillful delaying campaign against growing enemy strength. **215 Declaring Manila an open city, MacArthur, headquartered on Corregidor Island, put Lt. Gen. Jonathan M. Wainwright (q.v.) in battle command.** A combined U.S.–Philippine Army/Scouts force contested beaches, mountains, and rivers as it fell back into the Bataan Peninsula. MacArthur concentrated his dwindling forces and supplies in that area and by the first of the year held a fairly strong line.

216 People in the States expected action to save the American and Philippine troops, but several things made that impossible: first was the year-old "Germany first" decision; second, the Pearl Harbor disaster—combined with losing Guam, Wake Island, and critical

airplanes—made resupply and reinforcement impossible. Even so, USAFFE did wonders in chopping Japanese numbers and making Tokyo detach urgently needed men, ships, and planes to the Philippine campaign.

217 MacArthur vowed to stay to the end but was saved from this reckless promise by a direct order from the president to leave the Philippines. PT boats (q.v.) extracted MacArthur, his family, and some staff on the night of March 12, 1942; they went to Australia, where the general took command of Allied forces in the Southwest Pacific. Wainwright, who succeeded to command of United States Forces in the Philippines (USFIP), presided over a bad end. **218 Bataan was surrendered on April 9, and on May 6, Wainwright surrendered Corregidor—America's Gibraltar—to Lt. Gen. Masaharu Homma, who forced a surrender of all the Philippines by threatening prisoners.**

219 With their rallying cry—"Remember Pearl Harbor!"—Americans closed quickly behind the president in a kind of sober relief that the die had finally been cast. Churchill, ecstatically convinced of victory—"so we had won after all! [he gloated] . . . we had won the war. England would live. . . ."—pushed a swift war declaration against Japan on December 8. **220 With a picked group of advisers, the prime minister arrived in Washington on December 22, 1941, for Arcadia, the first war conference with FDR and his military staffs.** Meeting, talking, conferencing, the staffs bickered and brokered different strategies, logistics, methods, and pretty well proved George Bernard Shaw's dictum that "Great Britain and the United States are nations separated by a common language."

221 They differed seriously on how to run the war. American participants were uncertain of British martial competence—not only were things going bad for them in Europe and North Africa, the situation was also terrible in the Far East where Hong Kong was lost, Singapore threatened, and on December 10, HMS *Prince of Wales* and HMS *Repulse* were sunk by Japanese bombers. Conversely, British participants were appalled at American unreadiness, inexperience, and focus on the Western Hemisphere.

222 Concerned about casualties, the British favored an "indirect approach" strategy of air and sea raids at Axis edges in Europe while fending off the Japanese—essentially a policy of limited attrition. Marshall, Stark, and their colleagues favored an aggressive, direct strategy of fighting the Axis on their ground. They favored planning Operation Bolero, which would invade the European continent and provide the second front Russia's Joseph Stalin stridently demanded. American public opinion demanded some show of attack somewhere, and Marshall believed that Germany could only be beaten by a European invasion. British officers disagreed but hid it for a time. Churchill added gloom to the doom engulfing the Allies: Nazi submarine successes made a mockery of moving much of anything to France.

223 Twenty formal sessions and innumerable informal gatherings and personal talks reconfirmed the Germany first idea, forged a Combined Chiefs of Staff arrangement, and, at Marshall's insistence, accepted zonal commands (a theater supreme commander who would direct all services in his area) that short-circuited the usual alliance command tangles and began many long-lasting friendships. For instance: Marshall and Field Marshal Sir John Dill, former chief of the Imperial General Staff, now Britain's permanent representative in Washington, became bosom buddies—they were alike in manner, courtesy, and hobbies, and together they smoothed rough roads to victory.

224 Churchill and Roosevelt got along fine—in fact, they cemented a remarkable friendship of wisdom and wit. Disagreeing on several points, they compromised handily and their relationship shaped the course of the war. **225 Both won something at Arcadia— Churchill got reaffirmation of Germany first and FDR got the United Nations Declaration, his cherished scheme for lasting peace.** The declaration, issued on January 1, 1942, pledged to defeat the Axis and vowed that no separate peace would be made by any of the signing nations, all twenty-six of them (more later), including the Soviet Union.

Arcadia ranks as one of the most important war conferences—it set permanent Allied strategy and command decisions.

GERMANY, 1941

226 "Heil Hitler" resounded across Germany throughout the second war year. Germany now had *Lebensraum* (living room) and the anxious respect of the world—*Der Führer* delivered. True, England had not been conquered, but was adrift on its island and clinging to life by a sinking fleet of ships. After France's collapse, U-boats ranged the Atlantic from French ports, picking off merchant ships at a horrendous rate, with the Nazi submarine fleet steadily increasing. **227 From July to October 1940, 217 Allied ships were sunk—an average of eight a month per submarine.** No wonder U-boat captains remembered this as the "Happy Time" as they scouted along the

American coast, sinking any ships silhouetted against city lights. Even American warships went to the bottom as the U.S. Navy, daring war, increasingly covered Atlantic convoys to help Britain preserve its lifeline.

Everywhere *Wehrmacht* forces did impressive deeds. Not only had Nazi armies stormed Scandinavia, the Low Countries, and France but they also had saved Italian armies in the Balkans and Greece; with Luftwaffe cover they had mounted the airborne invasion of Crete in May 1941 and snatched the strategic initiative in the eastern Mediterranean.

Hitler's friend Mussolini kept sticking thorns in the Führer's side, however, and Italian ventures in North Africa sputtered toward collapse. **228 On February 6, 1941, British Tommies took Benghazi on the eastern shoulder of the Gulf of Sirte, some two hundred miles west of Tobruk, and the way yawned open to Tripoli and Tunisia.** Reluctantly the German leader decided he had, once again, to extricate the Duce from his ruinous ambition and sent troops to shore up the southern front.

229 In 1939 the German people had greeted war with a kind of grudging acceptance. Gone were the cheering crowds of 1914, the garlands and parties for gray-clad heroes marching to sustain Kaiser Wilhelm II's hopes for hegemony. Instead, as the British ambassador noted, "the mass of German people . . . was horror-struck at the whole idea of the war. . . . The whole general atmosphere in Berlin is one of utter gloom and depression." **230 Easy victories in Poland, the Low Countries, and France transmuted worry into enthusiasm;** Hitler's careful—if mistaken—early policy of producing consumer goods along with war matériel made his war acceptable, and Germans flocked to factories and war jobs as Hitler called out the faithful. During 1941, German workers built 5,200 tanks and 11,776 planes.

231 Normalcy pretty well characterized German life through the first half of 1941. True, the Nazi yoke fas-

tened tighter around the country, war taxation rose, industries were tuning for the war, but prosperity, military success, great expansion of territory (from 226,288 square miles in 1939 to 344,080 by summer 1941) and population (from 79.5 million in 1939 to 116 million), plus a national trait of obedience, shielded Hitler's errors—keeping up consumerism, idealizing motherhood and keeping women out of factories, canceling the invasion of Britain—and sustained national morale.

Restricted travel pinched a little, but people still vacationed, some to such conquered gems as Paris. **232 Late in 1941 most Germans were ignoring the gaps in their neighborhoods when families simply vanished after Hitler issued the *Nacht und Nebel Erlass* (Night and Fog Decree) that consigned so many to concentration camps.** Citizens knew that all constitutional trappings had been swept into an ironbound personal dictatorship—"The will of the Führer is law." Yet so much seemed the same, and if vaunted German organization yielded to "organized chaos," it was a Germanic chaos that somehow worked. Most opposition urges were muffled by too many diverting distractions, too many excitements and triumphs as the year progressed. While there was bounty there was satisfaction.

233 A nation of well-educated, inquisitive, philosophical people were deluded by a pseudoliterature under Goebbels' control, by such technically sound patriotic films as *Baptism of Fire*, a 1940 paean to the Luftwaffe, *Victory in the West*, touting triumph over the hated French, and, in 1941, *Submarines Head West*, glorifying U-boat action. Goebbels fed the German hunger for martial music with great military bands blaring marches, songs like "Deutschland Über Alles" ("Germany Above All") and the party anthem "Horst Wessel Lied" (which made martyrs of thugs). Old favorites like "I Had a Comrade" and "No More Beautiful Death in the World" joined with such sentimental pieces as "Do You Remember the Beautiful May Days" to nourish a deep national romanticism;

Flags high, ranks closed,
The S.A. marches with silent solid steps.
Comrades shot by the red front and reaction
march in spirit with us in our ranks.

The street free for the brown battalions,
The street free for the Storm Troopers,
Millions, full of hope, look up to the swastika;
The day breaks for freedom and for bread.

For the last time the call will now be blown;
For the struggle now we all stand ready.
Soon will fly the Hitler-flags over every street;
Slavery will last only a short time longer.

Flags high, ranks closed,
The S.A. marches with silent solid steps.
Comrades shot by the red front and reaction
march in spirit with us in our ranks.

Hitler's troops had a patriotic songbook as part of their kit.

Without Goebbels' knowledge, Leni Riefenstahl (q.v.), documentary filmmaker extraordinaire who was charmed by Hitler, agreed to put film to work for him and dazzled audiences with masterpieces of Nazi success. Goebbels' jealousy of her made him a mean enemy.

234 Late in the spring of 1941, Rudolf Richard Hess, longtime crony of Hitler's, borrowed a plane from Willi Messerschmitt (q.v.) and bailed out over Scotland. He had some crazy notion about contacting high British officials (including George VI) to make a deal for coexistence. Mortified, Hitler wailed, "Who will believe me when I say that Hess did not fly there in my name . . . ?" This weird flight of fancy neither intrigued nor fooled the British—they knew Hess was simply "around the bend" and arrested him—but they gleefully flaunted the defection of the number three Nazi!

All kinds of rumors touch this bizarre mission. Did Hess come to negotiate peace or to propose an alliance with England against Russia? Full details may never come to light.

Imprisoned for the rest of the war in various facilities (a military hospital, a castle, the Tower of London), Hess was found guilty of war crimes at the postwar Nuremberg trials (q.v.) and sentenced to life in prison. He died in Spandau prison in 1987, a possible suicide.

GERMAN LAND BATTLES, 1941

235 Hitler appeared to abandon the English invasion without much concern, almost as if all the huffing and puffing had been a charade. He still aimed at beating Britain, but, frustrated there, he turned toward another fixation—destruction of Russia. Some historians argue that Hitler really had no grand strategy for winning the war and that Russia loomed mainly as a target of opportunity, one loaded with Bolsheviks, Slavs, and other *Untermenschen*. But the Führer kept England in mind as he explained his drive to the east as early as July 1940: "*Russia is the factor by which England sets the greatest store . . . If Russia is beaten. England's last hope is gone.* Germany is then master of Europe and the Balkans . . . *Decision: As a result of this argument. Russia must be dealt with. Spring 1941.*"

236 Although warned of Hitler's notion, the German general staff scarcely believed it, dreaded it in a sense, even though the *Wehrmacht* had grown much stronger in two years. A Russian campaign would demand huge stores of oil, transport, munitions, supplies of all kinds, with every problem compounded by huge distances, possibly by weather. Success would depend on speed—an attack had to start no later than May to avoid the power of Russia's formidable ally, "General Winter." Hitler understood this but was distracted by Mussolini's foolish drive into Greece, distracted, too, by Yugoslavia's demeaning defection from the Tripartite Pact in March 1941.

237 On April 6, 1941, German forces invaded Yugoslavia in Operation Punishment, simultaneously invading Greece from Bulgaria and taking Salonika in two days. Air raids squashed Belgrade, and Yugoslavia surrendered on April 17. Britain scrambled to extract some 55,000 men and, in a mini-Dunkirk, saved 43,000 of them. Although a great and cheap German victory (5,000 casualties) that preserved the Balkans, the Greek campaign remains the focus of a historical argument: did it doom the Russian invasion?

238 The Afrika Korps (q.v.), led by *Generalleutnant* Erwin Rommel (q.v.), a Führer favorite, was sent to Libya in February 1941, charged with salvaging something from the wreckage of Mussolini's North African venture and opening the way for an Axis takeover of the Suez Canal. This also distracted Hitler from Russia.

239 The Führer decided to dispatch help to Rommel, whose supply lines were exposed in the Mediterranean. At 8:00 A.M. on May 20, 1941, Gen. Kurt Student's paratroops began landing on the strategically vital island of Crete. Largest of the Greek islands, Crete sat athwart both Allied and Axis communications in the eastern Mediterranean. A perfect stepping-stone between Greece and Egypt, it had good airfields and ports. Britain held it with a small garrison (many troops were in Greece and East Africa), thinking the Royal Navy could protect it; the navy tried at great cost, only to learn again the value of airpower.

240 The British lost a staggering 17,325 men, counting 11,800 prisoners and 2,000 sailors. Hitler was horrified at the loss of some 6,000 men and the wrecking of

Legend has it that Rommel heard a song over a German radio station in Belgrade and liked it so much that he asked that it be played every night for his desert forces. The song was not popular; Goebbels, in fact, wanted it banned, but "Lili Marlene" persisted to become one of the most famous songs of the war, sung by Allied and Axis soldiers with equal enthusiasm. An English version, by Tommie Connor, 1944, follows:

> *Underneath the lantern,*
> *By the barrack gate,*
> *Darling I remember,*
> *The way you used to wait.*
> *'Twas there that you whispered*
> *That you loved me,*
> *You'd always be,*
> *My Lili of the Lamplight,*
> *My own Lili Marlene. . . .*
>
> *Resting in our billets*
> *Just behind the lines,*
> *Even tho' we're parted,*
> *Your lips are close to mine.*
> *You wait where that lantern shines,*
> *Your sweet face seems,*
> *To haunt my dreams.*
> *My Lili of the Lamplight,*
> *My own Lili Marlene.*

Göring's crack 7th Air Division. At high cost, Rommel's and Mussolini's supply lines were protected.

Another Mediterranean island, though, troubled the memory of some German staff officers—Malta in the western Mediterranean came under heavy Luftwaffe bombing.

241 Rommel had arrived in Libya on February 12, 1941, six days after learning he would command what was left of Italy's mechanized forces and the new Afrika Korps (q.v.). On the way he checked logistical problems and tested the mood of the Italian *Commando*

The versatile German 88mm artillery gun—effective in antipersonnel, antitank, and antiaircraft action—shown here firing on British tanks at Mers-el-Brega, April 15, 1941, during Rommel's advance.

Supremo in Rome. After a quick look at his command he decided to forget defensive orders, gather whatever effectives he could find, and attack. Ahead of him lay new and bad ground. Sandy along the coastal strip, the Western Desert's reaches were limestone shale broken by plateaus and sharp ridges inland. One main ribbon of road along the coast beckoned battle, but that road had barely sustained Italian and British operations. Aware that British forces were scattering, Rommel launched a probing attack against El Agheila on March 24, 1941, took it quickly, and pressed ahead, beginning a long, sunbleached gavotte of armor, planes, guns, and blood.

242 With one German and elements of two Italian divisions rushing eastward, Rommel bypassed fortified Tobruk, destroyed most of the British armor, took many prisoners, including several British generals, and drove Gen. Sir Archibald P. Wavell's men from Libya by April 11. Wary of Tobruk's flanking threat, Rommel made an ill-considered attack there in mid-April, was repulsed, and failed again with a reinforced thrust on April 30. Still, British armor and tactics had proved no match for a hero now widely known as the "Desert Fox."

243 Churchill lost confidence in Wavell now—unfairly, because Wavell was responsible for too many fronts at once—and replaced him with Gen. Sir Claude Auchinleck, who had orders to attack and relieve pressure on the Russians. Rommel outnumbered the British and had better tanks, which forced Auchinleck to delay his advance. When the new British Eighth Army moved west on November 18, Rommel faced 700 tanks, seven British divisions, and about 1,000 Allied planes; he had 414 tanks (154 of them inferior Italian models), two panzer divisions, three

Junkers Ju-87 Stuka dive bombers en route to Ghobi to attack British tanks, November 23, 1941, during the ultimately successful British offensive, Operation Crusader.

motorized divisions, four Italian infantry divisions, and about 320 planes.

Initially surprised, Rommel reacted swiftly and fought a series of small actions south of Tobruk—the garrison broke out on November 21 and was driven back in—but could not contain reinforced British columns and retreated toward Gazala. By the end of the year he was back at El Agheila, where he waited for supplies made scarce by the Russian campaign. Hitler was disturbed by his "Sun Hero's" apparent failure, but Rommel planned redemption.

244 Hitler had issued his first order for invading Russia on December 18, 1940; all preparations would be made by May 15, 1941. That date offered enough time to complete blitzkrieg operations which he hoped would wipe out Russian forces before winter—but the actual attack began on June 22, 1941. Some historians argue that diversion of German strength to the Balkans and Greece forced the apparently fatal delay in Operation Barbarossa; others suggest that the plan itself had fatal flaws in that overall strategy and objectives were not agreed upon and preparations were incomplete.

245 There are, also, interesting speculations about the German jump-off date. Some experts suggest that Hitler chose the date deliberately (even though it sacrificed precious weeks) because he cherished similarities cited between his career and Napoleon Bonaparte's; Napoleon marched into Russia on that date in 1812. The truth is that an apparently superstitious Führer knew Napoleon's invasion began on June 21, 1812, and held off a day to avoid bad luck.

246 At any rate, massive movements of men, supplies, guns, armor, and munitions were orchestrated brilliantly by the "great general staff." Train schedules were honed to close tolerances, movements of all the sinews of war were tweaked toward perfection as all of Germany seemed to lean eastward. Perhaps because of these elaborate preparations the Führer remained convinced that it would be a short war and kept Germany's economy at peacetime levels through 1941. This short-war psychology, and persistent contempt for the feckless Russian mobs defeated by the Finns in 1939, also infected the general staff—almost no provisions were made for winter uniforms, petroleum, or equipment. Long-range planning appeared utterly unnecessary on the eve of the great offensive.

247 Some 250 Axis divisions, spread across a two-thousand mile front, rumbled into Russia at 3:00 A.M. on June 22, 1941. Hitler and his generals agreed that the whole campaign would be a reenactment of the great western blitzkrieg of 1940, with the main thrust aimed at Moscow to embroil Stalin's (q.v.) best forces in a great battle for the political, psychological, manufacturing, and logistical heart of Russia.

248 Ritter von Leeb's (q.v.) Army Group North held the left flank, streaking along the Baltic toward Leningrad; Fedor von Bock's (q.v.) Army Group Center raced straight at Smolensk and Moscow; Gerd von Rundstedt's (q.v.) Army Group South aimed at Kiev and the Ukraine.

Unbelievably, the Russians were totally surprised. Despite reports of German troop movements into Poland and warnings from Britain as well as from spies, Stalin simply would not see that invasion was coming and had planned to stab Hitler in the back whenever the chance came. Consequently, Red Army forces were deployed well forward, some engaged in maneuvers, others simply resting. Communications were primitive and news of the onslaught spread unevenly and met wide disbelief. A few divisions rallied and fought; most, though, were swept up in the demoralizing confusion of the Russian high command.

249 Initial successes surprised even the Germans. As the Luftwaffe wrested control of the air, fortifications of the vestigial "Stalin Line" were smashed by siege guns. Brest-Litovsk, scene of Russia's surrender in World War I and linchpin of its defenses on the central front, fell in two days.

Leeb's Army Group North swooped ahead in a series of encirclements, destroying more than a dozen Red divisions west of the Dvina River before moving on to difficult forest lands. Army Group Center had by far the best of it in the early weeks. With the Luftwaffe controlling the air, Bock's armies bagged nearly 300,000 men, more than 2,500 tanks, and 1,400 guns in a huge trap near Minsk and took that city on June 27, 1941. Another pincers closing near Smolensk in mid-July trapped another 100,000 men, 2,000 tanks, and nearly 2,000 guns. The only resistance the Germans met was from the Russian Fifth Army that attacked southward from the Pripet Marshes and slowed Rundstedt's drive.

German tanks forming up for attack on the open terrain characteristic of much of the Eastern Front, July 1941.

Early in July, momentum seeped from a Nazi advance that had raced ahead of supplies and sustained many tank and vehicular breakdowns due to the rough, dusty roads. A respite gave time for regrouping and repair—but also gave Stalin time to reorganize his scattered and often badly led legions. Even so, the threat to Moscow loomed greater each day.

250 Stalin, himself in a funk for several days after early German success, thought of evacuation before trying to turn the war into a crusade to save Mother Russia. On July 3 he addressed the people about the war. Speaking to "brothers and sisters," he said "we must immediately put our whole production to war footing," predicted Napoleon's fate for Hitler, justified the Russo-German pact as a cloak for mobilization, then urged a vital program—a "scorched earth policy" so that not "a single engine, or a single railway track, and not a pound of butter nor a pint of oil" could be found by the Nazis, and thanked Britain and the United States for offering help. This was a different Stalin, one frightened into nationalism. He even restored long lost privileges to officers and churchmen. And, in one of the war's colossal understatements, he admitted to Churchill on July 18 that the Soviet situation was "tense."

251 It had to be a miracle. Even the supposedly godless USSR high command believed it: Moscow was saved by a miracle. German Army Group Center, pressing swiftly beyond Smolensk, raced toward Moscow when, suddenly and unbelievably, Hitler—seeking to capture raw materials and oil—shifted one of Bock's panzer groups to AG South, the other to AG North, which left the main push to Moscow to infantry alone. General "Hurrying Heinz" Guderian (q.v.), brilliant leader of Panzer Group 2, fumed at Corporal Hitler's "brainstorm": "This meant that my Panzer Group would be advancing in a southwesterly direction, that is to say toward Germany."

A general furor among the high command stalled Hitler's actions for a confused period. In late August, the Führer, proclaiming that Moscow could be taken after Leningrad was handled and the Crimea and Donets areas seized, confirmed Guderian's (q.v.) southwesterly mission and shifted Bock's group boundary northward so that part of his panzers and one of his armies could aid the advance on Leningrad.

Moscow's miracle worker was Hitler himself.

In August, Rundstedt's Army Group South got rolling and destroyed some twenty Russian divisions near Uman, pushed to the Dnieper River, and connected with Guderian's panzers coming from the north. After desperate, confused fighting in the Kiev pocket, that city fell on September 19, and Rundstedt's men took some 665,000 prisoners and much equipment.

252 Hitler's brainstorm had conjured a sizable tactical victory, but strategically the diversion proved a major blunder. Although Rundstedt could now drive into the Caucasus and the Crimea, Stalin had been able to bring fresh divisions from the east—he had concluded a neutrality pact with Japan in April (which Hitler apparently ignored) ending the Khalkhin-Gol Incident and releasing many tough Siberian divisions to fight the "Great Patriotic War" against Germany.

253 Amidst Rundstedt's successes, Leeb plodded to an encirclement of Leningrad. Hitler, in another of his grandiose visions, decided to besiege that great northern city and starve it out. So began Leningrad's epic days of hunger and arctic cold (3,000 to 4,000 died every day that first winter), of quenchless heroism, of mass death and thin hope. Leeb hoped for Marshal Mannerheim's support in closing the siege of Leningrad from the north, but once back to the lines held before the Russo-Finnish war in 1939, Mannerheim stopped, not to start again—but the Finns did cut the Murmansk railroad, hindering Allied supply shipments to Russia by sea.

254 When Hitler turned back to his Moscow plan in September, he could boast of incredible successes: the USSR had taken 2,500,000 casualties, lost 22,000 guns, 18,000 tanks, and 14,000 planes. Axis losses amounted to some 800,000 men—about 25 percent of the original striking force.

255 In rare agreement, Hitler and his generals concentrated forces against the Red Army units bunched in front of their capital; they would be caught in another trap set by panzer and infantry forces from reinforced Army Group Center. Once the Moscow drive started, Russian reinforcements would be delayed by Rundstedt rolling toward Kharkov and Leeb hammering Leningrad. There were problems, however—numbers of guerrillas were cutting supply lines and foretastes of winter were in the air—but not enough yet to halt another blitzkrieg.

256 Operation *Taifun* (Typhoon) began with Guderian's panzer group making a surprise thrust on September 30, followed two days later by other Nazi tank groups that broke strong Red Army defensive positions and captured almost 660,000 prisoners within two weeks. When Mozhaisk (the last big town before Moscow) fell on October 20, Bock's troops were forty miles from the capital. Stalin transferred manufacturing east of the Urals and many government offices to Kuibyshev on the Volga, but he stayed behind to help cram reserves in front of Moscow.

Bock had committed all his reserves, his tanks were worn, his trucks rattling wrecks, and his supplies were thin. Rundstedt, though taking Rostov in mid-November and scoring other major gains, also suffered thinning supplies and a dangerous Red buildup near Rostov. Leeb had supplies coming by sea, was generally in better shape than his colleagues, and captured Tikhvin, northwest of Moscow, also in mid-November.

Bock launched another attack on Moscow on November 15, but ran into fierce cold, increasing numbers of modern Russian planes, some new British tanks, hordes of well-equipped Siberian ski troops, and numbers of new Russian T-34 tanks that outmatched German armor.

257 Suddenly temperatures dropped to forty degrees below zero Fahrenheit, and the general staff's earlier failure to provide winter clothes and equipment threatened disaster. Frostbitten German troops stole civilian clothes for warmth; some were captured wearing women's underwear, fur boas, and cloaks; they were gleefully labeled "Winter Fritz" by Soviet troops clad in heavy parkas, boots, and proper arctic gear.

Still the Germans attacked—Hitler refused to stop and consolidate a winter line. After all, Moscow was so close! It got closer. By early December, the 3rd and 4th Panzer Groups were in sight of Moscow's Khimke water tower. **258** On December 5, 1941, the greatest offensive in warfare stopped, halted by Russian courage, true, but mainly by snow, ice, hunger, frozen men, frozen tanks, frozen guns and planes.

259 Heavily counterattacked on December 6, the Germans fell back and Hitler at last consented to creating defensive winter positions. Angry at the loss of equipment in some of the withdrawals, Hitler sacked thirty-five generals and four field marshals (the three

The Russian winter complicated transport when it did not shut down movement altogether. Here a German tank is used to drag an assault gun out of a snowdrift, the Eastern Front, 1941–42.

army group commanders and army commander in chief Walther von Brauchitsch [q.v.]), then openly took personal command of the army—which he had, in fact, been running since the French campaign. He prohibited retreats and ordered the winter front in 1941–42 to be defended by hedgehog positions—strongholds fortified for all-around defense. A decision both praised and damned, hedgehogs did finally stop the enemy, but at a high cost in blood.

Both sides prepared for renewed war in the spring. Advantage for the first year in Russia went to the Nazis, though Red forces were growing in size and competence.

260 Hitler's prejudices had baneful effects on military operations but even worse effects on occupation policy. Viewing Russians as *Untermenschen*, Hitler proclaimed a harsh program from the start. The campaign, he said, could not be "conducted in a knightly fashion." He noted that Russia did not sign the Geneva convention so her troops need not be treated the same as others, and told Himmler (q.v.) to police occupied territories with SS and Gestapo units independently of the army. In June 1941 he issued his vicious "commissar order," which sentenced all captured Soviet political officers to death. Brutal treatment of civilians and prisoners of war turned potential friends in the Baltic area and the Ukraine into bitter enemies and dangerous guerrilla fighters.

Winter wore on.

GERMAN SEA BATTLES, 1941

261 On May 19, 1941, the Nazi battleship *Bismarck* and her consort cruiser *Prinz Eugen* left the port of Gdynia on the Baltic for the Atlantic. British authorities worried constantly about the big (42,000 tons), new (1941), fast (30½ knots despite heavy armor and armament) German battleship; they dreaded the day this "unsinkable" pride of Hitler's navy might sweep into the Atlantic and smash convoys heading to Rus-

sia. When firm reports came on May 20 that two enemy ships were seen in the Kattegat (the arm of the North Sea between Sweden and the Jutland Peninsula of Denmark), the Royal Navy pulled in ships from as far away as the Mediterranean. A new battleship, HMS *Prince of Wales*, and the old but powerful battle cruiser HMS *Hood* raced to make an early interception. Meanwhile, on May 21, a British reconnaissance plane photographed the two German warships in a fjord near Bergen, Norway.

262 Nazi fleet commander Günther Lütjens doubted that his two surface ships and six escorting U-boats could sweep the Royal Navy from the North Atlantic, but still headed for the Denmark Strait (between Greenland and Iceland) in foggy weather. Spotting the cruiser HMS *Nor-*

Admiral Günther Lütjens, who went down with his flagship, the *Bismarck*.

folk in the strait late on May 23, Lütjens opened fire but his quarry escaped. New radar (q.v.) kept the British in contact. Early on the twenty-fourth Lütjen's force was engaged by the Polish destroyer *Piorun*, then by *Hood* and *Prince of Wales*. *Bismarck*'s shells struck *Hood*'s magazine; she blew up and sank in three minutes, leaving only three survivors. *Prince of Wales*, not yet fully operational, left the battle after being hit—but not before scoring two hits on *Bismarck*.

His ship trailing oil, Lütjens broke radio silence to tell Berlin he was running to France for safety. At 10:30 A.M. on May 26—nearly within range of land-based air cover—*Bismarck* was spotted by a Catalina PBY flying boat flown by a U.S. Navy pilot who reported to British authorities. They reacted quickly. Torpedo planes (Swordfish, as at Taranto) from HMS *Ark Royal* hit *Bismarck*'s steering and left her running in circles. Harassing British cruisers fought *Bismarck* through the night. On the morning of the twenty-seventh, battleships HMS *King George V* and *Rodney* moved in for the kill, but their guns could not break the enemy's armored deck or stop her engines. Gradually, though, *Bismarck*'s guns were smashed, and the ship was scuttled at about 10:15 A.M., losing all but 115 of 2,222 men.

ITALY, 1941

263 **Surely if any nation vivifies Thomas Jefferson's idea of "the pursuit of happiness," it is Italy.** Wine is prized, women are glorified, and arias ring in restaurants. Tragic, then, that when the war began, Mussolini banned dancing. It was a Duce thing, a kind of petulant, dictatorial, foot stamping.

Italian temper had never really favored war, and those times when the Fascists had embroiled Italy in conflict had not been glorious moments. Victory in backward Abyssinia against Emperor Haile Selassie's unprepared and unequipped followers came at a high cost in world opinion. The Spanish Civil War intervention showed, more than anything else,

the woeful weakness of Italian armor, guns, and training. Invading southern France in 1940 had been *opera buffa* at its worst. Albania restored some dignity, but Greece revealed Duce's armed forces as sad comics before a guffawing audience. Hitler's hasty help confounded the humiliation.

Mussolini knew that Italians resented being played for buffoons. Jokes about their martial prowess stung—"What is the shortest book in the library? A history of Italian military victories!"—and demeaned heroic ancestors who had created a nation and sustained its freedoms.

After Mussolini had consolidated his power in 1925–26, the Fascists controlled virtually everything and the monarchy was reduced to puppetry. Italy's internal situation, though, restrained some Fascist excesses. More a collection of oligopolies than a dictatorship when war began, Italy posed irksome governing conundrums. The people could be handled by strong secret police that grew stronger every month—and the people made little trouble as rearmament created jobs and a shadow prosperity emerged.

So *Il Duce*'s problems weren't so much with the people as a whole. He was, instead, confounded by some of his industrialist friends. Needing help from Italy's manufacturers, Mussolini wooed such giants as Fiat and Ansaldo, which controlled manpower, market, money, and were fiefdoms of force. Monopolizing war production, they apportioned it to themselves plus a few cronies and, in effect, dominated most of the economy. Try as the government did, it could not break this oligopolistic system of production and had to accept the poor armor, guns, even planes miserably unveiled in Spain.

264 **Management of resources might have controlled the big producers, but Italy was also short of raw materials, especially coal and petroleum.** Only 2.3 million tons of steel were produced annually in the late thirties compared to France (over six million tons), Britain (over ten million), and Germany (twenty-three million tons). Diversification stimulated the electrical industry, but it, too, lagged behind allies and enemies. The automobile industry had a good reputation but was cramped by shortages, a situation that limited driver and mechanic training. Italian aircraft were overrated, their engines weak and first-line combat models few; many older types proved worse than useless. All of this stemmed from the strength of big industry.

ITALIAN LAND BATTLES, 1941

265 **Militarily, 1941 began badly for Italy.** Most East African territories were gone, including hard-won Ethiopia, even Italian Somaliland. Almost 45,000 soldiers were taken prisoner by the British at Bardia in early January, and late in the month 30,000 more were lost as Tobruk fell. As Marshal Rodolfo Graziani (q.v.) pulled the Tenth Army back toward Tripoli in February, a British corps surprised him by moving inland, swinging back, and cutting the coastal road at Beda Fomm. After hard fighting, Graziani's army and air force were wrecked, 25,000 more of his men became prisoners, and he lost his job. Total Italian losses to Wavell's (q.v.) offensive that ended on February 7, 1941, were 140,000 men, 845 guns, and 380 tanks. Wavell lost 1,928 men and minimal equipment. One thing became starkly clear in this campaign: Italian tanks, guns, and vehicles were hopelessly inferior.

Morale became a problem. Bad news yielded to shock when long casualty lists confirmed that the Duce had led the nation to ruin.

266 **After Beda Fomm, Rommel (q.v.) took firm command in North Africa, smashed the British back toward Egypt—and used the remaining Italian troops effectively.** He was, in fact, fooled by the unsuspected strength of the Italian Ariete Division. He had put it into the center of his line, expecting it to retreat and allow German troops on the flanks to win another Battle

of Marathon—but an unexpected Ariete attack drove the British back and left the Germans behind.

Rommel was appalled by Italy's small and flimsy M13 tanks—they would, he said, "make one's hair curl." Interspersed, though, with his panzers, they did fair service when manned by Ariete tank men.

During the rest of 1941, Italian troops took part in Rommel's thrusts and counterthrusts across the desert from Agheila to Sollum and back. Losses were high in men and matériel, but so were the stakes—and victories outnumbered defeats as the Desert Fox blended artillery (especially the splendid 88mm multipurpose gun) with armor, infantry, and brilliant personal leadership. By the end of 1941 Rommel and the desert had burnished much shame from Italy's shield.

ITALIAN SEA BATTLES, 1941

267 *Il Duce*'s navy was beautiful, its ships a naval architect's dream. His crews were also good, but poor leadership and technology failed both men and ships.

Ordered to stop any British convoys headed for Greece, Italy's main fleet put to sea on March 27, 1941, and was soon spotted by British patrol bombers. Admiral Andrew Cunningham (q.v.) led a Royal Navy cruiser force to intercept. Early the next day, one Italian battleship, six cruisers, and seven destroyers were seen near Crete; these were joined by two more cruisers and three destroyers. British ships tracked the Italian ships off Cape Matapan throughout the day and surprised them late in the afternoon. The British had radar, the Italians none; hence an Italian battleship was crippled, four cruisers and two destroyers were sunk, and 2,400 sailors were lost, at a British cost of one plane. The Italian remnants fled to port. From that time, main Italian units never strayed from coastal air cover.

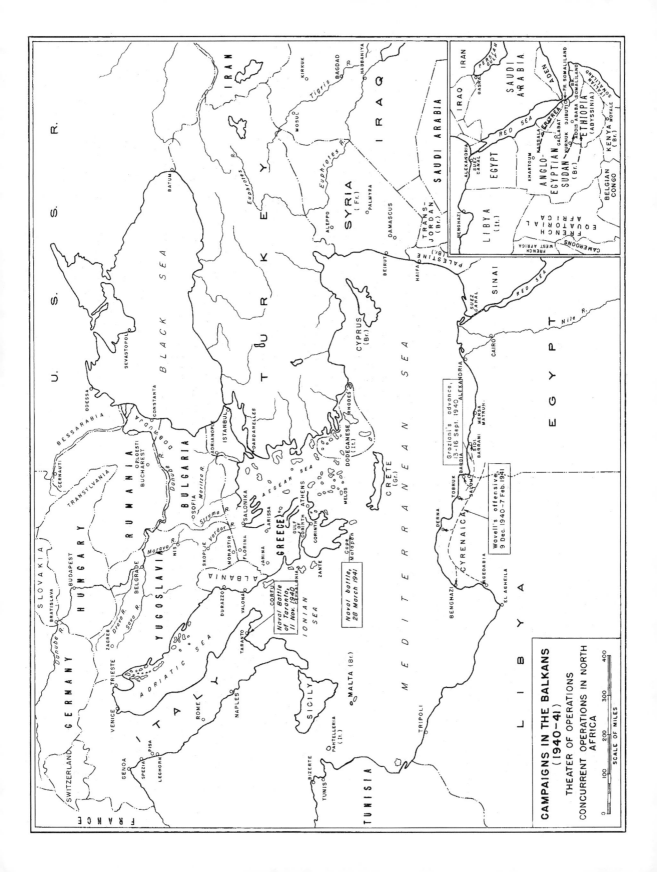

CAMPAIGNS IN THE BALKANS
(1940-41)
THEATER OF OPERATIONS
CONCURRENT OPERATIONS IN NORTH
AFRICA

SCALE OF MILES
0   100   200   300   400

By the middle of the summer 1941, Italian battleships were hors de combat because of fuel shortages. So ended any real Axis threat to the Mediterranean.

VICHY FRANCE, 1941

268 Pétain had saved France before at Verdun, and his words "they shall not pass" resonated in the French conscience. Called to lead when his country crumbled in 1940, the octogenarian marshal (q.v.) struggled to save some sovereignty by agreeing to an armistice with Germany and Italy. Thus France began a precarious dual existence partitioned into a *zone occupée* and a *zone libre*.

269 With his capital at the fashionable spa, Vichy, Pétain ran a dictator-

June 1940, Marshal Pétain shaking hands with the Führer (the "handshake of Montoire") while Hitler's interpreter, Colonel Schmidt, watches.

ship that twisted France's historic devotion to *liberté, égalité, fraternité* into an almost messianic national cleansing (which included anti-Semitism) embodied in a new motto: *travail, famille, patrie.*

Pétain is criticized for collaborating with the Germans, for allowing persecution of Jews and other *Untermenschen*, and for allowing French prisoners of war to be held hostage. Valid as are many criticisms, it should be said for the marshal that he worked from a position of eroding weakness.

Presiding over barely two-fifths of France, the southeastern part from the Swiss border near Geneva to a bit east of Tours and then southwest to the Spanish border, Pétain had few good people to work with. Pierre Laval, a longtime French political activist who swayed with left and right political winds and is aptly described as epitomizing "the worst morality and the best skills of French politics," did much to put the marshal in office, and his pro-Axis maneuvering made him invaluable to the new administration. As virtual head of

the government, Laval worked toward full "collaboration" with Germany, arguing that there was no other choice. Resistance would end even a shred of independence, probably under a harsh *Gauleiter*. At the end of 1940, Laval was arrested for fomenting a coup d'état in his own favor, but was freed by the Germans and would finally become Vichy's head man, with Pétain as figurehead. Admiral Jean Darlan replaced Laval for a time and moved to protect the French fleet. An Anglophobe, hence pro-German, Darlan also sought deals with Germany and the United States as he connived to protect the North African colonies. Pétain dampened the admiral's avid pro-German stance.

270 Hitler tolerated the new French state because it solved some occupation problems, kept many soldiers, sailors, and ships from the Allies, and concentrated French attention on independence while three-fifths of the country was systematically robbed of labor and natural resources.

VICHY FRENCH LAND BATTLES, 1941

271 Vichy's 100,000-man "armistice army" had little duty save internal security, but colonial forces were allowed to expand. There had been fighting when British naval units attacked a Vichy fleet at Mers-el-Kébir in July 1940. General de Gaulle (q.v.) sent some Free French troops, aided by the British, to take the big Vichy base at Dakar, West Africa, in September and failed. Syria saw some action in June 1941 when British and Free French forces invaded; Vichy defenders, aided by some naval units, were quickly defeated.

272 Vichy did not escape Barbarossa's effects. On August 27, 1941, the first contingent of the *Légion des volontaires Français contre le bolchevism* (LVF) left Versailles for the Russian front.

THE UNION OF SOVIET SOCIALIST REPUBLICS (USSR), 1941

273 Russia's greatest agony began on June 22, 1941. As the blitzkrieg engulfed the huge vastness of the western Soviet Union, it forced a command collapse—several generals and staffs were stranded on trains en route to their units—that sacrificed whole armies in a matter of days.

274 Within a week after invasion, the Politburo (the controlling hierarchy of the Central Committee) ordered evacuation of key war industries from cities in the enemy's path. With 60 percent of its armaments industry, more than 60 percent of its coal, 74 percent of its coke, 70 percent of its iron ore, nearly 70 percent of its pig iron, 60 percent of its aluminum, nearly 60 percent of its crude steel, 57 percent of its rolled steel production, and more than 40 percent of its electric power generating capacity lost to the enemy, every remaining factory or plant had to be saved, along with as many workers as possible.

275 From July to November, 1.5 million railway cars were used to move 1,500 factories and ten million people (one million from the Moscow area) to the Urals, Siberia, the trans-Volga area, and Kazakhstan—all while new plants were being built. This mass hegira—imperfect as it was—saved the USSR. Artillery plants expanded (Russia had specialized in big guns before the war), the rapid-firing *katyusha* rockets were mass produced, as were T-34 medium tanks (some of the best in the war). Of those 1,500 relocated plants, 1,200 were back in production by mid-1942.

Careful organization and frenetic zeal sustained Russian military production through 1941, but drastic increases were needed—statistics from the *Oxford Companion to World War II* tell a grim story: "Although aircraft factories produced 16% of the air force's front-line strength each month, monthly losses amounted to no less than 45%. While 18% of the front-line strength in armoured vehicles was replaced monthly, losses reached a staggering 57%.... By the winter artillery ammunition had been rationed to one or two shells per gun per day. During the last quarter of 1941 ... as strategic reserves were eaten up ... production of basic industries declined. Transport proved to be ... [a] major constraint. Army logistics had become so strained that in December horse battalions were reintroduced." There were a few bright spots—aircraft and tank production for the last seven months of 1941 almost equaled Germany's for the entire year.

276 A drastic drop in civilian goods hit by the end of 1941; new clothing and shoes nearly vanished and a scarcity of food threatened mass starvation. Yet morale rose as hatred replaced other necessities. Writers and poets went to war and wrote of hate. According to famous journalist Ilya Ehrenburg, Germans were not human. " 'German,' " he wrote, "has become the most terrible swear word.... Let us kill. If you do not kill the German, the German will kill you. ... If you have killed one German, kill another. There is nothing jollier than German corpses." A leading newspaper echoed the theme: "May holy hatred become our chief, our only feeling." V. I. Lebedev's poem "Holy War" appeared on June 24, 1941, was set to music, and became Russia's battle anthem. Other writers, composers, and artists worked in praise of heroes at the front and in the hospitals and factories, in the mines, on the rivers and oceans.

277 Human losses were astounding in the first weeks of Hitler's drive—nearly 40 percent of the USSR's 170 million people were caught behind German lines; the Red Army had thousands killed and more men captured than could be counted. Although surprised, frightened, and confused, many Russian civilians met the invaders with hope for release from the long Soviet reigns of terror and collectivization, release from shortages and hunger. But Hitler's "no quarter" orders quickly ruined the *Wehrmacht*'s chances to be greeted as liberators.

As Hitler's minions spread hatred wherever they went, Russians of all ages and stations flocked into war industries and factories, and worked on railroads, bridges, trenches. They fought more against repression than for the USSR, and the price they paid in blood that year remains untolled.

278 Stalin eventually took all reins of war-making to himself, proving good and bad in his varied jobs. His effective third of July speech to "brothers and sisters," ordering the whole country on a war footing and calling for a relentless "scorched earth" program, created the "holy war" to save Mother Russia. Even dissidents in the Ukraine and other parts of the USSR rallied to this call with an ancient and deep-running pulse of patriotism.

As he yielded to his old distrust of the army and military staff officers, much good from that speech was forgotten. True, he had resurrected some four thousand former high-ranking officers from the gulag before the war and began restoring such martial perquisites as rank and easier living conditions, but potential treason by the military lurked in the dark recesses of his oddly nimble brain. More than that, he nearly outdid the Nazis and Ivan the Terrible in repression. Nursing the ineluctable fear of coups that plague dictators, Stalin reinstated political commissars at all levels of government and all levels of the military. The commissars whom Hitler had ordered shot on capture appeared again—Hitler should have returned those captured because the commissars often confounded Russian field operations.

279 Like all leaders, Stalin had cronies, some from his early Bolshevik days, men who had been with him in the 1917 Revolution and were trusted because of shared sufferings. Several were with him on the Politburo (L. M. Kaganovich, M. I. Kalinin, A. I. Mikoyan [q.v.], V. M. Molotov [q.v.], K. Y. Voroshilov, A. A. Zhdanov) and some were in military positions (S. M. Budenny [q.v.], S. K. Timoshenko [q.v.], G. K. Zhukov [q.v.]). Not all were talented, but they shared the special skill of getting along with their old comrade. Not really gifted in picking able subordinates, Stalin did have luck.

280 Anastas Mikoyan proved invaluable as virtual chief quartermaster for the war; he procured and distributed supplies for all services and directed conversion of civilian industries to war production and also handled the baffling business of Lend-Lease (q.v.) aid from the United States. **281** Dour and stolid, Molotov served as deputy chair of the State Defense Committee and as foreign minister. Competent, ruthless, and demanding, Molotov fumed at Hitler's attack and made the first announcement of war to the Russian people. **282** Timoshenko, for a time people's commissar for defense, showed organizing ability, while Georgi Zhukov would rank among the best generals of World War II.

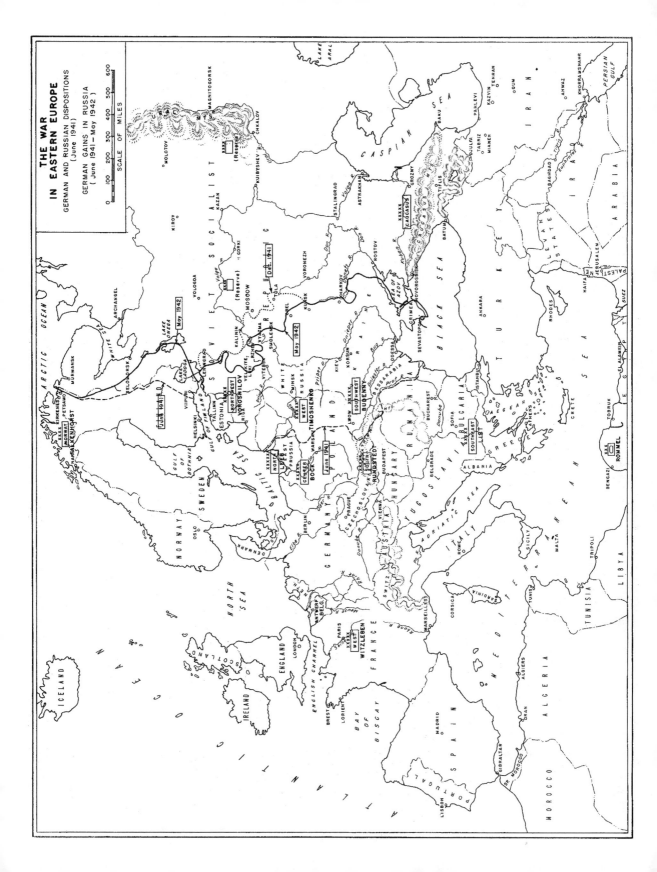

THE WAR
IN EASTERN EUROPE
GERMAN AND RUSSIAN DISPOSITIONS
(June 1941)
GERMAN GAINS IN RUSSIA
(June 1941 - May 1942)

SCALE OF MILES

0 100 200 300 400 500 600

As he sought to remake the war into a crusade to save Mother Russia, Stalin slowly earned support.

RUSSIAN LAND BATTLES, 1941

283 The *Wehrmacht*'s attack in June 1941 caught Red Army units and leaders in the midst of change. On paper things looked fairly good for the Soviets when Hitler struck. There were 2.9 million men available (more were coming) in the western theaters, supported by 10,000 tanks and 7,500 planes, while against them the Germans disposed 3.05 million men on the front, supported by 3,350 tanks and 2,770 planes. In reality, though, the Soviet situation was abysmal. Their planes and tanks were much older than German equipment and, worse than that, were badly handled. Swift Luftwaffe airfield strikes destroyed many Russian aircraft on the ground and won complete air control over the front on the first day. Soviet planners expected German forces to come slowly and start a regular offensive, not a blitzkrieg. Forward deployment along the Russo-Polish border accommodated those ideas, and had the war gone as expected, Red forces would have been ready.

284 *Wehrmacht* advances on the first day were astounding. In forty-eight hours German forces gobbled up Brest-Litovsk, site of Russia's WWI humbling by the Kaiser's troops and the command and control center for the Red Army's western front. Nazi heavy guns rolled up and smashed all illusions of the Stalin Line. A babble of confused messages jammed radio waves. "We are being fired on, what shall we do?" "You must be insane. Why is your signal not in code?" Hitler's armies swooped ahead in giant pincer movements.

285 Russia's defenses hinged on three *fronts* (army groups), commanded by trusted Stalin cronies; north under Voroshilov, south under Budenny, and the center under Timoshenko, the sole member of the troika

with a modicum of talent. All efforts to stem chaos failed as military and civilian refugees clogged the dirt roads, slowed trains, and snarled logistics as the gray juggernaut stabbed at the heart of the *Rodina*. Early orders to hold everywhere and counterattack proved absurd as German armor swiftly broke Russian lines. Bock's two panzer groups achieved a double envelopment near Minsk and by the end of June had captured the city and more than 300,000 prisoners, 2,400 tanks, and 1,400 artillery pieces. Army Group Center pushed on, Bock's thrusts and pincers wrecking twelve to fifteen Russian divisions west of the Dvina.

Disorganization itself may have saved the situation for a time; nobody could find out just how bad things were. Absence of news sustained hope as Timoshenko pulled up five reserve armies and the first formations of T-34 tanks to hold—Stalin, like Hitler, forbade retreat—on the upper Dvina and Dnieper Rivers. But with no air support and with most tanks gone, Timoshenko's strong resistance faded. **286** Bock snared the strategic city of Smolensk—the "gateway to Moscow"—on July 19, 1941, along with 100,000 prisoners, 2,000 tanks, and 1,900 guns. Here, though, the Nazis had their first experience with the fearsome *katyusha* rockets that would rive endless battle days.

Fortunately for Russia, Hitler kept a close eye on his front. Noting that his center advanced quickly while the flanks lagged, he shifted plans and men—Moscow could be mopped up after Leningrad and the resource-rich Crimea were taken. So Bock was ordered to divide his panzers between Leeb to the north and Rundstedt to the south. **287** This stalled the direct drive on Moscow and provided the "miracle" that stunned the Russian high command.

But Stalin made an astounding blunder when he refused to let his Southwest *front* retreat from Kiev and so presented the city and 665,000 prisoners to Rundstedt's armies at the end of September. The way was open to Kharkov and Rostov. **288** Then, in August 1941, Stalin issued Order No. 270, designed to make the Red Army fight to the last man. Instead it demoralized many and infuriated more—any soldier taken prisoner would be regarded as a traitor and his family would suffer.

Leeb's forces began to encircle Leningrad by the end of September and Hitler ordered him to besiege the city—let the Russians feed the citizens!

289 In August, Stalin appointed himself supreme commander in chief and created a seven-member group, the *Stavka,* to advise him. **290** These moves coincided with the German halt before Moscow and made Stalin look good to his people and the world; they also brought about the Three Power Conference (Lord Beaverbrook, minister of supply, represented the UK, and Averell Harriman the U.S.) in September, that settled on what Lend-Lease (q.v.) aid Russia needed immediately.

When the German drive on Moscow resumed in late September—Operation Typhoon—Bock, with his panzer and Luftwaffe units more than restored, hit two Soviet *fronts* and Budenny's big Reserve *front,* and in early October two of the *fronts,* comprising some ten armies, were surrounded and lost

some 660,000 prisoners. Bock drove ahead to encircle Moscow while Rundstedt headed for Rostov.

Now Russia's main ally, General Winter, joined the war, with rains coming on October 7 and the temperature dropping. German armor slithered, slipped, and stuck in the mud, but pushed on against all kinds of ragtag units thrown in to save the capital. **291** On October 20, 1941, the last big city in front of Moscow, Mozhaisk, fell and Guderian's (q.v.) tanks were near Tula. Hitler and his staff believed the Russians would evacuate Moscow and that the war was won. Not quite.

Trouble persisted for the Russians in the south, where Rundstedt took Rostov in late November and besieged Sevastopol. And when the roads froze over around Moscow, it looked as though General Winter had deserted Mother Russia. As Bock struck again on November 15, an entire Red Army collapsed and another was overrun by tanks. By November 24, with Guderian's armor only sixty miles southeast of the capital, Stalin was evacuating Moscow (though he stayed himself) and ordering desperate counterat-

Truck convoy crossing frozen Lake Ladoga with supplies for Leningrad during the unusually cold and early winter of 1941–42. These supplies helped sustain the blockaded city. An estimated one million noncombatants died during the 900-day siege.

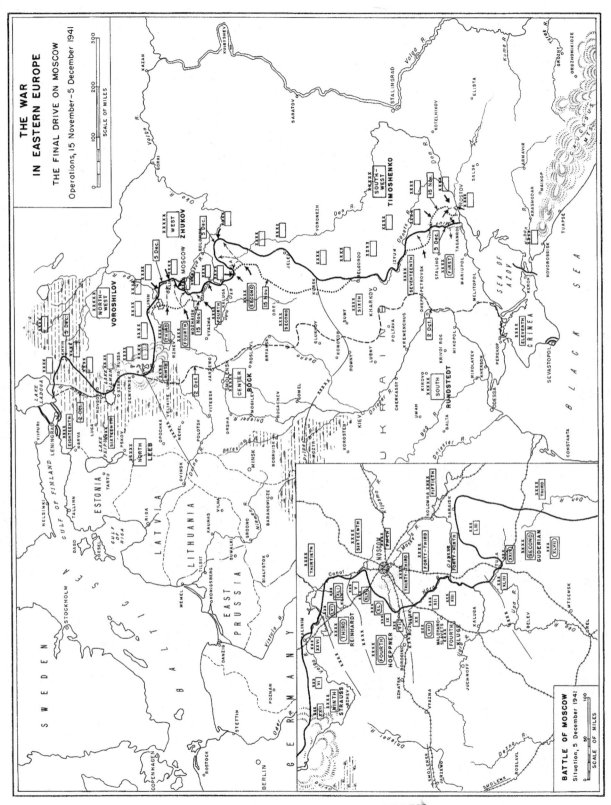

tacks. A few units equipped with British tanks and some with Soviet T-34s joined the battle, along with several fresh and tough divisions from Siberia—and General Winter returned as the temperature slipped suddenly to minus forty Fahrenheit, catching the Nazi armies short of winter clothing and lubricants. **292 The great German offensive stopped short of Moscow— but with much of it in sight—on December 5, 1941.**

293 A major Russian counterattack began on December 6 and the Russians scored big gains. Unready as they were, the Soviet high command fell back on historic Russian bravery and on a great population advantage to trade ground for time. The Germans underestimated the fanatical patriotism, the fighting qualities, and the large numbers of their enemy. But as Russian casualties mounted and prisoners flooded German POW depots, victory still looked certain.

THE BRITISH EMPIRE, 1941

294 Wintering through 1940–41 had been both exhilarating and terribly lonely for England. The "blitz" burned big parts of London, killed some twenty-eight thousand civilians, and wounded as many more, drove hosts to the "tube" (subway) shelters every night, strained all the emergency services, but somehow raised morale. Churchill, of course, contributed to raising morale—his dauntless rhetoric, his formidable walks through London's rubble, touched a deep strain of daring in the British soul. Nazi air raids, Nazi victories everywhere, combined with hard weather and unaccustomed things like clothes rationing and a manpower management program that tied male and female workers to their war jobs, were heavy burdens; but the people knew, somehow, that with all the "blood, toil, tears and sweat," they were making "their finest hour."

TOP: During the Blitz, the London underground or "tube" stations served as bomb shelters for many citizens. Here Londoners seeking safety bed down on escalators, 1940. BOTTOM: Elephant & Castle underground station, November 11, 1940.

TOP: The dome of St. Paul's Cathedral seems to float on dark clouds of smoke and flame during the fire raid of December 29, 1940. BOTTOM: Winston Churchill inspecting bomb damage, Ramsgate, 1940. As much as the unscathed St. Paul's Cathedral, Churchill symbolized Britain's indomitable spirit.

295 **An internal revolution was changing the life of Britain.** Before the war, English society had rested on a hereditary class system, and women's roles were limited. As military rolls expanded and men left home, and as women went beyond home, hospitals, and pageants to make planes, guns, tanks, and all kinds of weaponry, traditional roles shifted. Women became vital to the war. So did the handicapped, conscientious objectors, the "walking wounded." Total war had come to Britons by 1941.

296 **No money, no war—so goes a maxim worth remembering—and in 1941, Britain's credit really ran out.** Churchill confessed it to his war brother, President Roosevelt, and that canny politico translated the message into the war-winning Lend-Lease program. But Britain lacked more than money. U-boat successes in 1940 and 1941 nearly starved the United Kingdom. United States naval help in patrolling the North Atlantic and organizing convoys staved off British defeat, however, and Germany's unexpected invasion of the USSR in June brought universal joy. Churchill said it "seemed to be too good to be true."

297 **Churchill, fortunately, carried few ghosts from World War I.** Remembering his Dardanelles blunder, he kept an open mind about changes in war-making. Though some of his staff thought he did not appreciate modern military technology, he supported Sir Henry Tizard's scientific work on radar and George Thomson's initial studies of nuclear fission, and accepted another war-winning idea: let the Americans build an atomic bomb—a marriage of theory and resources that resulted in the Manhattan Project (q.v.). And despite the pressures of war, his government understood priorities, and scientific work flourished in wartime Britain.

298 **Literature, music, and art also flourished because of a governmental determination not to lose culture in the overwash of death.** Out of the awfulness came some remarkable creations in serious literature, theater,

music, and art. Fine battle paintings had been done during World War I, and Britain's cultural mavens in the second world clash helped found an artists' corps so that special human feelings in the anguish of war would forever be seen at fever pitch. Although an acting career did not earn an exemption from the draft, some slack was cut for performers who agreed to go on the circuit of service clubs and traveling shows. Laurence Olivier, Noel Coward, Sybil Thorndike, and other distinguished thespians played for soldiers and civilians in theaters, in air raid shelters, even factories. Funny Gracie Fields's Lancashire accent was heard widely and boosted the confidence of a rising working class. Vera Lynn's shapely figure titillated thousands at service shows as she sang "The White Cliffs of Dover" and "Lili Marlene." Popular music did much for morale, and dance bands like Henry Hall's were smash hits. So, too, was the monthly magazine *Lilliput*, which carried in each issue news, stories, and a picture of a girl in the buff.

Collectivized living brought unusual opportunities for reaching masses of people. Adult education, never keen in England, got a big boost from the war. Various universities, seeing their chance, offered off-duty factory workers varied classes in a kind of early "open campus" program.

In the down year of 1941, Britons' main pride came from the knowledge that they could "take it," that their home island alone boasted more than 2.5 million men under arms and more than 100,000 women in uniformed services.

299 **In 1941 the British Empire, though eroding in the Far East and stressed everywhere, still covered nearly a quarter of the globe, and without these dominions and colonies Britain would have lost the war.** Peoples in old dominions like Canada, Australia, New Zealand, and South Africa, joined by those in the viceroyalty of India, colonies in much of Africa, in the South Atlantic, South America, the Middle and Far East—all were subjects of the king, George VI. From them, the empire raised more than five million troops for the war and garnered invaluable raw materials.

By year's end, though, Russia, Lend-Lease (q.v.), and Pearl Harbor had changed the future of the world. **300 The United Kingdom declared war on Japan, December 8, 1941—even before the U.S.—and the empire soon followed.**

PROPAGANDA

301 Lord Haw Haw began daily broadcasts from Germany to England as the war began. William Joyce, a British fascist before 1939, went to Germany and Goebbels grabbed him for Berlin radio. In high sarcasm, "Lord Haw Haw" (Joyce borrowed the name from an earlier propagandist) ridiculed British efforts and beckoned Britons to quit the war and join in a great Nordic-Aryan crusade to exterminate degenerates, communists, and liberals. Nobody followed, but Britons remembered. Tried for treason after the war, Joyce went to the gallows on January 3, 1946.

302 Goebbels expanded his radio enticement by adding a female voice—Axis Sally. Mildred Gillars, American citizen, in Germany since the 1920s as a music student, accepted Goebbels' radio offer and, like Tokyo Rose (q.v.), mixed her calls for defection with good music. She, too, did more to increase Allied morale than anything else. Imprisoned for twelve years after the war, Gillars later taught in a convent and then finished her bachelor's degree in speech in 1973 at age seventy-three.

BRITISH LAND BATTLES, 1941

303 British land operations began smashingly in 1941. East Africa dangled out in the Somalilands, almost a forgotten drib of the war. But an Italian army under the duke of Aosta (veteran politician/soldier) had occupied British Somaliland in mid-1940, and late that year plans were made to get it back. Odds ran against British hopes. Aosta led 92,000 Italian and a quarter million Abyssinian troops, backed by tanks and more than 300 planes. The British had only 40,000 locals and a few more than 100 planes. Aosta, pessimistic and isolated, stayed on the defensive and wasted several opportunities to crush the British. Had Aosta known that British code-breakers revealed all his secrets to the British, he probably would have surrendered.

As it was, his pessimism grew with British successes in North Africa and dual offensives in January and February 1941 into Eritrea and Italian Somaliland; the surprising success of a small force under Lt. Col. Orde Wingate (q.v.) that restored Emperor Haile Selassie to his Ethiopian throne in May added to the duke's discomfort. Lieutenant General Alan Cunningham (older brother of "ABC" Cunningham [q.v.]), took the surrender of Italian East African forces that same month.

304 Victory in East Africa not only boosted British morale, it also opened the Red Sea and the Gulf of Aden, which allowed supplies through to Suez. That victory, too, contributed to another one against Vichy French forces in the Syrian campaign, June 1941. Crete, though, was evacuated—a la Dunkirk—the first of that month, after German airborne landings.

305 Although British strength was spread thin, troops were detached in mid-August to join Soviet forces in securing Iran. Germany imported much oil from what was still called Persia, and the Shah got along with Hitler. Britain needed Persia's oil, and Russia coveted the supply route from the Persian Gulf. By mid-September the invasion ended with a new administration friendly to the Allies.

306 In North Africa, General Wavell, although weakened from detachments to Greece, pushed his drive westward and, on January 22, 1941, his Australians took Tobruk. Wrecked tanks, abandoned equipment, and much generalized junk cluttered the enemy retreat toward Benghazi—which Wavell's men took on February 6. Six days later General Rommel took command in Libya and swung the momentum toward the Axis.

307 After he swept eastward through El Agheila in late March, the Desert Fox's small army picked up speed, bypassed Tobruk (a strategic mistake—he should have taken it), and by mid-April shoved Wavell's forces out of Libya. Then Rommel tried twice, unsuccessfully, to take Tobruk. Wavell tried two counterattacks from Egypt, which also failed and cost him his job. His replacement, Gen. Sir Claude Auchinleck, took the time to build his force while trying to stem problems in Syria and Iraq. The new Eighth Army, under Gen. Alan Cunningham, opened a successful attack on November 18 and relieved Tobruk as Rommel, his supplies rationed because of Barbarossa (q.v.), pulled back. Cunningham, his tanks almost gone, thought of retreat but Auchinleck replaced him with Maj. Gen. Neil Ritchie, who steadily pressed Rommel back to El Agheila by the end of the year.

Everyone knew, though, that Rommel was biding his time.

Problems persisted in the Mideast. Britain's fortunes sagged in Greece by midyear. **308** The 55,000-man expeditionary force sent to help the Greeks resist an Italian invasion was beaten by more than half a million invading Nazi troops. Some 43,000 survivors were evacuated in late April.

BRITISH SEA BATTLES, 1941

309 In May 1941 the British navy fought a rare warship to warship action. With "Sink the *Bismarck*!" becoming England's rallying call, Royal Navy sea and air units stalked the German giant and its escort in May. *Bismarck* (q.v.) sank HMS *Hood* on May 24, but was soon attacked by the *Prince of Wales* and other major vessels and sunk three days later. It was a kind of national crusade and every Briton gloried in the victory.

German photo of the battleship *Bismarck* engaging HMS *Hood* in the Denmark Strait, May 24, 1941. *Hood* would explode and sink, leaving three survivors out of a complement of 1,421.

310 As focus shifted to the Far East in December, HMS *Prince of Wales* and consort cruiser *Repulse* sallied from Singapore on December 8 to interdict Japanese troops and supplies headed for Thailand and Malaya. Admiral Tom Phillips expected air cover which never came, nor did other promised ships. The sovereign days of surface ships ended on the tenth when Japanese planes sank both British vessels in one of the Royal Navy's worst disasters.

German photograph of Gen. Erwin Rommel, between Tobruk and Sidi Omar, Libya, 1941.

311 Out on the restless reaches of the Atlantic the fiercest sea campaign of the war continued through the year. For U-boats the first "Happy Time" closed when U.S. Navy ships joined in convoy protection. But new Nazi submarines were coming, and Admiral Dönitz's wolf-pack tactics still took a steady toll. U-boats, planes, surface raiders, and mines sank some 3.1 million tons of Allied shipping in 1941—averaged to a little over 250,000 tons per month (the high point in April, 644,000 tons). But different packaging and port traffic management saved about three million tons, and some 1.3 million new tons were produced. Britain had a tonnage surplus for the year; nonetheless there were months of frightening scarcity in the Home Islands. **312** Dönitz and his canny *Frontboote* (Atlantic U-boats) captains did the most damage in the so-called air gaps—areas unprotected by Allied planes. A three-hundred-mile zone south of Greenland and an area known to the Nazis as the "black pit" west of the Azores remained open until 1943.

Although optimistic reports came from the Atlantic battle in 1941, the Allied situation remained bleak and the outlook dismal as Far Eastern losses escalated into catastrophe.

THE EMPIRE OF JAPAN, 1941

Who among Versailles' delegates could have known in those fateful weeks in 1919 that they really met to make war? Most of their high hopes for peace were already subverted by secret agreements and the vengeance of the victors. Germany and its allies had not been humbled; they were, they knew, undefeated, and hence angered and unrepentant, ripe ground for demagogues. Enter Hitler and Mussolini, and in the East, Hideki Tojo (q.v.).

313 But Tojo was a different sort of demagogue. Japan had evolved a matrix kind of government after it began emerging from its chrysalis of isolation in the Meiji era. Layers of influence clogged administration and diffused authority. Much government work was done through big

family corporations (*zaibatsu*) and various "associations," so Japanese society rested on genealogy and collaboration, a system resistant to bullyboy rhetoric.

314 Although one of the Allies in World War I, Japan suffered seriously during the postwar depression, again in the worldwide decline of the thirties, and from poorly negotiated naval treaties that restricted imperial fleet expansion. Occupying Manchuria in 1931, setting up the puppet state of Manchukuo there, and the "China Incident" (a war that began in 1937 as Japan contrived to attack China) had stretched imperial resources. Matériel weakness and continuing martial efforts in China and on the Manchukuo border with Russia forced Japan into a war economy by 1939. Shortages and the increasing truculence—including economic sanctions—of the United States, greatly increased the military's power.

A regular army officer, Tojo had taught at the staff college and commanded infantry in the China Incident. As a leading hardliner, he pushed for greater army influence in state affairs. Drawn into three cabinets during the late 1930s, he had supported the Tripartite Pact with Germany and Italy; but he blundered in urging the invasion of southern Indochina, which escalated American worries about Japan's restless expansionism and resulted in a total trade embargo in 1941. **315** Convinced that Japan's position would wither, Tojo, at an imperial conference, September 6, 1941, counseled war. Emperor Hirohito (q.v.) made him prime minister in October.

316 He showed his own brand of demagoguery in pushing his cabinet toward war. After Washington, on November 26, demanded Japanese withdrawal from China as a condition of peace, Tojo's emotions spilled over. He railed against the so-called ABCD (America, Britain, China, and the Dutch) League hemming in Japan and called for unity. A rash of spy arrests (including master spy Richard Sorge (q.v.) in October 1941) seemed to prove the growing national threat. Seizing on uncertainty, the new prime minister was daring and proclaimed in November, that there come moments in the lives of people and nations when high risks must be taken, moments "to jump with closed eyes from the veranda of the Kiyomizu Temple." The time had come to fight, "rather than await extinction it were better to face death by breaking through the encircling ring to find a way for existence."

317 Some historians argue that American economic policy forced Japan into war—that President Roosevelt deliberately blockaded the island empire to force conflict. In fact, after receiving some indication from incomplete Magic code analysis that war loomed, he made a last-ditch effort for peace by sending an urgent, highly conciliatory message for Hirohito's eyes on December 6—which reached Japan's foreign minister at about 3:00 A.M. on December 7, 1941. Whether or not the emperor saw it hardly mattered by that late date. Tojo's and the general staff's rhetoric propelled Japan into a decisive first strike.

1941 photo of the Type 97 Alphabetical Typewriter (*97-shiki O-bun In-ji-ki*), used for deciphering the Japanese Purple diplomatic code. It took eighteen months to break the Purple code. The first intelligence (produced September 24, 1940) so amazed one authority that he called the code-breakers "magicians"; and their code-work became known as Magic.

Most of the high command knew they could not win a long war with America, but believed Japan could earn a negotiated peace. The Imperial Navy concurred at the price of first attacking Pearl Harbor and the American Pacific Fleet—an operation which would clear Nipponese pathways to the resource-rich, if ill-defined, Greater East Asia Co-Prosperity Sphere.

318 Another controversy about Hirohito haunts the halls of history. How much did the emperor know about Japan's aggressive stances and how much did he approve? An active school suggests that Hirohito remained loftily above war decisions, that he opposed his country's march to Avernus. Again, there is not much to support this royalist idyll, since he gave imperial approval to major cabinet decisions and retained astounding influence throughout his reign. He liked to think of himself as a constitutional monarch in the British sense and certainly he reigned rather than ruled, but he listened and saw and sometimes tampered.

319 Hirohito accepted the logic for war, considering the constrictions from the United States, echoed by Great Britain. War, though, would have to be quick; the empire, already strained in China, could not survive a long conflict. Japan imported most essential raw materials: all of its scrap iron, bauxite, nickel, and rubber; nearly 80 percent of its crude oil (two-thirds of it came from the United States); over 80 percent of its iron ore; nearly 90 percent of its lead; almost 70 percent of its salt, along with varying amounts of tin, zinc, and copper. Almost 25 percent of the nation's rice was imported, as well as more than 80 percent of its sugar and over 70 percent of its soybeans. Synthetics and various substitutes were tried, and refineries were built, but the nation depended in 1941 on a merchant fleet of only 6 million tons and Southeast Asia's bounty.

Cold statistics are much like cold sake—unpalatable. Behind them though, is the stern reality of harsh national change. Increasing amounts of the annual budget went to war needs; in 1931 the military received less than 30 percent but that amount had doubled by 1940. War, by then, began to shape everything—appearances, diet, transport, education, medicine, entertainment, and morale.

320 **Morale received much official attention because it might affect loyalty.** While state control of personal lives did not reach Nazi or Fascist levels, programs were devised to prop up patriotism and monitor all kinds of dissent. The *Tokkō*, or Special Higher Police, roamed the Home Islands, arresting, sometimes torturing, and "retraining" backsliders. The word *Tokkō* brought the same fear as "Gestapo."

321 **For those who toed the line, civilian life continued fairly smoothly in 1941, save for increasing inflation.** Although the Japanese grumbled at increasing discipline and at short rationing of food and clothing, the arts, theater, music, and writing offered consolation, distraction, and humor. Many writers went to the front and wrote of high heroes and low enemies; poets flourished, and traditional Kabuki theater, Nō plays, and fairly good movies—mostly with patriotic themes—continued. Newspapers and magazines influenced millions and, early in the war, were reliable. Radios were the main mass attention getter. Radio stations—governmentally controlled—presented good programs that boosted morale and catered to a growing national craze for European classical music. Vapid propaganda would soon clot the public mind.

JAPANESE AIR/SEA/LAND BATTLES, 1941

322 **Japanese military leaders carefully planned the start of their Greater East Asian War.** Decision for war came at a September 6, 1941, imperial conference— at which Hirohito hinted his opposition to war with the British and Americans. But the militarists plunged ahead. **323** **A nonaggression pact signed with the USSR in April 1941 protected the empire's northern flank;** the pact survived Hitler's Russian invasion because the tripartite alliance required help only for invaded member states. With the Russian worry at least temporarily dimmed, Japanese planning jelled. First, the American fleet in Pearl Harbor would be smashed, which would open the way to the resource-rich Philippines, Malaya, Dutch East Indies, Borneo, even Burma—the indistinctly designed Greater East Asia Co-Prosperity Sphere. Then imperial forces would build a strong defense line around their new domains, hold on, and let high-cost attrition fatigue the United States into making peace in Asia so it could fight in Europe.

324 **Organizing a surprise attack on Pearl Harbor fell to a special staff working under the able Adm. Isoroku Yamamoto (q.v.), the Imperial Navy's commander in chief, who had long urged a preemptive strike.** A believer in combined operations (at which the Japanese had some experience), Yamamoto projected a fleet of six big aircraft carriers mounting 414 planes, supported by two fast battleships, two cruisers, and tankers, all screened by several destroyers and sixteen submarines.

325 **By November, with the task force ready in the Kurile Islands, Yamamoto told his officers that victory would make Japan a great power, but added that "the Americans are adversaries worthy of you."** "Climb Mount Niitaka," the order to go, came on December 2. By 0600 December 7, Yamamoto's fleet reached its launch point two hundred miles north of Oahu exactly on time and the first wave of bombers streaked for "battleship row," while others headed for American airfields where all the aircraft were conveniently lined up wingtip to wingtip to make them easier to guard and thus foil saboteurs. No American planes were seen, no antiaircraft fire intruded as the raiders enjoyed total surprise. This exclusively air attack

Admiral Yamamoto.

scored a victory rivaling Tsushima. Eighteen U.S. ships were hit, seven of eight battleships were sunk or badly damaged (Yamamoto had predicted the end of the battleship era). Of some 394 American planes on Oahu, 188 were destroyed and 159 more damaged. Yamamoto's fleet lost 29 planes and 6 submarines (5 of them midgets); his ships went untouched and undetected.

326 One surprise damped Nipponese excitement: no American aircraft carriers or heavy cruisers were in port that day, and a glaring mistake went temporarily unnoticed—Pearl Harbor's huge naval fuel tanks were untouched.

327 A seaborne blitzkrieg rolled into the Pacific and South China Sea to Guam, Wake Island, Hong Kong, the Philippines, Malaya and on toward Britain's great bastion and naval base at Singapore. This gigantic offensive should have outrun its supplies, but the Imperial

Navy guarded merchant ships and logistical routes—despite fierce interservice rivalry—and Japanese infantry lived lightly from sacks of rice and off the spoils they took. The Imperial Army picked off fragmented enemy resistance bit by bit.

328 Unfortified Guam, defended by about 700 U.S. Marines and Guamanians with no weapons larger than .30-caliber machine guns, resisted 6,000 Nipponese invaders from December 10 to 12 before surrendering.

At Wake Island, westernmost U.S. Pacific base, the defenders, four hundred Marines, a Marine fighter squadron, and some dug-in shore batteries, repulsed the first landing on December 12, and sank two destroyers and an escort vessel. A second Japanese attack, reinforced by two carriers from the Pearl Harbor force, overwhelmed the island on December 23, 1941, at a cost of four more ships along with twenty-one planes and nearly a thousand troops. Wake's heroic defense buoyed American morale in a period of bad news.

329 Earlier acquisition of Indochinese and Formosan airfields and ports made everything easier for the Japanese in their "strike south" strategy. Early on December 8, large Japanese air forces struck airfields supporting Hong Kong, Malaya, and major U.S. positions in the Philippines and almost eliminated scattered Allied air forces. Six old planes and six infantry battalions, all inadequately trained save two recently arrived from Canada, defended Hong Kong. The Allied troops, lacking mortar ammunition and transport, had scant hope of holding anything save the island itself. A Japanese division along with air and naval support broke the mainland bottleneck at what was familiarly known as the "Gin Drinker's Line" and by the tenth had forced the British back to the island. Expertly divided, then conquered, the defenders surrendered on Christmas Day. British casualties amounted to 11,848 for the eighteen days: the Japanese lost 2,754.

330 Malaya, a big and strategic peninsula jutting between India and China into the South China Sea, took a bit longer to fall. Lieutenant General Tomoyuki Yamashita's (q.v.) 60,000-strong Twenty-fifth Army, well covered by sea and air forces, had landed in south Thailand and northern Malaya ahead of the Pearl Harbor attack early on December 7, 1941. Then three jungle-trained divisions, China veterans, scampered through southern Thailand's wooded trails and into Malaya against fragmented opposition. About 139,000 British, Australian, Indian, and Malay troops were badly disposed to stop Yamashita. Lieutenant General Sir Arthur Percival deployed a couple of divisions to cover airfields in northern Malaya, but these dispositions hardly seemed sound since there were scarcely 150 old British planes available to contest the air over Malaya and Singapore. And with *Prince of Wales* and *Repulse* (q.v.) sunk right after the invasion, Percival had almost no naval help.

Yamashita drove two columns south along both sides of the mountains splitting Malaya, took several airfields, flanked several successive British positions, and by early January took Kuala Lumpur, Malaya's capital, and rushed toward Singapore itself.

331 Poorly prepared defenses failed (contrary to popular rumor, Singapore's big guns did not all point seaward), food and water ran short in the refugee-choked city, and, on February 15, 1942, Percival surrendered. Yamashita, now the "Tiger of Malaya," scored the greatest victory of the young war with less than 10,000 casualties. British casualties amounted to 138,708, more than 130,000 of them prisoners. Huge amounts of booty were taken: 740 guns, 2,500 machine guns, 65,000 rifles, 300 armored cars, several thousand vehicles, plus 1,000 railroad engines and cars.

332 Hirohito crowed, "Britain's base of operations in the Far East is overthrown and annihilated. I deeply approve of this"; while Churchill lamented, "I speak to you under the shadow of a heavy and far-reaching military defeat. All the Malaya Peninsula has been overrun." To which, thinking of Adm. Tom Phillips's flotilla, the prime minister added another regret: "In my whole experience I do not remember any naval blow so heavy or so painful."

333 The strategic results gave even greater cause for Allied lament. With two vital colonies gone, the Indian Ocean now opened to the Japanese, Borneo threatened as well as Java and Sumatra, Allied Far Eastern fortunes hinged on Gen. Douglas MacArthur's doings in the Philippines.

334 Formosa-based Japanese heavy bombers surprised U.S. airbases in the Philippines. Laziness, hubris, or just plan stupidity permitted a near repeat of Pearl Harbor at Manila on the morning of December 8, 1941. Although amply warned of war, MacArthur somehow failed to alert his main airbase at Clark Field of a likely attack. On the morning of December 8, 1941, most planes of the United States Army Forces Far East were caught on the ground. In quick time, half of MacArthur's air strength was burned or broken. Swift follow-up hits on other airfields and on navy air installations soon drove the tiny American Asiatic Fleet scurrying southward out of range of Formosa-based Japanese planes. By mid-December, MacArthur had only a handful of fighters left. He did have strong ground forces at hand—almost 130,000 men—but needed more guns, ammunition, and food. Japanese air and sea interdiction of supplies, combined with America's focus on Europe, doomed the Philippines.

335 On December 10, 1941, Lt. Gen. Masaharu Homma's (q.v.) Fourteenth Army (some 43,000 strong) landed on northern Luzon to begin an expected fifty-day Philippines conquest. First phases went well and Homma's two-pronged drive, reinforced by additional landings near the capital, took the open city of Manila in twenty-two days—January 2, 1942.

336 Homma found his progress stalled by MacArthur's long-standing plan to retire all his forces into a fortified Bataan Peninsula—a plan undiscovered by Japanese intelligence. Although defenses were incomplete and rushes of refugees derailed American logistics, Lt. Gen. Jonathan M. Wainwright pulled most remaining American and Filipino troops into the peninsula. Here good ground, short lines, and some previously stockpiled reserves of food and ammunition aided the defense.

By the end of January, Wainwright, commanding on Bataan, had a fairly strong defensive line ready. Homma, needing more men and supplies, made the mistake of asking for time. He got it but ruined his reputation in Tokyo.

337 For the Japanese, 1941 ended splendidly. In the month of December they had stunted the U.S. Navy, were taking the Philippines, had taken Hong Kong, invaded Burma and Borneo and attacked the Dutch East Indies, were about to take Malaya/Singapore, and were scaring Australia. The Greater East Asia Co-Prosperity Sphere looked more promising than ever.

338 How did all this happen; how had the United States, Britain, France, and Holland been so humbled so fast? Hubris is part of the answer, hubris combined with racism. Ernest Hemingway, always with a sense of the fitness of things, best explained what happened:

All through the Pacific and the Far East in 1941 I heard about the general incapacity and worthlessness of, 'those little monkeys.' Everywhere I heard what we would do to those little monkeys when the day of the great pushover came. One cruiser division and a couple of carriers would destroy Tokyo; another ditto Yokohama. No one ever specified what the little monkeys would be doing while all this was going on. I imagine they were supposed to be consulting oculists trying to remedy those famous defects in vision which kept them from being able to fly properly. Or else try-
ing to right all those battleships and cruisers which would capsize in a beam sea.

Rude awakenings happen in war.

HEADS OF STATE

339 Generalissimo Chiang Kai-shek (1887–1975), president of the Republic of China and commander of its armed forces, became Allied supreme commander of the China war theater in late 1941. A tough Nationalist, Chiang foiled kidnappers in late 1936 who wanted him to join forces with the Communists, but he refused; in 1941, the Communists, believing he alone could lead all of China in resistance to Japan's encroachments, paid lip service to helping him. Chiang was never fooled. Fearing indigenous Communist power more than Japan's transitory encroachment, he connived to fight them both. Trading space for time, he pulled his capital back into western China, to Chunking in Szechwan Province, fought at key places, screamed outrage to the world over such Japanese horrors as the Rape of Nanking, and held on in hope of getting outside help. With the spread of war, he became the Allied strongman in the Far East, and both Britain and the United States began massive aid programs to China.

340 Chiang's Kuomintang government seethed with corruption, but its uneasy alliance with Chinese warlords lent it strength, and Chiang kept respectability by fighting the Japanese. He never wavered in his belief that Communists in China were the real enemy, and his repression of them seemed, sometimes, like a purge of his countrymen. Focused on China, Chiang appeared ignorant of Allied global problems and projected an arrogance of obligation—the Chinese had been fighting the Japanese for years and he felt that the newcomers owed them much. Such attitudes chilled many would-be friends, including the U.S. Congress, and imperiled relations with his Allied chief of staff, Lt. Gen. Joseph W. ("Vinegar Joe")

Stilwell—whose curmudgeonly manner made him a wretched subordinate anyway.

Chiang kept his best troops (few enough) for later use against the Communists, which further irked the Allies. Divorced from military and civilian realities, Chiang pulled around him a gang of sycophants eager to shield him from the frightening truths stalking his country.

341 **In sum, Chiang rates as a poor general but a splendid military politico, and that talent enabled him not to lose China to Japan.** His stubbornness, though, would yield at last to Mao Tse-tung and his Communist rebels.

342 **Hirohito, the 124th emperor of Japan, reigned from 1926 until his death in 1989.** Revered as the "Son of Heaven," perched loftily in his palace, aloof from things of the world, Hirohito embodied the nation in the minds of his countrymen. Intelligent, enlightened beyond expectations, a serious marine biologist, Hirohito sought to end Japan's xenophobia and parochialism. He failed because he reigned but did not rule.

Opposed to war in 1941, the emperor could only express doubts; he could not command peace. He supported war once it came and backed his armed forces. But when defeat loomed in late 1944, he looked for ways to surrender. He urged acceptance of the Potsdam peace terms in July 1945, but the armed forces insisted on immolation. **343** **After the great fire raids of 1945 and the two atomic bombs in August, and with General Tojo out of government, Hirohito intervened and broadcast an imperial rescript on August 14, 1945, that called on the nation to "endure the unendurable" and accept defeat.**

344 **Bravely seeking to assume all blame for Japan's war actions, atrocities included, Hirohito earned Allied occupation leader Gen. Douglas MacArthur's (q.v.) respect.** Allowed to retain a ceremonial role as emperor, Hirohito undeified him-

Emperor Hirohito, September 1945, soon after Japan's surrender.

self and enjoyed the role he always wanted—constitutional monarch.

At his death after a sixty-three-year reign (the longest of Japanese record), Hirohito's war role remained controversial.

345 **Joseph Vissarionovich Djugashvili-Stalin, 1879–1953, was dictator of the Soviet Union throughout World War II.** Taking the name Stalin ("man of steel"), this cobbler's son early became a revolutionary and spent some time in Siberia because of his views. Rebellious views also earned him expulsion from a Tiflis theological seminary in his native Georgia. Exempted from service in the First World War, he enthusiastically followed Lenin and became commissar of nationalities in Russia's revolutionary government. During the civil war, Stalin served as political commissar on the southern front and worked with the Red Army in the Polish campaign of 1920. Never a real soldier, Stalin intruded on strategic decisions and believed in his military genius.

Stalin won a ten-year power struggle following Lenin's death in 1924. **346 Preferring the role of éminence grise to officeholding, Stalin ran the USSR through colleagues on the Politburo until 1941, when he took Molotov's (q.v.) post as chairman of the Council of People's Commissars and became dictator in name as well as fact.** Later he would assume command of the army and name himself marshal, then, much later, generalissimo. Russia's backwardness bothered him, and he launched a series of five-year modernization plans which strengthened the nation's military but dislocated and murdered masses of kulaks—wealthy, productive peasants—and nearly ruined the economy.

347 Dictators usually live in paranoia, and Stalin became convinced that Russia's military leadership represented some kind of imperialist cabal. During 1937–38 he began a series of blood purges to cleanse the country and the party, exterminating most of the officer corps (along with millions of civilians) and replacing them with younger men, presumably loyal to him. Some were competent, but most were inexperienced and ignorant, willing to stick with cavalry and infantry at the expense of modern planes, tanks, and mechanized units. **348 Finland's agile resistance to the 1939 Russian invasion rudely awakened Stalin and his high command to such new things as ski troops, air-land coordination, light armor, and light artillery.**

Stalin intensified aircraft and tank production, muttered privately about a possible war with Japan

Soviet foreign minister Molotov signing the German-Soviet Treaty of Nonaggression, August 23, 1939. German foreign minister Ribbentrop (in dark suit) and Stalin stand behind him; a portrait of Lenin overlooks the scene. This pact and the Treaty of Friendship, Cooperation, and Demarcation signed the next month governed Nazi-Soviet relations until June 22, 1941, when the German invasion of the USSR began.

(he remembered the Manchukuo episode) or Germany, but secretly courted Hitler. Stalin nursed a grudging admiration for Hitler and Mussolini—a kinship of terrorists perhaps—but publicly excoriated Nazism. **349 The Nazi-Soviet Pact of August 1939 stunned the world and especially Russians.** To Stalin, the pact offered convenient cover for a brutal assimilation of eastern Poland, Bessarabia, parts of Finland, and all of Latvia, Lithuania, and Estonia while Hitler turned westward.

Convinced for some arcane reason that Hitler would keep his diplomatic word, Stalin simply refused to believe information about a German invasion in June 1941. When the blitzkrieg rolled across the Bug River on the twenty-second of that month, Stalin sank into a paralytic daze. **350 After he pulled himself together, he directed an energetic and effective war effort.** Holding fast against despair, conjuring massive Allied help, and finally getting a coveted "second front," he adroitly shifted rhetoric from communistic babble to nationalistic exhortation and stirred a cauldron of patriotism that ultimately won his war.

Tough, energetic, stocky, his roundish face dominated by heavy brows and accented by an old-fashioned handlebar moustache, Stalin assumed an avuncular pose in Allied meetings that never quite convinced FDR or especially Churchill of his naive sweetness. Nonetheless, he proved an effective diplomat. Permitting himself to be talked into making war on Japan after Germany collapsed gained him part of Far Eastern spoils. After that he further consolidated Russia's military gains in the halls of talk, ultimately extending the USSR's reach far westward into a partitioned Germany, into Hungary, the Balkans, and Japan. He outmanipulated FDR and stymied Churchill's perceptive urge to curb his appetites before drawing the "Iron Curtain" across Europe.

Increasingly senile after the war, Stalin died on March 5, 1953.

351 He looms in history as the greatest mass murderer of all time. Still, he did great things to save his country. There is, in his paradox, a kind of Gogolian tragedy. "In him was joined," said one historian, "the criminal senselessness of a Caligula with the refinement of a Borgia and the brutality of Tsar Ivan the Terrible." True, but one other trait should be added—the iron determination of Peter the Great.

ALLIED LEADERS

352 Marshal Semyon Mikhaylovich Budenny, 1883–1973, was one of Stalin's civil war cronies and an important Russian commander in World War II. Handsome, tall, a jovial hard drinker, Budenny attracted unflattering descriptions. "A very large moustache, but a very small brain," said one observer, and another saw him as a "sly and durable toady of Stalin's." Loyalty to Stalin certainly opened doors for Budenny. His early military service as a noncommissioned officer in World War I had addicted him to cavalry. Without real martial training, he became commander of Stalin's pet creation, the First Cavalry Army; in the civil war, he proved a hero on horseback and became a marshal in 1935.

353 Given command of a *front* (army group) at the outset of Barbarossa, Budenny retreated with everyone else. In July 1941 he took command of half of the Red Army, ostensibly defending all of Russia south of the Pripet Marshes. Misreading German intentions, he led most of his forces into a gigantic encirclement at Kiev in September 1941 and lost more than half a million men. Stalin finally relieved him and he languished in reserve duty until the middle of October. Rising again, he led the North Caucasus theater from April until September 1942, by which time his forces were virtually driven out of the war.

Stalin kept his crony on the Main Military Council and created the job of commander in chief of cavalry for him. After the war he received several other honorific titles. This three-time Hero of the Soviet Union died on October 26, 1973, and was buried in the Kremlin Wall.

354 Oveta Culp Hobby, 1905–1995, organized and commanded the Women's Army Corps of the United States Army. Born in Killeen, Texas, daughter of a state legislator, she early developed an interest in public affairs and public service. Parliamentarian of the Texas House of Representatives, 1925–31,

Hobby honed her knowledge of government and worked with various state commissions and agencies. After helping organize the 1928 national Democratic Convention in Houston, she participated in Thomas T. Connally's successful U.S. Senate campaign, served as assistant to Houston's city attorney, lost a legislative race, and, on February 23, 1931, married former Texas governor William Pettus Hobby, president of the *Houston Post-Dispatch* publishing company. Learning the newspaper business with typical gusto, Hobby became book editor, assistant editor, and executive vice president of the company, did yeoman work for Hobby's radio station, KPRC, and had two children.

Board service on various charity, art, and cultural organizations consumed only part of Hobby's boundless energy. Asked in June 1941 to create a women's activities section for the U.S. Army, she refused but did agree to prepare an organizational chart for such a unit. **355 Asked to put the plan into effect she again refused, but her husband encouraged her acceptance and she became head of the Women's Interest Section, War Department Bureau of Public Relations, 1941–42.** General George Marshall then asked her to study the British and French women's armies and devise a better plan for the United States. After Pearl Harbor she presented a program to utilize women in many army jobs and a list of prospective commanders for such a corps. Marshall said, "I'd rather you took the job." She did and began a hectic, frustrating, exhilarating, wearying, satisfying career in creating and running the Women's Army Auxiliary Corps. Responsible for everything from personnel and deployment to uniform design, she encountered all kinds of rebuffs. Since the corps existed outside the army, it received strangely little help in funding, support, or courtesy. She herself confronted slights—Washington's Army and Navy Club admitted her (she held a commission as a colonel), but wanted her to enter by the back door.

Women proved themselves quickly, however, and demands for Hobby's volunteers flooded in from the field. **356 Evolved into the Women's Army Corps (WAC) in 1943, Hobby's command expanded until, by war's end, it boasted 100,000 members, with worldwide assignments.** The corps made an invaluable contribution to America's war effort and Hobby received the Distinguished Service Medal in January 1945.

One of America's most important women, Hobby changed the face of the army and of her country. She exuded calm competence mixed with grace, wit, and charm.

357 Douglas MacArthur, 1880–1964, ranks as the most controversial American general. He projected personae by the peck and generated such varied reactions that he is lost in different perspectives. His own perspective, bloated by rhetoric, is the most consistent: he is the greatest general who ever lived (the famous photograph of him wading ashore on the Philippines is flawed only by his not walking on the water). His mother's perspective is hardly less idyllic. She protected it zealously and pushed his career by shameless correspondence and social influence. His staff generally saw him in his own effulgence; General Marshall (q.v.) once said to him, "You don't have a staff, General. You have a court." Superiors generally admired him, even if they disliked him— General of the Armies John J. Pershing being an important example.

Born into a powerful family (his mother a socialite, his father a highly decorated army general), MacArthur entered the U.S. Military Academy in 1899 accompanied by his mother—she stayed in a hotel near the parade ground to cheer his performance—and emerged as first captain of the 1903 class with the highest grades in twenty-five years.

After a brief stint in the Philippines, MacArthur, promoted to first lieutenant, served as aide-de-camp to his father, an observer of the Russo-Japanese War, 1904–5. Young Major MacArthur helped bring the National Guard into the American Expeditionary Force (AEF) in 1917. Jumped to colonel in September 1917, MacArthur switched to the infantry and became chief of staff to the 42nd Division, which he suggested be composed of troops from many states—hence its name Rainbow Division.

358 In France, MacArthur's daring made him America's youngest brigadier general in June 1918—he did not know that his mother had written the AEF's commander, General Pershing, recommending the elevation. This "D'Artagnan of the Western Front" commanded a brigade in the AEF's major offensives, earned two Distinguished Service Crosses, a Distinguished Service Medal, six Silver Stars, two wound stripes, and led the 42nd during the last week of World War I. His meteor streaked higher. **359** Appointed the youngest superintendent in West Point's history in 1919, he revitalized an institution about to be closed, modernized the curriculum, and doubled the cadet corps. All this caused resentment among many superiors and brought a shortened tenure for the devoted superintendent.

Married in 1922 to New York socialite Henrietta Louise Cromwell (divorce came seven years later), MacArthur took command of the Military District of Manila and finally headed the Philippine Division. Another letter from his mother to army chief of staff Pershing in 1924 won MacArthur his second star. His morale sagged when his marriage crumbled in the late twenties, but his 1928 assignment to lead all U.S. troops in the Philippines revived him. **360** Appointed army chief of staff in August 1930, he fought with unusual success to enlarge the budget in bad Depression years and he upgraded antique mobilization plans. Involvement in the Bonus March troubles of 1932 unfairly tarnished his reputation.

On the way back to the Philippines to be Manuel Quezon's (q.v.) military adviser in 1935, MacArthur met Jean Faircloth and married her eighteen months later—it would be a lasting and happy venture.

361 Appointed field marshal in the Philippine army in 1936, he also assumed command of the new U.S. Army Forces in the Far East, July 1941, and began a rigorous training program.

His World War II career began inauspiciously. Informed of the Pearl Harbor attack, MacArthur inexplicably did not order proper air dispositions and lost most of his air force on the ground. After enemy landings on Luzon, December 10, 1941, MacArthur contested ground north and south of Manila and, as Japanese units pressed toward the capital, he authorized withdrawal of all forces to the Bataan Peninsula. His own headquarters moved to Corregidor Island in Manila Harbor on Christmas Eve 1941. His originally sound logistical arrangements for Bataan failed in the onrush of refugees, and supplies, especially food, were short from the start of the siege.

362 Vehemently opposed to America's Germany-first strategy, newly reappointed four-star general MacArthur urged reinforcements. Ordered out by FDR (Churchill urged it), MacArthur, his family, with a few staffers, boarded a PT boat on March 12, 1942, and after a dangerous trip, reached Australia, where he made the first MacArthur pronouncement: "I came through and I shall return." His words became a motto of hope. For his defense of the indefensible (General Eisenhower's view), MacArthur won the Congressional Medal of Honor.

Vainglory aside, MacArthur came into his own in 1942. **363** As supreme commander of the Southwest Pacific Area, he organized not only the defense of Australia but also of adjacent areas. Seeing the immediate enemy threat to Port Moresby, New Guinea, he erred in committing untrained and poorly supplied American troops to a jungle war against a bush-savvy enemy. With fighting going badly in the Buna area and faced with the ignominy of having Australians take over the fighting, MacArthur brought in energetic Gen. Robert Eichelberger and gave him a brief order to "take Buna, or do not come back alive." Eichelberger sacked the commanders of his debilitated command, brought in reinforcements, food, medicine, armor, and, taking heavy casualties, cleared the

Buna-Gona front by January 22, 1943, and saved MacArthur's reputation.

364 Famed for his island-hopping strategy—urged on him by the U.S. Joint Chiefs of Staff—MacArthur began bypassing strong points, taking weaker ones, and starving such major Japanese bases as Rabaul. These successes aside, MacArthur's pleas for more men and equipment ran into opposition from Adm. Ernest J. King (q.v.), commander in chief of the U.S. Fleet and chief of Naval Operations. A friend of FDR's, a powerful sailor and politico, King made the Pacific a U.S. Navy war, which, for a time, reduced MacArthur to a nearly adjunct role in the Southwest Pacific Area. Admiral Chester Nimitz (q.v.) led the main U.S. thrust in the Central Pacific. MacArthur improvised brilliantly, though, as he did more with less and finally worked well with the navy.

King insisted on bypassing the Philippines, opting for going to China instead; MacArthur, whose repute grew with achievement, won a tough argument and fulfilled his promise to return with his swashbuckling landing on Leyte, October 20, 1944. **365** Promotion to the five-star rank of general of the army came to MacArthur as resistance ended on Leyte and began on Luzon. The liberation of Manila came on March 3, 1945, and American forces regained all of the Philippines by July. Fortunately, Allied plans for attacking Japan's home islands were nullified by Hirohito's surrender rescript. **366** On August 15, 1945—the surrender date—MacArthur became Supreme Commander for the Allied Powers (SCAP), and staged the surrender ceremony aboard USS *Missouri* on September 2.

Displaying unsuspected tact and diplomacy, MacArthur did a remarkably able job of running occupied Japan. Sagaciously insisting on retaining the emperor as a national symbol, SCAP, brooking little Washington supervision, ran a successful personal satrapy. He designed a new constitution for the empire, which reformed its polity and policies.

He died at Walter Reed Hospital on April 5, 1964.

367 Anastas Ivanovich Mikoyan, 1895–1978, one of the USSR's most important trade officials, deserves comparison with Lazare Carnot as "the organizer of victory" for his logistical genius. An Armenian, Mikoyan took a theology degree in 1915 and joined the Communist Party. Siding with Stalin against Trotsky, Mikoyan held various high governmental trade posts into the 1940s.

In World War II, Mikoyan showed himself a logistical genius as he managed procurement and distribution of war matériel. He directed conversion of civilian industries to war production and supervised the Lend-Lease program for the USSR. For his outstanding work, Mikoyan became a Hero of Socialist Labor in 1943.

Deputy premier in 1946–53, Mikoyan fell victim to Stalin's growing paranoia and faced liquidation. Saved by his friend Nikita Khrushchev, he retired from office—a rare achievement for Old Bolsheviks—in the mid-1960s. But Mikoyan stayed on the Communist Party's Central Committee until 1976.

A dark, mustachioed, witty man, Mikoyan once described himself as an old "Armenian rug merchant," while others saw a highly intelligent, gifted negotiator whose wartime deeds may have saved the USSR. He died in Moscow on October 21, 1978.

368 Vyacheslav Mikhailovich Molotov, 1890–1986, Soviet diplomat and close aide to Stalin. Part of the antitsarist revolution in 1905, Molotov joined the Bolsheviks in 1906 and adopted the sobriquet Molotov (hammer). After editing *Pravda*, 1912–17, he became Stalin's right-hand man, second secretary of the Central Committee, and finally foreign minister, Politburo member, and premier from 1930 until 1941, when Stalin made himself premier.

A member of the GKO (State Committee of Defense) through the war, Molotov worked mainly in diplomacy and arranged several nonaggression pacts. He is rumored to have talked with Nazi diplomat Joachim von Ribbentrop in mid-1943 seeking terms, but nothing happened. **369** Molotov arranged the Moscow Conference in 1943 and attended the rest of the war conferences as well as the San Francisco meeting that established the UN. Despite Molotov's unswerving loyalty, Stalin, increasingly paranoiac after the war, suspected him of working for the U.S. and nearly eliminated him.

In and out of favor from 1953 until the 1970s, the stalwart Old Bolshevik died in 1986, a victim of the system he embodied.

Lenin described the stubborn, dour, undiplomatically harsh Molotov as "the best file clerk in Russia." Churchill considered him "above all men fitted to be the agent and instrument of an incalculable machine."

370 Harold Raynsford Stark, 1880–1972, U.S. chief of Naval Operations at the time of the Pearl Harbor attack. This conscientious and able Pennsylvanian became CNO in August 1939. Increasingly alarmed by reports through the Magic (q.v.) system of Japan's rising aggressiveness, Stark sent several warnings to all fleet commanders. Late in the year, though, he became convinced that Japan's first attack would come in the Far East and not at Pearl Harbor. Early on December 7, 1941, after Japan's last message arrived, he offered to send a flash alarm to Pearl Harbor via navy communications, but General Marshall told him the army would get it there speedily enough—it arrived after the attack began.

371 Swept up in the frenzied search for Pearl Harbor scapegoats, Stark lost his job in March 1942 and went to London as President Roosevelt's personal liaison with Churchill and governments-in-exile. Personable, Stark proved superbly effective in his diplomatic duties.

In October 1943, Stark took command of the Twelfth Fleet, which comprised all U.S. naval forces in British and European coastal waters. The admiral retired in April 1946, his career dimmed by Pearl Harbor's shadow. Many colleagues thought General Marshall more guilty of dereliction than Stark. The admiral died in Washington in August 1972.

372 Semyon Konstantinovich Timoshenko, 1895–1970,

was a Soviet general of some talent. A virtually illiterate Ukrainian, a machine gunner in World War I, Timoshenko did heroic duty in the civil war, in which he suffered five wounds and won the lasting respect of Stalin. A graduate of the Frunze Military Academy in 1922, he rose rapidly to various district commands and became a lifetime member of the Supreme Soviet. Sound service in the Polish campaign of 1939 brought him the dubious duty of rescuing Red Army honor in the Finnish War. Swift reorganization and stern discipline forced Finland's surrender after a ten-week campaign.

373 Promoted to field marshal, named a Hero of the Soviet Union, Timoshenko became minister of defense in May 1940. Taught the weaknesses of the Red Army on various battlefields, the defense minister struggled manfully to modernize the army's command, training, logistical, and morale structure. He blundered, along with many others, in not believing that Germany would attack and in fumbling early responses. Finally energized, Timoshenko took command of the western *front* near Smolensk. With Stalin as defense minister in July, Timoshenko concentrated on stopping Hitler's avalanche. He did slow it a bit but could not prevent the dissolution of the army in the Bialystok pocket disaster.

Ordered to the Ukraine, the marshal arrived in time to witness closure of another German pocket that bagged 665,000 prisoners. **374** Timoshenko yielded Rostov on November 19, 1941, but, reinforced, scored the first Russian victory in retaking that "gateway to the Caucasus" ten days later. Things began going badly for Timoshenko with his return to the Finnish front; this time he failed to achieve anything. Reassignment to the Ukraine brought him no better luck; he bungled a counterattack at Kharkov in May 1942 and, in August, Stalin plucked him from the field and gave him various training and liaison positions. Effective in early operations, Timoshenko lost his touch and became an irksome curmudgeon.

Commanding different military districts after the

war, Timoshenko did some ceremonial duty and died in Moscow on March 31, 1970.

375 **Jonathan Mayhew Wainwright, 1883–1953, was the U.S. general who surrendered Allied forces in the Philippines.** "Skinny" Wainwright was born into a military family, graduated from the U.S. Military Academy in 1906, joined the cavalry, fought against the formidable Moros in the Philippines, then became a staff officer with various units.

A brigadier general in 1938 and assigned to San Antonio, Texas, Wainwright became a major general in September 1940 with posting again to the Philippines. Given command of the North Luzon Force after Japanese landings in December 1941, he organized its withdrawal to the Bataan Peninsula. After General MacArthur (q.v.) left the Philippines for Australia in mid-March 1942, Wainwright assumed command of all U.S. forces in the islands and moved his headquarters to heavily fortified Corregidor Island on March 21. After resistance ended on Bataan in April, Wainwright continued fighting until May 6, 1942, when he surrendered his forces and finally, fearing for his men, all the U.S. Philippine forces.

376 **A prisoner for the rest of the war in Manchukuo, Wainwright, subjected to humiliating tasks to make him "lose face," often fought unsuccessfully to get better treatment for his men.** Liberated on August 25, 1945, Wainwright witnessed the Japanese surrender aboard USS *Missouri*. Returning home to a hero's welcome, Wainwright received the Congressional Medal of Honor and a continental command. He died in San Antonio, Texas, September 2, 1953.

No one else better exemplified West Point's motto: Duty, Honor, Country.

377 **Orde Charles Wingate, 1903–44, was an able and controversial British guerrilla leader.** Having learned guerrilla warfare in Palestine, in early 1941 he led a mixed force into Italian-occupied Abyssinia and bluffed, baffled, and fooled the enemy into abandoning the capital, whereupon he restored Emperor Haile Selassie to his throne. His unflattering views of superiors plus his fairly constant rudeness and emotionalism nearly got him kicked out of the army.

Field Marshal Wavell, who worked fairly well with Wingate, pulled him into India for special service. **378** **By June 1942 the newly appointed brigadier had proposed long-range penetration groups to be supplied and supported entirely by air—Wavell approved, and the Chindits, taken from the Burmese word *chinthe* (winged stone lions), were born.** From February to April 1943, Wingate led three thousand Chindits behind Japanese lines in Burma, lost more than two-thirds of his men, and won considerable fame. Churchill, who always cherished irregulars, greatly admired Wingate. Taking him to the Quebec Conference in August 1943, the prime minister pushed his new protégé, and Wingate found himself a major general commanding a division that had an American component—Brig. Gen. Frank Merrill's contingent soon known as Merrill's Marauders.

Wingate's Special Force went behind enemy lines to support Lt. Gen. Joseph Stilwell's expedition coming from Yunnan, China, but a large Japanese offensive aimed at Imphal forced the Chindits into conventional battles for which they were ill-prepared. Wingate died in a plane crash March 24, 1944.

Many traditional soldiers saw Wingate as bumptious to a fault, insubordinate, unstable, and outlandishly ambitious. Others saw genius in him and his campaigns. His men, charmed by his derring-do and battle zest, cherished him. With Wingate's death, Churchill said, "a bright flame was extinguished."

379 **Georgi Konstantinovich Zhukov, 1896–1974, was the USSR's most able and outspoken Soviet field marshal.** Peasant-born near Moscow on December 1, 1896, young Zhukov thirsted for education, won two St. George Crosses in World War I, joined the Red Army in 1918, and rode with the cavalry in the civil war. A powerful man, a bit under mid-height, vigorous and daring, Zhukov rose rapidly as he devoted himself to studying modern warfare—especially mechanization—and seized every opportunity to take advanced military courses in the 1920s and 1930s. Briefly suspected of political weakness, Zhukov went on to command various cavalry divisions and to recognition for his decisive defeat of the Japanese at Khalkhin-Gol (Nomonhan) in Outer Mongolia in August 1939.

380 Appointed chief of the Soviet general staff in January 1941, Zhukov worked to modernize the Red Army. Arriving to take charge of Leningrad's defense just as Hitler ordered the city besieged, Zhukov seemed a miracle worker, an image reinforced in October 1941 when he went to Moscow's defense just in time to have mud and bad weather stop the German advance. Zhukov reorganized, and after the Russian ally General Winter stalled a renewed Nazi drive in early December, Zhukov counterattacked to great success. Weather and general conditions blunted his continued attacks and he did not achieve his objective—the destruction of German Army Group Center.

381 Stalin made his successful general deputy supreme commander. Giving him and the new chief of the general staff, Gen. A. M. Vasilevsky, a free hand, Stalin watched the success of his move as Operation Uranus destroyed Hitler's Sixth Army at Stalingrad and led to a successful push to the Donets River—for all of which Zhukov received a marshal's star in January 1943.

382 Together with Vasilevsky, Zhukov planned and won the gigantic tank battle at Kursk in the summer of 1943 and, together, they launched the long offensive that resulted in Berlin's destruction and Hitler's death in 1945. Fiercely jealous of this thrice hero of the Soviet Union, Stalin, after the war, consigned him to remote, small commands. Zhukov rose again, right after Stalin's death, to become first deputy minister of defense and first minister in 1955. In that role he pressured Poland and brutally ended Hungary's brief flirtation with democracy. Suddenly sacked in 1957,

he lived in relative obscurity until 1965, when Leonid Brezhnev revived him and the marshal's memoirs became military classics. Zhukov died June 18, 1974, and was buried in the Kremlin Wall.

383 Some historians offer Georgi Zhukov as "the greatest general of the war," an evaluation to be balanced against the aid he received from the largely overlooked Marshal Aleksandr M. Vasilevsky.

AXIS LEADERS

384 Karl Dönitz, 1891–1980, was the Nazi admiral whom Hitler chose to be the last leader of the Third Reich. Commissioned in 1913 as a German naval officer, Dönitz commanded U-boats in the First World War. Fiercely loyal to Hitler, Dönitz became commander of all Nazi U-boats in 1935. **385** Drawing on experience, he devised the frighteningly successful "wolf pack" tactics—a group of U-boats vectored by radio to convoys which would be attacked by a horde of surfaced boats at night—that haunted Churchill and nearly won the Battle of the Atlantic. As Allied shipping increased and anti-submarine warfare swiftly improved when radar came into wide use, Admiral Dönitz speeded production of a new and larger all-electric U-boat equipped with a snorkeling system that permitted battery-charging while submerged. These vastly better boats came into service too late to change the war.

386 Dönitz became commander in chief of the German navy upon Admiral Raeder's retirement in January 1943, a position in which he did poorly. As the war worsened for the Nazis, he tried various desperate measures that wasted men and vessels.

387 Hitler, on April 30, 1945, named Dönitz his successor. The admiral arranged to surrender the tottering Third Reich on May 8–9. Captured by the Allies on May 22 and convicted at Nuremberg on two counts, he received a ten-year prison sentence. Upon

Admiral Karl Dönitz, architect of Germany's U-boat offensive.

his release in 1956, Dönitz published his memoirs and died in December 1980.

388 Heinz Wilhelm Guderian, 1888–1954, was a brilliant German panzer general. An argument continues about who had the panzer idea. Was it Guderian, the influential British military historian Basil Liddell Hart, Gen. J. F. C. Fuller, or perhaps Karl von Clausewitz himself? Guderian, almost unanimously, gets the credit for assimilating the various elements into a remarkable combination of air/armor formations that produced an entirely new type of warfare.

Son of a German regular army officer, Guderian trained in radio communications and served in the First World War. Between wars he studied Liddell Hart's and Fuller's works about tanks and the future of war. As he later said, "Since nobody else busied himself with this material, I was soon by way of be-

ing an expert." **389** In 1938, Guderian published a landmark book (untranslated into French or English), *Achtung Panzer*, which described the blitzkrieg idea in detail—bunched tanks would open a restricted area in an enemy line, penetrate to some depth, then spread out behind the line to flank and envelop troops, destroy artillery positions and reserve areas, and push ahead in a campaign of destruction and mystification.

Guderian applied his ideas to stunning effect in the Polish invasion of 1939. Then he switched to the west and blitzed through Allied positions in France, destroyed the Belgians, flanked main French positions, and brought quick, astounding victory. The blitzkrieg worked effectively in the opening phases of the Russian campaign in June 1941 as Colonel General Guderian's armored group raced for Moscow and joined in the staggeringly successful envelopments at Minsk and Smolensk. Shifted southward, his tanks helped close the huge trap at Kiev. Not only a superior tactician and strategist, Guderian also proved a popular leader of men—his troops fondly called him "Hurrying Heinz."

Although Guderian respected some of Hitler's insights and the two got along well in the glory days of war, the winter of 1941 etched rifts between them. Hitler's "no retreat" policy Guderian thought idiotic and they clashed; on December 26, Hitler relieved his brilliant tank man from command.

Recalled in March 1943 and appointed inspector general of armored troops, Guderian worked at repairing and refitting Germany's hard-worn tanks. **390** On July 21, 1944—significantly, the day after the try at killing Hitler—Guderian became chief of the German general staff and loudly condemned the would-be assassins. Hitler put him on the Court of Honor with Rundstedt (q.v.) and Field Marshal Wilhelm Keitel that indiscriminately drummed hundreds from the army and so gave them to a vindictive people's court.

391 As chief of staff, Guderian argued increasingly with Hitler's growing wrongheadedness and got fired for the last time on March 28, 1945. Captured but not sent to trial, Guderian wrote his excellent reminiscences, *Panzer Leader* (1954). He died in mid-May 1954.

Guderian's reputation has grown and he ranks in the pantheon of World War II's great generals.

392 Masaharu Homma, 1888–1946, was the Japanese general who conquered the Philippines in 1942. Intelligent, well-educated, westernized by long assignments with the British army, a major general by 1935, Homma fought in China before being tapped to lead the Philippine invasion in December 1941. Given command of the Japanese Fourteenth Army and supporting air forces, a total of some 43,000 men, he received orders to complete the mission in fifty days. He took Manila in twenty-two days, but MacArthur's (q.v.) unexpected retreat to Bataan skewed Homma's schedule.

His request for reorganization time infuriated the general staff and he lost face. He conquered Bataan by April 9, 1942, and MacArthur's successor in the Far East command, Lt. Gen. Jonathan M. Wainwright (q.v.), surrendered all the Philippines on May 6. Recalled to Japan in August 1942, Homma went on the shelf for the rest of the war.

393 Although Homma tried to restrain his troops from much rape and pillage and denied knowledge of high casualties during the Bataan Death March (q.v.), a war crimes commission found him responsible for many war crimes—including the Death March—and sentenced him to death. He went before a firing squad on April 6, 1946.

394 Erwin Johannes Eugen Rommel, 1891–1944, the Desert Fox, is one of the most famous generals of World War II. Swabian-born to middle-class parents, Rommel joined the army in 1910 and emerged from the Danzig War Academy as a lieutenant. This short, unprepossessing young infantry officer became, in World War I, "the perfect fighting animal, cold, cunning, ruthless, untiring, quick of decision, incredibly brave." Fighting on the Eastern, Western, and Italian Fronts, in mountains and trenches, he consistently exceeded the call of duty. For his sparkling initiative at Caporetto in October 1917 he won Prussia's most coveted decoration, the Pour le Mérite. Although he spent the rest of the war, unhappily, as a staff officer, he never qualified for the general staff—a deficiency still used against him by detractors in Germany.

395 A teacher at the Dresden Infantry School in the late twenties and early thirties, his lectures were finally published as *Infanterie greift an (Infantry Attacks* in the English translation of 1944) and won him international military fame. Hitler liked the book.

Rommel headed the Führer's headquarters guard during the Austrian Anschluss in 1938 and took over a cherished panzer division in February 1940. In France his quick attacks won his command the nickname of "Ghost Division" as his men dashed ahead of infantry support, reached the English Channel, swerved to the south, took Cherbourg in mid-June 1940, and streaked along the French coast to Spain in a textbook example of mobile warfare. He became a *Generalleutnant* in January 1941.

Crisis and symbolism shaped Rommel's coming fame.

396 Hitler, hearing Mussolini's cries for help in North Africa, debated creating an African hero—he had already anointed a "snow hero" (Eduard Dietl)—and decided to risk making politically naive Rommel his "sun hero." Rommel's African campaigns were the stuff of legend. Taking over a chaotic front and a ridiculously messy conglomeration of German and Italian remnants in mid-February 1941, Rommel began epic campaigns of infantry/tank/air energetics that flanked, surrounded, and baffled his British enemies for two incredible years and earned him field marshal's rank. His Afrika Korps became world famous.

Military historians sympathize with underdogs, and most students of the Desert Fox's North African ventures see him as a front-line hero rising above realities to the glories of another Napoleon. Napoleon he was not, but he nearly reached the Suez to change the war; and although defeated at El Alamein and driven finally to the environs of Tunis, he had forever stamped his genius on the rolls of war. Evacuated to Germany on sick leave, Rommel returned to Africa at Hitler's personal request.

Sadly for Rommel, he lost Hitler's confidence because of El Alamein, a battle where he arrived too late to fight. Partially recovered from illness, Rommel served at the Führer's headquarters, then commanded in northern Italy in August 1943 as that unhappy country crumbled out of the Axis at last.

397 Late in 1943, Rommel went to inspect the "Atlantic Wall" from Denmark to the Alps and found preparations for an expected Allied invasion hopelessly inadequate. He and CIC-West Field Marshal von Rundstedt argued about how to repulse invasion. Both field marshals met with Hitler soon after D-day. Rommel complained about Hitler's ignoring local commanders' recommendations from an isolationist distance, boldly asked how the Führer thought the war could still be won, and urged the Führer toward surrender. Badly wounded by a British air attack on July 17, Rommel lay unconscious while the July 1944 attempt to kill Hitler failed. Marginally implicated in the plot, Rommel, offered the choice of suicide and family protection or an appearance before the bloody People's Court, killed himself on October 14, 1944, the last of Germany's paladins.

398 Isoroku Yamamoto, 1884–1943, Japan's most famous admiral, planned the attack on Pearl Harbor. As a young Japanese naval officer, Yamamoto studied English in the United States and served as naval attaché in Washington, where he focused on the oil industry because he knew it would be a crucial factor in future war. He knew, too, that airpower would make scrap of battleships. These views did not sit well with the Imperial Navy's traditionalist leaders, but Yamamoto remained outspoken in urging naval modernization—though he seems to have missed the cruciality of radar. **399** His loud opposition to war

with the United States nearly got him assassinated, and when, in the late 1930s, the prime minister asked what Japan's chances were in such a war, the admiral answered: "We can run wild for six months or a year, but after that I have utterly no confidence." To the same question at a Tokyo meeting in September 1941: "Japan cannot vanquish the United States. Therefore we should not fight the United States."

He thought about war, though, and how best to give Japan some chance when it came. His conviction that the U.S. fleet in Hawaii must be destroyed frightened most navy planners—it would be too costly. Having studied the British 1940 victory over the Italians at Taranto (q.v.) he thought a preemptive strike might work—and it worked far better than he schemed.

Continuing to command the Combined Fleet, Yamamoto piled victory on victory in the South Pacific and supported successful conquests at Hong Kong, Malaya, Netherlands East Indies, invasions in the Solomons and New Guinea, and an intrusion as far as Ceylon. There had been losses in the Coral Sea battle in May 1942, but nothing really crippling.

Yamamoto knew, though, that future success hinged on luring the U.S. Navy's Pacific remnants into a battle of destruction. He finally sold the idea after the April 1942 Doolittle air raid on Tokyo, and he planned meticulously for the greatest naval effort in Japan's history.

400 Strategically sound, Yamamoto's plans were undone by poor intelligence: he believed that only two U.S. carriers were left—there were three—and that they would be overmatched easily by his four. Worse, he assumed that he had total surprise—he did not know that the Japanese naval code had been broken and that the Allies knew his every plan. So, in the decisive Battle of Midway, June 4–7, 1942, Yamamoto lost all four carriers and other ships while sinking only one U.S. carrier, the *Yorktown*. And although Yamamoto had some later success around Guadalcanal, the sea power balance shifted against him and he ran out of ideas.

Still vastly popular and highly dangerous, he decided to make an inspirational inspection of front-line bases in the Solomons on April 18, 1943. In a stupendous lapse of security, his itinerary and schedule went out in regular naval code, and waiting U.S. Army fighters shot his plane down. Japan did not reveal his death for a month and mourned him with a rare state funeral.

401 Tomoyuki (Hobun) Yamashita, 1885–1946, is widely regarded as Japan's best general. Nicknamed "Tiger of Malaya" for his brilliant conquest of that peninsula, Yamashita's participation in a failed military coup in 1936 made an enemy of Hideki Tojo (q.v.) and dogged Yamashita's later career. Shunted off on an inspection tour of Germany late in 1940, then off to command the Kwantung Army in Manchukuo, his banishment ended in November 1941 as Lieutenant General Yamashita took over the new Twenty-fifth Army for the invasion of Malaya. Landing far north of Singapore on December 8, 1941, he conducted a dazzling blitzkrieg through terrain the British thought impassable. Taking Johore on January 21, 1942, he landed at Singapore on February 8, and the British surrendered on the fifteenth.

Jealousy among army high commanders combined with lingering resentment denied him celebration or an imperial audience, and he dutifully trudged to eastern Manchukuo. Called back to the war after Tojo resigned in September 1944, Yamashita drew the dismal task of defending the exposed Philippines against MacArthur's onrushing hordes.

402 Doing better than most others could have, he consolidated his forces and received scant reinforcements. Knowing his weakness, he issued orders against the defense of Manila and directed that POWs on Luzon be freed as the enemy landed. Without planes or sea support, his men under constant air and guerrilla attack, his communications riddled, Yamashita burrowed and moved until his food supplies shrank to nothing. About ready for a ceremonial suicide after he consigned his ragged survivors to guerrilla warfare themselves, Yamashita heard of Japan's surrender and he walked into Allied lines.

403 His trial for war crimes, especially some atrocities in Manila when he thought it had been abandoned, came as a sad denouement to a great career. Vowing ignorance of barbarism, explaining that he did not, in fact, command many of the perpetrators, Yamashita appealed his death sentence. Legal and moral issues won stays of execution; however, the Philippine Supreme Court refused to act on the general's appeal; the U.S. Supreme Court said it could not intervene against MacArthur; President Truman refused clemency, and Yamashita went to the gallows on February 23, 1946, in what two Supreme Court justices branded a "legalized lynching."

PEOPLE

404 Richard Sorge, 1895–1944, ranks as one of history's great spies. Born in Baku, Russia, grandson of one of Karl Marx's aides, Sorge served in World War I, took a doctorate in political science, and, in 1924, began professional spying. By the 1930s, posted to Tokyo as correspondent for a German newspaper, the communist Sorge, masquerading as a loyal Nazi agent, became press attaché in the German embassy. Organizing and running an effective spy network with members in high places, he sent invaluable information to Moscow, less useful data to Berlin.

405 Unkempt, thuglike, with a cruel glint in his eyes, a notorious drinker and womanizer unlikely to be anyone important, Sorge learned of Japan's intention to join the Axis and even provided the exact date of Barbarossa (q.v.). Stalin ignored the information about the coming German attack because he did not want to believe it. **406** Sorge's September 1941 report that Japan would not attack the USSR but instead move south proved pivotal; it convinced Stalin to move Siberian reserves to the Eastern Front. Sorge also informed Moscow of Japan's decision to attack Pearl Harbor.

Years of trying to find the source of unauthorized radio messages finally paid off, and in October 1941 the *Tokkō* (q.v.) arrested Sorge and his main agents. Following long appeals, Sorge and a trusted lieutenant were executed in November 1944.

407 **Leni Riefenstahl, 1902– , German filmmaker who revolutionized the documentary genre.** Beautiful and athletic, Riefenstahl began as a dancer but became fascinated by movies. Breaking into the male-dominated film business by sheer talent, she wrote, directed, produced, and acted in a series of "mountain pictures" that made her reputation.

408 **Hitler admired her and asked her to make some documentaries for the Nazi party.** Taken in by the Führer's charisma, Riefenstahl agreed. Two early efforts were mediocre, but her highly innovative use of symbols, people, and multiple cameras in her panegyric to the 1934 Nazi Party rally in Nuremberg, *Triumph of the Will* (1935), shot her to filmdom's top ranks. Her four-hour celebration of the 1936 Berlin Olympiad, *Olympia* (1938), cemented her professional standing.

409 **Her close association with Hitler and her propaganda efforts for the Nazis in many ways ruined her life.** Questions dog her always about just how close she and Hitler were. Did she know (and perhaps silently condone) his "final solution" of Jewish genocide? Imprisoned after the war (she escaped twice), harassed by American and French officials until 1947, Riefenstahl, shunned by the movie community, turned to still photography and produced two superior books on life in Africa and published her memoirs in 1993.

Still dissatisfied with her creations, Riefenstahl took up scuba diving at age seventy-two and practiced it still in her nineties. Her underwater photography is proof of her continuing camera originality.

Willing Nazi or dupe? Her films offer conflicting evidence.

410 **Wilhelm Messerschmitt, 1898–1978, German aircraft designer and builder.** "Willi" Messerschmitt learned to fly at age fifteen and soon began designing planes. Establishing his own factory in 1923, he produced an all-metal aircraft in 1926. He unveiled his Me-109 fighter in 1936, at the Berlin Olympiad. Various versions of it appeared through the war years and it enjoyed probably the greatest production run of any warplane.

411 **Messerschmitt's Me-410 ranked among the finest heavy fighters and interceptors ever made, and his Me-262 introduced the jet age to war and terrified Allied aircrews.**

After the war Messerschmitt made jet planes for Germany and NATO. He died on September 15, 1978.

1942

THE THIRD YEAR
OF THE WAR

UNCERTAINTY

*It's the fashion now to make war and presumably
it will last a good long while.*

—Frederick the Great to Voltaire, 1742

Appearances all ran for the Axis as victory loomed in 1942. Everywhere their land, sea, and air forces were poised to make final blows across the globe. For the Allies, the new year boded more defeats to come. Everywhere their land, sea, and air forces seemed scattered, battered, weak, and confused. Appearances can be deceiving, of course, and there were those on both sides who looked behind exteriors to find the way the currents ran. For Winston Churchill, the currents ran deep and surgent for the Allies. When their total resources came to bear, they would win. Franklin D. Roosevelt banked on Britain and the prime minister and pressed for breathing room so that America could make tools and train men. Time was the x factor in the victory equation as crises pressed in from east and west.

THE UNITED STATES, 1942

412 FDR's promise that the U.S. would become the arsenal of democracy led to radical changes in the country right after war began. High goals proved undaunting: provide twelve million trained soldiers and sailors, many more than Roosevelt's fifty thousand planes, hundreds of ships, everything for the largest war effort in history. As the draft kicked in, and munitions, shipping, aircraft, tank, radio, radar, medical, and clothing orders swamped the nation, older men, women, and youths joined the labor force. High wages, good incentives, and better working conditions solved recruiting problems. By the end of 1942 the labor force boasted more than 7.5 million people.

Factories added second and third shifts and workers went into overtime at a 50 percent premium beyond a basic forty hours. With new assembly line and prefabrication techniques in place, former automobile plants switched to making planes, tanks, and engines, and production skyrocketed. A vast construction program built training camps, hospitals, munition plants, shipyards, chemical works; many of these were located in the South, so that America's former "number 1 economic problem," the South, boomed. Civil service rolls expanded as civilians did all kinds of military jobs in depots, posts, camps, and stations.

413 Growing U.S. forces consumed much of the output, but Lend-Lease got more than its share—the entire Allied effort increasingly relied on the men and women in America's workshops and on its farms. With fewer people but better methods, farmers produced more than enough for home needs and greatly helped the Allies.

Plentiful resources encouraged research into new and improved weapons and sustained work in nuclear fission.

414 Plentiful resources or not, rationing soon became necessary. Shoes, some foods (meat, coffee, and sugar hurt the most), gasoline, and other fuels were doled out according to ration stamps and "A," "B," or "C" stickers on car windshields. Strict egalitarianism

Night view of the final assembly section of the A-35 Vengeance bomber, Vultee Aircraft Corporation, Nashville, Tennessee, August 1942.

ruled the ration boards although varied black markets flourished.

While "don't you know there's a war on" soothed many irks, racism posed problems. Blacks made real progress in government jobs that paid the same for everyone, but still they were discriminated against in unions and in military rank.

415 **Japanese-Americans suffered the worst discrimination.** Some 110,000 of those on the West Coast were unceremoniously—and probably unconstitutionally (although the U.S. Supreme Court never said so)—herded into detention camps in March 1942. Conditions were not good and resentment lingered.

Discrimination sometimes ran according to convenience. **416** **Shortages of farm labor introduced the "bracero" program which brought thousands of formerly taboo Mexicans onto borderland farms.** Chinese and Filipino residents enjoyed expanded legal status.

417 **Latin American diplomacy claimed some administration attention.** In January 1942 a Pan-American conference convened in Rio de Janeiro. Here U.S. efforts focused on getting all Latin American countries to join the Allies. Not all agreed, but a resolution did suggest that all these countries sever relations with

A Japanese-American World War I veteran, dressed in uniform, entering Santa Anita Park, an assembly center in California for evacuees of Japanese ancestry, April 1942.

the Axis. Much progress came in the difficult area of hemispheric defense coordination.

418 **America's women won most from the war.** Not only did they flock to factories and office jobs where child care facilities were often provided, but they

"Rosie the Riveter" poster promoting women workers' contributions to the war effort. Note the scarf holding back her hair so that it won't interfere with work.

Women workers installing fixtures and assemblies to a fuselage tail section of a B-17 Flying Fortress bomber at Douglas Aircraft plant, Long Beach, California, October 1942.

also ferried aircraft to Europe and joined Col. Oveta Culp Hobby's (q.v.) Women's Army Corps (WAC). Housing shortages pinched in big industrial cities but the government provided modest subsidies for workers. A baby boom began in 1940 and families held together fairly well.

By the end of 1942, America's morale soared and the country geared up for a long, hard war.

High morale mixed with anger as the year passed. The story of what happened on Bataan after the Yanks surrendered dribbled home in bits of horror. **419 Full accounts of the infamous Death March would not be known for a year or so; meanwhile rumors and facts combined in a montage of barbarity.** Growing reports of Japanese brutality spread and fanned incipient racism into a revived hatred of the "yellow peril." Victory would bring vengeance.

420 That the war grew nastier could be seen in the daily news. That it grew more alarming could be seen in the growing involvement of scientists, notably physicists, as special warriors. Rumors about a possible uranium bomb had stimulated Albert Einstein's 1939 letter to President Roosevelt, and as more physicists came to the United States from Germany with more information, rumors became fact. **421 FDR expected Dr. Vannevar Bush's Office of Scientific Research and Development to push research.** In March 1942, Bush told the president that "recent developments indicate . . . that the [atomic bomb] is more important than I believed when I last spoke with you about it. The stuff [uranium] will apparently be more powerful than we thought, the amount necessary seems to be less, the possibilities of actual production appear more certain." Bush's report, sparked by evidence from such émigrés as Enrico Fermi, John Von Neumann, and Edward Teller, ended by saying work might begin in 1943 and would be difficult. Roosevelt replied that speed "is very much of the essence." **422 Dr. Arthur Holly Compton got the assignment to design a bomb, and he organized a group to do the work under the chairmanship of J. Robert Oppenheimer, professor of physics at both the University of California at Berkeley and the California Institute of Technology.** Oppenheimer turned out to be an entirely unlikely natural for the assignment. He pulled together a "galaxy of luminaries" at Berkeley during the second week of July 1942. Among the nine principals at the meeting were three future Nobel Prize winners, and the inspiration shared by all attendees remained with them as the richest exchange of ideas in memory.

They agreed quickly on the possibility of atomic fission, ruminated for a time on the design and nature of a "gadget," spent some time pondering possibilities of a hydrogen bomb, and puzzled over how far the brilliant German physicist, Nobel laureate Werner Heisenberg (a main architect of quantum mechanics) had gone with atomic research. He had been at it since the 1930s and had benefited from Lise Meitner's experiments as well as those of many others.

423 That meeting marked the real beginning of what became known as the Manhattan Project, the greatest engineering program yet launched by man to make history's greatest man-made threat to life. It metamorphosed from a purely scientific to a scientific/military project, with Oppenheimer running the science side and Brig. Gen. Leslie R. Groves (who built the Pentagon) managing the multi-installations around the United States. Historians would imply later that Groves appointed Oppenheimer, but they were co-team leaders whose complementing talents energized the drive to build the bomb.

424 On the medical front in the 1930s, infections from wounds and disease were attacked by sulfa drugs which, miraculous as they seemed, did not stop streptococcal infections, but in the 1940s new research produced new medications for bacteria that revolutionized battlefield medicine. By 1942, Alexander Fleming, Howard Florey, and Oxford colleagues had proved the value of the new penicillin and produced enough for battle treatments. Penicillin became a kind of standing miracle—bacteria evaporated before its onslaught and war fatalities dropped astoundingly.

UNITED STATES FAR EASTERN BATTLES, 1942

425 Militarily the new war year started badly for the United States, despite the fact that the Japanese stumbled after taking Manila on January 3, 1942. Orders diverted General Homma's good 48th Division for service in Java and forced redeployment of the general's units. Wainwright, recognizing the

Japanese photograph showing victorious Japanese troops on Bataan Peninsula, Philippines, 1942.

weakness of his positions northeast of the Bataan Peninsula, fell back into that prepared zone of last defense.

426 **Bataan posed tough problems for the offensive.** More or less well fortified, the twenty-mile-wide and twenty-five-mile-long peninsula was cut by mountains that drained alluvial streams to the east and the west where dense jungle covered the lowlands.

Heavy fighting steadily drove American and Filipino forces back toward the small port of Mariveles at the tip of Bataan jutting into Manila Harbor toward Corregidor Island. Furious hand-to-hand combat seared Bataan's landscape and the defenders stuck to their guns despite malaria, beriberi, various tropical debilities, and dwindling rations and ammunition. American supplies shrank as Japanese ships sank small supply vessels trying to bring in food, medicine, and ammunition; by January's end, rations

Surrender of American troops, Corregidor, May 6, 1942.

were halved—monkeys, dogs, mules, carabaos, iguanas, snakes, all became gourmet dishes for Bataan's defenders. Thousands of men languished in makeshift hospitals, unable to function.

When General MacArthur (q.v.) obeyed President Roosevelt's orders to leave on March 12 and turned over his command to Wainwright, the new lieutenant general had little to lead. Wainwright moved his headquarters to Corregidor and ordered the Bataan fight continued. Actually he had the right idea—Homma's effective strength had been cut to some 3,000—but the Filipino-American troops were too weak to attack. Major General Edward P. King surrendered Bataan on April 9, 1942. The Japanese took some 75,000 prisoners.

Corregidor held out until May 6, 1942, and Wainwright, to save prisoner lives, surrendered all of the Philippines.

427 **Heroic defense of a forlorn hope thrilled America.** The denouement, the Bataan Death March, ignited a fury that would be slaked only by immolation.

On April 10, the day after the surrender, the Japanese began rounding up prisoners for movement to Camp O'Donnell. **428** **Although General King offered trucks for some 75,000 men—about 12,000 of them Americans—most prisoners were put into a long column and marched northward in deadly, humid heat.** They marched in columns of fours or threes and soon learned that stragglers were usually bayoneted or shot; they marched mostly without food or water—Japanese guards taunted them, took their personal belongings, ate and drank in front of them, buried some alive, beheaded others—and those who tried to help weaker comrades were either severely beaten or killed. **429** **A few escaped as the march went on for six days and for sixty-five miles to San Fernando.** There the prisoners were crammed into boxcars with little ventilation; many suffocated and died during the three-hour ride. After another seven-mile march they reached Camp O'Donnell. Some made the whole march without any food at all, drinking only dribbles

Photo captured from the Japanese showing long line of U.S. prisoners along the Bataan Road. They carry their fallen comrades in improvised litters in what became known as the Bataan Death March.

of water from carabao wallows. The camp provided little relief. The hospital had no medicine; prisoners waited in line ten hours to get a drink; a little rice became the standard ration, and the daily death rate rose. Many prisoners were sent to hard labor in various islands, some went to camps in Manchukuo.

General Homma (q.v.) had made some provisions for transport and food, but there were far more prisoners than he anticipated and the guards had no supervision. **430 Of the 75,000 men who started on the march, about 54,000 made it to the end.**

431 Americans can be patient as long as they are doing something positive. Waiting while the Philippines fell built national frustration, and President Roosevelt knew that an American attack of some kind had to happen or he would face serious domestic trouble. Where and how? He and the staffs had agreed on the Germany first strategy and virtually written off the Far East. **432 Yet the sweeping Japanese conquests shamed and infuriated America.** General Marshall probed for ways to stem the onslaught. Martial resources were the problem. Short-

Chinese soldier guarding a line of P-40 fighter planes at an American Volunteer Group airfield in China. The Chinese called the planes the "flying tiger sharks" because of the shark-toothed emblems on their noses, but to everyone else they (and their pilots) were the Flying Tigers, whose victories destroyed the myth of Japanese air supremacy.

ages of manpower, equipment, transport, and naval assets plagued all far eastward planning. Australia called in alarm for help from the U.S. as the Rising Sun began searing all of Southeast Asia. What to do? Something dramatic had to happen.

First, jury rig an air raid on Japan. Odds ran absurdly against any carrier planes—much less bombers—getting close enough to hit Japan. **433 But Lt. Col. James H. Doolittle, peacetime air racer, perfected the idea of using modified B-25 Mitchell bombers which could carry a one-ton bomb load from a carrier about seven hundred miles east of Japan and then escape across it to Chinese airfields.** Doolittle trained volunteers on how to make short takeoffs from a measured landing strip. Early on April 18, 1942, sixteen Mitchells departed the U.S. carrier *Hornet* and completely surprised Tokyo air defenses.

Kobe, Nogoya, Yokosuka, and Yokohama also shared the surprise and damage. Fighters scrambled after the raiders, antiaircraft guns flailed the air, but all planes escaped toward China. Bad weather forced several down and a few landed in Japanese controlled parts of China, but seventy of the eighty-two

Doolittle Raid, April 18, 1942: a B-25 taking off from the deck of the USS *Hornet*.

airmen who flew the raid escaped, as did the *Hornet*. **434 Militarily insignificant, Doolittle's raid had a massive impact on morale—Americans were thrilled by the sharp reply to Pearl Harbor, and the Japanese lost a massive amount of face in addition to being suddenly aware of their homeland's vulnerability.**

Second, order Douglas MacArthur out of Corregidor and bring that somewhat battered paladin to Australia, from whence he could make noises of salvation. MacArthur, though, refused puppetry and fumed at the Germany first strategy that left him a symbol without substance. Acting while protesting, though, the new supreme commander of the Southwest Pacific Area (as of April 18, 1942) sought coordination of a disjointed and mutually suspicious group of Australian, Dutch, and British troops with the independent forces of Adm. Chester Nimitz (q.v.).

MacArthur—ordered by Roosevelt to protect Australia—desperately needed naval help.

435 In February a small Allied fleet tried to stop a huge Japanese invasion force heading for oil-rich Java and failed at heavy cost in the Battle of the Java Sea, February 27–March 1, 1942. Without increased air and sea cover, MacArthur could not prevent Borneo's loss and possibly Australia's invasion. Japanese coordination of all arms in various campaigns impressed and frightened all Allied commanders. **436 Japanese bombing of Darwin, the capture of New Britain, New Ireland, the Admiralty and Gilbert Islands, and a landing on New Guinea threatened the complete isolation of Australia and New Zealand.** MacArthur began to receive some reinforcements and learned from ULTRA (q.v.) traffic of enemy plans to send three invasion convoys—covered by aircraft carriers and heavy surface units—to Port Moresby, Papua.

437 Admiral Nimitz (q.v.), now the U.S. Pacific Fleet's CIC, moved to intercept, and the first major naval engagement fought entirely from carriers began on May 4, 1942. When the Battle of the Coral Sea ended on the eighth, the badly hurt U.S. carrier *Lexington* had to

A young Air Corps pilot, William E. Dyess, who made the Bataan Death March and later escaped, published one of the first full accounts of walking death in *The Dyess Story*.

This is part of his testimony:

There was no room to lie down. Some of us tried to rest in a half squat. . . . I heard a cry, followed by thudding blows. . . . An American soldier so tortured by thirst that he could not sleep had asked a Jap guard for water. The Jap fell on him with his fists, then slugged him into insensibility with a rifle butt. . . .

The rising sun cast its blinding light into our eyes as we marched. The temperature rose by the minute. Noon came and went. The midday heat was searing. At 1 P.M. the column was halted and Jap noncoms told American and Filipino soldiers they might fill their canteens from a dirty puddle beside the road. There was no food. . . .

We had learned by rough experience that efforts to assist our failing comrades served usually to hasten their deaths and add to our own misery and peril. So we tried the next best thing—encouraging them with words. . . .

"Hello, Doc. Taking a walk?"

"Ed," he said slowly, "I can't go another kilometer. A little farther and I'm finished."

"Well, Doc, I'm about in the same fix". . . . Every now and then Doc would begin to lag a little. [We would slip back and shove him.] He always took the hint and stepped up. . . . Doc didn't fall out. If he had his bones would be bleaching now somewhere along that road of death that led out of Bataan. . . .

Skulking along, a hundred yards behind our contingent, came a "clean-up squad" of murdering Jap buzzards. Their helpless victims [who had fallen out of the march] sprawled darkly against the white of the road, were easy targets. . . .

On through the night we were followed by orange flashes and thudding shots.

be scuttled, the carrier *Yorktown* had taken hard hits, while the heavily damaged Japanese carrier *Shokaku* and her consort carrier *Zuikaku* (short of aircraft) were out of action for several months. Tactically a victory for the Imperial Navy—it had better planes than the Americans—the battle amounted to a strategic defeat since the invasion forces turned back and MacArthur's command regrouped.

438 A frustrated and worried Admiral Yamamoto knew he had to finish off what remained of a U.S. Pacific fleet, especially the carriers he had missed at Pearl Harbor. ULTRA intelligence informed Nimitz and MacArthur that Yamamoto planned to lure what remained of a U.S. fleet into obliteration northwest of Hawaii. Always cunning, he schemed to lure part of the U.S. force northward to chase a Japanese diversionary invasion of the Aleutians while his main body struck strategic Midway Island. Angry arguments surrounded this plan in Imperial Navy discussions, but loss of face after the Doolittle Raid finally brought approval.

439 Since Nimitz knew enemy plans through Ultra, he concentrated, secretly, carriers *Hornet* and *Enterprise*, along with *Yorktown* (miraculously repaired in two instead of ninety days) and two task forces near Midway. On June 4, 1942, 145 Japanese warships attacked the island. U.S. Adm. Raymond Spruance's task force raced in and found Japanese carrier planes refueling after hitting Midway. Attacking low, Spruance's torpedo bombers not only smashed enemy planes on deck but also drew down enemy fighters and exposed the carriers to high flying dive bombers. Although only six of Spruance's bombers returned, they had set the stage for victory. Three enemy carriers were blazing; one escaped (*Hiryu*) and next day launched a heavy attack on USS *Yorktown*. Spruance's trusty dive bombers retaliated and *Hiryu*'s crew scuttled her.

ABOVE: Maymyo, Burma, April 19, 1942: (left to right) Generalissimo and Madame Chiang Kai-shek and Lt. Gen. Joseph E. Stilwell (commanding general, U.S. military mission in China) are all smiles on the day after the successful Doolittle Raid. BELOW: Marines on "alert" between Japanese attacks on Dutch Harbor, Alaska, June 3, 1942. These air strikes were diversionary; the main attack was made at Midway, June 4.

Both sides paid heavily for the three-day action—the Japanese lost four carriers (including 250 planes) and a heavy cruiser, and had another heavy cruiser damaged along with a battleship and other vessels; U.S. losses included *Yorktown* (finished off by an enemy submarine), a destroyer, plus 147 planes.

440 Midway may deserve rank as the most decisive naval battle of World War II. Yamamoto's plan fizzled and the balance of Pacific naval power shifted permanently to the U.S. and the Allies. More than all that, Midway certified that at sea as on land, a third dimension—airpower—truly dominated war.

SBD Dauntless dive bombers from the USS *Hornet* fly over the burning Japanese heavy cruiser *Mikuma* during the battle of Midway, June 6, 1942

441 As American strength grew slowly, new Pacific command arrangements solidified. MacArthur kept responsibility for Australia and all the islands northwestward to French Indochina and the Philippines; Admiral Nimitz's brief ran across the Pacific Ocean to Midway and south along the U.S. supply route from Hawaii to Australia, including Samoa, Fiji, the New Hebrides, and, for a time, the southern Solomon Islands. U.S. commanders might well have been

daunted as they looked at a map—Japanese conquests dotted the Pacific and not much remained to the Allies. Close looks, though, showed that, impressive as the emperor's empire seemed, it lacked cohesion and spread beyond control.

Where to hit that Japanese house of cards and start it tumbling down?

First, stop further incursions toward Australia, then push hard against weaker enemy island outposts. MacArthur kept calling for assets and urging action in the Pacific theater. When Admiral King joined in pushing for the Pacific and argued that the Japanese had to be stopped before they consolidated in the Bismarck-New Guinea-Solomons area and chopped the U.S. supply lanes to Australia, the Joint Chiefs of Staff decided to help. Temporarily men and matériel went to the Southwest Pacific and command disputes sank into the background. This happened just as the Japanese decided that, despite Midway, they had resources enough to drive ahead in their New Guinea endeavors, take Port Moresby, and expose Australia and New Zealand.

442 Orders issued in July committed U.S. forces to seizing the New Britain-New Guinea-New Ireland areas as quickly as possible—a foothold in that zone would threaten the large Japanese base at Rabaul, New Britain, as well as favored routes of enemy reinforcement. Vice Admiral Robert L. Ghormley, CIC, Southwest Pacific Area, helped by some of MacArthur's and Australia's air and naval strength, would take the Santa Cruz Islands as well as Tulagi and environs in the Solomons. So began the grinding struggle for Guadalcanal that started in August 1942.

Objections that the offensive came ahead of resources and without time for careful planning were negated by news of a new enemy airfield under construction on Guadalcanal. Neither Ghormley nor MacArthur had much reliable information about objectives. Rumor had it that some 5,000 enemy troops were on Guadalcanal and 2,000 on Tulagi, when, in actuality only 1,500 (600 of them labor troops) were

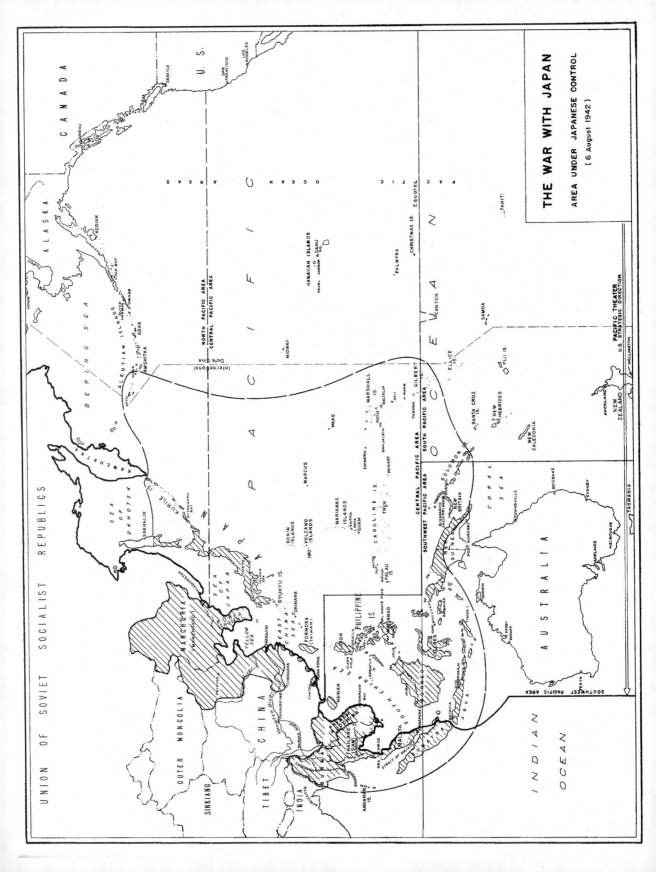

Most popular of American war songs in 1942 was one by Frank Loesser supposedly inspired by a line uttered by a military chaplain during a battle:

PRAISE THE LORD AND PASS THE AMMUNITION

Down went the gunner, a bullet was his fate
Down went the gunner, and then the gunner's
*   mate*
Up jumped the sky pilot, gave the boys a look
And manned the gun himself as he laid aside
*   The Book, shouting . . .*

(Refrain)
Praise the Lord and pass the ammunition
Praise the Lord and pass the ammunition

Praise the Lord and pass the ammunition
And we'll all stay free

Praise the Lord and swing into position
Can't afford to be a politician
Praise the Lord. We're all between perdition
And the deep blue sea
Yes the sky pilot said it
Ya gotta give him credit
For a sonofagun of a gunner was he

Shouting Praise Lord,
*   we're on a mighty mission*
All aboard, we ain't a-goin' fishin'
Praise the Lord and pass the ammunition
And we'll all stay free

(Refrain twice)

on Tulagi and 2,200 (1,700 labor troops) on the larger island—this faulty intelligence dogged the whole campaign with hesitation.

443 The reinforced 1st Marine Division (19,000 men) under Maj. Gen. Alexander Vandegrift went ashore at Guadalcanal, Tulagi, and three other islands on August 7, 1942, supported by three aircraft carriers and escorts. Some opposition developed in the twin islets of Gavutu-Tanambogo, but consolidation of defensive positions on Guadalcanal went swiftly. Vandegrift, overcounting the opposition, braced for counterattacks while he planned other landing sites; he did, at least, secure the airfield (soon known as Henderson Field) on August 9. Puzzles about enemy numbers proved to be only one problem on Guadalcanal. No good maps were available, and the sticky humidity, the rain forests, the baffling jungle, and the lack of roads presented problems unexpected by the Americans. So, too, did the sudden appearance of concentrated enemy resistance.

444 From Rabaul came bombers (fortunately reported in advance by an Australian coastwatcher [q.v.]) and a large enemy naval force that defeated U.S. covering warships in the Battle of Savo Island on August 9, 1942. The next day, U.S. Adm. Frank J. Fletcher, fearing a heavy air attack, abruptly took his carriers away, which forced the only partly unloaded transports to abandon the landings on Guadalcanal. Probably necessary, this precipitate withdrawal left the thinly supplied Marines brutally vulnerable until some air support arrived on August 20 as Henderson Field became partly operational.

Japanese reinforcements came ashore in bits and brigades from all parts of the sprawling new empire, and the Japanese commander happily underestimated U.S. strength—by the twentieth of August there were 3,700 Japanese on the island against 10,000 Americans; on September 11, 9,000 Japanese were ashore, while U.S. strength reached 11,000.

445 Feeling the security of superior numbers, the Japanese commander attacked U.S. positions piecemeal, and on August 21 he lost an entire detachment of 900 men in the Battle of the Tenaru River. American casualties, too, ran high because the Marines were unpracticed in jungle warfare.

Serious naval actions depleted U.S. strength in the Solomons as two aircraft carriers were out of action by mid-September, but slowly U.S. strength grew and held control of the sea. Despite large enemy reinforcements, U.S. forces defeated a major offensive in October, and in mid-November a last huge onslaught by combined Japanese land and sea forces brought on the naval Battle of Guadalcanal.

446 This twenty-four-minute action on the night of November 12/13 ranks as one of the grimmest in naval history; U.S. losses, six ships, Japanese three, including a battleship. The next night further efforts to land Japanese troops were foiled by U.S. naval remnants and Henderson Field's Cactus Air Force (a mixed collection of some thirty fighters and torpedo bombers).

Reinforcing contests continued after these decisive sea actions. By the end of 1942 the Marines were relieved by the U.S. 25th Infantry Division, and in January 1943 some 50,000 American soldiers attacked the remaining undersupplied enemy ranks. In one of the most impressive actions of the Guadalcanal campaign, some 13,000 Japanese survivors were secretly evacuated early in February 1943.

Tolls of Guadalcanal can best be cast in misery. Both sides struggled against each other in a relatively small place and against diseases unknown in impenetrable terrain, against clouds of flies and mosquitoes, against malaria, heat, and jungle rot, against burning thirsts and fevers and muddied slime and snakes. Both sides fought well. From that woeful, hellish place Americans took an appreciation that they had beaten some of the enemy's best, at a cost of 1,752 dead, very many wounded, and very many ships and sailors lost. The Japanese army nursed its first defeat in the war, having lost some 25,000 men; the Imperial Navy had been brutally handled and lots of irreplaceable carrier pilots were lost.

447 Guadalcanal, unknown to most Americans before August 1942, became a talisman of victory in the United States: the place where the march to Tokyo began.

Fighting on Guadalcanal raged while the Japanese, still intending to take Port Moresby and threaten Australia, sought to reinforce their landings on New Guinea. First efforts were thwarted by the Coral Sea battle in early May, but the few Japanese troops that did land at Gona, Papua, moved vigorously inland and by the end of July 1942 had seized Kokoda, gateway to a trail leading across the Owen Stanley Mountains to Port Moresby. **448** Fortunately for the Allies, the Imperial Navy could not support the Port Moresby offensive because of carrier losses at Midway. Nonetheless, the Japanese got within thirty miles of their objective by mid-September. Fighting in and around Lae, Salamaua, Milne Bay, and Buna flickered through the summer until, at last, MacArthur sent General Eichelberger to take Buna—which he did by late January 1943. Costs ran high on both sides in this grim jungle campaign—some 10,000 Allied casualties against probably 15,000 Japanese.

As the Joint Chiefs of Staff argued heatedly over what would happen the next year in the Southwest Pacific, MacArthur and Adm. William F. "Bull" Halsey (q.v.) (since mid-October 1942 tactical commander in the South Pacific) established a firm base in the Solomons for further advances north and west.

449 The year 1942 ranks as a time of change in the Pacific war. Allied forces, shattered and demoralized at the start, brandished their battered little fleets in myriad costly engagements with much stronger enemy task groups and, finally reinforced, began holding their own. The Japanese, everywhere triumphant at year's beginning, bungled many chances at sea and on land to annihilate Allied forces and by the end of 1942 found their conquests scattered almost beyond the protection of a far-stretched Imperial Navy.

ABOVE: The five Sullivan brothers received special permission from the Secretary of the Navy in order to serve aboard the same vessel. On November 13, 1942, that vessel, the USS *Juneau*, was sunk by Japanese submarine I-26. Only eleven of a crew of six hundred survived; and the five brothers all died. Their deaths resulted in Congress passing a law (the "Sullivan" act) prohibiting all military members of a family from serving in a combat zone at the same time. BELOW: 1943 poster promoting service and patriotism.

the five Sullivan brothers
'missing in action' off the Solomons

THEY DID THEIR PART

UNITED STATES WESTERN BATTLES, 1942

450 **While Americans paused to gird in earnest for a war of expanding dimensions, they managed to sustain the Allies around the globe.** Behind all the churning activities lurked a restive drive to get deeply into the war, a drive teased by pushes to such places as the new bases lent by Britain in return for destroyers and a substantial force which went to Iceland in July 1941.

But it all happened too slowly. All the planning, the to-ing and fro-ing between Washington and London, the seemingly endless talking, irked the public. It took no military genius to see what had to be done—just do it! Get "our boys" to England and then on to overwhelm the Nazis. And so schemed General Marshall and the Joint Chiefs of Staff.

They intended the UK as a staging area for Europe, a place to train masses of troops, a place to build mountains of supplies until the whole island kingdom bulged with military might. **451** Much of the arranging fell to the War Plans Division of the War Department general staff. Temporary brigadier general Dwight D. Eisenhower reported for duty there on December 12, 1941, largely because of his recent service in the Philippines. Two days later the somewhat austere and formal General Marshall asked "Ike" (nearly everybody called him that) what should be done for MacArthur and his command in the Far East.

Surprised—Ike did not yet know Marshall well—he asked for a few hours to give an answer. **452** At last he reported that the whole Philippine situation could not be saved. "Our base must be Australia," said Ike. "We must take great risks and spend any amount of money." The tall VMI man answered, "I agree with you." They agreed on another vital point—the need for unified command. Marshall's experience in the First World War in close proximity to Gen. John J. Pershing had exposed him to the vagaries of overlapping command arrangements. Eisenhower's experience in working as a member of Pershing's postwar staff had taught the amiable Kansan the same lessons. **453** Marshall set his new protégé the job of devising the right kind of orders for Allied theater and force commanders. On Monday, June 8, 1942, Ike presented a thirty-page plan for unified command of all U.S. forces going to Europe.

454 Just back from an inspection trip to England and refreshed in the need for unity in a coalition effort, Eisenhower suggested that the chief of staff read the document carefully since it likely would be important. Marshall surprised Ike with his response. "I certainly do want to read it. You may be the man who executes it. If that's the case, when can you leave?" Three days later Eisenhower got a job whose limits he could define. It is doubtful that anyone better could have been selected for an appointment demanding sensitive military and diplomatic negotiations among touchy allies.

455 As he reached London on June 24 to take up his assignment as commander of American forces in England, Eisenhower began growing into a new personal dimension—he became, first and last, a coalition man and insisted on the same devotion among his generals and staff. A story made Allied rounds about Ike's comment that he had no objection to an American officer calling a British officer a bastard, but if he said "a British bastard" he would swiftly be en route home. Some Allied colleagues noted, though, that their new leader insisted on American troops remaining under American command—another Pershing lesson.

456 Problems ringed him everywhere. Stalin called stridently for a "second front" and urged a swift cross-Channel effort—and Ike flirted with the idea of a nearly sacrificial feint into northern France. Recalling the disastrous Allied cross-Channel raid on Dieppe in 1942, British leaders opposed this notion and Ike appreciated the dangers. Typically balancing losses versus gains, he argued that "We should not forget that the prize we seek is to keep 8,000,000 Russians in the war"; small losses might be an acceptable exchange. Besides, most American strategists wanted a cross-Channel invasion at some future time. FDR added to pressures by insisting that some Allied offensive had to happen somewhere in 1942. Churchill and his staff urged an invasion of French North Africa that would perhaps stiffen Free French sentiments and might trap Rommel's Afrika Korps between Montgomery's Eighth Army and the American invaders.

457 Ike feared a North African diversion would sidetrack the main effort toward France, but he finally, and most reluctantly, agreed to Operation Torch, the invasion of Morocco and Algeria. Named commander, Allied Expeditionary Force for the venture, he threw himself into hectic months of planning, but his confidence flagged amid wild French political machinations involving General de Gaulle and various rivals, amid arguments about where the African landings should take place, amid worries about shortages of shipping, manpower, munitions, everything. On November 7, 1942, just before the attack, Ike continued his remarkable candid correspondence with Marshall: "We are standing . . . on the brink and must take the jump—whether the bottom contains a nice feather bed or a pile of brickbats!" Frequently during this first operation, Ike vented worries and irks to Marshall, who understood that his man was growing into whole new capacities and supported him staunchly.

Although the landings went well on November 8, supported by outstanding naval/air cooperation—some Vichyite resistance appeared—and these new combat realities forced Ike to evaluate himself. He had been slow, he realized, in getting his units into place, had tolerated incompetence in his Intelligence staff and laxness among some field commanders while, at the same time, micromanaging others, and he had lost the race to Tunis. More than those defects, he had been abysmally naive politically. Making a deal with French admiral Jean Darlan to neutralize Vichy defenses had been a disaster since most Allies thought Darlan among the world's worst fascists—a storm of anger burst over Allied Force Headquarters (AFHQ). Marshall sympathized and told Ike to let others worry about diplomacy and get on with the fighting. Eisenhower reorganized and in early November created the British First Army under Gen. Kenneth A. N. Anderson, a big, burly, fighting Scot.

German aggressiveness held the Allies back for the rest of 1942 as Rommel moved to link up with reinforcements. Both sides built reserves. Ike began thinking about the Tunisian endgame and what would happen next.

458 **It had been a tough summer for Erwin Rommel.** His amazing successes early in the year had soured in the Battles of El Alamein as Russia consumed increasing amounts of men and supplies became hard to get. During the first week of November 1942, General Montgomery's Eighth British Army completely broke through German positions at El Alamein, and Rommel told Hitler that his army, almost literally out of gas, faced annihilation. Hitler issued one of his stand-fast orders, which Rommel obeyed for a day before accelerating the German retreat westward.

459 **This retreat nearly coincided with Allied North African landings and did much to pull French forces over to the Allies.**

The Desert Fox's health broke but not his morale. Furious with Hitler's wasteful orders, Rommel nonetheless sought to rally his German and Italian troops to cooperate with another panzer army come to Tunisia under Gen. Hans Jürgen Theodor "Dieter" von Arnim. Happily for the Allies, Arnim's jealousy of Rommel confused German operations in Tunisia. This indecision may well have saved Eisenhower's first campaign.

460 **In 1942, America fought its toughest war in the North Atlantic.** While Nazi admiral Raeder (q.v.) pressed Hitler for unrestricted submarine construction, the few he had were doing serious damage to Allied shipping. Despite America's unrestricted war on U-boats in the Atlantic after U-652 and USS *Greer* exchanged torpedoes and depth charges in September 1941, submarines were nearly cutting the U.S. lifeline to Britain.

Sinkings were so common that numbers remained a deep secret. It is known now that from January to July 1942, 681 Allied ships were sunk. **461** **After America's entry into the war, U-boats began Operation *Paukenschlag* (Drumbeat); they often roamed the surface along the U.S. East Coast at night and easily picked off ships silhouetted against city lights.** Sinkings increased, too, when U-boat captains noticed the U.S. Navy tendency to drop convoys off too soon, leaving them once they were near the American coastline; U-boats began trolling waters close to major harbors and river mouths such as the St. Lawrence and Mississippi.

Alexander Werth, able English newsman aboard the Murmansk-bound merchantman *Empire Baffin*, described a Nazi air attack:

> I was standing amidships with the R.A.F. boys and . . . several others, and we realized that something had happened to our sister ship, the Empire Lawrence. . . . She was no longer steering a straight course. Her bows were pointing towards us—was she moving at all? She was showing a slight list. And we realized that she was being abandoned. Already two of her lifeboats were bobbing on the water, and beside her was a little corvette, taking more men off. As we watched her, we heard all our guns fire like mad. . . . [T]wo more of the yellow bellies swept over with roaring engines, almost touching our topmast, and . . . made a dead set at the helpless, dying ship. And suddenly from the yellow belly the five bombs detached themselves and went right into her. . . . [T]here was an explosion that did not sound very loud, and a flash which, in the sun, was not very bright, and like a vomiting volcano a huge pillar of fire, smoke and wreckage shot two hundred feet into the air— and then, slowly, terribly slowly, it went down to the sea. The Empire Lawrence was gone.

A worried Royal Navy gave some antisubmarine warfare (ASW) escorts to the U.S. fleet. U.S. warships did begin coastal convoying by May 1942, but U-boats, shifting to the Gulf of Mexico and Caribbean, claimed 160 more ships. Between May and September 1942, more than a million tons of Allied shipping went to the bottom of the Gulf of Mexico and the Caribbean.

462 What U-boat commanders called another Happy Time—the days of limitless targets and limited opposition—lingered throughout 1942, but wide use of such new things as radar, ASW aircraft, and amazing shipbuilding feats boded ill for the *Kriegsmarine*.

463 North Atlantic fighting ranked with the worst of the war—especially for the merchant mariners who endured nerve-racking stress, terrible weather, angry seas, gatherings of U-boats, and usually little chance of survival. By far the worst agonies were suffered by those seamen working the route to Russia via the Arctic Ocean around Norway. On this Murmansk run, U-boats were helped by awesomely bad weather, by equally awesome Nazi land-based bombers, and sometimes by surface vessels.

Stalin's demands for supplies forced the institution of the exposed northern convoy circuit that steadily sucked down men and ships. **464** In June 1942, Convoy PQ-17, thirty-five thinly guarded merchant ships, headed north from Iceland for the thousand-mile stretch through the Arctic Ocean into the Barents Sea and the big southward turn to Murmansk and Archangel. A U-boat alert on July 1 gathered a wolf pack while the British belatedly sent a large surface force, including battleships and carriers, for protection. The Germans responded with the huge dreadnought *Tirpitz*, two pocket battleships, and ten destroyers.

"RAF Liberator Attacks New Type of U-Boat" read the original caption for this photo which describes the U-boat as "straddled by the first stick of the depth charges" dropped by the Liberator. Gunners can be seen in the conning tower to the left of the blast.

The threatened naval battle fizzled as Hitler ordered his surface ships home. But things got worse for the convoy as the ships scattered and U-boats and aircraft attacked for several days. When the Germans broke off action, twenty-four of PQ-17's thirty-five ships were sunk, which accounted for 200 planes, 3,300 vehicles, 400 tanks, and masses of other supplies. Ten weeks later a heavily guarded PQ-18 sailed for the same ports. Attacked by planes and subs, the convoy fought back but lost thirteen of its forty-three ships. The Germans lost twenty-seven planes and three U-boats. In August, heavily escorted Convoy SC-94, eastbound from Canada, lost thirteen of its thirty-six ships while Nazi losses came to two U-boats sunk and two damaged.

Severe Atlantic losses continued through 1942 and beyond.

GERMANY, 1942

465 War enthusiasm waned as 1942 promised hard struggles in Russia and continued commitment in North Africa, on the oceans, and now even in the air over Germany. Any German who remembered the fearsome times after World War I would admit that things were much better than at any time since then. Still, the Third Reich had become by early 1942 both a totalitarian state and a dictatorship—and there were differences. Germany now belonged to Hitler; he was Germany. That had become increasingly true through the winter of 1941–42. Now, at season's changing, would his springtime come?

Who could doubt it? All omens ran for him. While German armies did not win in Russia in 1941, they had weathered the winter in fairly good shape and were poised to deliver a knockout offensive. Home conditions were about the same as before the war with Poland—plentiful food, clothing, shoes, and luxuries reflected an improved living standard and showed how little the war had touched the Fatherland.

466 Younger Nazis hardly noticed the erosion of law. Older generations realized that commissions, bureaus, and special agencies like SS *Obergruppenführer* Reinhard Heydrich's *Reichssicherheitshauptamt* (RSHA, the Reich Main Security Office) that pulled the Gestapo (q.v.), the criminal police (*Kripo*), and the Nazi Party security force, *Sicherheitsdienst* (SD) into a gatherum of oppression, had largely supplanted the courts. A few worried about obvious intrusions on personal freedoms. The need for laborers

---

The German anthem in English translation, "Deutschland über Alles":

Germany, Germany above all
Above everything in the world
When, always, for protection and defense
Brothers stand together.
From the Maas to the Memel
From the Etsch to the Belt,
Germany, Germany above all
Above all in the world.

German women, German fidelity,
German wine and German song,
Shall retain, throughout the world,
Their old respected fame,
To inspire us to noble deeds
For the length of our lives.
German women, German fidelity,
German wine and German song.

Unity and right and freedom
For the German Fatherland;
Let us all strive to this goal
Brotherly, with heart and hand.
Unity and rights and freedom
Are the pledge of fortune grand.
Prosper in this fortune's glory,
Prosper German Fatherland.

grew slowly into an emergency that dragooned increasing numbers of people into war work.

467 **Some citizens also found themselves pressed into various patriotic "associations" which became less voluntary by the day**—boys and girls (ages ten to fourteen) went into the *Deutsches Jungvolk*, while Hitler Youth groups were compulsory for young men and the *Bund Deutscher Mädel* for young women. An almost antique romanticism kept girls and women out of the labor force, as they were meant to be Germany's great mother figures.

Things at home may have been relatively good, but casualty lists kept coming, along with the trains full of wounded, reminders of a baleful darkness in the east.

468 **Statistics, though, seemed to validate the Führer's optimism.** Steel production still rose in 1942, as did the production of coal, lignite, synthetic oils, and rubber, while aluminum production jumped more than 10 percent; German aircraft production went from some 8,000 planes in 1939 to over 15,000 in 1942; 2,200 tanks were built in 1940 and 9,300 in 1942. Enemy production statistics were ignored or "adjusted."

469 **Serious political scientists puzzled over the chaotic administrative structure of the Reich.** Far from demonstrating vaunted German organizational skills, Hitler's administration ran a haphazard course, with top officials calling the governmental structure "organized improvisation." Hitler manipulated confusion by playing bureaus, departments, and officers against each other so that conflict resolution rested wholly in his hands.

470 **Hitler's friends never felt secure in their relationship with him**—manufacturing wizard Albert Speer once noted, "If Hitler had had any friends, I would certainly have been one of his close friends." By 1942, Hitler's often inexplicable personal friendships were becoming notorious. *Der Dickie*'s First World War heroics duly noted, Göring's revolting self-indulgence now made his bombast ridiculous and his ambition absurd. That the Führer tagged him as successor anguished those who heard it—and finally even the Führer began to shun Göring.

471 **More fears should have been raised at the rise of such personalities as Goebbels and Himmler, Heydrich and others—but hope infects judgment and Germans still hoped.**

Appearances added to hope, of course, as daily things remained mostly the same across Hitler's domain. Children went to school, theaters beckoned audiences, while books, newspapers, art, and music sustained popular curiosity and universities pursued learning.

472 **Subtle things reshaped German culture.** As Dr. Goebbels increased his control over national information, he found novel ways to co-opt cultural output. In the 1930s he had established a German Chamber of Culture, comprising separate chambers overseeing literature, cinema, fine arts, music, and theater. Performers in these chambers required racial and political vetting by Goebbels' propaganda ministry, and members self-policed their work for purity.

473 **Works by Jewish authors—even great ones—were banned, while bland tales of heroics and romance reached thousands.** Playwrights and players pandered to a national need for diversion of almost any caliber. The "Strength through Joy" campaign, which controlled every aspect of workers' entertainment and leisure time, even vacations, thrived through 1942.

Goebbels centralized all cinema production and used films as his most persuasive means of advancing anti-Jewish and anti-Allied feelings while bolstering morale. Composers and musicians received special scrutiny since music could touch the German soul. Jewish music disappeared from all repertoires while boisterous folk themes, light operas, and some classics flourished.

Certainly not all cultural efforts in 1942 were poor but, in general, standards sagged under "management" of themes and spirits. Where Germany had often led in creativity, the life of the mind sank so low that the formerly critical public gratefully accepted dreck.

474 **The Wannsee Conference. Hitler decided in late December 1941 to make a "clean sweep" of the Jews.** Reinhard Heydrich (he had the Wagnerian middle name of Tristan) (q.v.), already engaged in a genocidal pogrom, scheduled a meeting of fifteen potential exterminators in the Berlin suburb of Grossen-Wannsee for December 9, 1941. Pearl Harbor and two big December 8 air raids on Aachen and Cologne intervened and the meeting slipped to January 20, 1942. **475** **Conferees met at the call of Heydrich (invitations were sent by Adolf Eichmann) at Interpol's Berlin headquarters and were charged by Heydrich with producing a "final solution of the Jewish question."**

Heydrich reviewed emigration problems and said Jews must be handled differently. They would be shipped east in labor columns. Some, he guessed, "would fall through natural diminution." There would be no survivors. An inconclusive argument touched the issue of half-Jewish or mixed-race people. A conference protocol announced: "In the course of the execution of the Final Solution, Europe will be combed from west to east." **476** **The Wannsee Conference marked the nadir of human debasement and changed the face of Europe.**

As this gruesome campaign took firm course, it became increasingly public—although many Germans would not admit to knowing—and a grim Nazi efficiency accelerated death. **477** **In Czechoslovakia, for instance, a place filled with so many despised *Untermenschen,* Heydrich replaced Konstantin von Neurath as acting Reich protector of Bohemia and Moravia—Neurath had been too easy in his protective methods.** Shortly

after raising the SS flag over historic Hradcany Castle in Prague, September 27, 1941, Heydrich outlined his program for the staff: "We will try to Germanize these Czech vermin!" Using methods from his other commands, RSHA, and the Gestapo, he staged public mass executions of men, women, and children—decimating the nation's intellectual and political ranks. This tall, arrogant sociopath swiftly became known as *Der Henker* ("the Hangman"), a title he doubtless enjoyed.

Then he turned fiercely on resistance elements and captured a skilled informer named Franta, who turned out to be a local member of the German *Abwehr* (military intelligence organization), which gave the Hangman another chance to attack his enemy, Adm. Wilhelm Canaris, who headed the *Abwehr.* That whole agency Heydrich now branded a den of traitors.

478 **Heydrich's persistence sealed his fate.** British intelligence could not afford a superefficient Nazi counterintelligence operation in Prague. Hence the Czech secret service in exile (fully aware of the likely reprisals) parachuted in a two-man assassination team that tossed a bomb into Heydrich's open car on May 29, 1942. He died from his wounds on June 4.

479 **Hitler ordered swift, bestial reprisals.** Two towns, Lidiče and Lezaky, were razed, their men shot, their women sent to concentration camps, their children abducted. The "Lidiče massacre" stirred worldwide horror.

480 **After Wannsee, the systematic elimination of Jews began in March 1942.** SS *Brigadeführer* (brigadier) Odilo Globocnik and SS *Hauptsturmführer* (captain) Hermann Hofle headed this special program centered mainly at the Belzec, Sobibor, and Treblinka death camps in Poland. Jews inhabiting the so-called General Government of Poland were the main victims. Chelmno, Majdenek, and Auschwitz-Birkenau were also death camps, but not part of Globocnik's operation.

481 Adopting the name Operation Reinhard after Heydrich's death, Globocnik put his 450-person staff into high gear carrying out his special mandates: Plan and coordinate the collection and transportation of Jews from General Government areas to the death camps; build death camps and kill all those who entered them; gather all victims' belongings.

Using SS people who had experience with Hitler's euthanasia ventures, Operation Reinhard pumped Zyklon B gas into specially built chambers used for mass killings. Special crematoriums were also constructed to handle the surfeits of dead.

482 So efficient was Operation Reinhard—it murdered 2,284,000 Jews—that it was terminated in December 1943. By then only a few scattered Jews serving as forced laborers remained in the General Government.

483 Scientists now routinely worry about morality of research, but this is a relatively new concern. Before the world wars, research served as its own justification—a view still cherished by some. Pure science and unfettered research were the rich grounds of discovery in post–World War I Germany, especially so at the famed Kaiser Wilhelm Institute in Berlin. In 1941, freedom of inquiry, adequate resources, and brilliant colleagues lured Werner Karl Heisenberg there as director. It proved a difficult time for him as Nazism shadowed the German mind and Hitler expected scientists to work for the state.

Heisenberg did not resist this nationalistic notion and turned the institute heavily toward war projects. By the time he took over as director, his reputation as the father of quantum mechanics well established, Heisenberg knew the military potential of atomic physics. **484** He also knew that Hitler expected German scientists to make good his promise to unleash *Wunderwaffen* (wonder weapons), and the special

government research station at Peenemünde tried to oblige. The Führer's main interest focused on rockets and jet propulsion; he poured resources into fuels and design studies. **485** Back in the 1930s he had made Heisenberg head of the *Uranverein*, a project to make an atomic bomb. The Nobel laureate's research indicated that much more uranium would be needed than Germany could produce, even if the large, heavy water plant in Rjukan, Norway worked at capacity.

486 This gross miscalculation he later said had been deliberate, a way to prevent a Nazi bomb. True or not—Heisenberg's general reputation militates against so egregious a mistake—Germany did not get the bomb, but Nazi science did important research in various military areas.

RUSSO-GERMAN BATTLES, 1942

487 Fighting flickered throughout the winter along the USSR's Western Front. After the Soviet counteroffensive stalled in February 1942, both sides rested and refitted. Refitting proved harder than expected for the Germans. Hitler's overweening optimism foreclosed sound planning. When fighting came harder and took longer than expected, material deficiencies multiplied. Manpower reserves were no longer limitless. Save for Army Group South, which had been recruited almost to full complement, most Nazi divisions stood at half strength. Whole numbers looked fairly good because fifty-one Axis satellite divisions joined—Hungarian, Romanian, Italian, and Slovak, plus a Spanish volunteer division—but they were underequipped and unreliable. Since Hitler had not yet declared full war production, the whole German logistical chain squeaked. Tanks, other vehicles, munitions, spare parts, clothing, even food ran short.

Hitler's determination did not, as he plotted the German summer offensive. **488** New and stronger tanks, he knew, were coming—the extremely effective

Tiger I, weighing in at fifty-five tons, able to go nearly twenty-five miles per hour (thirty-eight kilometers per hour) and armed with the ubiquitous 88mm gun. From Leningrad south to Rostov at the eastern end of the Sea of Azov, Nazi armies held strong lines.

489 **Soviet supply problems compounded, too.** By the end of their offensive the Russian armies were exhausted, their logistical skein raddled, and, despite Lend-Lease aid, they even lacked rifles. Hitler's "hedgehog" defensive positions had chopped heavily into manpower during the winter and the Soviets were, for a time, unable to mount an offensive.

490 **Hitler's strategic ideas were not all bad.** The OKW (*Oberkommando der Wehrmacht*; military high command) staff, various field marshals, and generals argued strongly about scattering *Wehrmacht* strength too widely across the Caucasus. They thought it might still be possible to concentrate Army Groups Center and North into a Moscow drive while Army Group South stabilized the flank—a move expected by the Russians. Hitler, though, fixed on the real need for natural resources, proclaimed a complicated plan to secure the grain, oil, and mineral riches of the south. Issuing orders in April for the summer campaign (Operation Blue), he aimed the major effort toward the Crimea.

Grudgingly recalling Field Marshal von Bock, Hitler gave him command of Army Group South, which was later divided into army groups A and B. Army Group B (a mixed organization of infantry, panzer, and Hungarian armies), under Field Marshal Baron von Weichs had orders to hold a line from Kursk south to Izyum. Field Marshal Siegmund Wilhelm List, a burly "unpleasant-looking man with the aspect of a proletarian and uncultured manners," whom Hitler distrusted, took command of Army Group A (composed of infantry, panzer, and Romanian armies), which would operate on Weichs's right and clench the Caucasus oil fields. During this drive Hitler expected Stalingrad and a substantial number

of Russian armies to be encircled. List understood Hitler's pincer tactics and prepared to attack eastward and link up with Army Group B, coming south from Voronezh.

Various actions preceded the main drive. The Luftwaffe attacked Russia's Black Sea Fleet; once the fleet and bases were neutralized, Manstein, on May 8, 1942, launched his Eleventh Army in a drive to clear the Kerch Peninsula. Eleven days later he drove the enemy into the sea and inflicted 150,000 casualties.

491 **A Russian thrust behind massed tanks broke through on both sides of Kharkov by May 12 and Hitler responded with a May 17 drive against the Izyum salient.** After weeks of puzzling combat, Nazi troops pinched off the salient in late June; the Russians lost almost a quarter of a million men plus some 1,250 tanks, but avoided total envelopment.

492 **While Bock and List organized their fronts and logistics, and eliminated big partisan pockets behind the lines, Manstein thought it best merely to immobilize Sevastopol's gargantuan defenses and send men and equipment to the major summer offensive.** Hitler, though, loved spectaculars and knew that the complete devastation of Sevastopol's defenses would let Manstein show the world that the super guns built to break the Maginot Line could now reduce the Black Sea's great fortress city—thirty-three cannon of calibers ranging from 10.9 to 23 inches (one could hurl a 31-inch shell over thirty miles—faint shades of the "Paris gun" of World War I!). **493** **On June 2 more than six hundred Nazi guns launched the drive on Sevastopol to much less effect than expected.** Hitler wanted it over by June 23 but the heroically defended fortress did not yield until July 4, 1942, along with 100,000 prisoners. Meanwhile, on July 1, 1942, Manstein became a field marshal.

494 **Operation Blue's first phase was launched on June 28, 1942, toward Voronezh and the Don River; rain and**

mud slowed Bock's drive, but Voronezh fell on July 6. Hitler and his generals had expected to surround thousands of Red troops in the big bulge of the Don between Voronezh and Rostov, but the trap was ruined by Stalin, who permitted his only strategic retreat of the war. So instead of rounding up prisoners, Nazi troops found themselves in a melee with terrified Russian stragglers scrambling to escape. To stem the "strategic retreat," Stalin and his staff threw numbers of barely trained tankers into disorderly battles. By July's end, Stalin conceded complete disciplinary breakdown as the First Tank Army deserted en masse and had to be disbanded. Despite Bock's surprising success, failure to close the Don trap gave Hitler an excuse to fire him on July 13 and replace him with more pliable Field Marshal von Weichs.

495 Adept at self-destruction, Hitler switched his whole campaign plan southward again, ordering exploitation drives east and south of recently captured Rostov and on toward the Maikop-Amavir oil fields, with spurs thrusting toward the huge Baku oil reserves. This shift scrambled tactical and logistical plans and slowed reaction time.

Logistics became crucial. Hitler's random shifting of plans and units created fuel shortages at key locations. **496** General Friedrich Paulus's big Sixth Army, aimed at Stalingrad, ran out of gas for ten critical days and was briefly short of ammunition. Russians used the breather to rush fortifications at Stalingrad.

An early August success on the Don, which netted fifty thousand prisoners, earned Paulus special rations of supplies and he drove a fifty-five-mile spearhead to the Volga in two days, August 21–23. Ever the efficient staff officer and eager to prove himself as a field general, Paulus also did well with one of his panzer armies on the Don some ten miles north of Stalingrad. Building a screening line between the Don and the Volga, he reached south to meet the Fourth Panzer Army, which had crossed the Don east of Rostov and turned northeast for Stalingrad.

497 For different reasons both Stalin and Hitler became fixated on Stalingrad. Stalin's civil war experience in the city, then called Tsaritsyn, convinced him of its strategic value and he feared Hitler planned to take it, cross the Volga, and sweep northwestward toward Moscow. Stalingrad must be held.

This theory bestowed undeserved wisdom on the Führer. Normally he shunned city battles as too costly—witness Warsaw and Leningrad, even Stalingrad itself, which could have been taken easily several months earlier—but now, because publicity turned world eyes to the Volga bastion, he began herding air and ground reinforcements in behind Paulus's Sixth and Hermann Hoth's nimble Fourth Panzer Army. These reinforcements came mainly from Hitler's former major objective, the Caucasus, which weakened the huge salient sagging into the Caucasus and toward the Caspian Sea.

498 Temper fraying, irked at little things, Hitler began sacking generals as the Stalingrad fighting flared. List departed on September 9, 1942, for being slow with Group A, and army chief of staff Franz Halder left on September 24 for disagreeing with Hitler.

499 While Hitler changed commanders, so did Stalin. Failures along the whole Russian front finally indicated how seriously the military purges of the thirties had hurt the Red Army. Not that 1941's disasters had gone unnoticed, but how deeply amateurism had affected command became clearer by mid-1942 as more reserves and equipment were wasted in ineffective attacks and counterattacks. Although Stalin counted 5.5 million men at the front with eleven more armies in reserve, and Hitler mustered at most 4.5 million, differences in command and experience more than equalized these strengths. **500** While Stalin called loudly for an Allied second front to relieve pressure on the USSR—one of the reasons for the abortive, costly, but instructive mid-August 1942 Dieppe Raid on the French coast—he made his best war appointment on August 27 as he called Gen. Georgi Zhukov (q.v.)

to be deputy supreme commander of the Red Army and Navy and sent him to organize a Stalingrad counterattack.

Clearly the dictator saw that Russia stood in dire need of military professionalism for, along with the Zhukov choice, Stalin revived the word "officer," created several decorations for officers only, and relieved commanders from the baneful control of political commissars. Would these reactions be enough?

"Uncle Joe," as various Allied publics liked to call him, would have felt much relieved to know the summer pressures Hitler endured. Calls for a second front echoed in Hitler's headquarters and he expected some Allied response. Matériel shortages mounted as expanding partisan activities seriously interrupted logistical areas behind the German armies.

501 **Hitler did much to cause the partisan risings.** His declaration of "no quarter" in the Russian campaign turned many potential friends to furious foes; then, too, there were the *Einsatzgruppen*. These SS/SD killer squads roamed behind the armies to dispose of all Jews, Red political commissars, and other *Untermenschen*, along with such partisans as might be found. Since June 1941, five groups had trailed the Russian invaders, and by the beginning of 1942 an estimated six hundred thousand Jews had been liquidated. Nazi rear area security slowly became a nightmare—many veterans would long remember the wars behind the lines as being more savage than the battles at the fronts.

502 **These burgeoning worries intensified Hitler's megalomania; he isolated himself from the general staff and took counsel largely of his own visionary genius.** And he had some good news to validate his judgment— his vigorous "Sun Hero," Rommel, whom he had himself found and raised against the pompous views of old-line Prussians, once again drove the British pell-mell back toward Egypt and seemed poised, this time, to reach the Suez Canal. **503** **Rommel's cam-** paigns reflected Hitler's own—and Napoleon's—faith in *audace, toujours l'audace.* Hitler hinted that most of his generals lacked that driving force.

504 **The Führer ordered Stalingrad taken by Paulus, whose men began fighting street to street, house to house in what German soldiers branded a "rat's war."** Days came and went in a horrid cacophony of bombs, shells, machine guns, grenades, screeching dive bombers. At last Stalingrad became a warren of survivor-infested rubble.

Close combat snarled through September and October and winter again complicated German logistics. Hitler nearly agreed to let Paulus fight his way out and join Manstein, but Göring's boast that the Luftwaffe could deliver 600 tons of supplies a day to the Sixth Army (although only 120 tons arrived on the best days) convinced the Führer to hang on. During all this vacillation, large Red Army groups were gathering on the Volga north and south of Stalingrad.

505 **On November nineteenth and twentieth, awesome barrages signaled Operation Uranus, the most carefully orchestrated Soviet offensive of the war.** Nikolai Vatutin's and Konstantin Rokossovsky's *fronts* smashed across the Don north of Stalingrad, shattered the poorly led and poorly equipped Romanian Third Army, and swerved southward to link with Andrei Yeremenko's Stalingrad *front*, which crossed the Don south of the embattled bastion. This drive on the twentieth engulfed the Romanian Fourth Army, then headed northwest and encircled Stalingrad.

Manstein led a forlorn effort to break through with pitifully small forces in mid-December and got to within thirty-five miles of Paulus. Break out, ordered Manstein, but loyal Paulus, who could not reach Hitler (probably by design), writhed in indecision while the front collapsed. Russian forces almost trapped Manstein's men.

506 **When Paulus announced to his remnants that the Führer had declared the principle of fighting to the last**

Sixth Army commander and newly created field marshal Friedrich Paulus, shortly after surrendering at Stalingrad, January 31, 1943.

man, one general snorted that never before had he heard an absurdity erected into a principle! Paulus held out until divisions were regiments, regiments were companies, and companies parts of squads, the men mostly frozen or starving. However, Sixth Army's continuing resistance did pin down key Red units that could well have overwhelmed the overmatched army groups under Weichs (B), Manstein (Don), and Kleist (A). **507 Hours after being notified of his promotion to field marshal on January 31, 1943 (Hitler thought this act of high symbolism would stiffen resolve), Paulus surrendered the fragments of his command.** For his Stalingrad obsession Hitler lost some 300,000 men and much equipment.

508 Victory came at a crucial time for Russian morale; it soared as a new confidence energized the armies. Soviet losses in the Stalingrad campaign were never announced, but were doubtless heavier than German—skill in combat remained the *Wehrmacht*'s manifest advantage.

509 Although a real turning point had come in the war, it could hardly be seen at the time. Manstein fought frantically to hold the Rostov gateway open so Kleist's Group A could escape the exposed Caucasus salient—Hitler had finally approved a withdrawal! But the withdrawal faced disaster as Hitler insisted that some toehold be held in the Taman-Novorossisk oil area. This could be done only by isolating the Seventeenth Army in a pocket with its right flank on the Black Sea and its left on the Sea of Azov. Almost a hundred miles of the Azov's east coast gaped between Kleist's Seventeenth and First Armies. Kleist successfully pulled his First Army back through Rostov just as a big Soviet attack on January 25, 1943, threatened to collapse Manstein's left and trap Group Don's armies against the northern Azov coast.

510 For the Russians, 1942 ended with victories rolling forward from Leningrad (where close fighting shifted bits and pieces of the front and a slightly weakened blockade continued) and in front of Moscow (where the enemy had been pushed back toward Smolensk), and in the south where the Nazis were about to be expelled from the Caucasus.

After a brilliant beginning, 1942 proved an almost desperate year for Germany. Hitler's aim south to the Crimean oil areas had beckoned drives to the Black Sea and on toward the Caspian Sea. But this possibility vanished when the Führer's fascination with Stalingrad sucked men and equipment into a consuming maw that not only destroyed a huge German army but also threatened the loss of the initiative.

511 Still, skillful fighting by veterans had rescued the year for Hitler—a look at a map showed that, despite defeats, scares, and varied ineptitudes of Hitler himself, Nazi armies were about where they were when the year began.

AXIS AIR/SEA ACTION, 1942

512 Axis navies worked to keep the Mediterranean lanes open to North Africa throughout 1942. British warships operating out of Gibraltar and Malta, alerted by ULTRA of most enemy doings, frequently interfered with Italian naval convoys, but despite inferior numbers and equipment, Italy's navy did fairly well. Substantial losses in men and ships were offset by the fact that 91 percent of the men sent to North Africa arrived, as did 85 percent of supply tonnage.

Harassing Malta occupied much Italian naval time and effort. Submarines and torpedo bombers did serious damage to Malta shipping in 1942. Highly effective Italian 10th Light Flotilla attacks on vessels in Alexandria and Gibraltar often crippled the enemy. The flotilla's submarines also crippled Leningrad blockade-breaking efforts on Lake Ladoga.

513 Hitler's submarines might have won the war in 1942. German surface ships joined in effective attacks on Atlantic sea lanes and against the exposed convoys on the Murmansk run. Still, Hitler would not commit such big ships as the *Tirpitz* (q.v.) to battle, apparently preferring to use the "fleet in being" as a deterrent.

514 All sea and ground operations depended crucially throughout 1942 on airpower. Fighters, bombers, torpedo, and carrier planes sustained the fighting in North Africa, Russia, the Balkans, indeed everywhere. But the RAF thousand-bomber raids in May–June 1942 against Cologne, Essen, and Bremen were fairly effective morale crushers.

Italian planes generally ranked several cuts below Allied or German aircraft. A few fighter and bomber models were effective and played important roles in attempting to protect Axis Mediterranean

On May 30, 1942, Cologne was hit by the first thousand-bomber raid of the war. Chief of RAF Bomber Command Gen. Arthur T. "Bomber" Harris gave orders to avoid damaging the great cathedral. This 1945 photo shows the intact cathedral standing amid ruins.

supply routes throughout 1942. Italy's air force did well, also, in their continuing attacks on British Malta convoys. But a lack of carriers crippled Italy's long-range capabilities and prevented air-navy cooperation. By the end of 1942, Italy's air force had noticeably dwindled.

515 Although the Red Air Force grew amazingly by late 1942, the Luftwaffe remained a potent ally of the *Wehrmacht.* Unable to bring adequate supplies to Stalingrad, German planes did stave off defeat for a time and gave effective support to Manstein's AG Don. Statistics for the year, though, had alarming portent: Germany produced 14,700 planes against Russia's 21,700.

ITALY, 1942

516 Stressed by military efforts in so many directions, the Italian people settled into a kind of mediocre misery by mid-1942. Feeling rather like the Reich's stepchildren, condemned to a below-the-salt status by the end of 1941, Italians faced a hollow future. Cracks in the Nazi monolith at Stalingrad, in North Africa, in the Balkans, in France even, as well as America's entry into the war, shifted attitudes. Many Italians now began to change their mind, to think the Axis would lose. Shifts in attitude produced shifts in loyalties. People began to break out of their lethargic acceptance of Fascist society.

517 By 1942, Mussolini still had not achieved complete totalitarianism in Italy. Too many nearly feudal obligations militated against it. *Il Duce* had to work with the Catholic Church (hostile to shared centralization), with the crown, and with both public and private cartels (which kept working together for market control), with powerful business leaders, all of whom rose above regimentation. Most people accepted centralized education, many joined the burgeoning Fascist organizations for social and entertainment reasons; they all benefited from some of Mussolini's progressive programs. Behind even the "good" programs, though, lurked a massive bureaucracy created more for jobs than for business. Mussolini—a la Hitler—fostered competing agencies which gave him the power of mediation. Several paramilitary organizations such as the Blackshirts enrolled many unemployed former officers and so welded their loyalty. These organic differences in Mussolini's system had an important result—they prevented creation of a Fascistic monolith while intruding muffling layers of government that diffused power. While disgruntlement grew, Mussolini's perception dimmed; he seemed to sink into apathy while Italian intrigue seethed around him.

518 A tottering dictator unleashed opponents and party politics resurfaced. Old-line antifascist marshal Pietro Badoglio, who cautioned against war in 1939, kept contacts in high circles. With Princess Maria José of Savoy (the king's daughter-in-law), Badoglio tried to negotiate peace with the Allies in August 1942. The king found himself suddenly popular, as it seemed he might dump the Duce.

519 Fascism's machinery failed to make lasting inroads, which added to Mussolini's isolation. Whereas Hitler's Nazi Party structure had strong foundations in social and economic organizations, Fascist structures felt impermanent. Efforts to dragoon such cultural leaders as university professors, writers, philosophers, scientists, and musicians into props for the regime failed, although their work suffered some censorship in 1942—but the ignorant censors were often played for fools.

520 Mussolini's grandiloquence ruined him. He had promised that war would restore the "grandeur that was Rome," and Romans wanted to believe in the coming glory. So *Il Duce* faced rebellion at home by the end of 1942 as Rommel's legions retreated, as Italian forces disintegrated in Russia, and as the

RAF began to pummel northern Italy. **521 Aware of his shaky situation, Mussolini, in December 1942 (again in April 1943) urged the Führer to make a separate peace with Russia—with a bit more nerve he might have tried for a separate peace of his own.** Bankrupt of both ideas and popularity, Mussolini resorted to the old administrative dodge of blaming subordinates and sacked most of the *Commando Supremo* in January 1943, along with many cabinet ministers, including his son-in-law Galeazzo Ciano (q.v.), the foreign minister. But labor unrest grew and no one trusted *Il Duce* anymore. The Pact of Steel softened.

invited Mussolini's further aid and received the Eighth Army, commanded by Gen. Giovanni Messe. Although coping with inferior equipment and uncertain supplies, Messe held portions of the Eastern Front through most of the year. Ordered back to Italy in October 1942, he missed the near annihilation of his army in the Stalingrad debacle. Attempting to hold part of Army Group B's line on the Don north of that city in mid-November, Eighth Army cracked under Vatutin's massive attack on the nineteenth, took heavy casualties, and essentially disappeared from the war.

ITALIAN LAND/AIR BATTLES, 1942

522 Mendacious stories to the contrary notwithstanding, Italy's fighting men were excellent. Poor equipment, poor training, myopic strategy, outmoded tactics, and crushing assignments were what dimmed their chances for success.

Sadly for Italian troops, equipment had hardly improved. Tank production still suffered monopolistic control which delayed new models while stifling improvements. Worse, although armor officers knew what the army needed, the army did not control tank procurement. Frantic efforts to obtain good Czech tanks from the Skoda works or to build some licensed models of German tanks failed against the oligopolistic power of Fiat and Ansaldo. The army had to take what manufacturers offered and they refused even to modify their own tanks with Fiat airplane engines to give them greater speed. Cosmetic changes fooled no users.

523 Reluctantly accepting Italian help in Russia during 1941, Hitler changed his stance in 1942. Needing more men, he

THE DESERT WAR

524 Italian troops proved essential to Rommel's revival of the desert war in January 1942 and helped push the British nearly to El Alamein.

Both sides halted to build up reserves and supplies. Rommel struck again on May 26 when he noted that British dumps were outgrowing his own, reached Tobruk on June 19, then took it on the

British infantry advance in open order, Second El Alamein, October 1942.

twenty-first in Britain's worst defeat since Singapore. His German and Italian tanks and planes now amply fueled by the huge supply dump at Tobruk, he thought he could finish off the British.

525 Exulting in what must have been his most exciting week of the war, Hitler promoted Rommel to field marshal on the day of Barbarossa, June 22, and made the chancy decision not to invade Malta because of the Tobruk cornucopia. Rommel rolled eastward against Gen. Sir Claude Auchinleck's British Eighth Army, and pushed it to Gazala. **526** On the twenty-eighth the armies faced each other at a small Egyptian rail station, El Alamein.

Here the terrain favored defense. With his left flank on the Mediterranean and his right anchored some forty miles south against the impassable Qattara Depression—a squashy, rocky, wide canyon unsuited for men, tanks, or much else—Rommel had no room for his favorite swooping flank attacks. In front spread a shale-like, stony desert with scattered clumps of sandy thornbushes that discouraged initiative. In this forlorn place the campaign stalemated.

Auchinleck got reinforcements along with a visit in August from Churchill, who wanted a quick attack. **527** "The Auk," as most knew him, stalled, and Churchill, on August 13, made one of his hardest and best decisions: he moved Auchinleck back to India, put Gen. Harold R. L. G. Alexander in charge of the Middle East, and gave the replenishing Eighth Army to Lt. Gen. Bernard Law Montgomery.

An unlikely pair, it seemed, with Montgomery older, senior in service, egotistical; but the British chief of staff, General Brooke, thought they would be a good team. They were. "Monty" respected his new chief; worked hard to get to know his new army by going among the troops often, sporting his jaunty beret, making motivational speeches; and built a massive superiority in tanks, artillery, fuel, and munitions while preparing positions carefully as he schemed to fool the Desert Fox. He used detailed

British official photo: Gen. Bernard Montgomery watching tanks move up, North Africa, November 1942. Success at Second El Alamein, a set-piece operation unusual in desert warfare, earned him a knighthood, and he became one of Britain's most publicized generals.

ULTRA intelligence of enemy plans in getting his army ready.

528 Rommel struggled with logistical problems. Tobruk's largesse thinned sharply as supply lines to that base were strafed, bombed, and harassed continuously. And as Russia bulked larger in German concerns, Africa waned in view. Ordered to attack against his judgment, Rommel demanded and received the promise of large fuel reserves—which did not come. But, receiving a few reinforcements to both German and Italian units, he struck near Alam Halfa Ridge on August 30, 1942. British minefields slowed his drive. After fierce tank fighting, Axis forces began retreating by September 2 to former positions and the battle ended on the seventh. First round to the British. But, fearing a trap and not sure of his army's readiness, Monty did not pursue.

Both armies refitted. Montgomery received new U.S. Sherman tanks and massive supplies from the elongated Red Sea route. Rommel got some new units and began strewing his whole front with anti-tank and antipersonnel mines and consolidating static defenses—static proved the problem. Being forced away from his war of maneuver, Rommel had to play the enemy's game and he hated it. And thinking about it made him ill. Late in September he went to Germany on sick leave.

529 Recovering from digestive disorders at Zemmering, Rommel took a noon phone call on October 24, 1942. "Rommel, there is bad news from Africa," Hitler said. "The situation looks very black. No one seems to know what has happened to Stumme. Do you feel well enough to go back and would you be willing to go?" Still sick, he went and reached his headquarters by the evening of October 25 to learn of Monty's fierce attack two days before.

530 El Alamein ranks as one of the decisive battles of World War II. Careful preparation of a multiphased battle enabled British troops to open corridors through minefields, break through to rear areas, chop up defensive infantry positions, and take on main German armor in wasting engagements that eroded Rommel's strength. Forced by air attacks and fuel shortages to deploy his tanks piecemeal, the Desert Fox knew by November 2 that he had lost the battle (he had only 35 operational tanks out of 496 at day's end) and began retreating that night. Hitler demanded that he hold on, which Rommel did, reluctantly, for a day, and then he picked up his withdrawal in earnest. Later he said he should have ignored the Führer's senseless order.

As Axis stragglers fled westward to regroup and defend Tunisia with more troops, the remnants of Stalingrad followed another senseless order as the war took a true and lasting turn. **531 Churchill would say El Alamein marked the end of the beginning.**

VICHY FRANCE, 1942

532 A kind of somber melancholy settled over France in 1942 as meaner intrusions affected daily lives. Vichy's writ ran even into the *zone occupée*—under German supervision—and the regime tried to project something of a patriarchal empire theme (governmental decrees, for instance, began *"Nous, Philippe Pétain . . ."*) but few French were fooled. This government wanted to control thought and so intruded on family lives, managed education, and wallowed in an agrarian aridity. All the dismal portents of the previous year were realized as Laval pushed his brand of collaboration. **533 Trying to get something for the concessions made, he offered a slick deal to Hitler: he would send three French workers to Germany in return for one POW.** This miserable "compromise" added contempt to a nation's hatred.

534 During 1942 the government increasingly enforced two pogromist *Statuts des Juifs* (Jewish Statutes), ferreted Communists and Freemasons, and negated trade unions. By then, as one account says, "Vichy appeared as a force not of national integration but of political retribution. Its outsiders, mainly immigrant Jews, were interned in camps . . . in the south-west, and a General Commissariat to oversee all Jews and liquidate Jewish businesses was entrusted to Xavier Vallat. . . . In May 1942 his place was taken by Louis Darquier de Pellepoix, an open and venomous racist and advocate of deportation."

535 **Laval's most heinous crime came in August 1942** when he "surrendered thousands of families who believed they had found asylum in France, insisting that they 'must all go' including the very youngest children." Out in the country, even in the cities, people began hiding Jews in what, in many cases, were first acts of resistance.

536 **Resistance to persecution took many forms.** Jewish veterans, who had semiprotected status, protested along with elements of the Catholic Church—the archbishops of Toulouse and Lyon being notably outspoken—but, by the end of 1942, cattle trains from the French had transported some 45,000 Jews to the eastern death camps.

Sympathy and horror for Jewish and other harassed friends added to the general *tristesse* of the French. Respect for the venerable marshal continued in a historical sense, but the government managed to lose most of its support during the year.

537 **Any pretenses of sovereignty vanished with the November 8, 1942, Allied invasion of North Africa.** That action triggered Germany's takeover of the *zone libre* three days later because Hitler doubted France's loyalties. He left Vichy some scraps of authority but absorbed the economy almost fully into the Nazi war effort. By early 1943, France's tribute accounted for about a quarter of Germany's GNP. Labor felt the heaviest Nazi levies. **538** **A steady drain of workers had been going eastward, but by early 1943 the inauguration of the *Service du Travail Obligatoire* (Compulsory Labor Service) imposed conscription and gathered some six hundred thousand victims. A huge revolt erupted against this heinous sacrifice of Frenchmen.**

Resentments accelerated when the Gestapo infiltrated all of France in an ugly public humbling. Insults to the occupiers were harshly met, often by hostage-taking, torture, or by murder on the spot. So ran the new Reign of Terror as Vichy began consuming itself.

539 **Resistance provided an outlet for bitter frustration and became a kind of existentialist diversion.** Underground news sheets circulated across France; one of them, *Combat* (founded by Albert Camus), kept liberation alive across the land. A vigorous protest lit-

---

"Le Chant des Partisans," 1943, Hy Zaret, adapted from Resistance leader "Bernard," lyrics by Anna Marly:

When they poured across the border
I was cautioned to surrender
This I could not do;
I took my gun and vanished. . . .

There were three of us this morning
I'm the only one this evening
But I must go on;
The frontiers are my prison. . . .

I have changed names a hundred times.
I have lost my wife and children,
But I have so many friends,
I have all of France.

An old man, in an attic,
Hid us for the night.
The Germans captured him;
He died without surprise.

Oh, the wind is blowing,
Through the graves the wind is blowing,
Freedom soon will come;
Then we'll come from the shadows.

---

erature flourished, fostered in 1942 by the *Comité National des Ecrivains* that published important reviews. Resistance themes enriched French poetry, Paul Eluard's strong "Liberté" becoming a national rallying call.

Cultural leaders did not all rebel. A lively life of the mind prevailed among a pro-Nazi intellectual elite, including writers Alphonse de Chateaubriant, Céline, Lucien Rebatet, even, with a whiff of equivocation, Jean Cocteau.

People lived under Vichy, worked, and did the daily things of survival, but they carried a haunting shame, a sense that somehow they were less than French.

THE UNION OF SOVIET SOCIALIST REPUBLICS (USSR), 1942

540 If uncertainty persisted among the Western Allies about Communism's capacity to fight the war, that uncertainty haunted the Kremlin as well. Despite success in saving Moscow and in surviving 1941's winter, Stalin knew his country's future hung by threads of will, raw materials, munitions, foreign aid, and luck. Hitler's legions were poised for a huge new offensive. Much reordering of Soviet economy and society produced more centralization (along with some selective decentralization), better rationalization of priorities, greater war production, larger muster rolls. None of this came easily. Living standards tumbled as consumer goods nearly disappeared. Agricultural output shrank as laborers went to factories or the military, hence severe food shortages loomed for 1942. Stalin's personal anxiety grew along with his power—by the beginning of the year he was making virtually every important national or war decision.

This, of course, put serious pressure on the dictator to project a personal dedication to victory that would shape the national will. It had another, largely unanticipated, result. Total centralization had created a "pass the buck" attitude in all areas of administration over many years, an attitude nearly epidemic in the times of the Great Terror. Stalin massacred millions for good, bad, in some cases no, reasons; opposition simply drowned in blood. **541** By the time Barbarossa began, though, new generations were coming to prominence in the Communist Party and in most important economic areas. These younger men, many of them of peasant origin, graduates of rapidly improving Soviet universities, formed a kind of technocracy of expertise. While Stalin had doubts about too much higher learning, he sponsored many of the emerging "experts" because they were essential to modernizing the country. Future Soviet premiers Nikita Khrushchev, Leonid Brezhnev, and Alexei Kosygin represented this modernity and—though Stalin may not have recognized it—bypassed old-line Bolsheviks as allies of the people.

These new leaders maximized the industrial improvements that had, by 1941, strengthened the Soviet Union's readiness for war. Stalin sent these men to various areas threatened by Hitler's minions; they were expected to salvage factories, raw materials, and people—their advice helped the whole evacuation process. Still, rely on them though he did, Stalin could not completely trust this new meritocracy.

542 Distrust of the supreme commander ran fairly deep among the professional general staff by the beginning of 1942. His relentless demands for attack, his rejection of even strategic retreats, had lost Kiev and 665,000 POWs. His insistence on a winter offensive at the end of 1941 struck the high command as absurd, but what he demanded he usually got—including the costly offensive that fizzled early in 1942. Costs meant little to him; cold-bloodedly he calculated that the USSR's potential superiority in people and production permitted profligacy. He knew that a Red Army attack somewhere would boost national morale. It did. But it also confirmed him in his sense of military genius, a sense that nearly ruined his cause. He now began giving operational orders by whim—shades of the Führer himself!

543 In twin idiocies, the dictators issued orders forbidding retreat. Stalin spurred obedience to his July 28, 1942, edict by branding retreat as treason—an extension of his mid-1941 order making traitors of any Red soldiers who surrendered. Hitler's orders against retreat were oft-repeated and plumbed depths of inanity in the Stalingrad slaughter.

Oddly enough, the two dictators ordered an attack at almost the same time in May 1942—Stalin to push the Red Army forward, Hitler to develop the Caucasus conquest. Nazi forces, attacking in the Crimea on May 8, achieved a great victory that cost the enemy 150,000 men, but reinforcements were thinned by a Soviet drive at Kharkov that intruded a big salient into German lines south of that city. German armies pinched off the salient by the end of June, stopping the entire Red offensive that lost 240,000 men and almost 1,250 tanks; they then punched further into the Caucasus, strengthened their center, and kept grinding at Leningrad.

544 Pressing his original attack into a kind of counterthrust near Kharkov, Hitler began a decisive drive toward Stalingrad while sustaining the southern campaign. General Franz Halder, chief of the German General Staff, groused that such unsupportable plans "were the product of a violent nature following its momentary impulses, which recognized no limits to possibility and which made its wish-dreams the father of its acts." Infuriated when someone read a report about Soviet reserve strength, "Hitler flew at the man . . . with clenched fists and foam at the corners of his mouth," saying he wanted to hear no more "idiotic twaddle."

545 Temperament marked the biggest difference between the dictators. Egotism they shared, intransigence too, cruelty, cunning, but Stalin got the temperamental edge by listening and learning. During the first two years of war he had relied on his amateurish strategic notions in ordering foolish, costly operations. Then, although he resented disagree-

ment, Stalin came to accept advice from generals like Zhukov and Boris Mikhailovich Shaposhnikov, along with Aleksandr Mikhailovich Vasilevsky and Konstantin Konstantinovich Rokossovsky.

Shifting his attention from the battlefields did not mean Stalin pushed less hard. Physically tough and a workaholic, he coerced (the gulag threat was brandished often) procurement, manufacturing, and logistical marvels from subordinates. The new convulsion of plant removals in mid-1942 went more smoothly than the frantic upheavals of 1941—officials and managers knew their jobs and Stalin largely avoided micromanagement. Still, more than 32,000 enterprises fell into enemy hands—only about an eighth of productive capacity west of the Volga escaped. Combined with industries already saved, however, these were enough.

Distribution remained a crisis of logistics. Rail lines, vastly overworked, short of trained people, struggled against bomb damage, massive traffic snarls, misdirection, capture, wear, and parts shortages. In February 1942, Stalin chaired a special transport committee that put railroads directly under the army logistics chief. Things got better for a time.

546 Raw materials ranked high among Soviet deficiencies. An emergency program of fuel production began in September 1942, with slow results. Power generation sagged because of scarce plants and untrained workers. Metal sources were redirected, with much coming now from trans-Ural areas. Steel manufacturing declined from some 18 million tons in 1941 to 8.1 million in 1942.

547 Despite these shortages, shiftings and sortings, military production rose, totals being increased by an influx of Lend-Lease goods. Soviet factories made about 25,500 planes in 1942, compared with 15,500 in 1941; 24,500 tanks came off assembly lines in 1942, compared with 6,500 in 1941; Red artillery received 357,000 new pieces in 1942, compared with 68,000 in 1941; rifle production doubled in that year to 4,049,000; ammunition fabrication almost literally exploded!

548 **A realist who looked at these numbers would be forced to the dismal conclusion that they were simply not enough.** The Soviet Union needed more than Lend-Lease, more than production miracles; it needed foreign help, specifically a second front opened against Germany. Stalin resented bitterly British and American reluctance to attack somewhere on the Atlantic or Mediterranean coasts. Not that Churchill and Roosevelt rejected the idea—they both agreed with the need but disagreed on times and places. FDR thought of a trans-Channel attack on France, while Churchill doubted the Allies were ready for that stupendous effort; he suggested a North African invasion which would pin down Nazi troops and supplies. Churchill's plan won out, to Stalin's despair—he kept reminding his reluctant allies that the USSR paid in blood for delay. He also reminded them that the USSR was carrying the fighting—a point irksome to Churchill. Their counterreminders of the essential help getting to the USSR by Lend-Lease seemed specious to Stalin.

Clearly, until the Allies got their strategies together, the USSR must rely on another visit from General Winter and on luck. For luck it had Hitler.

549 **Dimitri Shostakovich lived and worked for a time in the rubble of Leningrad.** There he wrote his famous Seventh (Leningrad) Symphony, first performed in Kuibyshev in March 1942 and in Leningrad itself in August. Immensely admired, it became a talisman of Soviet bravery; western orchestras performed it widely as they did Shostakovich's patriotic Eighth and Ninth Symphonies. Other Soviet composers embedded war themes in some of their finest music—Sergei Prokofiev's Fifth Symphony and Aram Khatchaturian's Second were written in wartime; Prokofiev also produced several film scores and his tremendous opera *War and Peace* (1941–43). Dimitri

Kabalevsky's war work included a superior cantata, *Vast Motherland* (1941–42), a major opera, *In the Fire* (1942), and *Revenger of the People* (1942).

Good writing continued through 1942. Ilya Ehrenburg's *Fall of Paris* won 1942's Stalin Prize. Much superior work came from the legion of writers who went as correspondents to various fronts, where their presence and their readings perpetuated a deep-struck Russian love of literature. The "hate" theme sounded in 1941 continued but with new layers of patriotic sensitivity and even with some humor.

550 **The derring-do of Vasily Terkin, a kind of Soviet Good Soldier Schweik, captured in Alexander Tvardovsky's popular poem, became part of a new national folklore.** War smothered and inspired creativity. Many writers ignored the official demand for heroic descriptions of the Holy War and showed heroism in battle's squalor—and were themselves heroes.

THE BRITISH EMPIRE, 1942

London suffered under various fogs as 1942 began. Bleak weather was combined with war miasma to dampen place and spirit. For Churchill, though, America's coming to battle made a certainty of victory.

Quick to seize a chance for England and himself, Churchill rushed to Washington in late December 1941 and the resulting Arcadia Conference produced several important decisions about command and strategy. Military and civilian experts there agreed to Operation Torch, a North African landing in 1942—a decision much to Churchill's pleasure and to Roosevelt's doubt. The conference had a political result for Churchill—it cemented, for a time, his leadership of the Allied cause.

551 **That leadership trembled a bit in January as Singapore teetered toward surrender, shook with alarming U-boat successes in the Atlantic, and nearly toppled because of Gen. Erwin Rommel, new Nazi commander in North Africa,** who spurred his Afrika Korps and Italian allies on a devastating drive across North Africa. These setbacks encouraged rumors that the PM ran the war himself, brooked little help, and needed curbing.

With typical grasp of parliamentary timing, Churchill asked a vote of confidence in late January, contrasted what the government had done against resources, and won 464 to 1.

552 News from North Africa dimmed Western euphoria; Axis hammering of Malta increased and Rommel received about two-thirds of the supplies sent to him; enough to sustain his attacks. His swift drive from El Agheila to Gazala in January 1942, then his flanking victory against Neil Ritchie at Bir Hachim in May and June, his capture of Tobruk (a major British disaster) on June 21, brought the Afrika Korps to within striking distance of Alexandria by early August. All this reaffirmed the need to strengthen Malta as a choke point for Axis supplies.

553 Holding Malta proved necessary and Churchill made that decision. Oval, some sixty-five square miles in size, this island had been gruesomely punished by the Luftwaffe since mid-1940. The stepped-up tempo of North African operations increased the battering of Malta. Encouraged to hold on, the small garrison, sustained by heroic efforts of the Royal Navy, lived under worsening conditions, under bombing that dwarfed the worst of the London blitz. RAF resources were ground up (sixty Spitfires shipped in on the U.S. carrier *Wasp* in April 1942 were shot down in a few days) but the island persisted: King George VI, on April 15, bestowed the George Cross on all the island's people to commemorate their heroism. When Field Marshal Lord Gort took command in May, Malta's defense continued. Rommel's success in capturing Tobruk's massive supply dumps in late June saved Malta; Hitler postponed efforts to take it and told Rommel to drive on to Cairo.

554 The Tobruk disaster coupled with Rommel's subsequent advance signaled Churchill's lowest fortunes and, on July 1, 1942, brought his leadership again into serious question before Parliament. Fighting a vote of no-confidence led by former defense minister Leslie Hore-Belisha, who received support from both left and right, Churchill prevailed by a vote of 475–25. He had, nonetheless, lost some strategic perspective and had allowed Rommel to become an almost personal nemesis.

555 While clearly the Allies would win in the long run—they had four-fifths of the world behind them—they faced a period of dangerous weakness. If they tried to do too much in giving Comrade Stalin his second front, they might be critically weakened. Haunted by the possibility, the PM kept pushing his "peripheral" strategy, to the irritation of the U.S. Joint Chiefs, even FDR's and certainly Stalin's. If the Allied staffs would hold to Operation Torch, all would be well.

For his own part, Churchill largely gave responsibility for the Far East to the United States—a fact not entirely comforting to Australia and New Zealand, nor, for that matter to India.

556 Revelations from Germany confirmed hideous suspicions. In November 1942, Jan Karski (pseudonym of Jan Kozielewski) a liaison between London's Polish government-in-exile and the Polish Socialist Party, shocked the Allied leadership with eyewitness news of the Final Solution. Until his report, there was little hard evidence to confirm Hitler's genocidal Jewish program.

557 Karski had gone into Belzec camp disguised as a guard, witnessed the exterminations under way—gassings, cremations, starvings, shootings, humanity degraded below animalism—and emerged to tell the tale. So sordid, so incomprehensible to reason were the things he said that many rejected his story. When Karski told Anthony Eden and FDR, they were sickened. American judge Felix Frankfurter said he did not believe it. When assured of Karski's reliability, the judge said, "I did not say this young man was lying. I said I cannot believe him. There is a difference."

558 **The exiled Polish government appealed for Allied help for Europe's Jews.** The Allies issued a condemnation and called a conference to consider reaction.

559 **In April 1943 a joint British-American conference convened in Bermuda to consider the fate of Jews in various parts of Hitler's domains.** Proposals to approach Hitler directly and to relax Britain's current limitations on Jewish immigration to Palestine were rejected, but a refugee center was opened in North Africa. Reason could not yet deal with barbarities beyond history.

560 **Empire matters increasingly concerned London.** With all dominions and colonies being drained by their war efforts, with several feeling neglected, ties to Britain frayed. Loyal Canada contributed men, planes, ships, and munitions to capacity, but naturally turned toward the U.S. for continental defense. Australia had already confessed reliance on the U.S. for help against Japan; so, too, New Zealand. British Somaliland had been lost and regained, and now talked of independence. **561** **When Thailand surrendered to the Japanese, an easy route to Burma opened.** By April 1942 all Allied stopgap efforts having been beaten down, British and Chinese troops abandoned Burma—a move that dampened Chinese morale, yielded fine airfields and rich resources to Japan, and threatened India.

562 **India's situation became critical.** A nationalist movement there spearheaded by Mohandas Gandhi (q.v.), Jawaharlal Nehru (both pro-Allied), and the Indian National Congress gained strength by capitalizing on Britain's need for men and material. General Wavell (q.v.), the viceroy of India, inherited a simmering rebellion as the Congress Party refused to join Britain's war effort, in effect offering to trade cooperation for independence.

In late March 1942, Sir Stafford Cripps, former British ambassador to Moscow, member of the War Cabinet, prominent Labourite politico, man of keen intellect and chilly demeanor, went to Delhi as head of a mission to win India's assistance. His bargaining chip was what India wanted—independence—but not until after the war. The Indian Congress divided; Nehru's faction favored the deal, Gandhi's did not, and the Muslim League demanded a separate state.

Incensed, Gandhi quipped that "they are offering us a postdated check on a bank that is obviously crashing." A congressional faction announced that "British policy toward India seems to be based on delaying every advance and attempting to create new problems and fresh complications." Distrust on both sides festered. **563** **With the failure of Cripps' mission clear by summer, Gandhi proclaimed his "quit India" movement of passive resistance.** With India-wide civil disobedience looming, Wavell interned Gandhi on August 9 and later jailed Congress Party leaders, temporarily muffling trouble.

564 **Ireland remained a problem.** Although Ulster, or Northern Ireland, kept its loyalty to the Crown, Eire, the old Irish Free State, remained neutral under the strong, unwavering leadership of its prime minister, Eamon de Valera. Churchill considered Irish neutrality near treason; he pressed steadily for war commitment and connived for use of important southern ports. Both sides expected the worst of each other—the British remained convinced that Eire's neutrality cloaked cooperation with German spies and submarines while Eire's officials expected an invasion from Ulster daily. Nonetheless, many Irish men and women fought for Britain.

565 **London's "we can take it" toughness infused all of the United Kingdom.** The rest of the UK, of course, suffered far fewer than London's nearly thirty thousand casualties but boasted equal patriotic zeal. Complete control of everyone's life by the government brought little complaint—even when women were registered and put into war jobs (some six million by 1942).

566 **Rationing reached its peak in August 1942.** By then people were accustomed to using public transportation as gasoline had almost vanished; they ate far less butter, sugar, and meat than in 1940, wore clothes long out of fashion (they tried to freshen up at "salvage drives"), and survived on a pound of meat, four ounces of bacon, and eight ounces of sugar, of fats, and of cheese a week A pound of soap could be bought in a four-week period along with marmalade and "sweets"—this last was particularly tough on a candy-loving people. Every eight weeks adults could buy a package of a dozen dried eggs, though children, the sick, and pregnant women could get two packages. Tea, sadly enough, joined the rationed foods, but basics like fish, bread, potatoes, "veggies," and fruit did not. America's ignoble export, Spam, became a dietary fixture. Black markets

Dylan Thomas

"A REFUSAL TO MOURN, THE DEATH BY FIRE, OF A CHILD IN LONDON"

. . . .

The majesty and burning of the child's death.
I shall not murder
The mankind of her going with a grave truth
Nor blaspheme down the stations of the breath
With any further
Elegy of Innocence and youth.

Deep with the first dead lies London's daughter,
Robed in the long friends,
The grains beyond age, the dark veins of her
    mother,
Secret by the unmourning water
Of the riding Thames.
After the first death, there is no other.

helped ease the strain. Then, too, restaurants and factory canteens were unregulated. The shortage of housing after the bombing became and remained a large inconvenience. Many survivors lived in damaged, condemned hovels.

Morale rose inversely to dangers, inconveniences, and scarcities. An easy camaraderie of shared burdens brought the people together, as did the moving from town to town for jobs. Class differences eroded, too, since everybody could get employment and war workers all were equal. Taxes were high but equitable. Then, there came the promise of much good in the future.

567 **For most British, some of the most disruptive changes wrought by the war were those wrought by the American GIs who began flooding into England in January 1942.** They brought their own raucous humor, their gee-whiz tourism, their gum chewing flirtations, their post exchanges (PXs). From those depots of luxury they brought nylons and other attractions to women who traded favors. Englishmen soon damned the Yanks as "oversexed, overpaid and over here." The GI response: "You're sore because you're undersexed, underpaid and under Eisenhower." As more Yanks came, friction escalated until a hectic rivalry existed, with the Yanks often branded cowards. That label died in battle.

568 **Entertainment flourished at all levels.** Publicans encouraged music and often brought in local ensembles; denizens themselves often sang or played various instruments, while the BBC contributed a good deal. Factories had been piping in music for years; in wartime they mixed it with real orchestras or bands for lunch hour relief. Famed novelist John Boynton Priestly—who wrote during the war—etched such a moment: "I saw two thousand people put aside what remained of the meat pies and fried plaice and chips they'd had for lunch, lift their eyes toward an orchestra consisting of four young women in green silk and then, all two thousand of them, roar out 'Oh

Johnny, Oh Johnny, how you can love,' and having paid tribute to Johnny and applauding the four young women in green silk these two thousand people returned, much heartened, to another five or six hours at their machines."

Concert and music halls boomed as did theaters. Movies were usually good—even the propaganda ones often had real style: witness Noel Coward's *In Which We Serve*. Popular and highbrow literature—including fine poetry—reached wide audiences.

A hard year ended in hope.

BRITISH LAND BATTLES, 1942

569 Japan moved quickly to secure Burma in December 1941. Tucked between India and Thailand, Burma had important natural resources along with easy access to the Bay of Bengal and the Andaman Sea. More than that, it anchored the Burma Road, China's last remaining supply route to the outside world.

By late April 1942, combined British, Indian, Chinese, and other forces escaped the Japanese fifteenth Army's pursuit by retreating into India. For the Japanese the campaign had been a great success. In four months they had taken Malaya and Burma, wrecked the British Empire in the Far East, and inflicted 13,500 casualties—all at a cost of 5,000 men.

570 For the Allies, losing Burma amounted to a huge disaster. Not only were the rich resources, the Burma Road, and several fine airfields gone, but also what remained of shredded prestige. With the monsoon imminent, no chances beckoned to retake the area—even though hard-pressed General Wavell made several enfeebled tries late in the year.

571 North Africa, along with Churchill's bête noire, Rommel, absorbed most British martial attention throughout 1942. Despite Washington's reluctance to take the Mediterranean theater seriously, Churchill never wa-

vered in his devotion to holding Malta and invading North Africa. Rommel's activities had much to do with shaping the PM's views, but he also felt that basic strategy dictated controlling the whole Mediterranean basin. If Rommel succeeded in getting to the Suez Canal, perhaps farther, the Allies' supply routes would be compromised. As the Desert Fox drove eastward, these concerns escalated. Malta's interference with Axis supplies justified all efforts at preservation. Somehow, though, Rommel kept driving until he cost several British generals their jobs. Relief came only when Monty defeated him at El Alamein and drove him back past El Agheila toward the Mareth Line.

572 At 1942's end, the Allies were slowly pressing Axis forces back into a pocket at Tunis.

BRITISH NAVAL ACTIONS, 1942

573 In one of the most daring ventures of the *Kriegsmarine*, two German warships flouted the Royal Navy. At 22:45 February 11–12, 1942, German battle cruisers *Gneisenau* and *Scharnhorst* with their consort, heavy cruiser *Prinz Eugen*, screened by destroyers and massive air cover, sailed from Brest up the English Channel to Norway—in broad daylight!

574 This escapade—Operation Cerberus—stemmed from one of Hitler's brainstorms. Fearing Norway would be invaded, he wanted more steel on the scene. Horrified at the idea, Admiral Raeder washed his hands of the whole thing. The British had long expected something like the run and thought they were ready. They even knew, from ULTRA, about where the ships would be—but a series of errors and jammed British radar kept the matter of when secret. Not until the ships passed Boulogne in daylight did the Royal Navy wake up. Their plans for interception went to pieces and only scattered attacks were mounted.

A humiliated Royal Navy managed to claim serious damage to *Gneisenau*. The Germans boasted of the feat but privately felt that the ships were greater threats in Brest.

575 **Bad news came in torrents to the Royal Navy in early 1942.** In March, Vice Adm. Chuichi Nagumo's (q.v.) Japanese carrier force sailed into the Indian Ocean on a kind of victory venture.

Having successfully attacked Pearl Harbor and supported the invasions of New Britain and the Netherlands East Indies, Nagumo launched a raid to attack Ceylon and harass Royal Navy remnants in the ocean they usually owned.

576 **Odds were all with the Japanese.** Nagumo's large force, supported by a smaller one under Vice Adm. Jizaburo Ozawa in the Bay of Bengal, faced Adm. Sir James Somerville's Eastern Fleet of five antiquated battleships, three carriers (his planes were outclassed), and five cruisers.

Ozawa's force sank twenty merchantmen in one day and three more later while Nagumo's planes bombed Ceylon. Somerville had to send some ships for refueling, and on April 5 enemy planes sank his cruisers *Cornwall* and *Dorsetshire* plus a destroyer. On the ninth, Nagumo's planes raided Trincomalee and sank the carrier *Hermes* and cruiser *Vampire*.

Having lost only seventeen aircraft on their raid, Nagumo and Ozawa withdrew.

THE EMPIRE OF JAPAN, 1942

A bright rising sun welcomed the new year. For the first time in its history the nation had become its boast, *Dai Nippon*. The empire stood now among the foremost countries of the world, its new boundaries carried by the emperor's warships, his planes, and his dauntless *Nippon denji*.

577 **For the opening year the empire's main challenge would be consolidating conquests and circling its "new order" with impregnable defenses.** All this looked easy enough, but as it happened, the very speed and success of Japan's early campaigns created problems, problems complicated by the traditional rivalry between the Imperial Army and Navy. With armies and flotillas operating in the Western Pacific, the various China Seas down to the New Guinea, Java, Sumatra, Malaya line, and with active campaigning in China, French Indochina, and Burma, supply lines were stretched thinner than expected. True, some supplies were quickly extracted from the new possessions, but basic military needs had to come from the home islands. Navy leaders, who knew they should support the army, had unexpected trouble subduing fractured enemy resistance. Tattered Allied naval forces sniped at troop and supply convoys, harassed main routes, shadowboxed larger forces in "the Slot" (the narrows between the islands of the Solomons chain), held on, and built strength. These enemy counteractions coalesced into a campaign for Guadalcanal and upset imperial defensive plans.

Still, immense gains were consolidated and the Japanese people basked in success.

578 **At home, the government shifted gears for a long war.** Changes of all kinds permeated life already. Now, though, form and substance merged. Rationing, for a time restricted to the main conurbations, spread across Japan. Back in 1940, regular civilian clothing had yielded to a drab and sexless people's uniform. An attempt to copy Nazi civil management policies through an Imperial Rule Assistance Association failed, but local voluntary organizations were consolidated under the Ministry of Home Affairs—which had the baleful result of regimenting meeting times, starting salvage campaigns, and spreading propaganda that spawned an incipient national boredom despite heroic efforts of local assistance associations to foster pseudo-camaraderie.

Education certainly did not escape imperial zeal. Schools offered tempting opportunities for indoctrination. Again, Nazi precedent showed the way toward a national Youth Corps integrated into the school systems and curricula fostering strength through patriotism.

Rationing's chill grip tightened in January 1942 as far-flung legions drained food from home. Now local corporations became essential as they distributed rice and staples to neighborhood groups.

579 Not surprisingly, war production suffered. Only tiny increases over 1941 were counted—531 medium tanks rolled off assembly lines in 1942 compared to 495 in 1941; 8,861 planes in 1942 versus 5,088 in 1941; aircraft carriers: 5 to 6; cruisers: 1 to 2; destroyers: 9 to 9. Another highly secret number had to be considered in working the logistical equation: merchant shipping tonnage. And that number alarmed supply officials: during the past year Japan had gained by manufacture and by capture some 945,374 tons and lost 1,123,156—and with U.S. naval strength rebounding, that number could only get worse.

Japanese morale remained high since good news still prevailed. Makers of public opinion—writers, newsmen, intellectuals—were directed into various propaganda roles. **580** Again copying some Nazi methods, Tojo's government instituted a Japan Literature Patriotic Association, replete with such specialized sections as poetry, literary history, and fiction. Headed by a noted author, the association sponsored publications and conferences. An attempt to create Pan-Asian literary interests sparked the Greater East Asian Writers Congress, which organized symposia and international tours. Literary themes were predictably nationalistic and venomously anti-Western.

News media kept up a rich tradition without much adjusting, although military and some ministerial censorship arrived with the "China incident." **581** When news went bad with the fortunes of war, management became inventive. The Midway disaster appeared as a great victory; later "sideways advances" showed Nipponese tactical agility.

In April 1942, Japan, like most warring nations, sent artists to the battle fronts to present combat in personal perspective. Filmmaking enhanced visual art. Newsreels were taken in action, and filmed travelogues of conquered lands proved highly popular, especially as diversion became a necessity.

PROPAGANDA

Japanese officials thought the radio a highly effective propaganda tool. Several English speaking women were hired to make daily propaganda broadcasts to GIs in the Pacific. **582** Popularly known as Tokyo Rose, these women mixed discouraging words with good American jazz—their words ignored, their music welcomed. One such Rose had American citizenship, Los Angeles–born Iva Toguri, who happened to be caught visiting an aunt in Japan when war began. Hired for about forty dollars a month, she did daily radio stints for some time. Convicted of treason (probably an error) after the war and sentenced to ten

Iva Toguri, most well known of the "Tokyo Roses," interviewed by correspondents, September 1945.

years imprisonment and a ten-thousand-dollar fine, Toguri was released for good behavior in 1956. She finished paying her fine in 1975. President Gerald Ford pardoned her in 1977.

PEOPLE

583 Admiral Wilhelm Canaris, 1887–1945, a strangely dark figure who somehow earned a reputation as one of the war's master spies, joined the German Navy in 1905. Canaris became addicted to spying during WWI and in WWII organized and headed the *Abwehr*, the Nazi intelligence and counterintelligence agency. A member of Hitler's inner circle, Canaris rose swiftly to full admiral. He also formed the Foreign Intelligence Office.

584 Canaris became disgusted with Hitler—he called him "a madman"—during the Sudetenland crisis and steadily worked at getting rid of him. Ambivalent and uncertain of his duty, he saved many Jews while his Secret Field Police were almost outdoing the *Einsatzgruppen* in butchery.

The *Abwehr* harbored several traitors, and although Canaris still had high Nazi friends, his influence began dropping until his archenemy Heydrich (q.v.) usurped some of the *Abwehr*'s functions. Overt treason by one of his officers, bungled jobs by others, and his own disenchantment got him demoted to a minor position. Mistakenly arrested for involvement in the July 1944 bomb plot against Hitler, Canaris went to the gallows on April 9, 1945.

Rumor suggests that from the war's beginning he may have given the Allies information about Hitler's invasion plans.

585 Mohandas Karamchand Gandhi, 1869–1948, Indian nationalist and one of the most influential and revered spiritual leaders of the twentieth century. An English-trained lawyer whose advocacy of strength through love won him the honored title "Mahatma" (great soul), Gandhi was born in India but moved to South Africa and began a lifelong struggle against oppression. By 1921 he was leader of the Indian National Congress and directed it toward "the religion of non-violence." Clad in a loincloth, frequently at his spinning wheel, often in jail or fasting, he preached simplicity and truth while working steadily against British colonial rule.

Gandhi, who always supported the Allies, did lead massive nonresistance strikes against British India. He spurned Sir Stafford Cripps' offer of postwar independence, demanding instead, immediate freedom. **586** With a huge passive strike threatening, in August 1942, General Wavell (q.v.), the viceroy of India, interned Gandhi (whom he greatly admired) along with several Congress leaders. Gandhi remained in jail until May 1944.

A disgruntled Hindu fanatic assassinated the Mahatma on January 30, 1948.

587 Manuel Quezon (Manuel Luis Quezon Antonio y Molina), 1878–1944, was one of the founders of Philippine independence. Born on the island of Luzon on August 19, 1878, Quezon studied law, served in the Spanish-American War, then joined Emilio Aguinaldo's insurrection against the U.S.: after defeat, he spent six months in jail, turned to law practice, then entered politics. After election to the Philippine Assembly, he went to Washington (1909–16) as commissioner. Personable and persuasive, he became president of the Philippine Commonwealth in 1935, worked zealously for full independence, and worried about defense of the islands.

Late in 1935, Quezon brought Gen. Douglas MacArthur over as military adviser and finally made him Philippine field marshal. After the Japanese invasion in 1941, Quezon moved his family to Corregidor; on February 20, 1942, they were extracted and sent to the United States.

Sadly archpatriot Quezon did not live to witness independence. He died on August 1, 1944.

588 **Albert Speer, 1905–81, German architect and production wizard.** Anointed "architect of the thousand-year Reich" by Hitler, Speer became his close confidant and admirer. Addicted to grandeur, Speer designed the new Reichstag building while helping produce, with Leni Riefenstahl (q.v.), a spectacular Nuremberg rally. Appointed minister for armaments and munitions in February 1942, Speer showed a magician's touch at management and rationalization of production, and political savvy in edging military influence out of his realm, finessing Hitler's heavy-handed advice, and conniving against myriad Nazi rivals, all while increasing war production.

589 **Given total control of Germany's war economy (Himmler [q.v.] seethed) in 1943, Speer integrated much "slave labor" (he claimed to know nothing of concentration camps) into the main workforce and used industrialists as production experts.** While Allied bombers reduced much of the country to rubble, Speer's plants produced. In two years his program had almost quadrupled aircraft output and sextupled ammunition fabrication with only 30 percent more workers. His wisdom in spurring production of synthetic oil nearly sustained the Nazi war effort. His foresight in trying to stall Hitler's scorched earth policy saved much German industry.

Convicted at Nuremberg of using forced labor, Speer served a twenty-year prison sentence, during which he wrote interesting memoirs and a diary, both published in the 1970s. Speer died in August 1981.

SPECIAL WEAPONS

590 **Manhattan Project.** Code name: Trinity. The astoundingly complicated, huge U.S. scientific and engineering project that built the Allied atomic bombs. The entire effort came under the administrative control of Brig. Gen. Leslie R. Groves (q.v.). Groves took command in August 1942, and two bombs exploded over Japan in August 1945.

591 **Undoubtedly the most massive cooperative effort organized in American history to that time, Manhattan Engineer District remained an astonishingly well-kept secret, first to last—astonishing because 125,000 workers built huge plants operated by 65,000 men and women. Even Vice President Harry Truman knew nothing of the program.** Work progressed at two large installations—one at Oak Ridge, Tennessee, the other at the government-built town of Richland, Washington. Technical problems were handled at a special laboratory under the direction of Dr. J. Robert Oppenheimer, situated at Los Alamos, New Mexico.

592 **PT boat, nickname for Patrol Craft, Torpedo;** a high-speed, seventy-eight-foot-long wooden craft with two torpedo tubes. The Germans had an equivalent E-boat, and the British a motor torpedo boat.

PT-109, commanded by Lt. John F. Kennedy, was rammed by a Japanese destroyer in the South Pacific and sunk on the night of August 1–2, 1943. He and several others survived, and the adventure helped Kennedy's presidential election in 1960.

A PT boat patrolling off the New Guinea coast, 1943.

ALLIED LEADERS

593 Robert Lawrence Eichelberger, 1886–1961, hard-fighting U.S. general in the Pacific campaigns. Ohioan Eichelberger headed the U.S. Military Academy when the U.S. entered WWII. Taking command of the new 77th Division in March 1942, Eichelberger led the I Corps in Australia in June.

Receiving clear orders from MacArthur—"Take Buna or do not come back alive"—Eichelberger did just that after comprehensive command and logistical renovations. Involved in most of the island-hopping campaigns from New Guinea to Morotai, he then planned and executed an invasion of Hollandia, launched on April 22, 1944. **594** Particularly adept at the complicated business of amphibious landings, Lieutenant General Eichelberger's Eighth Army executed thirty-eight beach invasions from February to April 1945, including the reconquest of the Philippines.

Retiring in 1948 and promoted to full general in 1954, Eichelberger died on September 26, 1961.

595 Leslie Richard Groves, 1896–1970, U.S. Army engineer and master builder. Born in Albany, New York, Groves attended the University of Washington and MIT before entering the U.S. Military Academy. Graduating high in the wartime class of 1918, Groves served in the construction division of the chief of engineer's office and pushed construction of the Pentagon in Washington, D.C. Colonel Groves took charge of a "special weapons project" in August 1942. Promoted to brigadier general, tough, unpleasant, Groves seemed hardly the type to conjure cooperation from thousands of workers, scientists, all kinds of people; yet he did it, and did uncommon service. One authority says Groves directed "the greatest single project ever attempted by man; the vast construction jobs alone were the equivalent of the construction of a Panama Canal each year for three consecutive years."

Promoted to lieutenant general on January 24, 1948, the underappreciated Groves retired that February, then joined Remington Rand and published his account of the Manhattan Project in 1962. He died in Washington, D.C. July 13, 1970.

596 William Frederick Halsey Jr., 1882–1959, U.S. naval officer. "Bull" Halsey graduated from Annapolis in 1904, commanded destroyers in WWI, and became a qualified naval aviator in 1935; by 1940, Halsey ranked as senior carrier admiral in the Pacific. At sea with his flattops, he missed Pearl Harbor. Aggressive always, he urged the quickest possible offensive. During the first two months of 1942, under his equally aggressive commander, Admiral Nimitz (q.v.), Halsey led a carrier task force in the Marshall and Gilbert Islands.

After a few months of stateside sick leave, Halsey launched the Doolittle Raid on Japan, but he missed the Midway battle. Taking command of the South Pacific Force in October, Halsey had a big hand in key Guadalcanal naval engagements, including one in which his flotilla sank at least twenty-three enemy ships. Promoted to full admiral in late November 1942, Halsey, in command of the Third Fleet by March 1943, established close working arrangements with General MacArthur (q.v.) and successfully supported his island-hopping strategy.

597 Energetic, tough, bushy-browed and unconventional, Halsey, in mid-June 1944, moved Third Fleet to help Nimitz pick off the Carolines, island by island. All these operations were spiffily handled and Halsey became famous. But during MacArthur's landings on Leyte in October 1944, Halsey had trouble. He had two missions: cover the landings beginning on the twentieth; and destroy the main enemy fleet coming to wreck the invasion.

598 Knowing much about him, Japanese planners trapped him in his own combativeness. Assuming that Halsey's main force would give general cover to MacArthur's venture, the Japanese sent two strong surface forces to threaten Adm. Thomas Kinkaid's small Seventh Fleet directly supporting the U.S. landings. At the same time they ordered Admiral Ozawa's decoy carriers (with their few planes) to approach the Philippines from the north, astutely guessing that Halsey would go for the carriers and leave their two main forces free to annihilate the invaders.

599 **So began the "Battle of Bull's Run."** Underestimating the threat to Kinkaid, Halsey, on the night of October 24–25, swashbuckled off with Task Force 34 in search of Ozawa's decoys. Within a few hours Kinkaid called for help. Halsey almost had Ozawa by now—the carriers were nearly within gun range of his six battlewagons. A message arrived from Admiral Nimitz: "Where is Task Force 34? The world wonders." Halsey, who could not believe Nimitz would send so insulting a rocket, fumed. (Nimitz had not sent the message as received; nonsense phrases were added in encoding, and "the world wonders" should have been stripped off in decoding.) Then the Bull heard again from Kinkaid: "My situation is critical." There, close in front, Halsey thought, lay some of the richest pluckings of the war, but Kinkaid's situation was critical—Halsey wallowed in indecision. Finally he turned around and sped southward.

Arguments flew then and now: Was Halsey suckered into his biggest blunder, and did he then compound it by leaving Ozawa's ships unsunk? Nimitz defended him, and, at any rate, Kinkaid—helped by luck, two U.S. submarines, and enemy hesitation—not only saved the beachhead but also nearly destroyed the enemy fleets.

Questions did not slow the Bull's career. Japan formally surrendered on his flagship, USS *Missouri*. Following some stateside shore duty, Halsey became an Admiral of the Fleet in December 1945. He died August 16, 1959.

600 **Ernest Joseph King, 1878–1956, U.S. commander in chief of the fleet.** Ohio born of Scottish parents, he was commander of the brigade of midshipmen in the Naval Academy's 1901 class and ranked fourth of sixty-seven academically. His WWI service on Adm. H. T. Mayo's Atlantic Fleet staff taught him much about coalition campaigning as well as pertinacious leadership techniques.

601 **Willing himself to be a complete naval person, King mastered submarining and aviation between the wars.** Much like Gen. Billy Mitchell, King's persistent pushing of naval aviation earned him some enemies among old-line dreadnought types. Vice Admiral King headed the Air Battle Force in the thirties. A believer in rigorous training, he had his pilots practice night carrier landings—much to generalized horror. Despite (or perhaps because of) his skill and success in molding an effective carrier force, King failed to become CNO in 1939. When Frank Knox became secretary of the navy, he appointed King to command the Patrol Force in January 1941.

Able always to make the most of what he had, the admiral did important antisubmarine service with the Neutrality Patrol. As that command metamorphosed into the Atlantic Fleet in February, King became a full admiral with a broad Atlantic convoy mission. **602** **In the ruckus after Pearl Harbor, King became commander in chief, U.S. Fleet in late December with the new designation COMINCH, as opposed to the previously unintentional pun, CINCUS!** He and CNO Harold R. Stark got along well, but to King fell the real job of getting the U.S. Navy into the war.

603 **Grabbing the opportunity to make the Pacific theater the navy's own, he bullied, demanded, and "borrowed" resources until he ran the major operations in the Central and South Pacific areas that steadily eroded Japan's war capacity—he even managed to consign Douglas MacArthur (q.v.) to a secondary role, although they did cooperate.** Fortunately, his own strategic brilliance combined with a rare capacity to pick great subordinates brought a string of successes in the island campaigning of 1942–45. Thorny, stubborn, and egotistical, King had trouble with General Marshall, but they patched together something like a working partnership although disagreeing often on strategy and logistics.

After Knox's death in mid-1944, King's fortunes faded. He fought regularly with the new secretary, James Forrestal, who finally abolished the COMINCH slot. King reached five-star rank in December 1944, retired a year later, and wrote valuable memoirs.

An official U.S. Navy historian evaluated King as "the Navy's principal architect of victory . . . undoubtedly the best naval strategist and organizer in our history."

604 Chester William Nimitz, 1885–1966, the most important operational U.S. admiral in the war. Born in landlocked Fredericksburg, Texas, February 24, 1885, young Nimitz wanted to attend West Point but won an appointment to Annapolis, being graduated in the 1905 class, seventh out of 144.

After undistinguished service in the Philippines, Nimitz unwillingly transferred to submarines, soon becoming the navy's main authority on these boats. After commanding the Atlantic Submarine Flotilla, he found himself in Germany studying diesel engines. That experience fueled his successful crusade to replace the volatile gasoline engines in Yank "pig boats." A rear admiral in 1938, Nimitz commanded cruiser and battleship formations; by 1939 he headed the Bureau of Navigation (personnel).

At home in Washington, D.C., listening to a symphony on the radio, Nimitz heard about Pearl Harbor. **605** A bit more than a week later Secretary Knox appointed him CINC Pacific Fleet at Pearl Harbor with four-star rank. A tall, graceful, graying fifty-seven-year-old, Nimitz did not clean house, but made the existing staff his own to great goodwill. Picking his fighting team—Halsey (q.v.), Kelly Turner, Ray Spruance, Marc Mitscher, with Marine Corps generals Holland Smith and Alex Vandegrift—he set an aggressive tone from the start and pushed the enemy hard at every opportunity. His flagship submarine moved him around his domain, but he commanded most of the brilliantly successful amphibious campaigns from his Pearl Harbor headquarters. **606** An early believer in ULTRA data, he used it to plan his greatest coup—Midway. He never lost from then on, had a large hand in the later Philippine operations, and supported Halsey in the "Bull's Run" controversy.

Becoming a five-star admiral with Admirals Leahy and King on December 14, 1944, Nimitz performed his last war duty by signing the surrender documents for the United States in September 1945.

Living quietly after the war, Nimitz avoided memoir writing but did present a large collection of papers to the Navy History Division. He died in San Francisco on February 20, 1966.

1943

THE FOURTH YEAR
OF THE WAR

SCOURGING

*It is not the actual military structure of the moment
that matters but rather the will and determination
to use whatever military strength is available.*

—Hitler, Mein Kampf

Wars often set their own tempos. By 1943, all belligerents had settled into routines of hard conflict. Annual draft "classes" marched off, more and more civilians entered war work, economies tightened as consumerism virtually vanished. Things were still a little better in Germany—there some consumer goods yet stocked the stores as production of arms, munitions, planes, and tanks lagged. Hitler still hoped to appease his people while making war.

Everywhere people greeted the new year with more anxiety than enthusiasm as a grinding, drab dailiness dimmed the luster of life. A kind of mystical parallel between the two world wars could be seen in a growing belief in the endlessness of it all. Soldiers of the line came to feel that the war had always been and always would be and that the only true reality lay in the chaos of the front.

THE UNITED STATES, 1943

607 A large assembly of Allied leaders gathered near Casablanca, French Morocco, on January 14, 1943. Roosevelt and Churchill (Stalin begged off because of the Stalingrad crisis), replete with military and civilian staffs talked strategy. From the first it became clear that it was going to be difficult to reach agreements. Churchill, who came prepared with maps, diagrams, strategic dispatches, everything calculated to overwhelm the unprepared Yanks, urged his favorite "soft underbelly" strategy—he wanted to invade Sicily, sweep the Mediterranean clean of the enemy, then attack the Axis's weakest link, Italy, knock it out of the war, and possibly lure Turkey to join the Allies. Russia would be helped directly because Hitler would have to shift troops to the Italian front, and Germany's Western European defenses would be weaker when the cross-Channel offensive came.

Roosevelt, who looked and felt vigorous at this meeting, played his usual observer's role, watching the shifting wind. Especially he watched sober George Marshall's patient disagreement; the British strategy would slow preparations in England for the main attack on the Continent and would drain American support for the Pacific, which bulked ever larger in concern. The English bulldog stuck to his guns—statistics (he had them) showed that an attack on the French coast could not possibly be launched in 1943—there was not enough time to mobilize the supplies and training for the massive armies needed.

As with most conferences, a compromise emerged. **608** Sicily would be the next objective—Operation Husky, which Ike would lead after Tunisia—while Germany would suffer around-the-clock bombing. Marshall agreed to the Sicily move but nothing else for the moment.

A bit of behind-the-scenes humor tinged the conference. Both generals de Gaulle and Giraud were present as some of the discussions touched on the Free French, and they loathed each other. For unity's sake they had to forge some kind of working relationship. FDR supported Giraud; Churchill, de

January 14–24, 1943, the Casablanca Conference, formal portrait of Allied figures. Seated (left to right): Admiral E. J. King, Churchill, Roosevelt. Standing: (behind Churchill) Maj. Gen. Sir Hastings Ismay, Lord Louis Mountbatten, and (far right) Admiral Field Marshal Sir John Dill.

Gaulle. FDR put it all in perspective when he described their tasks: "My job was to produce the bride in the presence of General Giraud, while Churchill was to bring in General de Gaulle to play the role of bridegroom in a shotgun wedding." The resulting meeting produced one of the classic pictures of the war. Churchill's view of de Gaulle shows the difficulty in arranging that "wedding": "Here he was—a refugee, an exile from his own country under sentence of death, in a position entirely dependent upon the good will of the British Government, and also now of the United States. . . . He had no real foothold anywhere. Never mind; he defied all." Roosevelt suggested that de Gaulle thought of himself as a living Joan of Arc, "with whom it is said one of his ancestors served as a faithful adherent." Churchill replied, "Yes, but my bishops won't let me burn him!"

609 During the press conference on January 24, 1943, summing up what had happened at Casablanca, FDR told a story about Unconditional Surrender Grant, and unconditional surrender of the Axis then became the main Allied war aim. Churchill acquiesced. Critics argued that this pronouncement would stiffen enemy resistance, and certainly Goebbels used it to prove that there could be no surrender.

Much had been left untouched and there would be another meeting.

610 **Increased regimentation pinched in the U.S. more this year, but the wry reminder "Don't you know there's a war on?" usually salved irritation.** Which, to those who thought about it, showed that the war was a fairly unifying process. **611** **Probably for the first time since the American Revolution the country felt a strength in union.** A sense of gathering together in a great cause pulled often marginalized races into the effort and began eroding prejudice and ignorance. A great shifting and moving shuffled the country's people. A newness came to familiar things—new neighbors (often jammed closely), new places, new customs, even new accents and habits as war acted like a giant homogenizer of a new and different nation.

612 **Certainly grumbling continued but, in general, people helped each other win the war.** Most of what the government said it needed somehow appeared. Schemers in Washington sought to trim inflation by taking money out of circulation. They did that by raising taxes, by cutting consumer goods to the bone (no new cars or big appliances, cuffs cut from trousers, nylons became a kind of currency), by sponsoring voluntary drives—tin, aluminum, and clothing drives which whipped up much enthusiasm. Most popular were war bond drives, highly touted by tours of Hollywood stars buying them, waving them, singing about them. Kate Smith, well-known songstress, nearly outsold everybody when she boomed out "God Bless America."

Even when tobacco ran short—it went overseas in cigarettes—smokers grumbled mildly, bought Bull Durham shag, and rolled their own. Inventive advertising boasted of things absent—wearers could hardly feel the difference between a certain brand of lisle hose and nylon, Chrysler Motor Company made superior tanks. Sweet

tooths suffered: most of the highly prized Milky Ways, Mars bars, and Snickers were downsized and packed with 3-in-1 or 10-in-1 (one meal for three men, one meal for ten men) ration boxes for the services.

613 **By 1943 the huge male exodus could be seen.** By late 1943 some 2.7 million men were in the army, with another 1.8 million in the air corps and nearly three million in the navy, Coast Guard, and Marines. Men's places were filled now with large numbers of women in factories, government jobs, particularly in the WACS, WAVES, SPARS (Coast Guard), WASP (Women's Air Force Service Pilots who, by 1943, not only ferried new planes from factories to USAAF fields in the U.S. and foreign war zones but also trained pilots).

Men who stayed home did not necessarily stay put, as thousands joined in the national wanderlust from war job to war job. By December 1943, 10.7 million were in manufacturing as compared to 4.7

Office of War Information (OWI) cartoon by Hilda Terry. Home front humor: "We're just *made* for each other . . . I water his victory garden and he stakes my tomato plants."

OWI cartoon by Charles Shows making light of wartime shortages. Caption reads: "I'm conserving wool, this bathing suit's painted on."

million in 1940. Workdays and weeks grew longer, underwritten by overtime. Record amounts of steel came out of American smelters and, by 1943, after Japan had captured most of the world's rubber supply in the Southwest Pacific, the U.S. developed a highly successful synthetic product that sustained Allied needs. These successes were maximized by an equally amazing growth of the U.S. carrying fleet as mass production methods launched eighteen million tons of shipping in 1943 alone.

Women were encouraged into war work, and they demanded help in balancing homemaking with riveting. Factories and government offices created babysitting facilities while Congress established the Emergency Maternal and Infant Care program, with free obstetric and prenatal services for military wives. Requests for veterans benefits escalated—a

worry for any government—but Congress dawdled badly in catching up with the awareness of millions.

614 War, however, did not wave a magic wand and banish segregation. Certainly blacks shared equal war wages but this did not, in many minds, translate into racial equality. Blacks suffered (save in government slots) job insecurity and lived in uncertainty—Detroit writhed through a race riot in 1943 and there were other episodes in the South. The armed services remained segregated.

Organized labor sought to benefit from inequalities of any perception, but largely failed in a great swelling of patriotism which spawned vast numbers of voluntary organizations. **615** The United Service Organization, which helped service families and ran the popular USO canteens, vied with the Red Cross and Salvation Army to provide services that did wonders in smoothing life behind the lines.

616 As military intelligence grew exponentially in importance, so too did fears of spies and spying. Various service intelligence units were enlarged. FDR gave J. Edgar Hoover's (q.v.) Federal Bureau of Investigation (FBI) responsibility for keeping a eye on "subversive activities." While never a competitor with the Gestapo, the NKVD (the Soviet secret police), or *Tokkō*, Hoover's bureau infiltrated domestic life insidiously enough to win the nickname of the leading "subversive activity."

617 Probably a megalomaniac, Hoover established secret agencies within the FBI to keep tabs on "subversives" defined far beyond Webster. Employing thousands of new agents, he investigated German-Americans, Japanese-Americans, Communists, and Americans he thought might be subversive or somehow suspect. Borrowing heavily from his experience as Attorney General A. Mitchell Palmer's special assistant during the Red Scare of the 1920s, Hoover, not unlike Himmler, built a huge file on everyday Americans who might someday do something unpatriotic. He ex-

1944 poster by Schlaikjer. *Silence Means Security* admonished soldiers to watch what they said.

619 Some agencies like the Office of Price Administration, even the Office of Civilian Defense, were victimized by a congressional effort to punish FDR. A high-rolling conservative Congress hated to delegate power, especially to a chief executive it loathed.

620 Two hard fights erupted in 1943 over farm prices. Twice, in April and July, Congress passed acts upping prices on commodities, and twice FDR vetoed the bills to hold the inflation line. Embittered farm bloc legislators took aim at things FDR wanted. When he vetoed a harsh bill to curb coal miner strikes in June, Congress—amply backed by public opinion—overrode the president, who reacted by delegating much of his political and economic functions to new federal agencies that kept him out of day-to-day management. Congress and the president abraded each other increasingly in a classic example of a democracy's problems with war-making. Cooperation came quickly on issues of supporting the troops, of providing the tools of conflict; cooperation ebbed when executive peace-planning smacked of New Dealism.

panded his intrusions when FDR gave him wide wire-tapping power; some of the evil he did lives after him.

618 President Roosevelt trod a nimble course through the economic and social minefields appearing all around him. Unwilling to diffuse all his power throughout alphabet agencies, he resisted piling boards on commissions, on surveys and offices. Astutely aware of such economic needs as price controls and also aware that some rationalization of labor and agriculture must come, FDR fought some tough political battles in 1942 and 1943. After the November 1942 congressional elections, Democratic control teetered since a coalition of conservative Democrats and Republicans held the balance and cut back on residual New Deal programs (much hated by many) under the guise of trimming domestic spending to put more money into the war.

621 War excitement enhanced the whole entertainment business. Hordes of Hollywood stars went trouping to camps, posts, and USO canteens to entertain, to wait tables, to bring some touch of home and glamor to a frightening existence. Like the country, music was evolving. Swing and jazz were being challenged by bebop, and new vocalists like Frank Sinatra caused mass swooning among teenage girls, starting in 1943. Yanks took their amazing music with them and left it wherever they went. An American original, the musical, thrived during the war, with 1943's *Oklahoma* by Rodgers and Hammerstein setting all kinds of records for much time to come.

622 Most Hollywood movies had patriotic themes but kept a generally high quality. Ranking with the absolute best is 1943's *Casablanca*, starring Humphrey Bogart and Ingrid Bergman; Rommel sparked several

"COMIN' IN ON A WING AND A PRAYER"

We're coming in on a wing and a prayer
We're coming in on a wing and a prayer
Tho' there's one motor gone we will still
carry on
We're coming in on a wing and a prayer.

What a show, what a fight
Yes we really hit our target for tonight
How we sing as we fly through the air
Look below there's a field over there
With a full crew aboard and our trust in the Lord
We're coming in on a wing and a prayer.

films; one of the best is *Five Graves to Cairo* (1943), with formidable Erich von Stroheim as the Desert Fox. Bob Hope, Dorothy Lamour, and Bing Crosby offered broad and musical laughter in their various *Road* films.

At the end of 1943 the United States boasted soaring morale, massive effort, and a festering hatred of its enemies.

623 A sublime act of heroism pulled Americans' attention to the hard Atlantic war. A small Allied convoy, SG-19, left Saint John's, Newfoundland, on January 29, 1943, bound for Greenland. Of the three ships, one was the U.S. troopship *Dorchester*, filled with cargo and assorted troops. Torpedoed before dawn on February 3, *Dorchester* began sinking by the bow. Terrorized at the thought of landing in freezing water, passengers and crew mangled lowering the lifeboats and milled helplessly. Survivors remembered seeing four chaplains standing together near the bow, calming the panic, handing out life jackets, and urging men into the sea. When the jacket supply ran out, the chaplains, first lieutenants Clark V. Poling, John P. Washington, Alexander D. Goode, and George L. Fox—two were Protestants, one Jewish,

one Catholic—removed their own life jackets and gave them to other men. They were last seen linking arms and praying as the ship sank.

Their sacrifice touched the entire Allied world. In 1944 the chaplains were posthumously given Distinguished Service Crosses.

UNITED STATES WESTERN BATTLES, 1943

624 Everything seemed to go so slowly in North Africa. Landings were good, initial operations successful, even tricky relations with Vichyites smoothed, but green U.S. troops turned out to be a problem, along with their green generals.

625 During his self-assessment after the Africa landings, Ike found himself too kind to his subordinates (that question had bothered Marshall) and, in his February 1943 reorganization looking toward the Sicily invasion, he replaced the hesitant Lloyd Fredendall with George Patton as commander of the II Corps and then activated Fifteenth Army Group. Ike named Harold Alexander—Britain's Near East leader—as his deputy and commander of the new army group, made up of the First and Eighth Armies. Ike and Alex proved a formidable team through Operation Husky and beyond.

While Ike regrouped, Rommel disappeared from Africa; a sick man, he returned to Germany in March. Enemy resistance continued but obviously slackened as Axis forces were starved for supplies. The last opposition in Africa ended on May 13, 1943. Ike's command sustained 76,000 casualties in the campaign and captured some 238,000 POWs. Gloating would have to wait: Husky and what came next captured everyone's attention.

626 As mopping up continued around Tunis, Roosevelt, Churchill, and entourages gathered in Washington for a continuation of their Casablanca talks. Code-named Trident, the May 11–25 discussions centered on

France, Atlantic issues, the Far East, direct damage to Hitler, and help for Stalin by invading mainland Italy after Husky.

Thorny personalities enlivened the sessions. Major decisions were hammered out fairly solidly—France would not be invaded until 1944; one of Hitler's main oil sources, the Ploesti fields in Romania, a difficult and distant target, would be bombed (which first happened in August); and redoubled convoy efforts (which were working) would continue.

627 Two maverick generals brought a bitter China argument to the table. Lieutenant General Joseph W. ("Vinegar Joe") Stilwell, commander of the China-Burma-India (CBI) theater, manager of Chinese Lend-Lease, and by now at odds with his boss, Chiang Kai-shek, came to argue loudly for his long-germinating plan to recover Burma and aid China with a ground campaign. With him, equally strident, came airman Maj. Gen. Claire Lee Chennault—who organized the vital air route over "the Hump" from India to China—to plump for an expensive but attractive plan to build several Chinese airfields to sustain the new Fourteenth Air Force. In a memorable moment, Stilwell shouted: "It's the ground soldier slogging through the mud and fighting in the trenches who will win the war!" Chennault bellowed: "But God damn it Stilwell, there aren't any men in the trenches!" Chiang and FDR backed Chennault's boast that he could push the Japanese out of China and the war by airpower alone—that decision proved a costly blunder.

628 Planning for Husky degenerated into a messy series of arguments between the Allies about who would do what and with how much—and most especially where.

629 Some distrust persisted after the North African campaign. A few American strategists could see no real point to driving through terrible terrain across northern Italy into Austria. Some British doubts of Eisenhower intruded on preparations, despite General Marshall's having had Ike made a full general on February 11, 1943. General Sir Alan Francis Brooke, chief of Britain's Imperial General Staff, had dim regard for most Americans and, considering the whole North African venture, said that "Eisenhower . . . was far too much immersed in the political aspects of the situation . . . which he should have left to his Deputy, Clark. . . . Tactics, strategy and command were never his [Ike's] strong points."

Still, planning and preparations proceeded. For this first direct attack on Axis territory, Ike delegated command to General Alexander. He deployed two armies—Patton's new Seventh and Monty's Eighth—to make the Sicily landings, supported by British naval bombardments, by U.S. paratroopers, British glider-borne forces, and heavy air cover. **630 An elaborate diversionary effort (Operation Mincemeat)—partially successful—sought to point enemy attention to Greece.** Meanwhile an armada of 2,500 vessels, including new landing craft, converged from North Africa, Britain, and the U.S.—180,000 men, 600

LSTs (landing ship, tank—a 327-foot craft that could carry 175 troops that were also used to transport tanks and smaller landing craft), awaiting tanks at La Pecherie, French naval base, July 8, 1943, two days before the invasion of Sicily.

tanks, 14,000 vehicles, and 1,800 guns, with ammunition, food, medicine, and other equipment, were brought to the Sicilian invasion.

631 The invasion of Sicily began early on Saturday, July 10, 1943, as the weather worsened and high winds scattered parachutists and gliders widely, many dropping into the sea. Monty's landings on the east coast of the triangular-shaped island met light resistance and went almost as planned. His troops took Syracuse that day. Patton's landings on the wind-lashed southwestern beaches met stiffer resistance but were finally successful. Aggressive armored counterattacks against Patton at Gela on the eleventh failed, largely because of vital U.S. Navy gun support.

Alexander's armies faced formidable opposition and initially were outnumbered. Airborne landings were hampered by several miscues and deadly friendly fire. **632** Able general Alfred Guzzoni—in charge of the defenses—had some 350,000 men on the island deployed as infantry, with six mobile divisions and several less efficient ones in reserve; two of the mobile divisions were German Panzers. Axis theater commander Field Marshal "Smiling Albert" Kesselring had more armor en route across the Messina ferries the day the Allies landed.

633 As more German troops arrived so did a one-armed panzer general nicknamed *Der Mensch* ("the Man"), Hans Hube. He and Guzzoni extracted most of the Axis troops from western Sicily (Palermo fell to Patton on July 22) and began skillful withdrawals toward Messina. Making brilliant use of the tough terrain, scattering mines widely, counterattacking adroitly, they held up the Allies and prepared to evacuate their men and matériel.

July 11, 1943, off Gela, Sicily, during the invasion, an American cargo ship smokes after being bombed by a German plane and having its cargo of munitions explode.

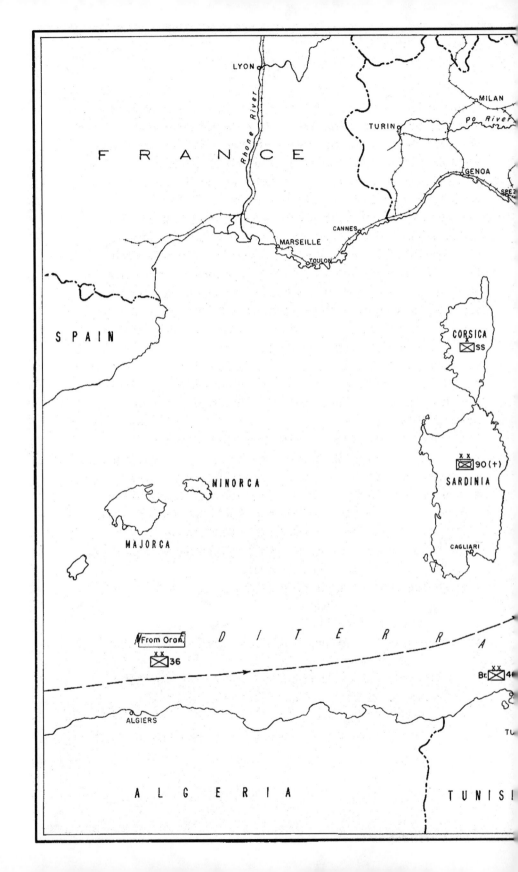

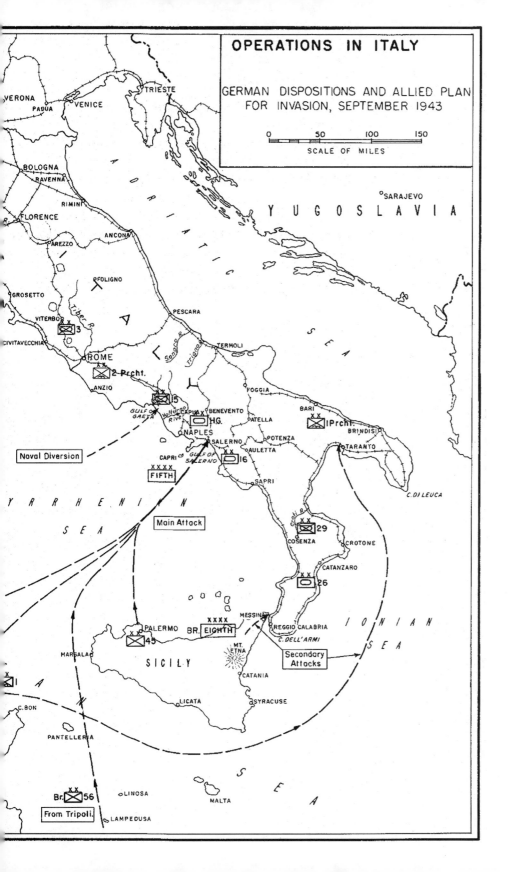

Montgomery's Eighth Army plowed northward toward and around Mount Etna, aiming at Messina against growing opposition and falling far behind schedule. Alexander ordered Patton to speed eastward across the northern coast and attack. Patton's men marched and fought brilliantly and reached Messina on the evening of August 16—to find the enemy gone. Guzzoni's Italians evacuated from the third to the sixteenth of August and Hube's Germans from the eleventh to early on the seventeenth—in a masterful operation they extracted some 62,000 Italian and 40,000 German soldiers, 9,800 vehicles, and 47 tanks. **634 Both sides paid dearly for Sicily: Close to 32,000 Allied casualties against 12,000 German and almost 150,000 Italian POWs.**

635 Thousands of superbly phrased leaflets, signed by Roosevelt and Churchill, fluttered over Rome on July 17, 1943: "The time has come for you, the Italian people, to decide whether Italians shall die for Mussolini and Hitler—or live for Italy and civilization."

636 Mussolini met Hitler at Feltre on July 19, 1943, as the Allies pushed ahead on Sicily. The Führer gave short advice. "Sicily must be made into a Stalingrad," he declaimed. "We must hold out until winter, when new secret weapons will be ready for use against England." Mussolini got no promises of more troops, and, in fact, Hitler was scheming to send in troops as occupation forces since the *Abwehr* and Gestapo had alerted him to the Duce's imminent overthrow.

637 Bereft of excuses, short of hope, Mussolini reluctantly summoned the Fascist Grand Council to its first meeting since 1939. In the Palazzo Venezia on July 24, 1943, he pulled out all the stops in a histrionic two-hour harangue to reconstitute his power with his henchmen. He failed. Fascism's promises of Roman reincarnation had come all too true—around them that day the delegates could see the new ruins of Rome. The council voted 19–7 against him; he called on King Victor Emmanuel on July 25, to be

1943 photograph of a mutilated poster of Mussolini attests to *Il Duce* becoming the "most hated man in Italy."

told he no longer headed the Italian government. "The soldiers don't want to fight anymore," the king said, adding that "at this moment you are the most hated man in Italy." As he left the palace, *carabinièri* arrested him and spirited him to the first of several hideaways. **638 Mussolini would be rescued on September 12, 1943, by a daring commando-type raid headed by Hitler's bold adventurer Otto Skorzeny, and flown to Germany. There the Führer installed him as puppet leader of the "Salo Republic."**

639 The king formed a new government headed by Marshal Pietro Badoglio, who continued negotiating with the Allies. At this point Allied policy wavered and negotiations stalled at a crucial instant, but Badoglio concluded a secret armistice agreement with the Allies on September 3, 1943, which came into force on the eighth; Italian troops were disarmed while the Italian fleet struck colors at Malta. Badoglio managed to get Allied cobelligerent status for Italy. **640 During the arrangements for Italy's defection, Hitler reinforced Kesselring with sixteen divisions—not from the Eastern Front.** The field marshal swiftly disarmed Italian troops in the north, secured Rome, and prepared to repulse invasion.

641 With Italy changing sides, the Allies anticipated easy mainland landings. Everything seemed set for swift success—Monty's army would land at Reggio di Calabria on September 3, while Mark Clark's U.S. Fifth Army would go ashore at Salerno on the ninth, then both would join in a concentric operation. Monty

landed against no opposition, but heavy German resistance met Clark and increased over several days; only desperate emergency reinforcement of the beachhead and Allied air cover prevented Clark's men from being thrown into the sea—German loudspeakers greeted them with "Come on in and give up. You're covered." Not until October 1 did the publicity-hungry Clark reach his first objective, Naples.

642 Kesselring successfully urged more men and stubborn defense on Hitler and began constructing heavy fortifications—the Gustav Line—south of Rome. Allied hopes wallowed in Italy's winter mud. Rocky terrain, river-drowned and mountain-dominated, turned every German defensive position into a minor fort

Marshal Badoglio (left) aboard the HMS *Nelson*, after signing armistice terms September 29, 1943. General Eisenhower walks beside him; behind them (left to right) Air Chief Marshal Tedder, Lieutenant General Mason-Macfarlane, and General Alexander.

and every battle into fearsome grapples for what the British called the PBI (poor bloody infantry). General Alexander, who commanded the advance, lacked decisive orders and underestimated German defensive skills, so his projected breakthrough attacks lacked punch and advanced by inches. The almost vertical terrain accentuated Alexander's strategic problems; first the Calabria and then the Apennines Ranges divided his armies, Monty's Eighth on the east, Clark's Fifth on the west, making liaison between them difficult and coordination nearly impossible.

Grinding battles of attrition—**643 in which the highly decorated Nisei 100th Infantry Battalion fought valiantly**—flared along the Volturno, Garigliano, and Sangro Rivers in dismal winter conditions. By year's end, Allied forces were strung out along the Garigliano and approaching the Rapido River. Casualties had been heavy and, so far, the Italian campaign had been a showcase for the pertinacity of Kesselring's troops.

DIPLOMACY

644 While reorganizing his forces to break the Gustav Line, Eisenhower learned, on December 10, 1943, of a vital decision taken at the mid-August Quebec Conference (Quadrant): he had been given the greatest military command ever given anybody. He had expected, along with most others, that a British general would lead the cross-Channel invasion of France (Overlord). During Quadrant, Churchill had proposed that America's preponderant strength dictated an American commander. FDR offered Ike to general agreement. As a trade-off, Lord Louis Mountbatten became Supreme Commander Southeast Asia (SEAC).

Eisenhower handed over the job of Supreme Allied Commander Mediterranean (SACMED) to British general "Jumbo" Wilson, went to London, and started planning.

645 Diverging Allied strategies and aims resulted in an important series of conferences during the last months of 1943. U.S. secretary of state Cordell Hull and British foreign secretary Anthony Eden conferred with Soviet foreign minister Vyacheslav Molotov in Moscow from October 18 to November 1, 1943. Hull and Eden soothed Russian concerns about a second front by promising to cross the Channel in the spring of 1944. Stubborn Molotov reciprocated by agreeing to the policy of unconditional surrender and to some kind of postwar world security organization as well as Allied occupation of a defeated Germany.

646 Churchill and Roosevelt soothed Chiang Kai-shek's feelings of estrangement at the second session of the Cairo Conference (Sextant), November 22–26, and December 3–7,

Air Transport Command (ATC) plane flying over the Egyptian pyramids, 1943. Begun in May 1941 as the U.S. Air Corps Ferrying Command to deliver Lend-Lease aircraft to Britain, and renamed in 1942, the ATC functioned as a global enterprise effectively linking the U.S. with every theater of the war.

Photograph taken in Tehran during the Eureka Conference of November 28–December 1, 1943: Soviet marshal Voroshilov shows President Roosevelt the sword presented to the people of Stalingrad by George VI of Britain. Among the onlookers are Stalin (left) and Churchill (far right).

1943. More resources were promised for the Far East along with amphibious operations in the Bay of Bengal as support for a Burma offensive to reopen communications with China. However, this promise was later canceled as the amphibious craft were needed more for the invasion of southern France in August 1944. More important to Chiang, China would get her lost territories back after the war, which would preserve the nation's "great power" status. The generalissimo came off badly at the conference. Arrogant, ill-informed, unwilling to throw out corrupt generals or to use his best troops against the Japanese (he hoarded them for use against his real enemies, the Communists), he showed a warlord's insularity and an egotist's myopia.

647 By the twenty-eighth of November, 1943, Churchill and FDR had reached Tehran for their first meeting with

Stalin (Eureka)—they would reconvene Sextant in a few days. Important agreements were reached in Big Three discussions lasting into December 1. Stalin and FDR ganged up on Churchill, convincing him to drop his stubborn plans for additional Mediterranean campaigning and winning his approval to send troops from Italy to support Overlord by a diversionary drive (Anvil) into southern France. Stalin pledged a big cooperating Soviet eastern offensive while agreeing to enter the Japanese war after the Nazi defeat. Some general talks centered on possible postwar Polish boundary shifts westward (a shoddy compromise), and on Finland's and Germany's future. Aid would go to Tito and his Yugoslav partisans.

648 Stalin made an offhanded suggestion that Roosevelt thought must be a joke, but that sickened realist

Churchill: alleviate any postwar German problems by eliminating 50,000 to 100,000 Nazi officers. Churchill knew that Stalin survived on terror and would export it to any occupied areas.

649 **A man called on the German embassy in Ankara, Turkey, one day in October 1943.** He offered, for ten thousand pounds, photographs of secret British documents. Wonder of wonders, this mysterious volunteer, Elyea Bazna (code name: "Cicero") served as valet to the British ambassador to Turkey, Sir Hughe Knatchbull-Hugessen. With a key to the ambassador's safe, Cicero provided copies of hundreds of secret documents for six months, including the date of the Tehran Conference and details of planned bombings of Germany.

Apparently not trusting their Albanian spy, the Germans paid him in counterfeit money.

ALLIED/JAPANESE FAR EASTERN BATTLES, 1943

650 **Japan's startling successes through most of 1942 had left Allied Far Eastern positions in a shambles.** American public opinion, combined with growing military conviction, had forced more resources eastward than planned. Those diversions from the "Germany first" program had made possible the beginning of an American counteroffensive which saved New Guinea and secured Guadalcanal. The powerful Imperial Navy still protected inner lines of supply and the main defense line running from the Aleutian Islands down through the Marshalls and Solomons to the big southern base at Rabaul. To keep the initiative and break the enemy defense line, Admiral King, General MacArthur, and Admiral Nimitz all wanted more assets. They were at a critical point—with help their combined offensives might achieve wonders.

Approval came at the Casablanca Conference in January to thrust on toward Rabaul, but by March, MacArthur made it clear he could not take that big

base in 1943. Instead, a scaled-down offensive, with Halsey going to Bougainville and MacArthur to western New Britain, would clear the Solomons and threaten the Bismarck Archipelago as soon as supplies permitted.

651 **America's increasing production capacity plus the recent arrival of the "Mighty Eighth" U.S. Air Force to join the RAF in the round-the-clock bombing of Germany justified sending more men and matériel to the Far East.** With the U.S. logistical situation improving rapidly, MacArthur, never really trusting non-U.S. generals, created **652** **Alamo Force (consisting mainly of Lt. Gen. Walter Krueger's Sixth Army) and effectively taking all U.S. troops away from the Southwest Pacific Area Allied land forces commander, Australian general Sir Thomas Blamey.** With Alamo Force and creative help from the U.S. Fifth Air Force, he stepped up his bypassing operations along New Guinea's north coast while using amphibious attacks on islands near Guadalcanal as he pressed toward Rabaul. MacArthur wanted Admiral Halsey's task force to strike straight from Guadalcanal to Bougainville, but the admiral talked him into securing additional air bases for the campaign.

653 **Japanese planners expected MacArthur to push on with his New Guinea occupation.** That he did, but not according to enemy guesses. Aware of the Japanese propensity to distribute occupation elements in ports or harbors on New Guinea's north coast, MacArthur decided to use this enclave strategy against them. If the major logistical ports could be captured, smaller bypassed posts would wither as supplies to them vanished. With good bases of his own at Milne Bay and Buna-Gona, MacArthur worked to secure the Lae-Salamaua complex on the Huon Gulf coast.

654 **Not entirely fooled, the Japanese sent Lt. Gen. Hatazo Adachi with headquarters elements of the Eighteenth Army from Rabaul to Lae and, on March 1, a huge Imperial Navy troop convoy was spotted heading for the**

Huon Gulf and into what would be known as the decisive Battle of the Bismarck Sea. Every available plane from the U.S. Fifth Air Force swooped on seventeen enemy ships from March 2 to 4, nearly annihilating the whole convoy (seven transports, four destroyers sunk; some 3,000 of 5,500 Japanese reinforcements drowned; sixty-one enemy planes destroyed against total U.S. losses of four aircraft) and clearing the gulf as U.S. forces feinted a late June drive on Salamaua. An attempted enemy concentration exposed Lae, which a brilliantly orchestrated U.S. air, amphibious, and land assault seized during the first week of September. Moving quickly, U.S. forces occupied the Huon Peninsula, thereby cutting off the enemy on New Guinea. By the end of 1943, MacArthur's combined forces had occupied Cape Gloucester on western New Britain and the 1st Marine Division—of Guadalcanal fame—held Long Island, off the Huon Peninsula.

655 **This adroit nullification of enemy strength would have been impossible without Admiral Halsey's deft attacks in the Solomons.** Halsey did not have an easy time. Command chains were kinked. As Commander, Pacific Ocean Areas he had nominal responsibility for Australia, New Caledonia, New Hebrides, Fiji, and part of the Solomons. He had ships, but they weren't his—his naval superior, Admiral Nimitz, attached some when needed; after March 1943 he also reported to General MacArthur for ground activities. Despite predictable entanglements, Halsey performed near miracles in combined and amphibious campaigns. He had two ground forces he used dextrously, along with some land-based naval air units mixed with the 13th USAAF.

656 **Halsey planned to skip up the Solomons, capturing airfields and isolating Japanese ground forces as he moved bombers and fighters ever closer to Rabaul.** His first objective, the Russell Islands, were unoccupied and seized on February 21, 1943; within a week two airstrips, a PT base, a radar station, and supply dumps were under construction. Halsey settled down for troop training (using Guadalcanal as a model) while he planned to attack Munda Airfield on New Georgia.

Enemy activity increased as the Seventeenth Army, headquartered on the southern end of Bougainville, worked to strengthen the entire central Solomons area. At the beginning of 1943, Seventeenth Army remained under the control of Gen. Hitoshi Imamura, commanding Eighth Area Army (which also included Eighteenth Army), and heavy reinforcements were distributed among various islands; a reinforced regiment went to New Georgia, more troops landed on Bougainville.

U.S. forces landed on Rendova Island, across a strait from Munda, on June 30, 1943. Light resistance evaporated and U.S. 155mm guns began firing on Munda Point. Elements of two divisions aided by Marine battalions hit the New Georgia beaches on July 2, expecting to mop up by the end of the month. The attackers met hard resistance as reinforcements came from Bougainville. By mid-July mud, malaria, heavy jungle, and inaccurate maps had all but stopped the invasion. Most of the 25th Division from Guadalcanal came to help. A coordinated offensive late in the month finally broke enemy lines. Munda fell on August 5, and three weeks later so did the island. Japanese aircraft losses—350 vs. 93—would be critical, especially in pilots.

657 **Mixing plane and ship thrusts like a fencing master, Halsey finessed attacking the fortified air base at Kolombangara by switching to lightly held Vella Lavella, which sat athwart Japanese communications to Kolombangara.** No opposition met landing forces on August 15; airstrip construction began immediately which, when completed on September 27, allowed the U.S. to bomb Rabaul much more heavily, causing enemy withdrawal from Kolombangara. **658** **U.S. forces won the New Georgia campaign by early October at a cost of 1,094 killed, 3,873 wounded, and thousands incapaci-**

tated by disease. The Japanese counted some 2,500 casualties out of 8,000 heroic defenders.

Obviously the "blockade and strangulation" strategy worked and would continue. Even though a series of naval battles happened during these land actions, results were about even and the basic strategy continued.

659 **Halsey had already started another operation.** General Nathan Twining's Thirteenth Air Force began plastering airfields in Bougainville's neighborhood; heavy bombers did real damage and finally restricted enemy action to night raids only. Bougainville had inviting possibilities. Airfields there would interdict enemy supplies in the whole area and likely would neutralize Rabaul—if that base could be isolated, a good many Allied lives would be saved, and the Joint Chiefs ordered it isolated. Bougainville must first be taken.

660 **Halsey seized the Treasury Islands which could be used as a landing craft base.** A night landing by New Zealanders October 26–27 shoved the few defenders inland, where they were swiftly dispatched. Then the Bull faked the enemy out of their confidence by making several diversionary landings on Choiseul Island—the Japanese took the bait—while on November 1, 1943, Gen. Alexander "Sunny Jim" Vandegrift's I Marine Amphibious Corps hit the beach on the shore of Bougainville's Empress Augusta Bay. Main enemy forces on the south end of the island were isolated as Marines built a defensive perimeter around an advanced naval base and three airstrips. From those airstrips U.S. planes dominated the island, completely isolated the Japanese Seventeenth Army, and continued hammering the wrecked remains of Rabaul. Action in the Solomons theater ended as U.S. energy aimed elsewhere.

661 **Action shifted to the Central Pacific Area where Admiral Nimitz continued the Allied attack.** He intended an intrusion into the Marshall Islands as the beginning of a sweep across the Central Pacific, during which he would pick up isolated Japanese garrisons as he took Tarawa, Makin,

Saipan, Guam, Ulithi, Yap, and the Palaus on the way to the Philippines.

Prospects improved dramatically. Japanese carrier and plane losses crippled their attack strength and U.S. submarines picked off enemy merchant tonnage at will. Although the Imperial Navy still boasted some formidable vessels, they were now the hunted in the air/sea war. Besides, taking Tarawa atoll looked like a snap. Betio, its main island, barely blipped on a map—its size about equal to New York's Central Park.

662 Although usually amply prepped by ULTRA intelligence, Nimitz missed a couple of essential points. Betio had some 4,500 crack Japanese defenders fiendishly hidden by natural and artificial defenses. Rear Adm. Shibasaki Keiji, commanding Betio, claimed that a million men could not take it in a hundred years.

Using Alligators (LTVs [land vehicle, tracked]) as personnel carriers, the 2nd Marine Division went ashore on November 20, 1943. Miscalculated tides grounded many Alligators, and men wading in far from shore were mowed down. Next day the Marines managed to divide the defenders and things got better as more Marines arrived. Fearsome fighting raged for two days as the Marines slowly edged defenders to Betio's eastern tip. Cramped there, they launched fanatical banzai charges but were cut to pieces. By November 23, the Marines overran them all. **663** This tiny bit of dirt cost 1,009 U.S. killed and 2,101 wounded, portents of things to come as another year ground down.

664 Both sides had changed strategy. The U.S. Joint Chiefs of Staff approved the idea of getting to the Philippines from two directions; along New Guinea's coast and through the Marianas. Japanese strategists reluctantly decided to contract their defensive perimeter, which now would run from the Kurile Islands down through the Marianas and Caro-

LEFT: **USS** *Casablanca* with airship escort, August 8, 1943. Fleet Airship Wings were organized as antisubmarine patrols, but the big soft-sided airships were also effective in raising morale. BELOW: Marines take cover on Red Beach #3, Tarawa, Gilbert Islands, November 1943.

lines to western New Guinea and on to the Dutch East Indies and Burma. This would release troops for retraining and give time to produce new carrier pilots and warships.

By the end of 1943, the Allies were confident. As for the Japanese, they faced a wilderness of impossibilities.

THE UNION OF SOVIET SOCIALIST REPUBLICS (USSR), 1943

665 **As the new year opened, the Soviet Union should have been exhausted.** Although Nazi legions had been held and then thrown back, they remained a terrible threat. Winter had been hard on everybody in the USSR. Hunger stalked the country since most people received barely a thousand calories a day (miners and industrial workers got more). Alarming shortages were felt in every area: clothes, shoes (all kinds of substitutes were tried), fuel for cooking and heating, paper, gasoline, money—even friends. Russians had a toughness to them, though, that surprised the enemy, and their morale rose in the midst of squalor.

666 **War wrought a sea change in government.** The Councils of People's Commissars, the Supreme Soviet, the now all-powerful State Defense Committee, even Stalin himself, now recognized the need to sustain the Russian war spirit. During 1943 governmental and party control relaxed somewhat; rhetoric shifted from constantly spouted Communist propaganda to more nationalistic encouragement. Political control of the army relaxed in the field and commissars gradually became soldiers. An old emphasis on "class warfare" faded as "comrades" now faced an enemy more dreadful than themselves.

Stalin, walking the edge of popularity, struck a deal with the Russian Orthodox Church as thousands of churches reopened, priests appeared, even bishops.

667 **By now professional cynics about the government, Soviet citizens knew the relaxation of controls for what it was**—a desperate gesture from a scared hierarchy, and the people did great deeds out of patriotism, not gratitude. Partly inured to sacrifice by the awful 1930s, they suffered, their strength sometimes failed, but they sustained this new and catastrophic revolution by iron will and terrible anger.

With so many men in the ranks or in heavy industry, most farm work fell to women, and in 1943 they upped their working days by half. Helped by children and the elderly, women pulled plows and rickety wagons, shoveled silage, and did agriculture's daily drudgery.

668 **Rising out of all these stresses came a quenchless Russian sense of humor and of art.** The antics of bumbling soldiers were captured in pulp—Vasily Terkin's exploits grew apace—and children's primers and poems offered fun instead of war. Good literature continued to be published. Konstantin Simonov's 1943 books, *No Quarter* and *Days and Nights*, ranked as best-sellers. Music filled the halls as Soviet composers orchestrated conflict.

Starting poorly for the USSR, 1943 became a year of the phoenix. All the tragedy, the effort, the fears, the hopes crested as the Red Army marched westward toward Berlin.

RUSSO-GERMAN BATTLES, 1943

669 **By January 1943, Stalin basked in the certainty that the Germans could not hold anything east of the River Dnieper.** Late that month General Vatutin plotted to pocket Army Group Don in the Donets Basin and launched a mobile tank force across the Donets east of Izyum aimed at the Sea of Azov. Less than a week later, on February 2, Generals Zhukov and Vasilevsky drove the Voronezh *front* armies in a two-pronged attack (Operation Star) south beyond Kharkov toward the Dnieper and north toward

Smolensk, with the overall objective of encircling Army Group Center.

These attacks pressed Manstein's left flank from Izyum; his front and right flank at Rostov were threatened by several Soviet armies. Hitler, finally grasping the disaster threatening the whole southern end of his line, recreated Army Group South under Manstein and told him to hold a line from Belgorod to the Sea of Azov. Manstein had some help for this daunting job. Besides giving him three fresh panzer divisions and solid air support, Hitler also authorized him to airlift one hundred thousand men from the 17th Army on the Taman Peninsula.

670 **Manstein counterattacked in mid-February with Hermann Hoth's Fourth Panzer Army.** Taking advantage of poor Russian front management, Manstein's spearheads surrounded herds of enemy troops. Some Red Army units dissolved, while others ran out of gas and joined the rout. Shifting direction in early March (a thaw threatened), Manstein retook Kharkov on the fourteenth and Belogrod on the eighteenth. This meant that he had restored the early 1942 German positions, save for a salient bulging around Kursk. "Manstein's counteroffensive was a masterpiece of mobile warfare," says one authority, adding, "It is sobering to consider what he might have accomplished if given a free hand from the beginning."

671 **Encouraged by Manstein's success, Hitler wanted to regain the initiative on the Eastern Front.** As he counted assets he noted that permitting a withdrawal from the Rzhev salient had shortened his front and released the Ninth Army for reassignment. More than that, the new Panther and Tiger tanks were arriving with fresh SS Panzer divisions. **672** **As Hitler and his generals assessed their situation in mid-1943, though, they realized the impossibility of another general offensive despite some added divisions and new equipment.** Serious crises in manpower approached after taking a half million casualties during the winter. Al-

though there were some three million German troops on the front, they faced over six and a half million Soviet troops. Few reserves could come from the West because Allied successes in North Africa raised the specter of invasion. Those numbers indicated that the Nazis could not simply dig in and hold—they would be overwhelmed.

673 **The best of bad options dictated a swift spoiling attack to chew up Soviet reserves and disrupt their strategy.** Place: the Kursk salient, 118 miles wide, 75 miles deep between Belgorod and Orel. Date: May 4, 1943. Tactics: Massed German tanks would hit the north and south angles and trap five Soviet armies.

674 **An uncertain, oddly worried Führer began looking for excuses.** Confessing to Guderian, recalled as inspector general of armor, that the very thought of Operation Citadel made him sick, Hitler had clearly lost faith in the plan. Delay proved doubly dangerous. Intelligence and observation revealed the whole scheme, which gave Stalin and his generals time to collect 1.3 million troops, 3,400 tanks, plus 2,100 planes, to ring the salient with antitank weapons, and complete several belts of trenches. They also built a handy six-army reserve.

These counterpreparations were detected by the Germans. Hitler's field commanders, Model, Manstein, and Kluge, advised scrapping the attack. Nonetheless, Hitler ordered 700,000 men, 2,400 tanks, and 1,800 planes into action on July 5. Model's Ninth Army from the north made slow progress and on July 9 stalled on a secondary defense line as Konstantin Rokossovsky committed masses of tanks that embroiled Model in a fierce melee of attrition. That day Model confessed that a breakthrough would be impossible. Hoth's attack, west of the Donets and heading north, almost broke Nikolai Vatutin's defenses. **675** **After a twenty-one-mile advance in six days against heavy resistance, Hoth ran into the Fifth Guards Tank Army, and the biggest tank battle of the war followed.** Some twelve hundred tanks were careening over open ground, chasing, evading, firing, burning, exploding. Hoth's panzers did more damage than they sustained, but numbers went against them. Hitler canceled Citadel on July 13, claiming that he needed the 2nd Panzer Corps to stop the invasion of Italy. On the twenty-fifth, hearing of Mussolini's arrest, the Führer warned Kluge that he must give up twenty-four divisions for Italy. Model, "the lion of the defense," went into carefully orchestrated withdrawals; he abandoned Orel on August 5 but fenced with three whole *fronts* until mid-August, and Manstein did the same.

676 German skill in retreat caused an important change in Stalin's mind—because of nimble Nazi maneuvering, Soviet encirclements usually failed and he banned any for the future. Another result: Stalin regained his faith in his military acumen and increasingly restricted his field commanders.

Kursk is often counted as part of the great Red Army offensive involving four million men, thirteen thousand armored vehicles, and twelve thousand planes that pinched off the German Orel and Kharkov salients in August 1943. The *Wehrmacht* permanently lost the initiative in those actions.

677 All military operations during the rest of 1943 proved anticlimactic for the Nazis. Although Leningrad remained under siege, the bonds were loosening. By August's end, eight Soviet *fronts* drove multiple attacks at Army Group Center's six-hundred-mile line, and Hitler permitted retreat behind the Dnieper. By October, AG Center had lost Smolensk and Hitler's Seventeenth Army remained isolated in the Crimea. German forces began a long, dogged, skillful but endless retreat westward.

By year's end German forces had been pushed back almost to their starting positions in 1941. A still strong *Wehrmacht* would regroup in the winter and fight hard for survival, but no longer for victory.

THE EMPIRE OF JAPAN, 1943

678 By the beginning of the new year the Japanese people knew that things were going wrong with the war. Scarcities scarred most parts of daily living; severe shortages of cloth, rice, and sugar had grown worse. Worse than material scarcities were demographic ones: fewer men on the streets, women shifting from homes to farms to factories. Somehow a strange hollowness infected society. People came more and more to draw on their own resources for such necessities as entertainment, hope, and happiness.

While the true results of Midway and Guadalcanal were carefully kept from the Japanese populace, the military leadership grasped them all too clearly. **679** Prime Minister Tojo took more control over the national economy under the March 1943 Special Wartime Administrative Law. Civilian needs, already neglected, suffered seriously against official demands for increases in aircraft, shipping, steel, and coal production.

680 Fault lines appeared in the war effort. Tojo's frustrations with the rivalry between the army and navy were constant. Although trained officers spoke of unified command with urgency, no one seemed able to bang heads and budgets hard enough to make it happen. Imperial General Headquarters, established in 1937, failed to coordinate anything except service selfishness; it operated above, around, and through the government while it coddled incompetence and belittled prudence. Service competition encouraged a growing black market as army and navy officers patronized it for such scarce commodities as aluminum and luxuries.

Tojo seized on this blatant illegality to make major administrative changes. Abolishing several useless ministries, he created a ministry of munitions (which he ran himself) and one of transportation. He hoped these agencies could rationalize aircraft production and improve home transportation policies. Again, Tojo found that his own military undermined effective action; he made no headway toward unified military command, a failure contributing to the total inadequacy of Japan's Intelligence service. Not only did the services not exchange intelligence data, they squandered resources spying on each other! One authority observed that Japan may well have lost the war by neglecting intelligence.

681 **Tojo did make some headway in war production despite service jealousies and an expanding black market—but at a brutal cost.** Aircraft production in 1943 reached 16,693, nearly doubling 1942's numbers. This proved a disastrous success, though, for in order to achieve it, the government had to dip into carefully hoarded raw material stockpiles. Since Allied submarines had effectively isolated the resource areas to the south, production could only decline—a stark state of affairs not shared with the people.

682 **Certainly the deepest fractures came in Japanese society.** As war pressures climbed, Tojo and his government faced a drastic necessity—to justify altering the national idealism of women as pedestaled nurturers of beauty and the future. To general shock in September, unmarried women were conscripted into a labor "volunteer corps." Working-hour limits on women and children were lifted. War finally hit education, one of Japan's proudest institutions, as middle school attendance time dropped. University students left privileged halls of academe to restore the emperor's legions as a nation began mortgaging its future. Internal integrity of the country eroded as food shortages drove more and more workers to scavenging farming areas around big conurbations, which weakened family units and aggravated worker absenteeism in key industries.

With Allied forces advancing in the south, with Burma threatened by a serious enemy buildup, Imperial General Headquarters, searching for ways to maintain its "impregnable" defense line strategy, found itself trapped by a serious tactical error.

683 **Incredible successes in the days after Pearl Harbor had induced both the Imperial Japanese Army and Imperial Japanese Navy to garrison lots of small islands scattered around the Central and Southwest Pacific.** Hard fighting on New Guinea and Guadalcanal combined with U.S. island-hopping had depleted many of these garrisons, and reinforcements were needed, particularly in China, Burma, and now along the Central Pacific defense barrier leading to the Philippines. The army had emphasized attacking just after Pearl Harbor and now, when reinforcements were needed, only untrained men, often unfit or too young, could be hastily dragooned and sent to replenish Field Marshal Count Hisaichi Terauchi's Southern Army. Terauchi's army had responsibility for everything south of the Philippines, and an influx of ill-trained, poorly armed recruits boded trouble. Terauchi scrambled to reorganize his vast domain and mix veterans with novices—not too successfully.

By late 1943 many garrisons could not be saved and were left to starve.

684 **Tojo and his advisers never understood the need to be honest with the people.** They expected the citizenry to have faith in them while they showed little in return.

Tokyo radio broadcasts offered a challenging ditty:

Why should we be afraid of air raids?
The big sky is protected with iron defenses.
For young and old it is time to stand up;
We are loaded with the honor of defending the
*   homeland.*
Come on, enemy planes! Come on many times!

But fear increased uncertainty late in 1943 as plans were announced for evacuation of nonessential personnel from the conurbations; uncertainty yielded to greater fear when thousands of homes were destroyed in order to make firebreaks. **685** **Mass hegiras from cities began.**

Looking back on a bleak 1943, the Japanese people looked ahead to much worse.

ITALY IN CONFUSION

686 Italians could be pardoned befuddlement as 1943 unfolded. In the beginning the situation seemed immutable. With his troops in Russia and his dreams almost intact, *Il Duce* strutted outlandishly. In fact, he could boast that Hitler's personal paladin, Rommel, had fizzled in North Africa and been extracted by Hitler to preserve his shaky reputation. In his place, taking over Rommel's troops, now called the 1st Italian Army, Mussolini sent Gen. Giovanni Messe. Veteran of Russian fighting, Messe stabilized the North African front, stopped Britain's Montgomery at the Mareth Line, and, when flanked out of that, gloriously stopped Monty at Enfidaville. After the Americans had gotten themselves untangled from their own mistakes at Kasserine Pass and begun to act like soldiers, Messe joined Nazi general Dieter von Arnim in a last-ditch defense of Tunis. He surrendered with honor on May 13, 1943, just after Mussolini made him a marshal.

687 After so much effort for so long, North Africa's loss amounted to a colossal disaster. This terrible collapse of Italy's martial ventures finished Mussolini. Booted out in July 1943, saved by Hitler, and ensconced somewhat uncomfortably in a puppet's theater, the Salo Republic, this diminished figure still tried strutting and screeching Fascist themes to a swiftly dwindling audience. **688** Nonetheless, he revenged himself on a few members of the Grand Council by having them, including his son-in-law Count Ciano, shot early in 1944.

689 Mussolini attempted conscription—raising some four divisions—and supported Germanization of industry, which brought half a million workers in Turin and Milan out on strike in November 1943. This was one of the first such spasms to hit the Axis. These and other repressive doings pushed a good many young Italians into a growing resistance movement.

690 Switching sides brought Italy new miseries. When Badoglio and the royal family escaped Rome for the south, they left most of the Italian army in the north without orders. As Nazi reinforcements came to Kesselring, he filled this void with mass captures, deportations to Germany, and mass murders. Some few strong Italian units held together and fought the Germans in isolated, bloody battles which ultimately were lost. In the postsurrender weeks, while Badoglio and the king worked to align their country with the Allies, Kesselring consolidated his grip on Rome and points north. In those weeks, too, Italian politics erupted in fragmented enthusiasm. Communists and anti-Fascists dominated these early debates and remained dominant through the rest of the war.

691 Italy north of Rome became, for all intents and purposes, another German occupied satellite. Laborers conscripted, resources plundered, national gold stolen, Italy suffered the usual intrusion of Gestapo and RSHA agents, who policed politics and thought and repressed resistance.

THE BRITISH EMPIRE, 1943

692 Twelve thousand people sat in front of Churchill at Harvard on Monday, September 6, 1943. He had come to receive an honorary degree and he felt deep stirring in his blood. History and blood, said Winston Churchill, pulled America and Britain together into almost common citizenship, and that seemed to him altogether good. Citing Bismarck, "for there were once great men in Germany," who said that "the most potent factor in human society at the end of the nineteenth century was the fact that the British and American peoples spoke the same language," the prime minister emphasized, "If we are together nothing is impossible. If we are divided all will fail."

Dedicated utterly to a vision of a transatlantic quasi-union, he conducted his own and his nation's business to foster that possibility. Which found him, sometimes, compromising his views on strategy, commanders, and, most especially, postwar planning.

693 In the matter of commanders he had compromised gracefully on the appointment of General Eisenhower to lead Overlord, though he had virtually promised the job to Alan Brooke. But he got a fair return on his affability—the acceptance in August 1943 of Lord Mountbatten as supreme commander of the new Southeast Asia Command (SEAC). This satisfying appointment made Churchill's protégé the youngest admiral at forty-three in the history of the Royal Navy. He had considerable naval experience, not all of it deft, and he had the best of all qualities for his position—boundless energy and great personal charm. The PM expected much from him.

694 The activities of General de Gaulle forced one of Churchill's longest, most difficult compromises. He thought de Gaulle a pain in the neck and avoided him to the limits of courtesy. Still, animosity did not prevent the PM from supporting the resistance movements proliferating in France, many of which rested on Gaullist enthusiasm. **695** In mid-May 1943 the French National Council for Resistance gathered in Paris, a result of remarkable coordinating work by the legendary "Max" (Jean Moulin). "Max," who represented de Gaulle, managed to pull representatives from most resistance groups, labor leaders, and political parties into the first effective coalescence of opposition. After Moulin's capture and death by torture in 1943, George Bidault became chairman. De Gaulle would take firmer control of France's war behind the lines when he headed the French Committee for National Liberation later in the year.

696 All these actions interested Churchill. Always a fan of irregularities, especially in war, he enjoyed the derring-do of the secret Special Operations Executive (SOE). This idiosyncratic collection of spies, saboteurs (a nine-man SOE group working with Norwegians wrecked the German heavy water plant in Norway, which all but finished their atomic bomb work), and rabble-rousers worked behind enemy lines to spread confusion and dissension, destroy strategic places, and aid resistance factions with money, men and women, advice, arms, and equipment.

697 Wrapped in mummylike secrecy, SOE became a kind of mythical kingdom that ran a war within a war. The public developed an erroneous (but helpful) view of a group of Etonion schoolboys strolling into Gestapo headquarters kicking a football on ahead. Churchill cherished this organization and gave it limitless money—which did not endear it to such professional agencies as MI5 and 6 (national security and secret service bureaus). Churchill backed the right horse in that SOE did outstanding service in disrupting enemy rear areas and encouraging resistance cadres to perform amazing feats.

Secret operations of all kinds received the PM's official blessing and by 1943 myriads of such actions were underway. **698** A special RAF project caught his imagination: 617 Squadron underwent special training with a new skipping bomb and attacked Ruhr River dams that were thought to sustain enemy industry. Nineteen bombers sortied on the night of May 16–17, flew in low, skip-bombed three dams, and breached two big ones. Eight planes returned from one of the boldest actions of the war. Churchill paid special attention to the code-breakers working out in Bletchley Park and gobbled up their ULTRA data.

699 Carefully monitoring developments among the atomic physicists, both Churchill and President Roosevelt welcomed news in December that Enrico Fermi and colleagues at the University of Chicago had achieved the first successful chain reaction. An atomic bomb could, indeed, be made and the world's weaponry affected even more drastically than by the advent of gunpowder.

700 **Not all news brought cheer.** In April 1943, London heard from Radio Berlin that mass graves of Polish officers had been found in the Katyn Forest near Smolensk. The Germans blamed the Russians for the atrocity (the officers' hands had been wired behind them and they had been shot in the back of the head); the Russians claimed the Germans had done it. When the Polish government requested a Red Cross investigation, the Soviet government broke off Polish diplomatic relations, adding fuel to Churchill's growing suspicions of his Red ally.

701 **Confirmation came later that the graves were those of some forty-four hundred Polish officers murdered in 1940 by the NKVD, the People's Commissariat for Internal Affairs, whose duties included liquidating anyone considered a danger to Soviet rule in the newly acquired territories.** In 1992 the Russian government released documents confirming that the murders had been ordered by Stalin and the Politburo.

702 **Looking at the year, Churchill knew that the tide had truly turned and that the Allies were winning.** Now, of course, came a time of fiercer combat because both the Germans and the Japanese would fight to the end. Planning for Overlord went on apace as the U.K. literally bulged with Yanks and their riches of equipment.

703 **England's looks were different now.** Instead of a somewhat battered, shabby land, it had become an armed camp. British and empire troops joined the Yankee bulk, trains hauled car after car of tarpaulined guns, lorries (trucks), bits of planes, tanks, stacks of munitions, strange looking boats, and boxes of rations as great rising stockpiles dotted the countryside.

704 **Society had changed shape as well.** Migrations redrew the human map of Britain. Children went to the country (even as far away as the U.S.), young men went to battle fronts, older men to factories or air raid duties, and women moved in an uneasy hegira from homes to wherever Ernest Bevin, Labour czar in the War Cabinet, said workers had to go.

Not privy to global views of the war, most Britons found 1943 much the same as earlier years: they felt dulled, gray, chilled, hungry, yet somehow survivors in a challenge of their faith. Not that certainty failed—they knew that Great Britain and its friends would win, but they languished in the matter of when. Nevertheless, the British remained optimistic, which produced a latent, saving humor. Accused of bravery, they eluded it—"It's not bravery. We English lack imagination." And so all of England tackled the things needed.

Coal, much the essence of life in England's winters, lagged in production, so when the need came clear, labor orders put miners' sons into the pits and later in 1943 dragooned that specially formed laboring class called Bevin boys (named after the Minister of Labour Ernest Bevin) to follow on behind.

Sometimes citizens simply had to have things "off ration," and dipped guiltily into the black market for such succulents as oranges. Most did the things suggested and planted little gardens to grow vegetables—there were 1.4 million such plots in 1943. These clearly were personal symbols of persistence as well as signatures of progress, of patriotism in action.

705 **War in the Atlantic loomed far above other wartime horizons in the scourging year of 1943.** In the first five months, some one hundred U-boats were sunk (forty-seven in May alone) as Allied losses dropped impressively, and all Allies were cheered when, in late May, the *Kriegsmarine* pulled its submarines out of the Atlantic. British and American convoy protection was winning the U-boat war.

Admiral Sir Bruce Fraser inspecting Royal Marines honor guard, 1943. Fraser won recognition for sinking the battle cruiser *Scharnhorst* in December 1943 and in November 1944 was appointed C-in-C of the new British Pacific Fleet (Task Force 57), which helped cover the Okinawa invasion.

Great Britain survived that difficult year, its people and their courage stolidly intact. Something the PM said, on the day he accepted Harvard's honorary degree, applied more truly than before: "The price of greatness is responsibility."

GERMANY, 1943

For Germany the new year opened with customary optimism but with an added, most un-German ingredient—uncertainty. **706 Goebbels' propaganda had, in a way, been too successful; it bred a national hubris that left no room for such military failures as Stalingrad.** Nor did it prepare the German public for the woeful casualty lists that insidiously drained morale—at Stalingrad alone the Germans lost nearly 300,000 men.

Russian war news ran generally bleak that year—Hitler's legions could not really resume an offensive. Badly beaten in the Kursk battles, the *Wehrmacht* had pulled out of the Crimea and began a stubborn, skillful retreat to the west. Although German troops kept their edge in combat, they kept losing men and equipment, and the disturbing news filtered back to the Fatherland along with rumors of a coming Allied invasion of France. A little comfort came from Italy, where a brilliant defensive campaign was stalling the Allies below Rome, but casualties continued and the enemy held the initiative. Everything got worse after the western invasion in June 1944. Bad luck or bad generalship failed to keep the Allies off the beaches and, once ashore, they drove German troops back relentlessly, taking thousands of prisoners and eliminating whole armies.

707 In late July and early August 1943, the RAF threw over three thousand bombers, equipped with new anti-

radar electronics, into a major night air offensive against Hamburg. The July 27 raids, using explosive and incendiary bombs, started a firestorm that destroyed half the city, killed over forty thousand people and left much of the remaining population homeless. These raids were aimed mainly at civilians but did substantial industrial damage. Another major RAF effort against Peenemünde in August hit rocket research installations with 4,000-pound Blockbuster bombs and forced relocation of further research.

Also in August, the England-based U.S. Eighth Air Force sent 376 bombers on a daylight raid against Schweinfurt (center of ball bearing manufacture) and Regensburg and lost 60 planes. High losses in a Schweinfurt raid in October stalled further daylight bombing until long-range fighter cover became available in early 1944.

While Speer's production program—his labor force bolstered in 1943 by some six million drafted laborers along with Soviet and Polish POWs and slave laborers from concentration camps—continued with minor glitches despite the bombing, the continued raids ruined many German cities and crippled civilian services.

German living standards began to drop by midyear, but Hitler, Himmler, Goebbels, and others made strenuous efforts to sustain the home ration. Not only did they urge increased farm production but they diverted foodstuffs from millions of Soviet civilians and war prisoners to Germany. "In its magnitude," says one historian, "this crime is comparable to the mass murder of the Jews."

708 A great evil hung over Germany, and although most German citizens did not know its full dimensions, it began to rot society—the Final Solution. Before Hitler came to power he had outlined clearly his racial supremacist views. Aryans only were fit to rule. He even adopted a Sparta-like attitude toward crippled or mentally retarded children by installing a national program of euthanasia in 1939—this he did as part of his drive to "purify" Germany. **709** Hitler's main hatred fell on Jews, and an open pogrom began after the invasion of Poland (with a Jewish population of one and a half million) in September 1939. It grew from small harassments to expulsion to emigration to self-accusation (a yellow Star of David on clothing) to extortion to ghettoization to starvation (two thousand a month were dying in the Warsaw ghetto by mid-1941) to organized assassinations by *Einsatzgruppen*, to the direct murder of millions in the streets, in homes, and relentlessly in death camps.

710 Jewish populations from conquered countries increased the problem. Death squads did fiendish work—at Babi Yar ravine, near Kiev, for instance, 33,000 men, women, and children were slaughtered in three days—but these disorganized efforts were inefficient. Organized genocide became Hitler's policy. A few protests were ignored or chastised, even one from the commissioner-general of Belorussia who wrote from Minsk on October 27, 1941: "To have buried alive seriously wounded people, who then worked their way out of their graves again, is such extreme beastliness that this incident must be reported to the Führer."

711 In the autumn of 1941, Adolf Eichmann became head of the Race and Resettlement Office of the RSHA and gave orders to exterminate every European Jew. He expanded and perfected extermination camps and by 1943 was devising designer deaths. He addressed the matter of killing massive numbers of people by applying regular logistical methods of procurement, storage, packaging, and distribution. Procurement devolved on SS formations that relied heavily on such local police teams as the *Milice Française* in ferreting Jews from hiding places, collecting them in boxcars, and shipping them to concentration camps for storage as labor (replete with identity numbers tattooed on an arm) or for immediate death by shooting or gassing. To allay suspicion, the gas chambers were labeled "shower," "dressing room," or "hospital"; even inside, the deception continued with instructions on bathing or fumigation.

712 **At Chelmno, Poland, one of the first "extermination camps," carbon monoxide pumped into hermetically sealed vans did the work.** That same procedure recurred in Belzec, Sobibor, and Treblinka, also in Poland. **713** **Later, in complexes like Auschwitz-Birkenau, Poland (the largest extermination center), big chambers were sealed and crystalline hydrogen cyanide (Zyklon-B) gas killed in a few minutes.** Selected prisoners, sometimes POWs, cleared the bodies for the next installment. The huge number of bodies outstripped burial efficiency and many—supposedly dead—went to gas ovens.

714 **Inmates at Auschwitz faced an additional abomination—the ministrations of Dr. Josef Mengele, known to prisoners as the "Angel of Death," because, in white-coated professionalism, he decided who lived and died, unless he decided to do some mutational surgery on them.** His practices nearly outdid the Marquis de Sade. He did exploratory experiments on Siamese twins, hoping to enhance the Nazi population as the number of dead increased.

A careful methodology governed the dead. **715** **Designated officials stripped them (their fumigated clothes went to Germany), cut their hair (for mattresses), picked the gold from their teeth (for the Reich's treasury or the picker), some saved skin for lampshades; others fed bodies into gas ovens for final disposal.**

716 **A few concentration camps had existed in Germany since the 1930s, though the early ones were not death warrens.** Hitler wanted these for "protective custody" of four prisoner categories: political opponents, *Untermenschen* (including Gypsies), criminals, as well as "asocial shiftless elements." All categories were liberally defined so that Jehovah's Witnesses (who refused an oath to Hitler) mixed with illegal radio listeners and foreign exchange violators. *Untermenschen* received special attention from the start —segregated barracks, deadly work schedules, starvation.

717 **Cunning deceptions were practiced on victims, mainly to lull them, and to blind the eyes of neighbors— they were being "relocated" "somewhere in the east."** The grim boxcars into which so many went were for resettlement. Fact: new extermination camps were ready in Poland, even in Russia. From way out there no word would come—and, true enough, it took at least two years for believable accounts of the unimaginable to filter into Germany and the outer world.

718 **Fear swept the camp administrations as 1943 brought Soviet legions inexorably toward Poland; fear based on repressed guilt, fear of world retribution.** As the Red Army kept coming, frantic efforts were made to banish all evidence of the camps (the gas chambers defied extinction), to plow them under and plant trees in their wake, but Red Army forces encountered masses of dead and living dead as they moved into Poland. **719** **When U.S. troops marched into Germany in April 1945, they liberated Buchenwald to find some 20,000 prisoners in varied stages of starvation and disease;** they encountered similar conditions at Dora-Mittelbau, Flossenburg, and especially Dachau. Several other camps liberated in May were no better. British troops freeing the huge complex of Bergen-Belsen in April found 60,000 prisoners in terrible condition, many of whom died within a few weeks of liberation.

These places, these numbers, at first numbed, then stunned, then outraged the Allies. Eisenhower's anger never abated, neither did Churchill's nor Truman's. All of which tended to harden the future for ex-Nazis.

ABOVE: Truckload of corpses, Buchenwald concentration camp, Weimar, Germany, April 14, 1945. The bodies were about to be burned when the U.S. Third Army arrived. BELOW: Buchenwald crematorium ovens, April 1945.

720 **Words are inadequate for dealing with the *Churban, Shoah*, the Holocaust.** Stalin, no mean expert on murder, once observed that "the death of one person is a tragedy; the death of millions is a statistic." Statistics, though, can convey their own horror.

Estimated number of Jews murdered by country and percentage of Jewish population:

> Belgium 40,000 (60%)
> France 90,000 (26%)
> Germany/Austria 210,000 (90%)
> Hungary 450,000 (70%)
> Poland 3,000,000 (90%)
> Romania 300,000 (50%)
> Russian Soviet Federated Socialist
>   Republic (Russia) 107,000 (11%)
> Soviet Socialist Republic of the Ukraine
>   900,000 (60%)

721 **Smaller nations had fewer deaths, and some helped their Jewish populations escape the cattle trains.** Italy's 50,000 remained fairly intact, largely because Mussolini delayed shipments. Danes, with their king's connivance, smuggled their 6,000 on small boats to Sweden. Most of Holland's Jews were sheltered. Of the 16,000 there, about 2,000 were lost, including young diarist Anne Frank, who died in Bergen-Belsen in March 1945.

722 **It is important to know that not all inmates took their abominable condition peacefully.** There were camp insurrections; prisoners killed some guards in the pitifully few successful escape attempts—but hundreds did rebel in full knowledge of reprisals, which were brutal and abrupt.

723 **It is important to know, too, that many Nazis involved in this savagery knew what they did and found it cleansing.** Hear a speech by Heinrich Himmler to some one hundred SS group leaders in Posen, Poland, October 4, 1943, telling about a special German virtue:

It is absolutely wrong to project our own harmless soul with its deep feelings, our kindheartness, our idealism, upon alien peoples.

One principle must be absolute for the SS man: we must be honest, decent, loyal and friendly to members of our blood and to no one else. What happens to the Russians, what happens to the Czechs, is a matter of utter indifference to me.

Whether the other races live in comfort or perish of hunger interests me only in so far as we need them as slaves for our culture; apart from that it does not interest me.

Whether or not 10,000 Russian women collapse from exhaustion while digging a tank ditch interests me only in so far as the tank ditch is completed for Germany.

We shall never be rough or heartless where it is not necessary; that is clear. We Germans, who are the only decent people in the world who have a decent attitude to animals, will also adopt a decent attitude to these human animals. But it is a crime against our own blood to worry about them and to bring them ideals.

Most of you know what it means to see a hundred corpses lying together, five hundred, or a thousand. To have gone through this and yet—apart from a few exceptions, examples of human weakness—to have remained decent fellows, this is what has made us hard. This is a glorious page in our history that has never been written and shall never be written.

We had the moral right, we had the duty to our people, to destroy this people [Jews] which wanted to destroy us.

Altogether, however, we can say, that we have fulfilled this most difficult duty for the love of our people. And our spirit, our soul, our character has not suffered injury from it.

724 **Here are the gross totals.** Of an estimated prewar European Jewish population of 8,861,800, some 5,993,900 (67 percent) died. Their ghosts would haunt Nuremberg in long echoes of horror.

1944
THE FIFTH YEAR OF THE WAR

SEARING

This grievous and obstinate war.

—Winston Churchill

THE UNITED STATES, 1944

725 **Long wars can become entities in themselves.** So many agencies of so many sizes sprang up in the U.S. during the first two years of conflict that bureaucratic confusion complicated war management. Something of that same confusion beset far-flung military commands. That fragmentation, though, produced something like reverse cohesion, so that in the U.S. by 1944, war had become a familiar entity with demands, attitudes, and powers that tended to co-opt its managers.

726 **Politics ranked high among the things first affected in 1944.** President Roosevelt's skill in charming people from the hustings did not carry over to relations with Congress. Democrats from farm areas hated New Deal "plow under" agricultural policies. Many Republicans nursed an old hatred of anything that smelled of the New Deal. Adroit themselves in congressional maneuvering, the conservatives forged a marriage of convenience with Southern Democrats—who resented the New Deal's catering to blacks in new federal agencies. This combination proved strong enough to stymie most of FDR's liberal social programs, strong enough, even, to roll back some legislation already enacted and to deny the tax levels Treasury thought the war demanded.

727 **These pickings at old wounds finally wore down the president's patience.** He devised a marvelously bureaucratic way to buffer himself. In the previous

Victory cargo ships (these mass-produced American freighters were later versions of the Liberty ships) line up at a U.S. West Coast shipyard before being loaded with supplies for navy depots and advance bases in the Pacific, 1944.

year he had created the Office of War Mobilization (OWM) to coordinate all government agencies involved in the war effort and named as its director James F. Byrnes, former senator from South Carolina. Fred Vinson, former congressman, moved up to replace Byrnes as head of the Office of Economic Stabilization. FDR chose Marvin Jones to be war food administrator. These three appointments showed that the president had not lost his political sense—though they were moderate Democrats, the triumvirate kept good congressional relations. FDR had, essentially, shifted responsibility for domestic political and economic matters. Byrnes proved so effective that he became virtually a deputy president. Congressmen found it politically dangerous to balk Roosevelt's war measures.

Veterans affairs became a vital issue for Congress. Several early administration efforts to enact veterans benefits bills had either been defeated outright or talked to death. Late in 1943, though, FDR tried again. By early 1944 so many veterans were looming on the horizon that a definitely New Dealish measure won solid approval in June—**728** **the Servicemen's Readjustment Act, popularly called the GI Bill of Rights.** A remarkably sweeping law, it provided liberal education allowances, readjustment payments, and low interest housing loans—and it changed the whole structure of America's higher education.

Women, too, followed money, and by 1944 they came to have a veteranlike importance as they moved into many formerly male jobs all over the country. By 1944 women comprised over 35 percent of the labor force. Becoming aware of an entirely new power in their hands, they intended to have large voices for the future.

729 **Unlike Great Britain, the U.S. did not have to coerce people into war work.** It simply never became necessary since good wages provided effective lures. Employment peaked early in 1944 at more than ten and a half million jobs—a growth of six million in three years.

730 **FDR and especially his socially conscious wife Eleanor tried valiantly to advance the cause of blacks.** But the time had not come, despite the persistence and power of the Roosevelts. Blacks were paid equally in war industries and in government jobs and their wages in general increased, but they still suffered

Brigadier General Benjamin Oliver Davis, the first black soldier to hold the rank of general (Oct. 1940), watching a Signal Corps crew at work in France, August 8, 1944. He served as adviser on race relations in the European theater.

last-hired, first-fired dangers, and not just in the South. Housing discrimination in such worker intensive cities as Detroit had led to a race riot in 1943, and to lesser protests in Mobile, Alabama, and Beaumont, Texas.

731 **For a long time America had been known as a "nation of tinkerers."** Although original inventions had certainly been produced here, the U.S. had lagged behind the industrial and scientific achievements of Europe and Britain. War changed that situation drastically. While it was no surprise that U.S. industrial power could produce masses of things, now American ingenuity took on sophisticated and scientific dimensions. Take, for instance, machine tools. Demand far exceeded supply in 1940, especially since the tools were complicated to make and workers were untrained to make them. Engineers simply designed simpler tools that nearly trained their users.

732 Engineers colluded with physicists to provide new tools of war; their teamwork produced and improved the radio-guided proximity fuze, which exploded when it received a preset frequency from a target. Chemists and industrialists cooperated in the mass production of aviation gasoline. University researchers finally devised acceptable synthetic rubber. Advances came, too, in chemical warfare weaponry, and by 1944 the U.S. had made great strides in the military uses of germs and biological warfare. **733** Only the Japanese and perhaps the Polish underground attempted tactical use of such weapons.

During the year, the Manhattan Project expanded exponentially. The Los Alamos, New Mexico, laboratory's scientific staff continued to grow, and large plants were at work in Oak Ridge, Tennessee, and Richland, Washington.

734 Government cooperated with industry in myriad ways—even spilling over into subsidizing production. Big automobile manufacturers retooled for war, shifting assembly lines from auto bodies to tanks and planes. Such a massive changeover cost astounding amounts of money. Knowing the problems these companies would face, the government stepped in and built Ford a huge plant at Willow Run, west of Detroit, and built Dodge a large engine works in Chicago.

735 War news throughout the year had been almost astoundingly good. This produced mixed reactions. The public now began to focus on "after the war," which tended to make the war itself less urgent; it also raised expectations of better living and caused some unhappiness with things as they were. **736** At the same time, a growing certainty of victory relieved everyone and made FDR's campaign for a remarkable fourth term a snap. He defeated Republican Thomas E. Dewey by 53.4 percent of ballots cast and swamped him in the electoral college.

THE WAR
IN EASTERN EUROPE
ALLIED GAINS IN EUROPE
(July 1943 – May 1945)
LEND-LEASE ROUTES TO RUSSIA
FINNISH CAMPAIGN OF 1944

0   100 200 300 400 500 600
SCALE OF MILES

By the end of the year optimism spilled toward joy. The nation boasted an army of seven and a half million men plus a navy of nearly three million engaged in the great crusade for freedom.

737 **Desertion is an endemic military condition.** Men (and women) depart ranks for all kinds of reasons. The United States has taken a largely liberal attitude toward it, save in wartime when the death penalty can come into play. Still, only one U.S. soldier has been executed for wartime desertion since 1864.

On November 11, 1944, Pvt. Ernie Slovik's court-martial sentenced him to death. General Eisenhower confirmed the verdict and President Roosevelt did not intervene. Slovik's case still rankles the military conscience, because he was judged "very poor combat material," had been classified 4F (disqualified) for the draft and then shifted to 1-A, and also because the whole U.S. Army had 6.3 percent desertion levels in 1944.

During the war the U.S. counted 40,000 deserters (the charge was usually changed to Absent Without Leave); the British had more than 100,000 deserters during the war. Germany's deserters amounted to 35,000, of which 15,000 were executed.

Soviet Armies were riddled with desertion—one in sixteen Red Army POWs had actually left their units.

DIPLOMACY

738 **As the Allies moved toward victory, they began serious consideration of a postwar world.** Outlines of a world peace organization had been discussed in the Atlantic Charter (August 1941), the Four-Power Declaration (signed at the Moscow Conference of October 1943), and at the Tehran Conference (November-December 1943). Representatives of the U.S., the U.K., China, and the Soviet Union gathered at an estate named Dumbarton Oaks near Washington, D.C., and in various sessions held

from August 21 to October 7, 1944, thrashed out some key issues crossing the path of what would become the United Nations. The Soviets plumped for the veto power for all of their republics, to general disagreement, but a compromise scheme called **739** **the Dumbarton Oaks Plan that posited a peace-keeping agency and promotion of world economic and social stability won approval.** This conference proved an important intermediary step in the history of the United Nations because its proposals shaped much discussion at the San Francisco Conference in 1945.

740 **A follow-up conference at Bretton Woods, New Hampshire, July 1–22, 1944, worked on postwar financial and monetary cooperation.** From it came the beginnings of the World Bank and the International Monetary Fund.

ALLIED WESTERN BATTLES, 1944

741 **As 1944 opened, all operations in Italy were hamstrung by preparations for the upcoming Allied invasion of France.** Still, General Alexander, showing the optimism of ambition, felt that the German decision to fight south of Rome offered a real opportunity. Allied drives against rail lines supporting Nazi positions might lure Kesselring into wasting battles to save his communications. Sound strategy is often ruined by reality. Sadly for Alexander, the Combined Chiefs of Staff transferred seven of his veteran divisions to England for Overlord, and replacements were still training; shipping for a possible flank landing behind main enemy positions ran scarce, again because of Overlord.

With prospects as bleak as the mountains blocking the front, Lt. Gen. Mark W. Clark's attack to reach the Liri Valley route to Rome started at 0550, January 5, 1944. Streaks of sunshine allowed air cover for the early stages of battle, but conditions worsened. Intense, brutal, close combat for a series

Field marshals Wolfram von Richthofen (far right) and Albert Kesselring at a forward command post, Nettuno sector, near Anzio, Italy, 1944.

of mountain positions inched the Allied lines forward beyond San Pietro to San Vittore, Casale, Mount Majo, Mount LaChiaia, and Cedro Hill. On January 15 the U.S. II Corps attacked Mount Trocchio, to find it abandoned as the Germans retired behind the Rapido River and into the main defenses of the Gustav Line.

742 Alexander reorganized his front, pulled in some Moroccans and New Zealanders (the Germans labeled these the Allies' best), and the French Expeditionary Corps under Lt. Gen. Alphonse Juin, an able, experienced officer whose stubborn defense of Lille probably made Dunkirk possible. Several U.S. divisions were sent to rest areas—winter fighting in the mountains had worn down men, animals (mule pack trains were used to move supplies in rugged alpine combat), guns, everything.

743 Sobered and aware that breaking the Gustav Line would involve a bloody and massive effort, Alexander re-

vived the idea of an amphibious landing behind enemy lines at Anzio. He had to beg for minimum shipping—he had almost complete air superiority—but in late January won approval for the operation which might flank Kesselring's lines and open the way to Rome; failing that, the attack might possibly drain German reserves and ease the way for troops attacking the city of Cassino at the base of a huge massif at the junction of the Rapido and Liri Rivers, key to the Gustav Line. General Clark planned to resume attacking toward Monte Cassino to split Gen. Heinrich von Vietinghoff's German Tenth Army reserves, once the Anzio landings began.

Clark's first assault on Monte Cassino did not go well, although the X Corps stormed the Garigliano in fine style on January 17, 1944. By the twentieth it had attracted Vietinghoff's reserves and much trouble. **744** That day the U.S. 36th Division (mainly Texans) made a poorly organized try to cross the Rapido River below Cassino and was bloodily repulsed (the Texans never forgave Clark).

745 U.S. Maj. Gen. John P. Lucas took his 6th Corps to a virtually unopposed landing at Anzio early in the morning of January 22, 1944. Surprised, Kesselring, who had expected some kind of amphibious try, rushed reserves from the north and from quiet parts of the Gustav Line. Lucas stopped to organize and suddenly found himself stuck on the beach with enemy fire coming from three directions. He could not advance and Clark could not reach him.

When bad weather interfered with Allied air and naval support on February 15, elements of the German Fourteenth Army launched a massive attack on Lucas's positions and all but eliminated the beachhead. German follow-up came in slow dribbles. Lu-

155mm gun ("Long Tom") fired by U.S. troops, Nettuno, Italy, February 13, 1944.

cas counterattacked on the nineteenth and stabilized his front. Both sides began fortifying.

746 Clark's desperate efforts to relieve his expected relievers by attacking Cassino and its overlooking Monastery Hill (the hill often called Monte Cassino) produced nothing but blood and woe. This first Battle of Monte Cassino cost Clark sixteen thousand casualties for an advance of barely seven miles, with no major objectives taken. Another assault would be equally difficult, likely as costly, and of questionable value.

747 General Alexander, though, decided to press on and for the next venture turned to Gen. Bernard Freyberg's New Zealand Corps in the British Eighth Army. Scheduled for February 15, this second Battle of Monte Cassino would be launched by the 2nd New Zealand Division and the 4th Indian Division. The 4th's commanding officer worried that the monastery—first built by Saint Benedict in A.D. 520—sheltered German troops and wanted it destroyed. Clark objected, saying that ruins would be easy to defend; others objected that destruction of the monastery would bring worldwide condemnation, but Freyberg and Alexander insisted. Warning leaflets were dropped over the mountain on February 14, and on the fifteenth Allied planes dropped 576 tons of bombs on the ancient building and courtyards.

748 Nothing survived the bombing save Saint Benedict's cell and his tomb—a small salve to the faithful.

Later it would be known that the Germans had promised the Vatican that they would not use the monastery, and kept their word—though they used it after the bombing! The abbot, monks, and many refugees were killed. **749 General Clark's prediction came true as panzer grenadiers and paratroopers swarmed the ruins and rained deadly fire on anyone daring to come up the hill.**

Predictions of world condemnation also came true.

Forebodings of failure were confirmed as the New Zealanders and Indians were stopped cold. Although Alexander tried a third attack on Monte Cassino, the campaign had clearly collapsed as the Germans continued their rain of death from the hill.

750 Reinforced and reinvigorated, Alexander now plotted Operation Diadem, a maximum effort to destroy Kesselring's whole command and take Rome. A good plan envisioned the VI Corps breaking out of the Anzio beaches toward Valmontone as the Fifth Army came up the coast to join the British Eighth Army driving inland toward Valmontone, neatly pocketing enemy forces.

On May 11, 1944, American, British, and French units attacked with considerable success, Polish troops taking Cassino on the eighteenth. Breaking out of Anzio on the twenty-third, VI Corps moved toward Valmontone and on the twenty-fifth met elements of the Fifth Army as Alexander's trap threatened to close around Kesselring.

751 Glory hungry Clark suddenly decided to deviate from the entrapment plan and make a surge to take Rome as he aimed northwest. Deft rearguard actions stalled Clark just long enough to insure Tenth Army's escape. Consolation came to Clark as his troops entered Rome on June 4, 1944, and the first Axis capital to be captured welcomed its conquerors in ecstasy. Two days later Overlord started.

Smaller, largely uncoordinated operations tied down German divisions, and partisan efforts sapped their strength. Still, at the end of 1944 the Germans held most of northern Italy. The question lingers: Did results in Italy justify the cost of 188,000 Fifth Army casualties, 123,000 for the Eighth, against enemy losses of some 400,000?

May 1944, men of Gen. Wladyslaw Anders' 2nd Polish Corps using grenades in the mountains above Cassino. In April 1945, Anders' army took Bologna in the last major battle of the Italian campaign.

Normandy landings, June 1944. American landing ships unload while engineers clear the beaches and prepare routes inland. Overhead barrage balloons provide defense against low-flying aircraft.

752 **A morning radio announcement on June 6, 1944: "Under the command of General Eisenhower, Allied naval forces, supported by strong air forces, began landing Allied armies this morning on the northern coast of France."** No one quite knew how it would go. Ike himself nursed cautious optimism but some of the staff bit their nails in worry. Certainly portents ran bad enough. Weather in the English Channel area went from bad to terrible in early June—gale force winds whirled huge waves, and naval units, landing craft, and auxiliary vessels gyrated violently while a vast gathered host grew seasick—some troops said that nothing could be worse, bring on the Germans!

753 **A mighty armada, one to dwarf Spain's, wallowed, waiting for the word to go.** Fifty-three hundred vessels of all sizes, shapes, and purposes waited to take 150,000 troops, 1,500 tanks, and many thousands of vehicles across the English Channel.

All waited on a decision from Ike: when? Consulting his meteorological staff, checking with unit commanders about morale among the waiting and with his air staff about possibilities, the Supreme Commander, Allied Expeditionary Force, finally consulted himself. Conditions on June 4 made going impossible, but weather experts prophesied a thirty-six-hour break, starting on June 6. Ike decided to go. Overlord began, and a great ironsided engine of men, machines, guns, and landing craft, all covered by a canopy of planes, began a measured, intricately choreographed surge toward France. Some on the ships thought of Shakespeare's words:

He that outlives this day and comes safe home,
Will stand a tip-toe when this day is named. . . .
And gentlemen in England, now a-bed
Shall think themselves accursed they were not
here.

A New York radio station told of the invasion at 3:32 A.M. and read Ike's Order of the Day: "The tide has turned. The free men of the world are marching together to victory." Not long after, the president led Americans in prayer: "Almighty God: Our sons, pride of our Nation, this day have set out upon a mighty endeavor, a struggle to preserve our Republic, our religion, and our civilization and to set free a suffering humanity. . . ." **754 By then, Ike had settled into lonesome, anguished waiting—with two messages ready, one for success, another for failure.**

In that waiting time he could think back over past hectic months of planning, gathering the myriad needs of war together and organizing those awesome sprawls of people and things so that they would move out and arrive together at the right place to meet the enemy.

755 Planning had begun right after Dunkirk, with Mountbatten heading a small planning staff which expanded and changed commanders in the spring of 1943. **756 British Lt. Gen. Frederick Morgan, who became Chief of Staff to the Supreme Allied Commander (COSSAC), added some more people to the planning group, opened a London office, and tried to stick a plan together without knowing who the supreme commander would be, and without knowing how many men, how much shipping, air assets, or naval support might be available.** Dedicated, tireless, easy to work with, Morgan virtually performed miracles in his year of uncertainty. Later, Ike would say that Morgan made D-day possible. He collected a talented group of staff officers expert in all military fields and orchestrated their work artistically. Originality sparked most planning. **757 Intelligence people created a huge fictional Allied army group somewhere in north England, ostensibly commanded by General Patton.** The German general staff bit on this diversion because Patton's daring made him just the man for such a command. Morgan himself conjured the idea of huge floating docks ("mulberries") to solve supply delivery problems in the first days of invasion.

758 Zeal and cunning kept the actual invasion date and place amazingly obscure. German agents picked up bits and pieces—carefully planted hints—of the place (Hitler actually guessed it), but fragmented spy reports and inadequate air observation—there were only 119 Luftwaffe fighters in the whole Channel area—created a miasma of uncertainty in the Nazi defense command.

Most of these activities were underway when General Eisenhower established Supreme Headquarters Allied Expeditionary Force (SHAEF) at a country place not far from London. By the first week in January 1944, when the doors opened, some operations had just started—bombing of bridges, rail yards, industrial sites, and German gun emplacements all across northern France had the dual purpose of tactical destruction and also diversion, since many targets were picked to convince enemy observers that the planes were softening up the Pas de Calais for landings. **759 The real objective would be a sixty-mile swath in the Baie de la Seine sector where five Normandy beaches, designated west to east Utah, Omaha, Gold, Juno, and Sword, offered some housekeeping room, and Utah lay within striking distance of Cherbourg with its needed port.** Heavy bombers aimed deep into Germany, attacking oil reserves, factories, and lines of communication.

Several times the previous year General Morgan noted that he had planned around a three-division attack, an entirely inadequate number. Force structure became a major concern and ideas shifted with numbers. **760 The decision came to use five divisions, two British, two American, one Canadian, for across-the-beach assaults; one British and two U.S. airborne divisions would secure the flanks by going in first.**

Much depended on separate smaller forces completing their special tasks, and on the active help of the French resistance, whose large numbers in northern France had been aided by arms and information from the SOE.

The whole venture all spread on the map for Ike as he waited for first words from the paratroops and from naval units about the greatest bombardment from sea to shore in history. Planning had been superb, but plans are ever hostage to battle. First words were mixed.

More than 23,000 paratroopers and glider men sailed to the flanks, missed their landing sites, and landed dispersed and confused. **761 Major General Maxwell Taylor, CO of the 101st Airborne Division, dropped in to find a corporal's guard of soldiers and quipped, "Never have so few been commanded by so many."** Regrouped, the flank guards held out and were relieved during the day.

762 News got better and better, and by nightfall Ike knew the invasion had succeeded—more than 130,000 men were in France at a cost of 9,000 casualties, far fewer than feared. Never had there been a day like it nor a venture to match. Even Stalin stood in awe of Ike's achievement. "The history of warfare," he said, "knows no other undertaking from the point of view of its scale, its vast conception, and its masterly execution."

Though the Allies held some eighty miles of French territory, they were cramped in a relatively small space for handling the massive supplies designed to sustain them. Breaking out posed problems. Easy enough, probably, to get off the beaches, but just beyond loomed the *bocage* country of Normandy, crisscrossed by dense hedgerows. In all the meticulous planning the resistance potential of hedgerows had not been calculated, and it definitely helped the Germans.

763 For the Germans, though, nearly everything went wrong on D-day. With troops fixed in remote positions, the normally nimble Nazis' recovery time had been slow, fragmented, and confused. In addition, there was the weather, which at least in this case had been impartial in hostility. Field Marshal Rommel, who commanded ground forces in the invasion area, thinking the lousy weather would preclude any invasion, had gone to Berlin to beg for more panzers and artillery and to make one more plea to let local commanders make command decisions—Rommel's superior, Field Marshal Rundstedt, commanding the West (*Oberbefehlshaber West*), could not move divisions without the Führer's permission!

764 When reports of the invasion arrived, neither Rundstedt nor Gen. Alfred Jodl, chief of staff, reacted swiftly—this might be a diversion, the real invasion would come elsewhere. Several coastal command generals were also missing that day. No one dared wake Hitler, who was asleep when the news arrived; when he got the word in the afternoon, he guessed it was another Dieppe sortie and told Rundstedt to throw the raiders into the sea.

Even when local commanders got things right and directed reserves toward the front, strong French resistance units (helped by SOE) deranged Nazi communications, wrecked railroads, cut phone lines, and attacked troop convoys.

765 A deep strategic disagreement fractured German command. Rommel, who had come to France in November 1943 as inspector general of coastal defenses, had made herculean efforts to shore up weaknesses with four million mines, half a million various tank and landing craft impediments, even with what became known as "Rommel's asparagus"—stakes connected by barbed wire, often tipped with mines or shells. He believed the Allies must be stopped at the beaches as opposed to Rundstedt, who accepted the classic idea of keeping mobile reserves some distance inland. Rommel's experience in Africa and his knowledge of Allied landing tactics in Sicily and Italy convinced him that their total control of the air would wipe out mobile German reserves. **766 On June 17, both men argued their ideas to Hitler who made the worst**

First Allied airborne paratroopers descend on Holland during the Netherlands invasion (Market-Garden), September 1944.

possible decision—a compromise that split reserves and confused commanders. Nor did he delegate any tactical authority. The field marshals' best hope rested in holding the enemy in the hedgerows as long as possible while getting heavy armor into battle.

Anguished, Rundstedt and Rommel met Hitler again at Berchtesgaden on the twenty-ninth. Rommel, struggling for civility, finally asked the Führer how he thought the war could still be won. Hitler sacked Rundstedt again on July 1 and Rommel got a stern lecture on defeatism after he sent a memo implying the need for surrender. **767 On July 17, Rommel's staff car was attacked by British planes; critically wounded, hospitalized, he recovered in time to hear that he had been accidentally implicated in the July 20 attempt on Hitler's life at the Führer's East Prussian headquarters at Rastenburg.** Given the choice of execution and public disgrace for his family or suicide, family protection, and a state funeral, Rommel took poison October 14, 1944. By that time his predictions had come all too true.

Airpower controlled most of the battlefields as the Allies fought out of Normandy; captured Caen, Cherbourg, and Brest; after that they landed an army group in the south of France; opened the port of Marseille; nearly trapped the northern group of German armies in the Falaise pocket; suffered the

Oscar Hammerstein II and Jerome Kern (1941):

"THE LAST TIME I SAW PARIS"

*The last time I saw Paris, her heart was warm
and gay,
I heard the laughter of her heart in every street
café.*

*The last time I saw Paris, her trees were
dressed for spring,
And lovers walked beneath those trees and
birds found songs to sing.*

*I dodged the same old taxi cabs that I had
dodged for years.
The chorus of their squeaky horns was music
to my ears.*

*The last time I saw Paris, her heart was warm
and gay,
No matter how they change her, I'll remember
her that way.*

first attacks of "secret weapons," liberated Paris (in August), then the rest of France; were stopped bloodily for a time near Arnhem in Monty's failed Operation Market-Garden, and were advancing into the Reich from Arnhem to Belfort.

768 **The Allies had strategic disagreements of their own.** Eisenhower, who is occasionally criticized still for overcaution, favored a broad front attack across Europe to the Rhine. He thought that pressing the Germans along a wide front would prevent sectored reinforcement and strain their logistics. This strategy would also give Allied airpower full sweep and make best use of superior numbers.

General Montgomery, for a time in command of ground operations, favored a pencil-like thrust of his army group straight for Berlin. He thought this strategy would not only take Hitler's capital but also take

the heart out of Germany and bring swift victory. Ike was probably right but arguments continue.

769 **Serious disagreements also erupted between British advocates of general area night bombing of German cities and American proponents of daylight "precision" strategic bombing.** The differences persisted as the saturation bombing of Germany began in February 1944.

770 **Logistical concerns led Eisenhower to keep pressing for a landing in southern France.** Cherbourg's port facilities were wrecked by the retreating Germans and out of service for months; Caen, too, had been savaged. Having Antwerp would help but the Germans fought to keep it. Marseilles seemed essential to the Supreme Allied Commander. On August 15, 1944, Operation Dragoon (previously called Anvil) began as U.S. general Jacob Devers's Sixth Army Group landed in southern France with much help from the French *maquis* and other resistance units. Marseille and Toulon fell on August 28, and Devers's U.S. Seventh and French First Armies started up the Rhone River, hoping to link up with Gen. Omar Bradley's Twelfth Army Group and trap the enemy caught between.

The Germans largely escaped, but Devers's advance eased Ike's logistical problems and protected his right flank while threatening the enemy's left at Cannes.

771 **Few events in the war attracted as much sentimental attention as the liberation of Paris.** For Eisenhower and his staff, Paris loomed as a military inconvenience. It would have comported more with higher strategy to go on around Paris in direct pursuit of retreating Germans than to get stuck feeding four million Parisians, but some symbols matter more than others. Paris mattered a great deal more—not just to Frenchmen but also to the millions worldwide on whom Paris had worked its enduring charms.

Eisenhower specifically ordered French general

ABOVE: U.S. 60th Infantry Regiment troops advancing under protection of a heavy tank, Belgium, September 1944.
BELOW: Nijmegen, Holland, was hit by both German and Allied bombardments during the Netherlands invasion, September 1944.

Pierre Koenig, heading the formidable French Forces of the Interior (FFI), to permit no uprisings in Paris or anywhere else without his personal orders. **772 De Gaulle, behind Ike's back, ordered Koenig to free the capital as soon as possible and instructed Gen. Jacques Leclerc, leading a French division under Ike, to ignore other orders and march to Paris.** Mixed orders resulted in the Metropolitan Police going on strike and three thousand of them seizing police headquarters on August 19, building barricades and shooting Germans. **773 Hitler reacted by ordering Paris destroyed, but the local Nazi commander, Gen. Dietrich von Choltitz, aided by the Swedish consul general, Raoul Nordling, negotiated a surrender that let him get his men out of an undestroyed city.**

Reluctantly, Ike accepted reality. Leclerc's armored division and the U.S. 4th Infantry Division marched in and formally accepted Choltitz's surren-

der. The next day General de Gaulle made an imperial entrance to thunderous cries of "Vive de Gaulle." To the French he said, "These are moments which surpass every one of our poor lives."

De Gaulle embodied France's image of itself. It was his persistent, nearly monolithic belief that made others believe in France. His greatness rose from a deep-struck love of his country. And it came, too, from a knowledge in his heart that what his countrymen needed most in their despairing time was a return of Gallic grandeur. He gave them grandeur in defeat when he called for war, when he shouldered the burdens of succoring a nation, when he made that nation a power in the Grand Alliance, when he provoked Churchill's comment that "of all the crosses I have had to bear, the heaviest has been the Cross of Lorraine," which de Gaulle accepted as a compliment to France. *Le Grand Charles* gave his

De Gaulle's triumphant return to Paris, the Champs Elysées, August 26, 1944. The Arc de Triomphe is in the background.

Parisians line the Champs Elysées, August 29, 1944, welcoming the American infantry units marching toward the Arc de Triomphe.

countrymen special glory that day when he spoke as he arrived in Paris and the old flags waved and *gloire* filled the air.

774 On June 13, the first of Hitler's *Vergeltungswaffen* (reprisal weapons), a V-1 "buzz bomb," landed on England. The Führer repeatedly boasted that at the right moment he would snatch victory with secret weapons such as these unmanned small guided monoplanes which sputtered and shrieked in flight. At some point their motors shut off and when the eerie silence came, people dove for shelter. Made mostly of wood and steel, they carried 150 gallons of gas plus a ton of explosive that blew up on impact. Visible in the air, they wracked nerves, but the damage they caused was bearable. Thousands of these rockets were dispatched, but many were shot down by spotter volunteers' antiaircraft and an alerted RAF. One

of the first rockets launched nearly got Hitler when it went off course! He had thought of targeting the invasion buildup in England, but, with a fanatic's denial of reality, went back to targeting London, whose population, he knew, would finally break and demand peace.

775 The later V-2s, much larger and deadlier than V-1s, were true guided rockets. Liquid oxygen fueled, they flew above the earth's atmosphere and weighed in at fourteen tons, with a payload of one ton.

At year's end U.S. troops had taken Aachen, the first German city. The Allies in the West concentrated some of their armies to pierce the Rhine while others drove at the Po River in Italy, and Tito's Yugoslav partisans systematically consumed Nazi units in the strange, wild, disorganized carnage that typified the Balkan wars.

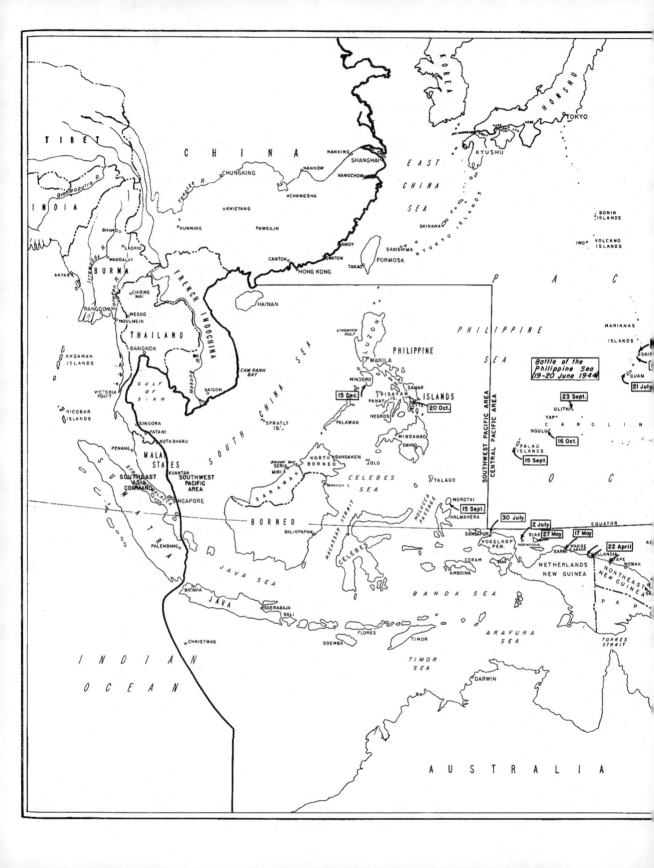

LANDINGS IN THE GILBERT ISLANDS,
21 NOVEMBER 1943 AND OPERATIONS
IN THE CENTRAL AND SOUTHWEST PACIFIC
AREAS, JANUARY—DECEMBER 1944

| 0 | 200 | 400 | 600 | 800 |
SCALE OF MILES

MARCUS

F I C

WAKE

17 Feb.1944

ENIWETOK

M A R S H A L L

WOTJE

31 Jan. 1944

KWAJALEIN

MALEOLAP

MAJURO

ISLANDS

MILI

TRUK

PONAPE

JALUIT

MAKIN

21 Nov.1943

GILBERT

TARAWA

ISLANDS

A N

NAURU

CENTRAL PACIFIC AREA

SOUTHWEST PACIFIC SOUTH PACIFIC
AREA

MATTHIAS

20 Mar.

NEW
IRELAND

ELLICE
ISLANDS

GREEN

15 Feb. 1944

RABAUL

BOUGAINVILLE

SOLOMON

RITAIN

ISLANDS

RUSSELL

GUADALCANAL

SOLOMON SEA

SANTA CRUZ
ISLANDS

MILNE
BAY

A L

ESPIRITU SANTO

NEW
HEBRIDES

NEW
CALEDONIA

Final refueling and adjustment of controls of a V-2 ballistic rocket. Most of the V-2s were built by using forced labor from the Mittelbau concentration camp working in a huge underground factory at Nordhausen.

U.S. First Army soldier wearing new snow cape, Belgium, December 1944. White rags are wrapped around the rifle barrel for additional camouflage.

Pathfinder unit, 101st Airborne, setting up radar equipment near Bastogne, Belgium, December 23, 1944.

UNITED STATES/JAPANESE PACIFIC BATTLES, 1944

776 By New Year's 1944, the Allies in the Far East faced an embarrassment of riches. They had discovered and developed island-hopping, the right tactics to beat the Japanese; they needed only to settle on the strategy. Strategically they were pursuing two options: MacArthur's leapfrog campaign along New Guinea's northern coast as he jumped closer to the Philippines, and Admiral Nimitz's island-grabbing drive across the Central Pacific, starting with the Gilberts and moving on to the Marshalls and Carolines, as he, too, aimed at the Philippines. In order to support the new, big B-29 Superfortress bombers on Philippine and Japan raids, the Joint Chiefs of Staff in Washington debated for a time whether or not to push a China landing so that airfields could be built. **777** Admiral King wanted to skip the Philippines and hit Formosa directly, arguing that was the quickest way to Japan itself. MacArthur urged a strike at the island of Leyte in the Philippines as a key base for several roads to Tokyo—

On tour in the Hawaiian Islands in 1944, President Roosevelt in conference with General MacArthur (in profile), Admiral Nimitz (standing at the map), and Admiral Leahy.

USS *Iowa* firing her sixteen-inch guns during a battle drill in the Pacific. The *Iowa* carried President Roosevelt to and from the Casablanca Conference in 1943 before being sent to the Pacific in early 1944.

plus the fact that he could then fulfill his promise to return.

778 **President Roosevelt tried to compromise by agreeing with both ideas, which proved impractical, and he finally supported MacArthur.** As air and ground assets went to MacArthur, Admiral Halsey's task force came under his operational control and led the right wing of the upcoming campaign.

779 **Beginning by harassing enemy units retreating from Lae and Salamaua, MacArthur leapfrogged to Saidor (it had a good airfield) and in April left the starving, increasingly desperate Japanese remnants to Australian clearing battalions.** Now in control of the New Guinea coast, MacArthur kept pressure on New Britain by attacking Cape Gloucester. There the reinforced 1st Marine Division fought the elements and Japanese in about equal doses as, by March, they established a solid front across the island. The enemy withdrew northeastward toward their great staging base at Rabaul, fighting as they went. By year's end the Japanese were literally penned in around Rabaul, on the northern tip of the island. Rabaul had been further isolated by Admiral Halsey's landings on Green

Island in February; then he pushed on to the north and west to take several small isles that threatened to surround the bombed and battered enemy base.

To close the ring, MacArthur pondered a skip to the Admiralty Islands in February. Air reconnaissance indicated only a tiny garrison left, but U.S. Intelligence estimated that some four thousand enemy troops were in place. **780** **The general, in typical swashbuckling fashion, went with a 1,000-man scouting party to Manus Island on February 29, to find that Intelligence had been right.** Instead of pulling out, MacArthur told the scouting party to hold on while he organized reinforcements. Quickly overrunning the Admiralties, MacArthur directed a brilliant shift back to New Guinea in April, seized Aitape with Hollandia, then hopped to Wakde and Biak in May, and Noemfoor Island in July; later that month Vogelkop Peninsula fell to the Allies, leaving trapped the Eighteenth Japanese Army and completing New Guinea's conquest. By September, MacArthur's advance reached Morotai, just about three hundred miles southeast of Mindanao Island in the Philippines.

Soldier beside his tank named "Killer," on which a captured Japanese light tank is mounted, Kwajalein, February 2, 1944.

U.S. 7th Division troops using flamethrowers, Kwajalein, February 4, 1944. These devices usually consisted of canisters of flamethrowing fluid (thickened gasoline) and a tank of pressurized nitrogen that would propel the liquid flame about fifty yards; they were an excellent and much feared means of flushing out the enemy.

Navajo communications men, Saipan, June 1944. Some three hundred Navajo "code-talkers" served with the Marines in the Pacific. Using a code based on the Navajo language (unintelligible to the Japanese), they could send messages without time lost enciphering and deciphering. This was especially helpful during amphibious assault operations.

781 Swinging the right wing of the general Allied push in a hook through the Marshall Islands, taking Kwajalein in a model amphibious landing on February 1, 1944, Nimitz, in June, moved toward Guam, Tinian, and Saipan in the Marianas. Japan's other great central Pacific base, Truk, had been completely isolated.

782 The 530 ships and 127,000 men of Adm. Raymond Spruance's fleet put two Marine divisions ashore on Saipan, June 15, 1944. A big island, some fourteen miles long, it had the usual depressing appearance to the attackers—broad beaches, tangled undergrowth inland, high hills overlooking landing areas, ridges honeycombed with caves, cliffs, all enhanced by massed mortars. No one knew exactly how many Japanese held the island, but guesses ran high—the island ranked as a major base. There were 77,000 men in Marine lieutenant general Holland M. ("Howlin' Mad") Smith's V Amphibious Corps; bitter experience had taught the need of overwhelming force in Pacific island operations. U.S. experience would quickly get even more bitter.

783 Lieutenant General Yoshitsugo Saito's Thirty-first Army boasted thirty-two thousand highly confident men, bafflingly entrenched or hidden. They expected to hold the Americans on the beaches until the Japanese Mobile Fleet arrived to annihilate enemy beachheads and transports. They nearly succeeded.

No sooner were they on the way to shore behind an inadequate naval bombardment than the Yanks ran into the hottest fire of the whole campaign; the three days allotted to conquering the island became mere whimsy. Had the missing Japanese fleet arrived—it was busy elsewhere, losing the Battle of the Philippine Sea—Smith probably would have been badly beaten, for in the first forty-eight hours he took four thousand casualties. Chillingly accurate mortar fire scoured every bit of shelter as men were hurt and killed and freight disintegrated until most of the landing area looked like a sodden, rusty scrap heap.

Finally, when the fleet failed to arrive, defenders fell back to the island's interior and dug in.

Inching ahead behind their artillery, Marines and GIs took a pile of rubble called Garapan, Saipan's main town. Using satchel charges and flamethrowers they dug defenders from caves and crevices under a constant cacophony of shells, machine guns, mortars, grenades, the cries of human agony.

784 On the night July 6–7, 1944, Saito's remnants launched the war's biggest banzai charge into sheets of American fire. With the end near, General Saito knelt in his command cave. Shouting "Hurrah for the emperor," he committed hara-kiri. Admiral Nagumo (q.v.), leader at Pearl Harbor, who commanded small craft at Saipan, shot himself.

785 On July 9, the last day of resistance, hundreds of Japanese civilians, who had hidden in caves on Saipan's northern coast, showed their special sense of honor. "In one of the war's most dreadful episodes," writes one historian, mothers and fathers shot, stabbed, and strangled their children, and threw babies over the cliffs; the women combed their hair and then, with their husbands, jumped over or blew themselves up with grenades.

Another Saipan tragedy: of Saito's 32,000 de-

fenders, only 2,068 surrendered. American losses were high: 3,126 killed, 326 missing, 13,160 wounded, for a total of 16,612.

786 The U.S. Fifth Fleet's appearance off Saipan triggered a major Japanese naval reaction. Admiral Soemu Toyoda, commander in chief of the Imperial Fleet, had planned Operation A-Go which would hand the U.S. naval forces attacking Saipan a climactic defeat. Giving the honor of victory to Vice Adm. Jizaburo Ozawa's Mobile Fleet, Toyoda echoed Adm. Heihachiro Togo's order before the victory over the Russians at Tsushima in 1905: "The fate of the Empire rests on this one battle. Everyone must give all he has."

787 Ozawa led a formidable force in search of a "decisive" battle—nine carriers, among them the new armor-decked *Taiho;* 473 carrier aircraft; five battleships, thirteen cruisers; thirty-three destroyers. Poorly trained pilots and the fact that unrefined Borneo fuel filled the tanks of some ships were the fleet's weaknesses. Although outnumbered in every ship category save heavy cruisers (eleven to eight) and almost doubled in planes, Ozawa counted on ground-based aircraft from Tinian and Guam to counterbalance his air inferiority.

Admiral Spruance knew all about A-Go and foiled the first part of it by not rushing to intercept the Japanese. He waited on their next moves as he delegated the coming action to Adm. Marc Mitscher's Task Force 58. Twenty-five Japanese submarines skirmished with Spruance's vanguard; seventeen soon were lost.

788 At 0830 June 19, 1944, the greatest carrier battle of the war began. Ozawa found himself in serious trouble from his first launch of 197 planes. U.S. bombs had already destroyed most of his expected land-based air support; the battle suddenly depended on his hastily trained naval aviators. At 10:00 A.M., "bogeys" appeared on U.S. radar, and started what

Americans would call the "Great Marianas Turkey Shoot."

789 **None of the Japanese bombers and fighters sent to sink U.S. carriers reached them and in really a matter of minutes 45 of the 69 attackers were destroyed.** That terrible ratio continued all the rest of a wild, dogfight-seared day as aircraft whirled, zigzagged, crashed, and exploded in a sky puffed with clouds and flak. Ozawa's second attack lost 98 of the 130 planes launched. His third attack did better, losing only seven of 47, but the fourth attack cost 73 of 82. On the day, Ozawa launched 374 planes; only 130 returned. In addition, 50 land-based Japanese aircraft were lost. Ozawa's fleet took serious ship losses as U.S. submarines sank two carriers, the *Shokaku* and *Taiho*, his flagship.

Mitscher's losses amounted to 29 carrier planes; 9 more went down from mechanical failure or on rescue missions—this despite a late-night carrier recovery for many.

Task Force 58 pursued the retreating enemy and on the afternoon of the twentieth attacked with 226 planes, sank a third carrier, *Hiyu*, plus two oilers and left Ozawa with only 35 operational aircraft. Twenty U.S. planes were lost in action, but 80 more were lost when, out of fuel, they ditched or crash-landed on carrier decks—even though Mitscher had the fleet's lights on to help recovery.

790 The Battle of the Philippine Sea finished Japanese naval airpower—few planes and few trained pilots remained.

791 **Guam, the largest Mariana island, came next.** A U.S. possession since the Spanish-American War, Guam had potable water and good

airfields defended by 19,000 toughened troops behind formidable beach defenses. The 55,000 men of U.S. III Amphibious Corps hit those defenses on July 21, 1944, after frogmen had blown pathways through beach obstacles and after a fearsome, seemingly endless air/sea bombardment which demoralized defenders. Sporadic resistance wilted in some three weeks, though individuals kept fighting for a time and some delivered chilling banzai charges. Japanese losses were over 10,500 killed, against a tenth of that for the Americans.

Next came Tinian, which lay a scant three miles from Saipan. This ten-mile-long islet shuddered under a forty-three-day air/sea bombardment before the 2nd and 4th Marine Divisions of the V Amphibious Corps went ashore on July 24, 1944. Opposed by more than 8,000 Japanese soldiers, the Marines overwhelmed organized resistance by August 1, with a little mopping up left to be done. U.S. losses came

Two U.S. officers plant the American flag on Guam eight minutes after Marine and army assault troops landed on the island, July 20, 1944.

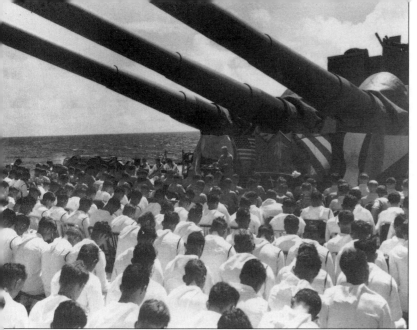

Crew of USS *South Dakota* attends a service honoring shipmates killed in the air action off Guam, July 1, 1944.

Yap. U.S. air forces bombed the Palaus twenty-one times during August and September 1944.

795 Intense offshore gunfire churned Peleliu's beaches on September 15, then the U.S. 1st Marine Division landed. Marines were close to the airfield as they came ashore against light resistance, but as they got onto hard ground, a series of sharp, tank-supported counterattacks hit them. After a week's fierce combat the airfield fell as the enemy retreated to hill positions. Colonel Nakasawa Kunio's 10,600 men had cunningly dug themselves into a hive of caves on a dominating massif the Americans called Bloody Nose Ridge. There the enemy put up a fanatical fight until the end of November—some held out longer.

Peleliu ranked among the Marine's bloodiest fights and cost them 6,526 casualties, including 1,252 killed.

to 295 killed and 1,554 wounded while the Japanese lost 7,000 killed along with 316 prisoners. **792** Marine lieutenant general Holland M. Smith, heading the Marianas Expeditionary Troops, thought Tinian the best amphibious operation of the Pacific campaign.

793 With Marianas-based heavy bombers, the first phase of the strategic air campaign against the home islands began. Raids also hit Luzon and the Visayas in the Philippines. During these destructive raids in August and September, the Japanese lost 978 planes and had 122 ships sunk and 137 damaged while the U.S. lost 114 planes and no ships.

794 To cover MacArthur's right flank as he advanced toward the Philippines, invasions of the Palau Islands followed Saipan. Babelthuap Island, biggest of the Palaus, had the largest garrison but no other attractions, so it would be bypassed. Angaur, six miles south of Peleliu, offered a fine site for construction of a heavy bomber base; it would be occupied. So would Ulithi; it had the best anchorage for large surface vessels in the area. Ngulu's occupation would isolate

796 Most of the U.S. 81st Division invaded Angaur Island on September 17 and secured it by the twentieth. On the twenty-third a regimental combat team took Ulithi without resistance and moved on to take Ngulu on October 16, also without resistance. Yap could now wither in isolation.

797 Flanks protected, MacArthur and Nimitz concentrated on a Philippine incursion. This clearly would be no "turkey shoot." Heavily garrisoned, all the Philippines were vital to Tokyo. Once ensconced in the Philippines, U.S. ships and planes could dominate the South China Sea, the Central Pacific, even the East China Sea, which would cut Japan off from China and from its newly won possessions. Japanese planners may not have known of the arguments surrounding U.S. strategy about objectives after the Allies occupied Leyte in the Philippines: where next, Luzon or Formosa? But this they knew: the Philippines must be held. Reinforcements went to Luzon; the other islands would be defended by planes—if any were left.

798 Occupation experience in those Spanish-American islands had taught the Japanese an interesting lesson. In March 1944, Imperial General Headquarters admitted that "even after their independence [proclaimed by Japan on October 14, 1943], there remains among all classes in the Philippines a strong undercurrent of pro-American sentiment. . . . something steadfast, which cannot be destroyed. . . . Guerrilla activities are gradually increasing." As the Americans came closer, they were about to rejoin old allies. And the closer they came to Leyte, the more an internally wobbling Japan became alarmed.

799 Admiral Nimitz, firm advocate of establishing a Leyte base, offered MacArthur the XXIV Corps (en route to Yap) and carrier air support, since Leyte lay beyond land-based air. MacArthur grabbed the offer, announcing that Leyte would be invaded on October 20, 1944.

800 The U.S. Sixth Army, under Lt. Gen. Walter Krueger, would be the attacking force, which proved extremely lucky. Krueger, Prussian-born and a "maverick" up from the ranks, had fought as an enlisted man in the Philippine Insurrection and knew something of the people and the ground. He also understood the primacy of Leyte in tactical geography. Bases there would permit U.S. forces to isolate Mindanao (where the Moros would help them), sanitize the Visayas, and threaten the China coast while opening the way to Luzon.

Krueger punched into Leyte with a three-phased plan: one to clear the string of islands ringing Leyte Gulf; another to establish beachheads with his X and XXIV Corps on Leyte's eastern coast and take Leyte Valley; the third, to secure the island and part of its neighbor, Samar. The Seventh Fleet would carry the Sixth Army and provide carrier air cover. Fortunately umbrellalike air cover supported the entire opera-

tion, with planes from the Third Fleet and ground-based planes from Morotai.

801 True to his word, MacArthur returned to the Philippines on October 20, 1944, as a gargantuan flotilla of 700 ships put some 160,000 men on Leyte after a four-hour barrage. Meeting light resistance, Krueger's men had a firm beachhead and an airstrip by nightfall. During that day MacArthur, with a group of staffers, sloshed ashore and he spoke to the Philippine people: "I have returned." A few days later his return looked doubtful.

802 A new Japanese government dispatched a renewed fleet to a cataclysmic duel for the Philippines. Admiral Toyoda activated his Sho-Go (Victory Operation) plan which postulated breaking the huge covering U.S. fleet at Leyte into defeatable parts—Admiral Halsey's big carrier group would be lured north out of the way while a pincers attack would demolish Adm. Thomas Kinkaid's relatively small U.S. Seventh Fleet and eliminate Krueger's beachhead. The scheme turned on Halsey speeding off to follow a Japanese carrier group—that had no planes—long enough for another Japanese flotilla to sink Kinkaid's ships and bombard the beaches. Halsey (q.v.) followed the lure as the Battle of Leyte Gulf began.

803 But Kinkaid put up an astounding defense of the beaches and nearly annihilated the Japanese fleet in a catastrophic battle that witnessed the first instances of Japanese planes deliberately crashing into U.S. ships—the first breeze of the *Kamikaze* (divine wind).

This battle effectively finished the Imperial Navy as a factor in the war.

804 Chaos ruled on the Leyte beachheads while the naval battle raged. Afterward, Krueger's troops moved fairly quickly to consolidate positions in central and northern Leyte. The general soon discovered that Japanese general Tomoyuki Yamashita, the "tiger of Malaya," commanding the Philippines, had found novel ways to reinforce his Leyte garrison. Sailing

Assault troops crawling onto the beach, Leyte Island, October 1944.

vessels of all kinds and sizes put 45,000 men and 10,000 tons of supplies ashore on the west coast at Ormoc. Fighting flared in the center as U.S. forces made little progress in getting control of Leyte Valley. Tropical rains in late October and early November turned roads to sluices and bogged everything down. Americans found the airfields they captured useless or too small, and naval air support languished after the clash in Leyte Gulf.

805 Krueger's delays irritated MacArthur, who thought of relieving him. Krueger, irked himself, took to his tent for a refresher course in military history. He carried with him Col. G. F. R. Henderson's classic *Stonewall Jackson and the American Civil War*. Exactly when he reread it is unknown, but results could be seen on a map as several U.S. columns began cutting Japanese forces into small groups, flanking and surrounding them until the last Japanese port fell on

In one of the war's most well-known images, General MacArthur wades ashore at Leyte Island, fulfilling his promise to return. Although staged, the photo effectively symbolized U.S. determination to wrest from Japan its imperial conquests.

Christmas Day and Yamashita informed his local commander and friend, Gen. Sosaku Suzuki, that the Leyte force had been written off. Japanese ground losses amounted to some 70,000, while total U.S. casualties were 15,584.

806 General Eichelberger's Eighth Army took charge of Leyte on December 26 and Krueger began planning another invasion.

THE UNION OF SOVIET SOCIALIST REPUBLICS (USSR), 1944

Rolling forward all along the great front, Red Army forces were bringing forth a New Russia as they smashed the Nazi "occupationists." New spirit buoyed the people, new strength revived the weakest army units, a renewed certitude in the *Rodina*'s destiny made a shining vision even in the chill and dreadful gulag.

807 For the Germans, going back toward the Reich meant hardships unimaginable, terrible losses, blighted hopes, and a damning desperation in the SS and *Einsatzgruppen*.

For Russians, German retreat meant much the same things—though most would not realize it for a time. At this point, all they saw was large areas of western Russia slowly being freed of an accursed enemy. **808** Stalin and his government thought of these occupied areas differently than might have been expected. Could such areas, such "infected" peoples, be trusted, be welcomed again into Soviet comradeship?

Stalin attacked this problem in a typically personal way. He picked trusted friends close to the State Committee for Defense and sent them as his "deputies on mission," to borrow a Charlemagne title, with the task of reinstalling into such places as the Ukraine, Belorussia, the Baltic states, all previous rights, duties, and obligations of the USSR. With Stalin's deputies came the NKVD (secret police), po-

litical commissars—all the trappings of oppression redivivus. Reintegration of western Russia stood high among Stalin's necessities since he wanted to continue prewar plans of modernization.

809 Reintegration went slowly, not only because the Nazis retreated slowly but also because too much too soon might ignite resistance—which came anyway in many places. Resistance might be expected in the Ukraine, where foreign leaders were rarely popular, but the Baltic states fought with special venom as the NKVD deported trainloads to eastern Russia because of Machiavellian suspicion.

810 Stalin exported this paranoia to all invaded areas. Bulgaria, Romania, Poland (especially loathed), Hungary, Czechoslovakia, even Austria, would be stamped under the iron rubric of Communistic "independence." Stalin made little effort to hide his determination to expand Communism into the areas taken by his armies. Awash in new territories as the year progressed, Stalin's veneer of Communistic patriotism sloughed to simple greed.

811 Churchill's fears were prophetic as the Red Army pushed its "iron curtain" of conquest rapidly westward. Greece, too, could have succumbed had Churchill not intruded his own forces to save a toehold in the Balkans.

Coming victory brings its own disturbances. When people who have suffered long for a cause sense success, they tend to behave like horses who suddenly see the barn—and override the reins in rushing to the feed bin. **812** The Russian people had had an addictive whiff of freedom for nearly three years, a fact that worried Stalin. He pulled the reins tight by curt reminders of destiny unfulfilled, of quotas and labor heroes. Collective farming remained part of the nation; as war work slowed, exhortations came to stick to the great national goal of industrializing—which, after all, had turned back the Nazis. Population increase ranked high on Communist agendas because people were an important unit of production. **813** **But behind all the stirring propaganda lurked a truth too sad to tell: the USSR stood bereft of people.** So many were dead that those left would have to do more than ever if the nation were to live—a fact that directed much of Stalin's thinking as on his legions went.

814 **To an initiate, numbers gave a fairly accurate history of the war.** War production still grew, even in the agonies of 1943, but nonetheless it had been a nearly even year in new planes and tanks built and a year of decline in artillery and rifle deliveries. In some areas, despite the Red Army's inexorable march west, the Third Reich still did better than the USSR. In 1943 the USSR produced 93.1 million tons of coal to Germany's 26.9 million tons, while a year later the USSR, doing better, had unearthed 121.5 million tons while Germany dug 28.1 million tons. Unfavorable ratios continued in steel production. The USSR in 1943: 8.5 million tons; Germany: 34.6, while in 1944 the USSR produced 10.9 million tons of steel versus Germany's 35.2 million tons. These depressing calculations showed that Russia needed more workers, a fact that triggered near press-gang efforts to recruit laborers wherever the Red Army went.

815 **Measured against civilian production, these figures were alarming.** A people coming out of hell expected hope, despite Stalin's hackneyed calls for redoubled efforts. The future looked bleak as no more clothes or cloth came to stores than the last year and even fewer shoes. People watched with pride the massive tanks and heavy artillery, the warehouses of machine guns, shiploads of small arms all oiled and primed for battle—but they did it bareheaded, in rags and papered shoes, in mended coats, darned socks, frayed gloves, with eyes dimmed from machine shops and days too long in the fields. They were what Stalin expected them to be—stalwart, strong, fixed on Lenin's goal, dauntless survivors of a land too tough to die.

816 **Despite shortages morale remained high, soared in fact.** By the end of 1944, Russia braced in hopeful expectation of the coming of the end.

RUSSO-GERMAN BATTLES, 1944

817 **Things looked better than ever for the *Stavka* (Supreme High Command) as its members opened the January 1944 campaign.** Hitler's lackeys were barely holding on in their collapsing southern salient, were pulling back in the center, and inert in the frozen north around Leningrad where they ignored the beachhead lingering west of the city. In January, Gen. Leonid A. Govorov pushed in reinforcements over a frozen Gulf of Finland and, on the fifteenth, struck southwest, broke through the German Eighteenth Army's front, and sought to trap it between his men and Gen. Kirill A. Meretskov's Volkhov *front*. Swift German reaction saved their army as thawing weather aided in the reestablishment of their line. These northern operations were mere opening skirmishes. The main offensive was launched in the south against Manstein's AG South. This massive drive isolated two Nazi corps. Manstein ordered them to break out, which most of them did, leaving behind the wounded and heavy equipment.

818 **Continued pressure in the south finally pushed Kleist's Sixth Army out of Nikopol, and as the left flank of his Army Group A sagged, it nearly uncovered the major rail center at Lvov.** During the March thaws, Manstein tried to reinforce the Fourth Panzer Army near Lvov and consolidate as much of the front as possible—all while keeping a eye on the wilting Sixth Army under pressure from Malinovsky's Third Ukrainian *front*. Again, doing more with less, Manstein shored things up effectively until Nikolai Vatutin and Ivan Konev thrust their *fronts* into a salient that bent his left back toward Lvov in March. The greater flotation of their wide-tracked tanks and the cross-country ability of many American trucks enabled the Soviets to wreck a German corps at Uman.

819 During this drive, Hans Hube's First Panzer Army became isolated, and the one-armed general charged it up and down behind enemy lines, wrecking communications, picking off small units, and making a massive nuisance of his command. Manstein finally badgered Hitler into sending reinforcements to save Hube—who helped by fighting in all directions as he extracted most of his men and heavy equipment.

820 Irked at Manstein's persistent arguments, Hitler sacked him along with Kleist. Manstein went into permanent retirement. Other generals still pestered the Führer. The high command pointed out that the stabilized line now, in mid-1944, ran too long to be held with the troops available. One suggestion: Use the thaw respite to establish a new front line from Riga on the north to Lvov in the center and anchor it on the Dnieper River in the south—thus freeing enough divisions for a hefty mobile reserve. Do it? No.

821 Hitler reverted to his old inspiration—he designated important communications centers as "fortresses" (hedgehogs), ordered them held at all costs, and refused to permit frontal fortifications. Nor would he pull in idle divisions from Crete, Greece, or even Norway.

822 At the Tehran Conference, Stalin had agreed to launch an Eastern Front attack in conjunction with Overlord. Carrying out that promise, Zhukov unleashed Operation Bagration (named after a hero in the war against Napoleon) on the night of June 23–24, 1944. The greatest Soviet offensive of the war to that time began slyly with intense partisan activities confounding communications and logistics for Field Marshal Ernst Busch's AG Center. In the morning of the twenty-third a thunderous barrage of artillery—400 guns per mile on a 350-mile front—smashed into AG Center; Busch rushed forces to protect Hitler's "fortresses." Without air cover—the Luftwaffe had been paralyzed by the Atlantic landings—and under fearsome pressure, Busch found his divisions surrounded, bypassed, and finally encircled. **823** In ten searing days Bagration knocked a 250-mile hole in the German front and handed the Germans their worst defeat in the war by bagging twenty-five divisions and destroying AG Center.

824 Hitler sent his "fireman," newly minted Field Marshal Walther Model, to collect what remnants he could find and restore the front. Heading the new AG North Ukraine (the old AG South), gathering stragglers of AG Center, bits and pieces of the Third Panzer Army, and elements of the Second Army, Model unsuccessfully kept urging Hitler's permission for strategic withdrawals. Locked into positions beyond hope, Model, in July, lost most of his old Ninth as well as the First Army. But he took swift advantage of a Soviet pause for supplies in mid-August and built a defense "a hair's breadth" outside the East Prussian border and on the Vistula.

For his desperate scrambling, hailed as a savior in the East, Model received the diamonds to his Knight's Cross in August, with orders to go west for more rescue work.

825 With the Russians nearly at the gates, the Polish underground in Warsaw rose a second time (the first had been in April 1943) and seized much of the city. Fierce fighting followed. Soviet troops watched idly because the Polish Home Army underground was a creature of the Polish government-in-exile in London, not of the Communist Polish government aligned with Moscow.

Some 37,000 Polish Home Army members fought to help the Allies and to show that the Soviets alone were not liberating Poland. **826** Organized to last ten days, the fighting lasted sixty-three; efforts were made from the Western Allies to airdrop supplies, but the Russians, at first, denied landing strips. Well planned,

Staged German photograph of Gen. Tadeusz Bor-Komorowski, Polish Home Army commander, surrendering to SS *Obergruppenführer* Erich von dem Bach-Zelewski, Warsaw, October 1944. Komorowski would be imprisoned at Colditz.

fronts, then fell back slowly until a massive Soviet flank rush drove toward Riga and the Baltic coast. At this, AG North abandoned Estonia and eastern Latvia and maneuvered some thirty divisions into a relatively secure cul-de-sac on the Courland Peninsula during August and September. This force could have been extracted by sea whenever Hitler called, but he wanted some threat still on the enemy right and to protect submarine training facilities in the Baltic.

829 Finland sued for peace when Estonia fell—that had been its base of German support and supplies. Two quick Russian drives finished resistance and an armistice went into effect on September 2, 1944.

well sustained by civilian medical, commissary, and fire organizations, the resistance forced a heavy response. Himmler brought in over 21,000 German troops, including Oskar Dirlewanger's Police Brigade (a gang of loosed criminals), a Russian POW brigade, and an Azerbaijani infantry brigade. At first all captured Poles were shot, but finally mass executions stopped. **827** Polish Home Army leader Gen. Tadeusz Bor-Komorowski surrendered on October 1, to surprising terms, considering the German commander's bestial reputation. General Erich von dem Bach-Zelewski signed an agreement recognizing the rebels as combatants and pronouncing the city to be totally evacuated. Casualties were high—more than 15,000 rebels were killed along with some 200,000 to 250,000 civilians; Bach-Zelewski admitted 17,000 casualties.

828 While Model was plugging the huge gap yawning toward northern Poland, Zhukov, in July, widened his attack to engage Gen. Ferdinand Schörner's AG North. This group stood firm for awhile against three Baltic

830 Stalin, now directing operations (with some *Stavka* advice), began to combine military and political strategy. Beginning on August 20, the 2nd and 3rd Ukrainian *fronts* attacked along the Romanian border in a "march of liberation," a series of drives to seize southeastern Europe ahead of the British and Americans. This strategy came as no surprise to Hitler, who hoped that just such a conflict of British and Soviet ambitions might be turned to some eleventh-hour advantage.

831 After Romania quit the war on August 23, Stalin faced a peculiar dilemma. Bulgaria, at war with the Western nations but not with the USSR, suddenly sought an alliance with Stalin and to negotiate peace with Britain and the U.S. Wanting no Western interference and no interruption of now largely surplus Lend-Lease, Stalin, on September 5, declared war instead and poured the 3rd Ukrainian *front* into the unfortunate country on September 8. Bulgaria achieved an armistice the next day, though Soviet troops stayed to support the inauguration of a Bulgarian Communist government.

832 With enemy forces probing toward inner Germany, Hitler guessed that restive regent Miklós Vités Horthy de Nagybánya, of Hungary, would seek to get out of the Axis and out of the war. This would be disastrous since German retreat routes into Hungary were vital. When the Führer learned that Horthy's son, Nicholas, had met with Soviet agents on October 15 to sign surrender articles, he called on his master of derring-do, Otto Skorzeny, who suddenly swooped in, bound up young Horthy, and flew him to Germany. Horthy senior, vainly seeking asylum with a relative of the former kaiser, also became a Skorzeny captive and spent the rest of the war in a Bavarian castle—safe from any armistice possibilities.

These personal adventures did Hungary no good. Both Hitler and Stalin saw Budapest as a political, military, and international gem. By December 1944, Budapest had been partly surrounded by the Red Army, but only partly. As the year ended, the German front ran from eastern Estonia, through eastern Poland, along the western Carpathian and Transylvanian Alps into western Bulgaria. The borders of the Third Reich were on the Russian horizon with hard, corruptive miles to go.

THE EMPIRE OF JAPAN, 1944

By 1944 the Japanese people could see that something magical needed to happen to prolong hope and restore serenity.

Clothes were drab and ragged and most hung loose on thinner frames, houses were shabby, cities unkempt. **833** There were many new family shrines as the casualty lists grew long and fear lurked in the national mind. Fear had come slowly but taken root. The government feared the fear because it sapped morale and might soften loyalty.

What did the people fear? Losing the war? That unlikelihood would bring unbearable dishonor, certainly a cause for fear. But it seemed deeper than that, almost a palpable terror. **834** It seemed as though the people knew the war would come to them.

Omens pointed to that happening. In April the kindergartens closed, there were hints that sugar had run out, passenger train schedules were cut drastically to make room for military freight, food shortages brought packs of wild dogs out on Tokyo streets, and rumor had it that some were killed for meat markets. Due to fuel scarcity people walked great distances in the country to find rice and vegetables—these long hikes increased factory absenteeism in a kind of doleful cycle of erosion. Interisland ferry travel had become uncertain. **835** Japan's Axis allies were being beaten in Italy and Russia. And now in Japan there were urgent calls for more warships and aircraft, calls for redoubled production. What would be used to build these things? Similar calls from last year had used up most raw materials. Where were new resources, where the promised wealth of the New Order? What had gone wrong with the manpower supply? Where were the merchant ships that were the people's lifeline? With daily news of the endless raids on Germany, officials talked more seriously about air raid precautions and about fire drills, talked more about sacrifice and spirit than about warmth and clothes and food. **836** In the summer, thousands of city schoolteachers worked to convince parents to let their children be evacuated to the country. By the end of the year nearly half a million children and their teachers had gone.

Was Japan being beaten?

837 Bolstering morale became a large government enterprise. Officials in the home ministry (in charge of internal security) stepped up activities of all the volunteer associations, especially exhorting work within the Imperial Rule Assistance Association and the neighborhood self-help committees and groups. Even fortune-tellers were dragooned to boost morale—see only good things ahead, they were told. Stricter rules governed writing, publication, and speaking. Several instances of important opposition members of the Diet being muffled or arrested made the news. The Special Emergency Act of 1942 had opened the way for repressive arrests by the dread *Tokkō*, and they increased now—but still not to the levels of the Gestapo or NKVD.

Serious efforts were made to encourage interest in civilian defense and mass city evacuations. Though this action might scare people it would also show that the government cared about their future.

838 War news forced changes in Japanese strategy and tactics. U.S. efforts, led by Major General Chennault, to bomb Japan from Chinese air bases resurrected the Chinese war. Although land operations had lapsed there for nearly two years, now a new Japanese ground offensive was ordered to capture these airfields and protect the home islands. Allied activity in India and Burma also focused Imperial General Headquarters' attention there; orders went to the Burma command to stabilize the area.

839 War news also forced a change in government. Bad news coming from Guadalcanal, northern New Guinea, the Solomons, Rabaul, and Truk had shaken Tojo and his government. When Tojo made himself army chief of staff in February 1944 so he could direct operations, this added fuel to criticism. Opposition to him in the Diet, at court, even in the news, expanded—many thought he must go if Japan wanted to negotiate peace. Various maneuvers by him to save the administration failed, and when Saipan fell, so did Tojo; in July he resigned all of his offices.

840 The new prime minister, Gen. Kuniaki Koiso, tried to improve relations between the services by creating the Supreme Council for the Direction of the War with the PM, service chiefs of staff, and the foreign minister as mem-

bers. It made little difference. War policy-making devolved to the chiefs of staff of the army and navy—with the rivalry still rampant. Much stronger leadership might have helped. Some officials thought of declaring martial law, but Japan's constitutional heritage doomed that idea, and even martial law could not dislodge the Allies from Saipan and its airfields in range of the home islands. The people were right in their fear—war was coming to them.

ALLIED/JAPANESE LAND BATTLES, 1944

841 A two-year lull immobilized troops in Burma. After Wavell's 1942–43 offensive against Akyab sputtered out, he began building ground reserves, air support, and supply bases across India. When the Quadrant Conference in 1943 ordered that land communications be restored with China. U.S. engineers started construction of a road from Ledo in India into northern Burma.

"Vinegar Joe" Stilwell flew in reinforcements from China to help the Chinese troops he had brought into India in wake of the Burma disaster. **842** As part of an Allied drive to retake Burma and open routes to China, he prepared to attack southward toward Myitkyina (pronounced "Mitchinna"), aided by Wingate's Chindits, plus the 5307th Composite Unit, a specially trained jungle fighting force better known as Merrill's Marauders. Chindits (q.v.) and Brig. Gen. Frank Merrill's men, largely supplied by air (with medical support provided by the legendary "Burma surgeon," Dr. Gordon Seagrave and his staff), would get behind the enemy, harass his flanks, build roadblocks, and cut off bits and pieces of his infantry. Stilwell began his drive from Ledo in February 1944. The Marauders set up a roadblock on the main enemy supply line and cut off seven thousand troops of their 18th Division. By late April, Myitkyina—it had the only hard-surfaced airfield in northern Burma—came under Marauder attack.

ABOVE: American medics treating casualties at a portable surgical hospital during the drive on Pinwe, Burma, November 1944. BELOW: A barge, powered by outboard motors, ferries men, a truck, and ammunition across the Irrawaddy River, near Tigyaing, Burma, December 1944.

843 But Merrill's men were fought out; they had been in action for almost a hundred days, fought five battles and thirty-two skirmishes victoriously, marched over 750 miles in horrendous mountain/scrub terrain, were ravaged by malaria, typhus, dysentery, short of food and ammunition, almost useless. Too weak to take the town, they hung on to the edge of the airfield by their fingertips until relieved on August 3.

While Stilwell made ready, the Allies started two other campaigns to stress the Japanese. The XV Corps would attack toward Akyab again, and IV Corps would attack to the Chindwin River.

Lieutenant General Renya Mutaguchi, commanding Japan's Fifteenth Army, encouraged by new armies arriving in support, conceived Operation U-Go, a "March on Delhi." He had somehow become convinced that masses of dissident Indians would flock to a Japanese liberation campaign. Mutaguchi's superior, Gen. Masakazu Kawabe, commanding the Burma Area Army, endorsed the March on Delhi. The campaign began with a diversionary push by Lt. Gen. Tadashi Hanaya's 55th Division against Gen. Philip Christison's XV Indian Army Corps (of William Slim's Fourteenth British Army), on the move southward once more in the Arakan toward Maungdaw.

844 Christison constructed an 1,100-yard-square administrative supply base near Sinzweya that became the objective of diversionary Operation Ha-Go. On February 4, 1944, what became known as the Admin Box Battle began. Aware of enemy plans but tactically surprised, the British fought fiercely. Japanese troops overran Maj. Gen. Frank Messervy's 7th Indian Division headquarters. Messervy managed to pull most of his command into the Box. Convinced they could easily break this British "square," the Japanese attacked time and again; the British held out for two weeks. The encirclers were themselves encircled and Hanaya's force destroyed. **845** The Admin Box battle, the first major engagement the British won over the Japanese in Burma, changed the tempo of fighting there.

After the Admin Box fighting, the Japanese

should have canceled the March on Delhi. Overconfident, outgunned, outnumbered, and outplaned, Mutaguchi's Fifteenth Army started Operation U-Go on March 7, 1944. Objective: preempt the initiative by cutting Lt. Gen. William Slim's supply line at Imphal, stranding and perhaps destroying the Fourteenth Army. Nothing went right for Mutaguchi. Slim's men held on at Imphal and at another base at Kohima. An odd sort of fluid siege lasted some four months; Slim received massive supplies by air and threw some tanks into the campaign. By mid-July, General Kawabe called off further operations. While Mutaguchi retreated across the Chindwin, Slim's continuing pressure created a rout. **846** The Imphal offensive or the March on Delhi became a decisive disaster for the Japanese. They lost 53,000 men out of 85,000, almost all of their heavy equipment, western Burma, and failed to install Subhas Chandra Bose's turncoat Indian National Army on home ground.

British losses came to 17,000. They not only gained Burma and opened the Ledo Road to China, but they also were in position to move toward Malaya, Indochina, and into China itself. Further offensives were delayed, though, by the Japanese Operation Ichi-Go in China, that began in April and continued into December 1944.

847 Imperial General Headquarters approved Operation Ichi-Go in April 1944. This last major Japanese offensive of the war started as a drive to capture the Chinese mainland airfields used by Maj. Gen. Claire Chennault's U.S. Fourteenth Air Force's strategic air offensive against Japanese island shipping. Ichi-Go accomplished its main objective by seizing seven airfields built at terrific expense in sweat and money, then continued on to threaten Chiang's capital at Chungking and open direct communications with Indochina. The nearly total collapse of Chinese resistance proved beyond doubt the fecklessness of Chiang and his Kuomintang government. Ichi-Go's success had little direct effect on the war, however, since the other Allies had pretty well written off China as a factor.

848 **At year's end Japan's fate had been sealed.** Heavy bombers came steadily from Saipan, from some bases in the Philippines, and other islands. Fire bombs on paper houses swept Japanese hopes into swirling ashes that spread a funerary pall all across the land. Imperial General Headquarters and many in the army and navy urged a fight to the finish, but this pursuit of futility found fewer and fewer fanatics.

THE BRITISH EMPIRE, 1944

The Lion was still roaring when the year began—perhaps a slightly weary roar but a roar nonetheless. Suffering, sacrifice, and death had tempered the people. Now that they had no doubts about the end, they picked up the hard burdens of hanging on with a kind of cheery stolidity. With their armies and the Yanks and other allies spreading out across France and to the Rhine, Britons hoped it soon would end. Churchill warned them, though, that their enemies were strong still and would fight with desperate fury.

849 **Britons taking stock for the coming year could be proud of themselves.** They bore heavy burdens with grace, stood to their ack-acks and factory machines in dark hours, ate and drank less (even in pubs), missed their kids, planted truck gardens all over the kingdom, sat with the dying in London and at empire hospitals and graves, came to cherish imperial friends, clasped hands with the ubiquitous Yanks, and worked beyond all kinds of calls of duty.

Of all things, these years of war had reaffirmed the persistence of the people, the persistence of humanity itself. These war years turned Britons' hearts inward once again to feel the force of being British. Their war record deserved boasting. "The Royals" had never left; two little princesses spoke bravely from embattled Buckingham. Parliament met through all the fury and the bobtail ravens stayed steadfast in the Tower. Churchill's strength still armed the nation.

850 **Minister of Labour and National Service Ernest**

Bevin kept strict controls despite the good news. With almost 100 percent employment—true, much of it conscripted—Britain's production records grew better each war year, except for deep-mined coal, which remained an essentially unregimented activity. Despite Bevin's ban on strikes, 1944 saw more than two thousand in the coal and engineering areas. Mostly short, they did not dangerously disrupt production. **851** **Aircraft manufacturing, under the astute management of Lord Beaverbrook, literally soared year after year (he had a large hand in the Battle of Britain) and by 1944 reached nearly 90,000 planes.** Rapid warship and merchant ship construction vastly helped the war against U-boats, and the proliferation of aircraft carriers—from five to more than fifty—would make an impact in the Far East. Production began tapering off by the end of 1944, both because war needs slowed and because U.S. production was carrying most of the war effort.

852 **Churchill, in his role of icon, did a kind of double service.** The cherished hero of England, he irked the Nazis into happily erroneous parody. Goebbels (q.v.) in an article for *Das Reich*, tried to unscramble the "riddle" of Churchill's grip on the English. The answer, he thought, lay in the fact that "although Mr. Churchill lacks all strategic sense in both politics and military leadership, he is an extraordinarily capable tactician." Goebbels speculated that in any other country Churchill would be sacked, but England liked him. "He is its curse, its evil spirit, a man who has all the abilities to be Great Britain's gravedigger. . . . We are happy that Mr. Churchill is there. We certainly do not want to be rid of him. . . . since he is the pathfinder for our total and radical victory."

853 **Happy enough with victory on the horizon, Churchill began to have serious worries about a postwar world in which Stalin and his Bolsheviks would bulk too large for comfort.** For the majority of Britons, though, the USSR seemed, still, a cherished, even essential, ally.

1944: THE FIFTH YEAR OF THE WAR

854 Churchill and his chiefs of staff had reason to be happy with the selection of Lord Mountbatten as Supreme Allied Commander of Southeast Asia (SEAC). He energized an area that was used to being the war's backwater. His local commanders—the brilliant Lt. Gen. William Slim, the steady Lt. Gen. Philip Christison, Lt. Gen. "Vinegar Joe" Stilwell, and later, U.S. Lt. Gen. Daniel I. Sultan—proved outstanding in overruling Mountbatten's often arcane strategies and in winning when it counted. Together this team reconquered Burma.

855 British leaders had reason to be happy, also, with Royal Navy operations in the Atlantic. Combined antisubmarine tactics had virtually extinguished the U-boat menace in 1944 and supply lines were open in all directions—although the Murmansk freighters still ran risks.

856 Monty's men drove on in Germany, hewing to Ike's broad front strategy. Field Marshal Harold Alexander, after Rome fell, pushed on in northern Italy, keeping pressure on Kesselring so he could not detach divisions to France or the USSR. Churchill still hoped that FDR might be persuaded to check Stalin's territorial ambitions by running an Allied campaign through the Alps into Europe. The prime minister thought Alexander the man both to help persuade and to do the job.

Britain's challenge for 1945 would be to do the thing it always did best—keep a stiff upper lip and "stick it."

GERMANY, 1944

857 Germany looked worse than drab as the new year began. Bremen, Cologne, Dusseldorf, Essen, Lübeck, hit with the huge (eleven-plus ton) "blockbuster" bombs, had swaths of rubble where streets had been—the RAF's constant night bombing had changed the looks of the Fatherland. More than

German prisoners, captured after the surrender of Aachen, marching into captivity, October 1944.

changing looks, though, these raids were now pinching daily life. Rail schedules were uncertain, roads needed work, nightly raid warnings abraded nerves and shortened tempers. Germans were getting back in heavy doses what the British had long borne. It all grew worse when the U.S. Eighth and Ninth Air Forces picked up the slack with fighter-escorted daylight raids in February.

858 Pressed now on all sides, Hitler had to change his way of war. His policy of producing both civilian goods and war matériel had to shift. War mobilization of the whole economy came at last. **859** Albert Speer, given the job of gearing the war effort to its realities, began closing small firms and redirecting labor, changing factory locations and—in a spectacular effort—moving aircraft production underground, achieving what some called the "Speer miracle." Even under what amounted to an air siege, the Reich constructed more than 24,000 planes in 1943 and nearly 40,000 in 1944. Nearly 20,000 tanks rolled off assembly lines in 1943 while almost 28,000 appeared in 1944. Two and half million tons of munitions were fabricated in 1943 compared to four and a half million in 1944. A dramatic rise in antiaircraft gun construction (157,000 in 1943 against 361,000 in 1944) showed a change in air defense tactics from reliance on Göring's tattered Luftwaffe to intense flak barrages.

860 Speer's "miracle" came at a high human cost. POWs, slave laborers from Poland and the USSR (where children were kidnapped for German factories, some girls for other duties), many of them from labor chief Fritz Sauckel's pools of condemned humanity, Jews from wherever the Nazis spread, these provided power for Deutschland's new war. Speer's plan gave these *Untermenschen* unexpected value, and by 1944 survival conditions had slightly improved for Soviet prisoners, Poles, even for some skilled Jewish workers. But, in the words of one authority: "The Nazis condemned millions of POWs and large parts of the Soviet population to death by starvation and endemic diseases in order to feed the *Wehrmacht* and the German population."

861 Morale remained fairly high as 1944 began but seeped slowly away with the year's disasters. With the Red Army boring in from the east, the Allies pressing up from Italy and in from the skies, and after D-day in June, in from the west, the people nursed a sense of there being nowhere to run. Hitler, calling on ingrained German discipline, held the country together. Goebbels mustered all the propaganda sources he could use to remind his countrymen about "unconditional surrender," about the fiends who bombed women and children, about glorious last stands turned to victory in German history.

862 Then in midyear came a new series of decrees levying food rationing, strictly regulating working conditions, and freezing wages and prices. Hard war had come at last. These measures, coming so late, sent signals of attrition.

863 A population survey of the cities must have frustrated the army high command. There were too many men still around. True, most were in uniform, but usually that of some competing, ancillary, or police agency, since Germany's system of controlling everything made bureaucracy balloon. SS uniforms were swarming, along with Gestapo and *Kripo* garb. Army commanders were infuriated by the SS and the Luftwaffe having their own fighting divisions. And there were many exemptions from the draft—thousands of men were detailed to factories. Nothing apparently could be done about that because most were highly skilled workers in areas where only Germans could be trusted.

864 Remarkably enough, all these police forces were hardly needed. Fear seemed to link Germans to Hitler and his cause with desperation and strength. There were opponents in the country, scattered, generally disorganized, and usually known by the security forces. Many were most brave in propaganda efforts and in trying for conspiracies, but brutal penalties chilled their ardor. Several attempts had been made on Hitler's life, but he seemed to be under some charmed protection.

865 Hitler's persistent stupidities in Russia finally jelled strong army opposition. His refusal to listen to generals who urged flexible defense against Red Army attacks cost thousands of men, masses of equipment, and nearly always brought disaster. A relatively small officer cabal decided, at last, that he must go—not a unified cabal to be sure, but one strong enough to act. Some wanted him killed, others arrested and tried. All were troubled by their oath of personal loyalty to the Führer. Most of the conspirators in the *Schwarze Kapelle* (Black Orchestra)—the Gestapo name for the group—were amateurs at conniving. Most were honorably Christian and disliked what they were planning. Innocent of security matters, many kept diaries, talked openly on the phone, and some talked too much, too often.

866 Their putative leader, former chief of the general staff Gen. Ludwig Beck, longtime Nazi opponent, brought prestige to the movement, as did Admiral Canaris, head of the *Abwehr.* A good many generals and other officers at least talked about joining. When a young nobleman, Count Claus Schenk von Stauffenberg, joined, the conspiracy had found its man. A badly wounded war hero, great-grandson of fabled nineteenth-century Prussian army reformer Field Marshal August, Count Neidthardt von Gneisenau, Stauffenberg loathed what he had seen of German atrocities on the Eastern Front.

He devised Operation Valkyrie in which a standby government in Berlin would seize power and sue for peace when word arrived of Hitler's death. A staff officer often present at Hitler's Rastenburg, East Prussia, headquarters, Stauffenberg had access and opportunity.

867 On July 20, 1944, he placed a briefcase containing a kilogram of SOE's time-fused plastic explosive under Hitler's conference table. Leaving "to make a phone call," he heard the bomb go off, thought all was well, and flew to Berlin to start the new government.

868 Although *sans culottes*, Hitler survived. Insufficient explosives, an accidental repositioning of the briefcase, and a change in the meeting place all worked to save the Führer.

Hitler, Himmler, and Goebbels (who did much to defuse the expected Berlin uprising) seized the moment to exterminate not only the conspirators (some were garroted by wire or hung on meat hooks) but also many other "enemies." An estimated five thousand died in a bloodbath of revenge. Army command structure tottered.

Hitler inspects bomb damage, 1944. Photo captured by U.S. Army Signal Corps on the Western Front.

This attempt caused a brief wave of sympathy and renewed loyalty to Hitler.

869 **Command problems multiplied as the Western Allies drew close to Germany's borders.** In a new paranoia about army commanders, Hitler reduced their authority to the immediate combat zone and distributed governmental power to Reich defense commissioners in the various political regions. The commissioners were run by Himmler, so the Nazi Party at last controlled the army.

870 **War naturally affected law.** Regular courts lost most powers and ad hoc tribunals expanded. **871** **Police agencies were beyond the law—in fact were law themselves—and deprived the people of the last shreds of legal rights while a vast, roofless facade of courts busily did a vigorous paper business in such routine matters as wills, private suits, and land transfers.** Something much like a Court of the Star Chamber appeared—the juryless People's Court, presided over by sadists doling inquisitional penalties for military, political, and civil offenses.

872 **Then came the *Fliegendes Standgericht*, the "flying courts-martial," which, late in the war, cruised army rear areas to pick up stragglers or deserters, try them, and shoot them. In effect, the courts practiced treason against the people.**

873 **By late 1944 the Third Reich began slowly unraveling.** Speer still produced something like a miracle with synthetic gasoline, but his increased numbers of planes could not fly because Allied strategic bombing of storage tanks and railroads created fuel shortages. Dwindling manpower cut the size of Nazi divisions, sabotage in factories moved from irritation to threat, inflation began rising, and recruiters saw the bottom of the barrel.

874 **Hitler met the manpower crisis by creating a whole new class of recruits.** Always sensitive to impor-

Dr. Joseph Goebbels, as propaganda minister, toured bombed cities, 1944.

tant dates, he decreed his new force on October 18, the date of the 1813 victory over Napoleon at Leipzig. This civil defense force he called the *Deutscher Volkssturm*, probably hoping it would spark a mass levy of the people. No such luck. A people awash in falsities now recognized it for what it was—an act of despair. All males between sixteen and sixty would be called in a series of levies. This pulled men from factories, universities, some schools—they took rudimentary training at off hours. They were slated for home defense but were ultimately in the front line. Pictures tell the terrible tale of boys in ill-fitting uniforms, clutching rifles, going to the guns.

875 **It came at last to seem as though no icons, no monuments would be saved.** A good deal of Nazi pride had clustered around the huge behemoths of the sea, *Bismarck* and *Tirpitz*. Loss of *Bismarck* stung that pride, but *Tirpitz* remained and amounted to a fleet in being by itself. **876** **The British, desperate to sink it,**

Men of M-51 antiaircraft battery are silhouetted against a sky streaked with vapor trails from Allied and enemy planes engaged in a dogfight, Christmas Day, 1944, near Puffendorf, Germany.

had struck at it several times—one notable strike in September 1943 came from British midget submarines, two of which got close enough to lay mines that seriously crippled the huge battleship—the two attackers won Victoria Crosses. Air attacks continued after *Tirpitz* moved to Tromso. On November 12, 1944, a famous British bombing squadron, 617, nicknamed "the Dambusters" for earlier feats, made a run with eighteen Tallboys (12,000-pound bombs), faked off a Luftwaffe protecting force, and unloaded on the battleship—sixteen bombs came close, two hit, and in less than an hour the "fleet in being" capsized. As *Tirpitz* began rolling, her 1,204-man crew's last act touched all German hearts—they sang "Deutschland über Alles."

1945

THE SIXTH YEAR
OF THE WAR

CLOSURE

*The winner is asked no questions—
the loser has to answer for everything.*

—Sir Ian Hamilton, Gallipoli Diary, 1920

Peace now became a vital Allied concern. FDR and Churchill, de Gaulle, all the major players, most particularly Stalin, toyed with the coming configurations in Europe. Victory brought new priorities. **877 The wonderful solidity of the Grand Alliance began crumbling as greed succeeded need.** Idealist Roosevelt, reacting to haunting memories of Versailles and the League of Nations, sought a new organization to keep peace in the world. Churchill paid lip service to the idea but preferred an Anglo-American axis as the best guarantee for democratic principles. Stalin, too, paid lip service to some kind of United Nations idea, but relied mainly on Red Army presence and neo-Soviet institutions to make the world he wanted.

THE UNITED STATES, 1945

878 Despite euphoria about the war's progress, FDR still fought a running skirmish with Congress. The conservative bloc still had strength to derail anything looking like New Deal ideas. The president learned that quickly in the new year as two proposed appointments ran into trouble. Having shifted to Harry Truman for his vice president, FDR wanted to do something for Henry Wallace, whom he admired. Wallace's nomination to be secretary of commerce won approval only after Congress largely emasculated the job. Aubrey W. Williams's nomination as head of the Rural Electrification Administration failed miserably. Obviously there would be no "victory honeymoon" for an embattled president.

879 Pressure showed in the president's posture, the lines of his face, a look of near exhaustion in the black smudges under his eyes, the gaunt cheeks, and increased use of his wheelchair. Roosevelt's war had been as hard, perhaps, as that of troops in the line. He found it difficult to delegate total authority, especially in Allied matters, strategy, even sometimes in tactics. Domestic battles added daily vexation. The steel braces on his legs compounded the burden. A good many colleagues had worried about his health for some time. An upcoming Allied conference would add more strain.

880 All kinds of problems began to clog Allied relations. With the Red Army storming into the Reich and the Western Allies driving Nazi troops into a huge pocket in northern Germany, protocols of rendezvous had to be decided. Questions of dividing up the spoils mounted. High on a list of problems stood the matter of an international peacekeeping body to monitor an unfolding world. Stalin, Churchill, and Roosevelt—with some seven hundred attending staff—decided to meet at Yalta in the ravaged Crimea.

881 They gathered on February 4, 1945, in bedraggled former vacationing palaces of the czars. Roosevelt's first view of Yalta city's remains infuriated him and he raged later to Congress about the "reckless, senseless fury" of the Nazis. Evidence of enemy barbarism added impact to the meeting. A kind of relentless

The Big Three at the Yalta Conference, February 1945, seated left to right: Churchill, Roosevelt, Stalin.

bonhomie veneered the sessions, which lasted through February 11.

882 **Each of the principals had a private agenda and nursed varying degrees of distrust.** Roosevelt, surely the most idealistic, hoped to charm "Uncle Joe" into giving firm support to a peacekeeping agency and making a promise to attack Japan. He also sought decisions on German occupation, Polish border issues, and Balkan turmoil. **883** **Churchill came more from anxiety than anything else.** Alarmed at Stalin's overt coldness to things like the Warsaw uprising and his insertion of pro-Communist governments in Romania and Bulgaria, the PM hoped to win FDR's agreement to take a harder line with the USSR in protecting oc-

cupied territories. Then, too, Churchill came with designs on recovering Britain's prewar Far Eastern possessions. **884** **Stalin came to win acceptance of the idea that possession followed the flag—that is, what his armies took, the USSR would keep.**

885 **Results were a hodgepodge of compromises.** Germany would be cut into four zones, one for the USSR, one for Great Britain, one for the US, and one, after considerable debate, for France (which was not represented, to de Gaulle's enduring resentment) to be carved from the U.S. and British zones. Germany would be administered by a four-power control commission. **886** **Although FDR and Churchill were reluctant, Stalin demanded reparations**

from Germany to be paid by such infrastructure as machinery and machine tools to the tune of twenty billion dollars, half going to the USSR. Trials of war criminals would be considered by the Allied foreign secretaries. Yugoslavia would be reconstituted under Tito; Italo-Yugoslav and Yugoslav-Bulgarian problems would be adjudicated by Moscow. Italo-Austrian questions were postponed.

887 Struggling for some consensus about a nascent peacekeeping group, all parties agreed to attend a United Nations organizational meeting in San Francisco on April 25, 1945, and all accepted the idea of a big power veto in the Security Council.

Poland troubled the whole conference. Churchill, representing one of Poland's guaranteeing allies, and FDR, now worrying about Soviet expansion in Eastern Europe, both wanted a free and sovereign Poland. Stalin agreed. For Soviet security, though, he wanted a Poland friendly to the USSR. Nonetheless, he accepted the idea of "free and unfettered elections as soon as possible on the basis of universal suffrage and the secret ballot." But although this sounded good, the so-called Lublin Polish group was already running a government. In addition, even though Stalin verbally accepted the notion of some representation from the exile government in England, the feel of sham hung in the Crimean air. **888** Discussions of Poland's forthcoming borders showed the Allies at their worst. Churchill and FDR finally compromised the Atlantic Charter by bartering Polish interests for expediency. The rump Lublin government would be reorganized to accept outside representatives—presumably some from the exiles. Poland's boundaries shifted as Stalin asked; its eastern limit would run along the old Curzon Line down to Czechoslovakia's prewar border while the question of how much of old Germany would go to Poland in compensation remained open. **889** Stalin answered that question upon Germany's conquest: the Oder-Neisse Rivers line marked the Polish-German border.

890 Pacific War decisions were signed without Churchill's knowledge—although he suspected what they were and essentially did not care. His interests were in the Southeast Asia areas. What happened in the Pacific he consigned largely to the U.S. **891** Here FDR became overgenerous in his desire to get the USSR's commitment to fight Japan. In return for this pledge, FDR accepted the Communist regime in Outer Mongolia, approved return of most of the territories taken from Russia in the Russo-Japanese War (including southern Sakhalin Island), approved various Russian land and rail lease arrangements in China, and left the Kurile Islands to Stalin. As a shabbily belated sop to Chiang Kai-shek, the secret protocol stipulated that he must approve the Chinese arrangements, FDR offering to broker the approval.

892 Probably the worst decision centered on refugees, deserters, and POWs from tyranny; they would be returned to tyranny's mercies.

893 Yalta's agreements still cause turmoil. Critics of Roosevelt claim that illness clouded his vision or that he simply gave away too much at Yalta. Defenders say that he argued from a position of weakness in that Soviet forces controlled most of Eastern Europe and were not likely to leave; that he and Churchill had saved as much as possible at the time. As for the Far Eastern agreements, they hinged on what FDR considered an urgent necessity to get Stalin into the war against Japan. Roosevelt did not know at Yalta whether the atomic bomb would work and sought to curtail an expected one million U.S. casualties in a ground campaign against the home islands. Questions remain open.

In reality, the armies' positions essentially dictated the peace.

894 Still hopeful, FDR reported to Congress about the good progress made at Yalta. He said, "Unless you here . . . with the support of the American people—concur in the general conclusions reached at Yalta

... the meeting will not have produced lasting results. . . . We shall have to take responsibility for world collaboration, or we shall have to bear the responsibility for another world conflict." In personal contacts his skepticism showed. "I didn't say the result was good," he told an inquirer, "I said it was the best I could do," and he doubted that Stalin would deliver on his promises.

Hardly surprised in the next few weeks at Stalin's machinations in Poland and in Eastern Europe, he chided "Uncle Joe" that the American people's opinion of Yalta would be vital—if they viewed it as a failure, all the dangers of distorted peace would rise again. FDR had hope tainted with weary realism and spoke of tougher stances to Churchill.

895 Franklin D. Roosevelt died suddenly at Warm Springs, Georgia, on April 12, 1945, following a stroke. The whole world mourned. People wept in Moscow's streets. Churchill intoned a world requiem: "A loss of the British nation and of the cause of freedom in every land." Goebbels, though, glowed: "My Führer, I congratulate you! Roosevelt is dead! It is written in the stars that the second half of April will be a turning point for us."

President Harry S Truman, who followed FDR, had scant knowledge of foreign affairs—indeed, scant knowledge of the war's secrets—but he had a Midwestern savvy and toughness that helped realize something of the world FDR envisioned.

Americans were doing better than ever. They certainly were making more money than before the war, and although housing shortages pinched a bit, general living standards soared. True, government infiltrated at various new levels but in ways that helped the war without outrageously inhibiting thought or activities. **896** A new national vision emerged as Americans came to know the power of their country and grasp the idea that it had a global role to play. Isolationism shrank drastically. Americans knew, too, how fortunate they were to have no war damage—save for a few almost comical efforts to send balloon bombs over the West Coast and rumored episodes of submarines shelling coastal states. **897** Taxes had gone up along with wages, and the national debt went from $28 billion to $247 billion in an expansion that baffled most people, but they did not worry much about it anyway. Americans knew they had done good things to win the war. FDR had been right when he said the U.S. would be the "arsenal of democracy." **898** Look at production figures: aircraft in 1939, 5,856 to a peak of 96,318 in 1944 for a total of almost 325,000. Tanks: around 400 in 1940 to a peak of 29,497 in 1943 for a total of nearly 88,500. America probably scored its most important war contribution in shipbuilding, with more than 5,700 merchantmen put into service.

War is what really mattered as victorious news came from all battle fronts.

ALLIED WESTERN BATTLES, 1945

899 Allied operations had essentially stalled in November 1944. Ike wanted to move his armies to the Rhine, but heavy enemy resistance, bad weather, and the December German counteroffensive in the Ardennes slowed everything down. Monty had been held up in an attempt to close the Falaise pocket and by fanatical Nazi resistance. **900** The new (September 1944) British field marshal, smarting from the bloody failure of his Market-Garden fiasco, still argued for his narrow-front thrust at Berlin, but plugged doggedly ahead from the Netherlands toward North Germany. He and his 21st Army Group played a large part in halting Hitler's Ardennes gamble in December 1944–January 1945.

901 On December 16, 1944, Hitler threw some twenty-five carefully picked divisions into one of his greatest war gambles. Attacking on about a sixty-mile front, the "Rundstedt offensive" (the name affronted the field marshal, who thought the attack absurd) aimed at dashing through the Ardennes to Antwerp, splitting

Circa 1945, men who led the U.S. military to victory. Seated, left to right: Simpson, Patton, Spaatz, Eisenhower, Bradley, Hodges, and Gerow; standing, left to right: Stearley, Vandenberg, Smith, Weyland, and Nugent.

the Allied armies, knocking out one of their main logistical bases, and stalling them in wreckage and confusion. Then, apparently, the Führer expected to take his best units back to the Eastern Front for a knockout smash there and win at least a negotiated peace. **902 Good planning took advantage of bad weather as Allied planes sat helplessly grounded.** Special German units, in U.S. uniforms, infiltrated the inhospitable Ardennes forest to confuse Allied reaction while strong panzer divisions raced through snows and cold toward the coast.

903 Lieutenant General Courtney Hodges' U.S. First Army took the main hit—its thin line in the Ardennes quickly unraveled. Surprised and confused, Hodges tried to get in touch with his scattered forces.

On a cold, gray, blustery, draggled day, a motorcycle courier arrived at Hodges' headquarters van. Having made his way somehow through the enemy

and the elements, he handed the general a top secret envelope and collapsed in bed.

Isolating himself to read the message from General Patton, whose Third Army had turned to help, Hodges opened the envelope to find a picture of Patton, helmet pulled low over his eyes and inscribed boldly, "Fuck You, Courtney!" Choking with laughter, Hodges suddenly saw the war in true perspective. **904 His army recovered quickly.** Hitler's offensive clotted around the town of Bastogne, where U.S. brigadier general Anthony McAuliffe, his forces surrounded, met a German surrender demand with a historic reply: "Nuts." The word baffled the Germans.

Clearing skies finally put Allied planes to work destroying German supply and reinforcement columns. Rundstedt wanted to end the attack but Hitler refused. By the middle of January, though, Germany's effort had fizzled. Hitler not only lost the

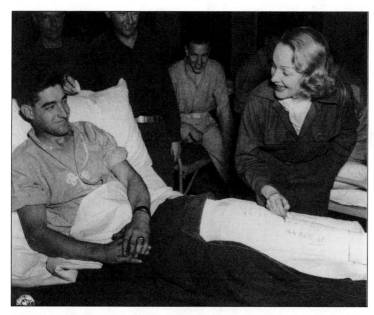

Actress Marlene Dietrich autographs a soldier's leg cast, U.S. hospital in Belgium, November 1944. During the war she gave over five hundred performances and made countless visits to the wounded.

chance to cross a river not crossed in war since 1805.

908 No doubt about it—luck is often decisive in war. On March 7, 1945, as the U.S. 9th Armored Division rumbled toward the town of Remagen, a German prisoner warned that at 4:00 P.M.—forty-five minutes ahead—the huge Rhine bridge there would be blown up by Nazi engineers. GIs won the race, seized the slightly damaged bridge, and changed the course of the campaign. In a day, eight thousand men and armor were across, consolidating, expanding their toehold and building other bridges. By the end of March seven armies had crossed and were speeding into Germany.

campaign but also priceless reserves needed in the east. **905** Patton's astonishing quickness in shifting his third Army attack from east to north had really turned the tide in what became known as the Battle of the Bulge.

906 General Devers's Sixth Army Group moved northeast to begin a drive in Alsace, aiming toward Karlsruhe. Before the Americans got started they were hit by sudden German offensives between Mulhouse and Colmar, near Switzerland, and further north in Lorraine. Some German divisions were caught in the "Colmar pocket." Ike ordered the pocket reduced, which the French First Army accomplished by February 9, 1945. All enemy bridgeheads west of the Rhine were eliminated.

907 A campaign to clear the Rhineland began with Monty's army group attacking from the Nijmegen area on the Allied left. He planned to link up with Bradley's men along the river. Devers's group also rolled to the Rhine, and Ike told all commanders to grab any

909 A furious Führer had four officers shot for losing the span; he replaced his Army Group West commander Rundstedt with Kesselring, who later remarked: "Never was there more concentrated bad luck at one place than at Remagen." Various things were tried to wreck the bridge—air attacks, V-2 attacks, frogmen, floating mines. All too late.

910 Pressing on after the Rhine crossings, Bradley and Devers ganged up on the German Seventh Army. Hitting it from north and south, they trapped a good part of it, destroyed the rest, and also almost finished the German First Army in a fitting ending for the Rhineland campaign. Estimates put German losses in that series of battles at 60,000 casualties and 250,000 prisoners.

911 Hard fighting lay ahead, but Hitler's maniacal stupidity in forbidding tactical freedom to his field commanders had cost him most of his men—resistance now would be a sporadic, increasingly desperate futility.

THE WAR IN
WESTERN EUROPE
ALLIED GAINS IN EUROPE

15 December 1944–21 March 1945

22 March–18 April 1945

19 April–7 May 1945

0   100   200

0   200

SCALE OF MILES/KILOMETERS

© 2001 Jeffrey L. Ward

GIs watch the Copacabana All Girl Review, at the Glenn Miller Theater, near Marseilles, France, August 29, 1945.

912 Ike gave Bradley the job of leading the drive into Germany—to Monty's discomfort. "Brad" had proved his daring, initiative, as well as affability and he would push without limit, using every advantage available. In early April two German armies under Model (Army Group B) were surrounded in what became known as the Ruhr Pocket. Hitler ordered the usual last stand but added instructions to destroy all communications and industrial equipment—which Model would not do. With serious supply shortages, Model fought on to keep some Allied divisions from continuing their main eastern drive. As his pocket

shrank, Hitler finally ordered him to break out—far too late. Model disbanded his army (yielding 317,000 prisoners) in mid-April, then shot himself.

913 Hitler conscripted new armies of *Volksgrenadier.* Mainly Himmler's Replacement Army troops, these were recruited from rear area units and from formations shattered in action. They were not first-liners. With these, Hitler also sent some of the *Volkssturm* to battle, indicating that the Third Reich had started grinding the seed corn.

Nothing helped. **914** The Allies pushed into Germany from three sides. Ike's forces bagged army after army, taking thousands of prisoners and ending any chance of strategic withdrawal to some last-ditch redoubt. Devers's Sixth Army Group headed south for Austria, and Bradley's Twelfth marched east to the Elbe where it would meet the Red Army.

915 After Rome fell in June 1944—sparking an FDR comment: "One down and two to go"—Mark Clark plotted a new offensive. Mission: crack the Gothic Line and destroy Nazi armies in Italy. Cracking the Gothic Line proved difficult. When Kesselring left to replace Rundstedt in the West, Gen. Heinrich von Vietinghoff took over in Italy. A canny old Prussian infantryman, he conducted a series of masterful retreats into the northern Apennines.

916 By the time Allied forces descended from the Apennines into the Po Valley for their last great offensive in early April 1945, peace negotiations were underway in Italy, and Vietinghoff signed surrender documents on May 2, 1945.

917 Vietinghoff performed a last, vital service before becoming a POW. As Allied armies overran Germany, a group of prisoners known as the *Prominente* (relatives of Allied leaders, including Dawyck Haig, son of Britain's WWI commander, titled Germans, condemned generals) were collected from various concentration camps by the SS, shoved into buses and

trucks accompanied by what looked ominously like a mobile gas chamber, and moved through the Brenner Pass into Italy. Fortunately, Hitler had given confusing orders to the escort and they fumbled around wondering what they should do with the prisoners, who expected execution. **918 Early on April 27, 1945, as the group approached the Tyrolean village of Niederhoff, one of the prisoners, Colonel von Bogislav Bonin, bluffed his way into the town.** Spotting old friend General von Vietinghoff, he whispered for help. Shortly an army force arrived, disarmed the SS guards, and saved the prisoners for American rescue on May 4, 1945.

919 *Il Duce* **and his mistress Clara, captured again by partisans, were shot on April 23, 1945, and their bodies, hanged by the feet, displayed in the Piazalle Loreto, Milan—a shabby end for the "sawdust Caesar."**

Hitler heard the news as he hunkered in the *Führerbunker*.

ABOVE: American soldiers of Japanese descent, 42nd Infantry Regiment, run for cover as German artillery shell is about to land. Italy, April 4, 1945. BELOW: Mussolini (third from left) and his mistress Clara Petacci (fourth from left) and cohorts, Milan, April 1945.

ALLIED/JAPANESE FAR EASTERN BATTLES, 1945

920 **Having decided to invade Luzon, MacArthur gave the job to Krueger's Sixth Army.** Starting north from Leyte on January 2, 1945, the U.S. fleet encountered heavy *Kamikaze* interference that nearly stopped it cold. In steady attacks from December 13 to January 13, the "divine wind" sank twenty-four ships, heavily damaged thirty, and lightly damaged thirty-seven.

Krueger landed four divisions on the difficult part of Lingayen Gulf beaches January 9, 1945. Paying close attention to his flanks—respecting his opponent, the Tiger of Malaya, General Yamashita—Krueger advanced slowly against many more Japanese troops than originally expected. Moving less rapidly than MacArthur wanted, Krueger received nearly constant complaints from his superior. Nevertheless, by February 3–4, 1945, elements of the Sixth Army were fighting their way into Manila.

USS *Pennsylvania* and a battleship of *Colorado* class followed by three cruisers move into Lingayen Gulf prior to the landings on Luzon, Philippines.

921 **Inside the city the enemy escalated resistance, fought almost house to house.** Finally they retreated into what they thought might be a sacrosanct haven, the medieval Spanish walled community, Intramuros. MacArthur did cherish that old place and, in fact, ordered Krueger not to use artillery against it. Two attacks were bloodily repulsed. Another artillery request to headquarters brought the same denial. Krueger then technically obeyed orders and drove tanks through the walls. The stronghold collapsed after MacArthur finally approved artillery fire. Amid brutal fighting, a badly battered Manila fell on March 4, 1945.

922 **Yamashita, critically short of supplies, sustained resistance until his starving, outgunned force broke into bits but even then continued fragmentary, ineffectual opposition until the war ended.** The Philippine campaign cost the Japanese some 450,000 men against 62,000 Allied ground casualties, with 13,700 killed.

The way opened now for a drive against the home islands.

General Yamashita, the "Tiger of Malaya."

923 The strategic bombing tempo against Japan speeded up now that Saipan, Guam, and Tinian sprouted B-29 bases. Earlier China-based precision bombing attacks had brought questionable results, so Gen. "Hap" Arnold put Maj. Gen. Curtis LeMay (the "Iron Eagle") in command of a new firebombing program aimed at burning Japan out of the war. **924** On the night of March 9–10, 1945, 334 B-29s from the Marianas flew over Tokyo at about 8,000 feet, dropping 2,000 tons of incendiaries on the city's paper houses. For some two hours the bombs rained and a great firestorm erupted over the capital. Twenty major industrial sites burned in addition to hundreds of homes. Some 90,000 people died, 125,000 were injured, and 1.2 million were left homeless. For the next ten days Nagoya, Kobe, Osaka, and Tokyo-Kawasaki again were seared by incendiaries. By mid-May even larger raids swarmed Japanese skies.

925 Not everyone liked the idea of blistering Japan. Some high-ranking officers argued that these raids, and the ones that wrecked Hamburg and Dresden earlier, were beyond the rules of war, but the rationale remained strong—the enemies had started it and "War is hell."

926 Air strategy dictated the next phase of island operations. Saipan provided a usable base for big bombers against Japan, but early raids proved costly. Closer bases were needed so Allied fighters could escort the bombers into Japanese defensive air space. Iwo Jima at last got the nod. An island of about eight square miles in area, halfway between Saipan and Tokyo, it offered the best emergency landing sites for damaged B-29s on home island routes and for fields from which medium bombers and fighters could reach Japan.

U.S. intelligence—backed up by ULTRA—confirmed the island's inhospitality. **927** As one Japanese defender said, it "was an island of sulphur, no water, no sparrow, and no swallow...." What it did have was about 23,000 Japanese troops, well dug into caves, shelters, and pillboxes, protected by minefields supported by cunningly hidden artillery emplacements. It also had an able commander, Lt. Gen. Tadamichi

B-29 Superfortress. With its 3,700-mile range, the B-29 was earmarked for use in the Pacific theater. It was the first bomber to house its crew in pressurized compartments. The first B-29 combat mission was an attack on railway yards in Bangkok, Thailand, June 5, 1944.

Kuribayashi. **928** **The Japanese commander decided on a static defense—he would not waste men and munitions on contesting the beaches but would counterattack with tanks when possible.** Two airfields were operational on the island, with a third under construction—these, plus lofty Mount Suribachi on the southwestern tip of the island would be key defensive points.

929 **Maj. Gen. Harry Schmidt's Marine V Amphibious Corps landed two Marine divisions on Iwo Jima at 0900 February 19, 1945.** The island—the most strongly fortified yet assaulted—had been battered for seventy-four days by fierce air attacks and naval bombardments, yet heavy, crisscrossing fire swept the first wave going ashore. With no room for maneuver, fighting raged head on, soon hand-to-hand. Volcanic ash added to the invaders' misery—it slowed everything down as vehicles bogged down in it and men slithered and slid forward. Accurate artillery plastered landing craft and heavy surf compli-

cated unloading. **930** **Still, landings were made along with progress toward cutting the island in two by the end of D-day, at a cost of 2,420 Marine casualties.**

931 **After four days of clenching combat, Marines took Mount Suribachi, a heroic feat memorialized in the famous photograph.** After committing his reserve division, General Schmidt pushed the attack against Kuribayashi's main defenses. **932** **By the end of February the worst fighting had ended, but sporadic encounters continued until March 21. Costs were fearsome on both sides: 24,891 U.S. casualties, including 6,821 killed; Japanese losses amounted to 21,000 dead and 212 prisoners—these numbers are inaccurate, though, since many Japanese were sealed in caves and shelters.**

In a matter of days the island began to save B-29 crews and by the end of the war 2,251 emergency landings were made, possibly saving 25,000 crewmen.

933 **The Joint Chiefs of Staff had for some time considered the Ryukyu Islands as a target for invasion. Since abandoning the idea of taking Formosa, army and navy planners settled on Okinawa as the best target.** Sitting between Formosa and Kyushu, it offered airfields for bombing the enemy's industrial heartland, good anchorages, and could handle large numbers of troops staging for an invasion of Japan. Forces working from there could cut completely all Japanese communications with the south.

Admiral Nimitz, commanding the Okinawa operation, faced unusual problems—especially logistical problems. **934** **Okinawa's size—sixty-five miles long and from two to eighteen miles wide—meant that masses of supplies would be needed for not only an invasion force, but also for**

Coast Guard and Navy landing craft unloading Marines and supplies onto Iwo Jima's black volcanic sand beaches, February 1945.

Joe Rosenthal's photograph of the flag-raising on Mount Suribachi, February 23, 1945, has come to symbolize the Marines' hard-won victory at Iwo Jima. Twenty-two of eighty-two Medals of Honor awarded to Marines during WWII were given for action on Iwo Jima.

naval construction battalions (Seabees) that would be building bases and airfields during the campaign. Another thing: 450,000 native Okinawans lived on the island. These constituted the first large group of civilians encountered in the Pacific campaigns—military government agencies would be required, along with extra food.

Supplies were collected, packaged, and shipped on staggered schedules to rendezvous with a flotilla of thirteen hundred ships gathering to sustain the launching of Operation Iceberg on April 1, 1945.

935 Main assault forces consisted of the U.S. Tenth Army (four army and three Marine divisions plus garrison, service, and military government personnel) commanded by Lt. Gen. Simon Bolivar Buckner Jr., commander of

American forces in the earlier Aleutians campaign. Heavy interdiction air strikes isolated Okinawa as numerous carriers and naval support units moved to cover landing operations.

936 Enemy reaction was slow but became fanatical as furious waves of *Kamikazes* struck naval forces around Okinawa—and did serious damage. But U.S. planes soon established control of the air over the island. Frogmen probed for underwater obstacles, minesweepers crept in to cleanse the approaches.

937 At 0530, twenty minutes before dawn, April 1, 1945, battleships, cruisers, and destroyers all began firing on the island and especially the designated beaches in the fiercest bombardments ever to cover a Pacific landing. At 0745 carrier planes napalmed the beach defenses and in ten minutes a general barrage churned the landing zones. Intelligence predicted heavy resistance as a factor from the start, and Buckner's timetable stipulated daily objectives with victory coming in seventy days.

938 **L-day dawned to clearing skies, light surf, soft east winds, and a temperature of seventy-five degrees as 180,000 men boarded landing craft.** "Finally, at 0820," says one authority, "an almost unbroken eight-mile line of armored fire-support craft and troop-carrying amphibious vehicles swept forward toward the seemingly lifeless [Hagushi] beaches."

For the moment they were lifeless. **939** **Lieutenant General Mitsuru Ushijima, commanding Japan's Thirty-second Army, did not contest the beaches, and by the end of L-day, Buckner's men had gone as far as expected for L+3.** Ushijima, who did not expect to beat the Americans but to make them pay an exorbitant price for Okinawa, followed an Imperial General Headquarters plan to hold the island at virtually any cost—if taken, the imperial inner line of defense would be broken. If all went well, the Imperial Navy's Special Attack Corps (*Kamikaze*), would, in conjunction with a large surface squadron and small suicide boats, destroy the U.S. covering fleet off Okinawa. That done, Ushijima's army would attack the unsupported Americans and push them into the sea.

Sadly for the defenders, the plan went awry really before it got started. A cache of the suicide boats had been captured on a tiny out island, while *Kamikaze* attacks did serious but not crippling damage to U.S. naval units. A sortie by the last big Japanese surface fleet, including the huge battleship *Yamato*, was destroyed by Admiral Spruance's carrier planes.

Ushijima's men had a great number of guns and knew how to use their artillery better than most imperial troops; they also had built a series of extremely strong defensive positions in the southern

Kamikaze pilot narrowly missing the USS *Missouri* (battleship on which Japan's formal surrender ceremony would take place five months later) during the battle for Okinawa, April 1945.

end of the island—many of which were unknown to U.S. forces.

Buckner's advance went speedily eastward and northwestward toward Zampa Peninsula with its Yontan airfield. **940** **By April 4 the expeditionary force had reached its projected L+15 positions.** Seabees went to work repairing existing landing strips and laying new ones. Few civilians were encountered—most apparently were with the Japanese troops.

As U.S. troops headed south they ran into Ushijima's main lines and close, brutal, remorseless fighting followed. **941** **Skillfully pulling back, line to line, Ushijima stalled Buckner's advance; by April's end an angry stalemate gave U.S. commanders a chance to relieve their exhausted divisions.** A big Japanese counteroffensive began on May 4—against Ushijima's better judgment. It proved a costly failure and consumed most Japanese reserves while also exposing hidden gun positions.

942 **Now, though, the Americans were up against the fantastically strong Shuri Line—possibly the strongest position U.S. forces faced in the Pacific, "a system of defenses in depth, employing mutually supporting strong**

points, pillboxes, and elaborate caves with connecting tunnels and several entrances. Many burial shrines were used, artillery and mortars were emplaced in caves, and reverse slopes were skillfully organized." Nevertheless, a crucial hill fell to the Americans in mid-May, and a month later major opposition cracked and fighting ended by the end of June.

Artillery fire killed General Buckner on the eighteenth and General Ushijima committed hara-kiri four days later. Okinawa cost the U.S. 49,251 casualties (12,520 killed); the Japanese lost 117,472 (110,071 killed). Between April 6 and June 22, *Kamikazes* flew 1,900 raids. They and the new guided suicide *(Baka)* bombs caused terrific casualties (4,900 seamen dead, 4,824 wounded) and ship damage (36 sunk, 368 crippled).

Planning proceeded for Japan's invasion—which doubtless would cost infinitely more.

USS *Bunker Hill* hit by two *Kamikazes* (or suicide dive bombers) in thirty seconds, off Okinawa in the Ryukyus, May 11, 1945.

Ship-to-ship transfer of wounded man (injured in fires following *Kamikaze* attacks) from USS *Bunker Hill* to USS *Wilkes Barre*, May 11, 1945.

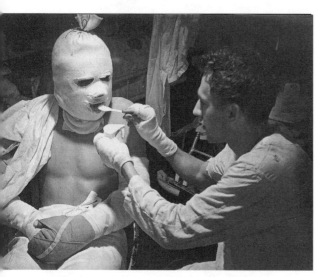

ABOVE: Encased in pressure bandages covering burns suffered in fires, a mummy-like patient is fed by medic on the hospital ship USS *Solace*, May 1945. RIGHT: A soldier unloaded from the tank that retrieved him from the front lines. Enemy artillery and small-arms fire prevented ambulances from removing wounded to the rear. Okinawa, April–June 1945. BELOW: View of #4 90mm AAA (antiaircraft artillery) gun emplacement with crew in pit. "D" Battery, 98th AAA Gun Battalion, 137th AAA Group, Okinawa, July 18, 1945.

THE UNION OF SOVIET SOCIALIST REPUBLICS (USSR), 1945

943 With the rolling wave of victories recorded every day, Soviet morale soared. Conservative military leadership pressed for continued production miracles but volume began to wane. More consumer goods were appearing, here and there new clothes could be seen. Although internal civilian travel did not yet revive, news sources expanded and people were aware of what was happening at the front as well as fairly well informed on Mother Russia's economy.

944 In such broken parts of the country as the Ukraine, the Crimea, and western Russia into Poland, human agonies were not so much reported as felt. Horrors of Nazi occupation were banked in Russian memories. Different logistical problems began to surface: how to provide food, clothing, and especially shelter to millions in the devastated areas; how to restore essential services such as water supplies, power, transportation—these became problems nearly as colossal as supplying the war itself.

945 Certainly the USSR now had a vast infrastructure for economic mobilization, but it was geared for destruction, not reconstruction. Shifting priorities would take time, labor, money—and certainly organization. Would the Communist Party provide revivification in those vast areas where life struggled against chaos? If not the party, who? These humane questions played against unspoken ones. Would the party govern in the liberated and captured sections where the Red Army ran? **946** If the party governed, would it bring with it all the tokens of Stalin's terror that shuttered life in Russia? For that matter, what could prevent it as his legions installed his puppets at his bidding? Who would oppose Beria's repression where the NKVD marched in behind the tanks? The Western Allies? Not likely. They were stressed nearly to the limit advancing from the west and clearly wanted an early end. **947** Those in the USSR who hated their op-

pression had almost no hope that it would change, nor could they expect outside help.

Such worries were uncommon, though, as Germany crumbled. **948** If once Stalin ruled by blood, who could doubt his greatness now? He had mustered Mother Russia's millions in a Great Patriotic War; his determination had held them all together against the world's most awesome armies; he did not spare himself in calling for total sacrifice. If he was hard still, he was also great. As the war wound down, Joseph Vissarionovich Stalin loomed as the greatest hero of them all—and accepted the title of generalissimo.

949 The Soviet people, though, had ample reason for pride in what they did to advance victory. Raw numbers are usually dry and uninteresting, but the USSR's production record deserves special consideration; the statistics provided in I. C. B. Dear and M. R. D. Foot, eds., *The Oxford Companion to World War II*, show that Soviet aircraft production climbed steadily during the war, from 10,382 in 1939 to a peak of 40,300 in 1944—for a total of nearly 160,000. Some 36,000 of the total were Ilyushin II-2s (Stormoviks), a kind of flying tank, which Stalin said were "as necessary to the Red Army as air or bread." Tank production soared: 2,950 in 1939 to a peak of 28,963 in 1944—for a total of over 100,000. Soviet artillerists justifiably prided themselves on their homemade guns: 17,348 made in 1939 to a peak of 130,000 in 1943—for a total of over 500,000.

RUSSO-GERMAN BATTLES, 1945

950 Taking personal command of the army, Stalin reorganized his *fronts*. He sent Zhukov to head the 1st Belorussian *front* which would have the honor of taking Berlin. Plans to end the war were set: the Red Army would smash from the Vistula to the Oder River in fifteen days, thence to the Elbe in another thirty. In this offensive the Red Army would hurl about 2.2 million men against German Army Group A, some

400,000 strong, while another 1.6 million would overwhelm Army Group Center and swing through East Prussia while clearing the Baltic coastline. Soviet planes would dominate the skies against a skeletonized Luftwaffe.

951 On Friday, January 12, 1945, the greatest World War II drive began when Zhukov's(q.v.) and Ivan Konevs's *fronts* erupted from Vistula bridgeheads with a ten-to-one superiority in troops. Hitler scrambled to find someone to stop the drive against Army Group A; finally in a flight of lunacy he gave command of a scratch new group to Heinrich Himmler (q.v.). Again nothing helped. By early February both Soviet *fronts* were strung along the Oder's banks from thirty-five miles east of Berlin to Czechoslovakia, temporarily stalled for supplies. **952** A smaller northern campaign cleared East Prussia, and here Stalin called a halt, delaying to let the Germans remind the Allies how much they needed the Red Army.

For their part, the Western Allies responded to Yalta requests for bombing help during the Soviet offensive. On the night of Tuesday, February 13, 1945, RAF Bomber Command sent 796 Lancasters on a general raid against Dresden, a city internationally renowned as an architectural gem and home of the famed Dresden china. Tons of high explosives and incendiaries rained on the city, spawning an all-consuming firestorm. The next day 311 U.S. B-17s worsened the massive damage; some fifty thousand people perished as the city nearly disappeared. An indiscreet press briefing at Supreme Headquarters

Dresden, 1945. Churchill said the bombing of this city "remains a serious query against the conduct of Allied bombing."

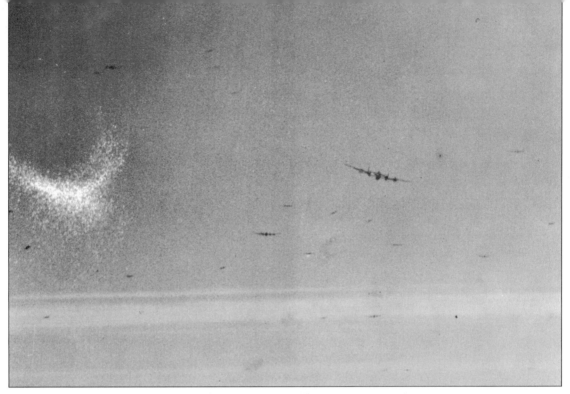

"Window" (far left of photo), strips of metal foil, released by Lancaster bombers during raid on Essen, March 11, 1945. Called "chaff" in the U.S., the countermeasure was designed to confuse enemy radar.

Allied Expeditionary Force explained that the new Operation Thunderclap deliberately targeted population centers to create chaos and interdict relief.

Headlines about Allied terror bombing brought loud condemnation—even from Churchill—and the Dresden affair remains a blot on the Allied record. It did not bother Stalin, who appreciated the help.

In March a renewed Soviet drive in the south toward Vienna brushed aside a senseless Hitler offensive in Hungary and pushed along the Danube. Vienna fell in mid-April and the whole Soviet front resumed a slow march westward.

953 News from the Allies, and especially a cable from Ike, energized Stalin. Across the Rhine, Ike's men encircled the Ruhr and were rapidly approaching the Elbe, where they had agreed to meet the Red Army. Their rapid tempo of operations might propel them into Berlin. Eisenhower's cable astounded the Soviet leader: the general declared that Berlin no longer remained an important ob- jective! A far more politically astute Stalin simply could not believe this, and, assuming there was some hidden plan, redoubled his suspicion of his Allies. Then he redeployed his *fronts* to let Zhukov roll on to and beyond Berlin while Rokossovsky's 2nd Belorussian *front* and Konev's 1st Ukrainian flanked Zhukov's drive to the Elbe. Getting to Berlin took longer than expected. During some reshuffling of Soviet troops, Eisenhower's forces moved well beyond the southern reaches of the Elbe.

Information reaching Ike from various sources indicated that Hitler had moved the Nazi government to the long-touted "National Redoubt" in the mountains south of Munich, and a dogged last-stand campaign was expected. Two things flawed Ike's reasoning: one, there was no "National Redoubt," despite Goebbels's efforts to invent one; two, Berlin had vast political importance, as Stalin clearly understood. Churchill also understood and fumed at Ike's naivete—the PM knew Berlin would be a vital

American troops enter Germany, marching through the Siegfried Line, 1945.

April 12, 1945, Supreme Allied Commander General Eisenhower with General Bradley (left) and General Patton (behind Eisenhower) inspect art treasures stolen by the Nazis and stored in a salt mine. One of Hitler's postwar plans was to use this plunder to create a world-class art center in Linz, his childhood home in Austria.

bargaining chip in the postwar Allied infighting. Perhaps Hitler understood the city's significance best of all the contenders, realizing that he would have to die in Berlin's rubble if anything were to be preserved of his life's work.

GERMANY, 1945

954 With enemies coming from three sides, with German troops fighting from fragmented pockets, with bombs pulverizing city rubble day and night, Germany collapsed. Some fanatics remained who urged war to the death—these, though, were mainly Hitler Youth and the few who had stayed home and miraculously avoided the bombers, the strafers, the big, long guns. Even Albert Speer's genius could no longer find the resources to make planes or tanks, nor the fuel for them.

955 Hitler had finally made his country a burning hell on earth. Not a hollow but a broken shell now, the Reich's ruins remained. A kind of acceptance of extinction infused the people, most of whom welcomed the sur-

May 3, 1945, following their surrender to U.S. troops in Austria, left to right: Maj. Gen. Walther Dornberger (commander of the V-weapons research station at Peenemünde), Lt. Gen. Herbert Axter, Dr. Werner von Braun (arm in cast), and, far right, Hans Lindenberg.

render. But fear remained, and thousands of Germans, including soldiers, panicked and streamed westward to reach the Allies before the Soviets reached them—a decision for the lesser of evils.

956 **There were sound reasons to flee the Russians.** As one Russian major later admitted:

a few regrettable things happened from time to time but, on the whole, a fairly strict discipline was maintained as regards "rape." The most common offense in Poland was "dai chasy"—give me your wristwatch. . . . But the looting and raping in a big way did not start until our soldiers got to Germany. Our fellows were so sex-starved that they often raped old women of sixty, or seventy or even eighty—much to these grandmothers' surprise, if not downright delight. But I admit it was a nasty business, and the

record of the Kazakhs and other Asiatic troops was particularly bad.

957 **As the Allies clustered, they began to divide Germany along the four-power scheme devised at Yalta.** Some heart-wrenching scenes followed when British, American, and French troops were compelled to hand over refugees and others to the Russians.

958 **The material costs of Hitler's war could be felt in the rubble around them, but Germans also suffered stupefying casualties.** Nazi armed forces suffered combined losses of nearly eight and a half million. Many thousands of civilians, perhaps more than a million, died in air raids—statistics are seriously distorted by urban devastation.

959 **Hitler had moved into the Berlin *Führerbunker* (a big air raid shelter under the Chancellery) in January 1945.** A physical and nervous wreck, the Führer dragged his right foot (a result of the assassination attempt) and lived day to day on various injections from his personal doctor, Theodore Morrell. People who visited the bunker found him dwelling increasingly on past glories and false hopes. With Albert Speer he talked of the great buildings to come after the war. But the secret weapons he had hoped would turn the tide had failed him—the new submarines were too slow in coming, there were too few of the fearsome M-262 jet planes—the Führer fell back on German mythology for solace. When FDR died, Hitler jubilantly recalled the collapse of the alliance against Frederick the Great in 1762 when Russia's Empress Elizabeth had died. By April, Hitler huddled in the bunker, unable to leave and barely functioning.

960 **Goebbels knew the need for a glorious Hitlerian end and there is no doubt that he had a hand in stage-managing the Führer's last hours.** As Russian troops smashed through the last blocks of rubble, Hitler gathered the Goebbels family, a few others, and his longtime mistress Eva Braun. Early on Sunday, April

29, 1945, he married Eva Braun. Then he finished dictating a political testament, wrote his will, napped until midday, and learned of Mussolini's terrible end. At about 3:30 Monday afternoon, he put a pistol to his mouth and pulled the trigger; Eva took poison. Their bodies were taken to the garden above, drenched with gasoline, and set afire. Reports vary about what happened then—according to some accounts the bodies burned and the ashes were scattered later by Russian artillery; other accounts say Russian troops found the bodies.

On May 1, Goebbels and his wife, faithful to the Third Reich, had their six children poisoned. Then they were either shot by an SS orderly or they tried to kill themselves and were then shot by the orderly. Their bodies, too, were burned.

961 As directed in Hitler's will, Grand Adm. Karl Dönitz became head of what was left of the Third Reich. The surprised admiral immediately began negotiating the surrender of Germany.

962 On April 25, 1945, U.S. troops and Red Army elements made first contact at Stehla, a small village southeast of Torgau. Torgau—seventy-five miles south of Berlin—gets the honors in most accounts because there a large and jubilant gathering of Russians and Americans celebrated splitting the Third Reich in two.

963 Fragmented surrenders of Nazi troops began on all fronts. General Vietinghoff surrendered Italy on May 2; General-Admiral Hans von Friedeburg surrendered German troops in Denmark, northwest Germany, and Holland to Montgomery at Lüneburg Heath on May 4; **964** General Alfred Jodl signed, for the German government, the unconditional surrender of all German forces at Eisenhower's headquarters in Reims on May 7. Eisenhower, enraged by the concentration camps he had seen, sent a grimly laconic cable to the Combined Chiefs of Staff: "The mission of this Allied force was fulfilled at 0241 local time, May 7, 1945."

Russian flag-raising over the Reichstag, Berlin, May 2, 1945. The arm of one soldier has been retouched to conceal a bracelet of "liberated" watches.

Field Marshal Wilhelm Keitel signing ratified surrender terms for the German army at Russian headquarters, Berlin, May 8, 1945. This was full circle for Keitel, who personally had conducted the French armistice negotiations after the fall of France, June 1940.

965 Stalin demanded a ratification in the Soviet zone, which occurred in Berlin on May 8. Field Marshal Wilhelm Keitel signed for Germany before representatives of the four Allied powers.

966 V-E (Victory in Europe) Day, May 8, 1945, brought millions into the streets all over the world. But everybody waited for the Asian sequel.

THE BRITISH EMPIRE, 1945

967 Now that the Nazis were finished and Hitler disposed of, Britons looked to the Far East eagerly to have the war truly done. From an economist's perspective, Britain faced serious debtor problems. Inflation lurked in the wings, the national debt stood at three times the national income; shipping had been seriously crippled, which meant foreign trade would return slowly, which meant Britain's normally hefty balance of trade would go into the red. The housing shortage caused by earlier bombing had not improved, and although the Allies won the Battle of the Atlantic, Britons still endured food and clothing shortages and a large array of war regulations.

968 War casualties were surprisingly light—total military and civilian, somewhere around 600,000, while in the First World War, Britain had counted a million military dead alone. As for the rest of the empire's states, casualties amounted to around 100,000.

969 The British Empire emerged from the war in some political disarray, with nationalist movements threatening unity. And the empire did shrink, but it shrank shrewdly into a Commonwealth with largely friendly independents that preserved some of the amity and cooperation of earlier days.

970 Victorious or not, the British people were war weary. Politics had lapsed for the war but interest revived. Churchill and others in the War Cabinet

ABOVE: Convalescent American soldiers attending Mother's Day services at the blitzed Coventry cathedral, May 13, 1945. BELOW: General George S. Patton waves to cheering crowds during a parade in Los Angeles, in his home state of California.

sought to preserve the coalition government until Japan surrendered. Labour Party leaders wanted a swift election, so one was laid on for July 1945. **971 Victory clearly at hand, Britons, turning from war and those who led the country through it, voted for the Labour Party.** Quickly the new prime minister, Clement Attlee, headed to Potsdam to take Churchill's place midway through the last conference of Grand Alliance leaders.

DIPLOMACY, 1945

972 Franklin Roosevelt's fervent wish came true at San Francisco, starting on April 25, 1945, as the United Nations Conference on International Organization opened. Delegates and staffs from fifty nations came to flesh out the agenda devised at the Dumbarton Oaks Conference in August–September 1944. Excitement tinged the air—most of the delegates and the masses of press representatives looked on this meeting as one of the most important in history.

That turned out to be true. Long and often heated debates swirled around the draft charter of a United Nations organization to keep peace in the world. For nine weeks so many changes, deletions, and amendments filled the days that talk seemed likely to kill a good idea. In the end, though, issues were resolved or suitably sloughed, and from all the arguments and discussions came a UN Charter that pledged goodwill in keeping peace, common support of human rights, and the equal rights of men and women; pledged, too, cooperation for the betterment of economic and social conditions everywhere, as well as a

British official photograph of Allied commanders meeting at Eisenhower's headquarters, Frankfurt-am-Main, June 10, 1945: (left to right) Field Marshal Montgomery (in beret), General Eisenhower leaning over to speak to Marshal Zhukov, who is presenting Montgomery with the Russian Order of Victory, and Montgomery's chief of staff, Major General de Guingand.

Stalin, arriving at Churchill's residence during the Terminal Conference, Potsdam, Germany, July 1945.

structure to prevent the use of armed force "save in the common interest."

973 Born in the aftermath of a terrible war, the UN held together through a little thick and much thin and still stands as a monument to reason.

974 Terminal, the last of the major Allied conferences, opened in Potsdam on July 17, 1945. Of the Big Three there, only Stalin boasted continuity. President Truman was still feeling his way into his job and Churchill's attention wandered to the general election in the United Kingdom. **975** Much needed to be decided, and Stalin came bolstered by the success of his legions' drive to Berlin. Truman, uncertain at first, waiting for historic news, and a preoccupied Churchill, listened glumly to Stalin's pseudodemocratic proposals for the myriad countries his armies had overrun.

Untutored as he was in diplomacy as a system of deceit, Truman came to balk at some of FDR's concessions at Yalta. Truman, not yet the consummate conniver he would become, had some compensating

stubbornness that Stalin could understand. And the day after he arrived he had the news he needed.

976 Churchill could tell by the way Truman's attitude suddenly turned tough at Potsdam that the atomic bomb was ready. Tests had been done at Alamogordo, New Mexico, on July 16, 1945. The weapon worked—beyond even the most optimistic expectations. Although designed to subdue Hitler and Hirohito, the bomb suddenly gave Truman and American officials generally the feeling of holding a royal flush—they now held the Russian bear by the throat.

977 In discussions of thorny issues, Truman talked cryptically of the U.S. having a powerful weapon (not unsuspected by the Soviets) and Stalin riposted with the hope that the U.S. "would make good use of it." Discussions did get easier though. While hashing over German and European boundary issues, Attlee and Churchill flew to England for the results of the general election. Churchill lost and Prime Minister Attlee returned to the conference and sustained Truman's views.

978 Out of the discussions came the Potsdam Declaration which settled much of Germany's future. "It is not the intention of the Allies to destroy or enslave the German people," the victors said, pointing out that the Germans, by changing their ways, could "in due course take their place among the free and peaceful peoples of the world." General peace treaties would be arranged with Allied foreign ministers and the former enemy powers.

979 After consulting with Chiang, the conferees, realizing Japan would fight to keep the emperor, modified the idea of unconditional surrender as they proclaimed the Potsdam Declaration on July 26, 1945. Japan, it said, should surrender its armed forces unconditionally, and expunge those who had steered Japan to "world conquest"; it reaffirmed the total commitment of all the Allies to Japan's defeat, declared that Japan would retain its four main islands, and promised no intention to enslave the Japanese people but threatened justice to war criminals. An ultimatum: surrender unconditionally or face "the utter devastation of Japanese homeland"—that was about the only forewarning the Japanese got about the atomic bomb. The Japanese announced they would *mokusatsu* (kill with silence) the declaration, which the Allies took as a rejection.

980 That same day, July 26, 1945, the U.S. cruiser *Indianapolis* arrived at Tinian with the U-235 core of the atomic bomb called "Little Boy." There came a sad denouement to the ship's mission. Returning to Guam, the *Indianapolis* received orders to proceed to Leyte Gulf in the Philippines to support an invasion. Captain Charles B. McVay asked for a destroyer escort, since his ship lacked sophisticated submarine detection gear. Assured by higher-ups that there was no threat present and no escort needed, he sailed. Just after midnight, July 30, 1945, a Japanese submarine torpedoed the *Indianapolis;* she sank in less than fifteen minutes. Some 900 of the 1,196 men aboard made it into the water, most of them wearing life jackets. Shark attacks began at dawn and built into a feeding frenzy that lasted until the survivors were accidentally found four days later and rescued the next day. By then only 317 men were alive.

In an unprecedented move, the navy court-martialed Captain McVay—he alone of all U.S. commanders was court-martialed for losing a ship in action against the enemy. Charges were vague but included failure to zigzag in good visibility—this despite the fact that McVay had discretionary authority to do it or not. The whole trial seems a sham in retrospect. The Japanese submarine commander testified that he could have sunk even a zigzagging *Indianapolis*, and a veteran U.S. submarine captain said the same.

Lurking in the background and not adequately presented by the defense: ULTRA data known in Guam indicated that two enemy submarines were in the waters between there and Leyte, and no one informed McVay. Visibility at the time of the attack was peculiarly bad—a condition noted in statements made by survivors which were not used at the trial and only recently discovered in navy archives.

A general feeling lingers that the trial was distorted to protect those who should have warned McVay and should have made better efforts to track his ship so that its disappearance would have been noted much earlier. Even the Japanese commander said, "I had a feeling it [the court-martial] was contrived from the beginning."

Although later restored to duty and given a retirement promotion to rear admiral, McVay never recovered from the humiliation and committed suicide. He was recently vindicated by an act of Congress.

981 Through the Japanese ambassador to Moscow, Emperor Hirohito hinted at a desire for peace, which Stalin reported with the caveat that the emperor would have to be retained. No immediate action followed, nor were the Japanese aware of Stalin's Yalta promise to enter the war. As the Western Allies' victory in the Pacific became certain, Stalin wanted to get in on the spoils and reclaim lost territories.

Convoy ascending the famous twenty-one curves of the road at Annan, China, March 26, 1945. The 517th Quartermaster Group used a relay system of convoys to transport food, fuel, and military supplies between Chen-Yi and Kweiyang; Annan was on this route.

ALLIED MILITARY OPERATIONS AGAINST JAPAN, 1945

982 Burma fighting went steadily against the Japanese. While General Kimura maneuvered feverishly to negate Allied superiority in men, matériel, and especially logistics, he failed. **983** Lashio fell to a combined Chinese-U.S. force on March 7, 1945, and truck convoys once more reached Kunming. General Slim slipped British troops through jungle routes and snatched Kimura's supply base at Meiktila. Mandalay fell on March 20, and Slim's forces raced Kimura southward.

Rangoon fell to Slim's XV Corps on May 2, 1945, effectively ending the war in Burma.

984 All through the war Japan maintained the Kwantung Army as a strong buffer in Manchukuo. True, it had been bested in the Nomonhan battles against Zhukov in the summer of 1939, and, true, it had supplied reserves to China and the South Pacific, but it cherished its own honor and stood ready. **985** By August 1945, Soviet marshal Aleksandr Vasilevsky's three *fronts* had eighty divisions, a million men, 5,000 armored vehicles, 26,000 artillery pieces, and 5,000 planes ready for the Japanese on the Siberian-Manchukuo border. This avalanche rolled into Manchukuo and Korea from both east and west just before midnight, August 9, 1945. In six days Vasilevsky's offensive knocked out forty Japanese divisions—the Kwantung Army lost 80,000 killed against a little more than 8,000 Soviet dead and 22,000 wounded. By August 20, Japanese resistance fragmented.

986 This smashing victory by a signatory of the Potsdam Declaration did much to convince the Japanese to end the war—some authorities think it had more effect than the atomic bombs. Certainly it left no place to hide.

987 While Japan struggled against the USSR and against lingering war fanatics in the government, American officials struggled over whether to use the atomic bomb. Secretary of War Henry L. Stimson and Undersecretary of State Joseph C. Grew advocated warning the Japanese before the drops and also assuring them that the emperor could remain. Secretary of State Byrnes objected. President Truman had asked Stimson to chair an interim committee of scientists and statesmen to advise on the use of the atomic bomb. Various approaches were discussed, including whether or not to share the secret and what to do with it. The committee heard scientific and military testimony and recommended the bomb be used to end the war as soon as possible and without warning the Japanese. Military testimony was significant. When Truman assumed office in April 1945, American casualties were running at about nine hundred a day, and rising. A military debate about what would be needed to force a Japanese surrender divided the generals. Hap Arnold's and Curtis LeMay's view was that B-29s could do it alone, while General Marshall and General MacArthur held the view that a home island invasion using ground troops would be required. Truman accepted the idea that an invasion would be necessary, but the estimated losses appalled him. Marshall talked of a two-stage attack, one on Kyushu Island in November 1945 and the second on Honshu in March 1946—at a cost of no less than half a million casualties, possibly even a million.

Those numbers had a serious impact on Truman as he made the personal decision to use the bomb without warning. He never second-guessed himself, and Churchill staunchly supported him then and later.

988 **Targets were selected by a committee, which put Kyoto at the top of its list.** Stimson personally intervened and forbade Kyoto being hit. Although it had some war industry, it was a world renowned cultural, architectural, and religious center, and he feared bombing it might drive Japan into Russia's orbit after the war. His intervention resulted in the addition of Nagasaki (large shipyards and steel works) to the committee's target list of Kokura (munitions), Hiroshima (major army and navy installations), and Niigata (large port).

THE LAST ACTS

989 **From the island of Tinian at about 2:00 A.M. on August 6, 1945, a B-29, the "Enola Gay," commanded by Col. Paul W. Tibbets Jr., took off for Japan.** Tibbets ranked as the most experienced U.S. B-29 pilot. The plane was one of those he had prepared carefully over several months of training for delivering an atomic bomb on

Colonel Paul W. Tibbets Jr., pilot of the B-29 Superfortress "Enola Gay," before the mission to drop the atomic bomb on Hiroshima, August 6, 1945.

Japan. After 6:00 A.M. the bomb, named "Little Boy," was armed, and Tibbets told his crew they were carrying the world's first atomic bomb.

In good weather the crew saw Hiroshima spread out under them a little past eight in the morning. The bomb was dropped at 8:16. Tibbets said "a bright light filled the plane. We turned back to look at Hiroshima. The city was hidden by that awful cloud . . . boiling up, mushrooming." Everybody pointed, "Look at that! Look at that!" yelled copilot Robert Lewis, who noted the leaden taste of fission and then turned to write in his diary: "My God, what have we done?"

990 **Under a 20,000-foot-high mushroom cloud more than 60,000 people perished—again that many would die later. More than 80 percent of the city's buildings vanished or collapsed.**

991 At 10:58 A.M., August 9, a plutonium implosion bomb, "Fat Man," detonated over Nagasaki, initially killing more than 35,000 (40,000 later) and flattening half the city. As Truman renewed massive air raids, the Japanese government debated the future. **992** Finally the unprecedented happened. The prime minister, unable to get a cabinet consensus, asked the emperor's intervention. Hirohito said he felt compelled to accept the Potsdam terms and made an imperial broadcast to his people: the war was over.

Allied prisoners of war at the Aomori camp near Yokohama cheer their U.S. Navy liberators, August 29, 1945.

Mushroom cloud column rising over 60,000 feet in the air over Nagasaki, site of the second atomic bomb dropped on Japan, August 9, 1945.

Spectators and photographers crowd decks of USS *Missouri*, awaiting the surrender ceremony, September 2, 1945.

ABOVE: Japanese representatives led by Foreign Minister Shigemitsu and Gen. Yoshijiro Umezu arrive aboard the *Missouri*, which was moored in Tokyo Bay. BELOW: General Douglas MacArthur signs the formal surrender documents. Behind him stand two gaunt figures: U.S. Lt. Gen. Jonathan Wainwright (front) and British Lt. Gen. Arthur E. Percival, both of whom had been POWs of the Japanese.

993 **Soviet troops continued driving into Manchukuo until the Kwantung Army surrendered.** Stalin wanted to grab what had been promised him at Yalta and sent paratroops and some of the Red Fleet to Dairen and Port Arthur, then scooped up the Kuriles and southern Sakhalin Island. Various imperial forces quickly surrendered all over the Pacific and in Southeast Asia—save for occasional diehards who held out.

994 **MacArthur fittingly stage-managed the last act of a war that killed between fifty and seventy million people.** Scrubbed and trimmed, the USS *Missouri* would be the site of the formal ceremony. There came now a truly "Skinny" General Wainwright and another emaciated former POW, Gen. Arthur Percival of Singapore, plus scribes and pundits and photographers to record a moment that looked somehow greater than the Fall of Rome. Brass shining, all at attention, the Allies waited for the enemy that sunny Sunday, September 2, 1945.

995 **MacArthur opened with short and courteous remarks, then Foreign Minister Mamoru Shigemitsu, in striped pants and top hat, came forward to a table on the foredeck. Hat off, pen in hand, he signed the unconditional surrender document for the Japanese empire, as did a representative of the Imperial General Staff.** Flanked by Wainwright and Percival, MacArthur came forward and signed, as did Admiral Nimitz and other Allied delegates.

996 **MacArthur, a noted rhetorician, made one of his best speeches, concluding with a ringing peroration:**

It is my earnest hope . . . that from this solemn occasion a better world shall emerge . . . a world dedicated to the dignity of man. . . . Let us pray that peace be now restored to the world, and that God will preserve it always.

These proceedings are closed.

Holding up copies of a special "Japs Quit" edition of the *Paris Post,* jubilant American military personnel celebrate at the Rainbow Corner Red Cross Club in Paris, August 10, 1945.

President Harry S Truman announces Japan's surrender, White House, Washington, D.C., August 14, 1945.

997 But not all proceedings were closed: in the Moscow Declaration after the Moscow Conference in October 1943, the Big Three Allies—USA, Britain, USSR—announced that "war criminals" would, somehow, be brought to book for the atrocities they committed during the war. Victors usually exact some sort of spoils, of course, but this war had spawned mass horrors beyond belief, and something would have to be done to insure that such inhumanities never happened again. Just how this would be achieved remained vague until two days after the atomic bomb mushroomed over Hiroshima—August 8, 1945—when a Four-Power Agreement signed in London set a legal framework. There would be two major jurisdictions—Europe and the Far East, with separate trials for each.

998 Some argument stirred around procedures. The U.S. wanted full trials, while the British argued that punishment was a political rather than a judicial matter and should be handled summarily. Finally the USSR backed the U.S. view. A special jurisdiction—the International Military Tribunal—would be created with one judge and one alternate from each of the signatory states.

Prosecutors in the European trials, centered at Nuremberg—although the IMT's official seat was Berlin—encountered some embarrassments in pushing indictments because of such historical precedents as Britain and France offering Hitler a virtually free hand before and at the Munich settlement, the USSR's condoning German expansion in central Europe, and U.S./British mass bombing of such cities as Dresden and Hamburg.

999 Official proceedings began in October 1945 with a joint statement of indictment for twenty-four prisoners. The indictments came under four broad areas: execution of a "common plan or conspiracy"; "crimes against peace"; "war crimes"; "crimes against humanity." The third category had the best base in Geneva Convention precedent. An early attempt to bring whole categories of functionaries to trial—such as the SS, various security corps, medical experimenters, and concentration camp administrators—gave way quickly to concern for the individual guilt of those accused.

The accused had legal representation and all received fairly good opportunities for defense. Among them were Göring, now cured of drugs and impressively cogent in his own behalf, Rudolf Hess, whose attention wavered; former diplomat Joachim von Ribbentrop, who appeared astounded to be on trial; such military figures as Field Marshal Keitel, whose arrogance never flagged; General Jodl, Admirals Raeder and Dönitz—all of whom argued for immunity under the rubric of following orders; Ernst Kaltenbrunner of the SS, who made little effort to hide his brutality; the apparently regenerate Albert Speer, who denied personal culpability for using slave laborers but surprised the court by accepting general guilt for being a member of the Nazi government.

1000 Verdicts were announced in October 1946. Eleven defendants got a death sentence, others were given various jail stints, and Franz von Papen, wily manipulator, was acquitted. All those sentenced to death were hanged in mid-October, all save Göring, who took poison scant hours before the hanging.

No further sessions of the full IMT were held. Burgeoning troubles between the Allies ended them, although individual countries carried out their own trials in their respective zones of Germany. The U.S. conducted a dozen trials, acquitted thirty-five defendants, executed twenty-four, and sentenced eighty-seven others to jail terms.

Unprecedented, perhaps of uncertain legality, the Nuremberg trials did reveal to Germans and to the world irrefutable evidence of Nazi horrors.

1001 Far Eastern trials began in Tokyo in May 1946 and continued to November 1948. Twenty-eight Japanese military and civilian leaders were indicted as the most serious war criminals, including Tojo; there were other lesser categories. The defense did a sound

ABOVE: Gaunt prisoners at Ebensee, Austria, a concentration camp whose inmates were used for "scientific" experiments, May 7, 1945. BELOW: Defendants at the International Military Tribunal trials, Nuremberg, 1945-46 (front row): Hermann Göring (facing forward), Rudolf Hess, Joachim von Ribbentrop, and Wilhelm Keitel. The white-helmeted guards were called "snowdrops."

job in exposing the fragile bases of the trials, indicating time and again that international law did not condemn people for acts of state, nor for failing to prevent others from breaking laws and committing war crimes. These objections were dismissed and the indictments stood.

Dubious procedures further disturbed the Far Eastern trials—defendants were selected with a view to the weight of evidence against them; certain likely defendants were arbitrarily exempted (Hirohito, for instance); some judges were hardly qualified and obviously prejudiced (one of them had been on the Bataan Death March). Rules of evidence wavered and charges were inconsistently drawn.

Seven defendants were condemned to the gallows, including Tojo, and, after MacArthur personally approved the sentences, they died on December 23, 1948. The court was divided in its judgment, with several justices dissenting, and at least one arguing that all the defendants were not guilty.

There were also regional trials held in various places of former Japanese domination, but they were generally less infamous than the ones in Tokyo.

The case of General Yamashita (q.v.), though, who was tried in October 1945 by an American military tribunal in Manila, exemplified the highly biased intervention of General MacArthur and seriously damaged the court's image. These judicial farces demeaned the entire concept of the postwar attempts to hold accountable the war's criminals.

Some people argue that the trials, the dressing up of the ritual of "winners take all" in robes of justice, were obscene. But the problem was the enormity of crimes in World War II. So enormous, so far beyond conception were they, so soiling, that it seems mankind itself wanted some sort of damnation for humanity's failure in the worst war of recorded history.

INDEX

Page numbers of photographs and illustrations appear in italics.

PERMISSIONS

Excerpts from *Men at War*, copyright © 1942 by Crown Publishers, and *Year at Stalingrad*, copyright © 1946 by Alexander Werth, reprinted by permission of Random House.

"A Refusal to Mourn the Death, by Fire, of a Child in London," by Dylan Thomas, from *The Poems of Dylan Thomas*, copyright © 1945 by The Trustees for the Copyrights of Dylan Thomas, reprinted (U.S.) by permission of New Directions Publishing Corp. Reprinted (Canada and U.K.) by permission of David Higham Associates.

"The Last Time I Saw Paris," words, lyrics by Oscar Hammerstein II and music by Jerome Kern, copyright © 1941, reprinted by permission of Universal Music Company.

"Praise the Lord and Pass the Ammunition," words and music by Frank Loesser, copyright © 1942 (renewed 1969) by Famous Music Corporation, reprinted by permission of Hal Leonard Corporation.

Maps from *The West Point Atlas of American Wars, Vol. II, 1900–1953*, Section 2: World War II, copyright © 1959 by Frederick A. Praeger, Inc., reprinted by permission of Greenwood Publishing Group, Inc.

"Comin' in on a Wing and a Prayer," lyrics by Harold Adamson and music by Jimmy McHugh, copyright © 1942.

PHOTOGRAPHIC SOURCES

The author and publisher wish to thank the following who have kindly given permission to reproduce the photographs on the following pages.

IWM (Imperial War Museum)
NA (National Archives and Records Administration; public domain)
NASM (National Air and Space Museum, Smithsonian Institution)

Page 3 (*top*) IWM 01, (*bottom*) IWM HU 55569; page 5 (*top*) NA 208-PR-10L-3, (*bottom*) IWM A42; page 6 (*top*) NA 208-PP10A-1, (*bottom*) IWM A23442; page 7 NA 242-EB-7-35; page 8 (*top*) IWM MH1926, (*bottom*) NA 242-HLB-5073-20; page 9 IWM HU 68019; page 10 IWM C 5422; page 11 (*top*) NA 306-NT-2743-V, (*bottom*) NA 306-NT-3160-V; page 12 IWM E839; page 14 IWM 46; page 18 German Private Collection, Bild Nr. 2, Gruppe 33; page 19 German Private Collection, Bild Nr. 92, Gruppe 28; page 20 NA 242-EB 7-38; page 21 IWM H 3277; page 23 IWM 4255; page 31 IWM MH 13143; page 32 German Private Collection, Bild Nr. 145, Gruppe 31; page 36 NA 242-HB-47721-306; page 43 NA 080-G-30550; page 44 (*top*) NA 080-G-3240, (*bottom*) NA 080-G-19947; page 45 (*top left*) NA 080-G-19943, (*top right*) NA 080-G-32915, (*bottom*) NA 080-G-16871; page 47 NA 079-AR-92; page 48 NASM A-43680-E; page 53 IWM HU 1205; page 54 IWM MH5591; page 55 IWM HU 39586; page 57 IWM HU 40176; page 58 IWM A14897; page 62 IWM HU 76027; page 67 IWM MISC 54424; page 69 (*top*) IWM HU 65956, (*bottom*) IWM D1568; page 70 (*top*) NA 306-NT-3173V, (*bottom*) IWM H3514; page 73 (*left*) NA 242-EAPC-6-713A, (*right*) IWM HU 381; page 75 NA 064-M-276; page 77 NA 80-JO-63430; page 80 IWM NAP 284316; page 81 NA 242-JRPE-44; page 89 IWM A14899; page 97 (*top*) NA 208-X-6177-D, (*bottom*) NA 210-G-3B-424; page 98 (*left*) NA 179-WP-1563, (*right*) NA 208-AA-352X-1; page 99 NA 111-SC-334265; page 100 NA 208-AA-80B-1; page 101 (*top*) NA 208-AA-288-BB2, (*bottom*) NA 208-11-12X-21; page 102 NA 080-G-41196; page 104 (*top*) NA 111-SC-134627, (*bottom*) NA 080-G-12076; page 105 NA 080-G-17054; page 109 (*top*) NA 208-PU-195GG-1, (*bottom*) NA 044-PA-777; page 112 IWM C5816; page 120 IWM MH 9704; page 121 NA 111-SC-206174; page 123 IWM E18511; page 124 NA 208-PU-138LL-3; page 135 NA 080-G-490488; page 137 NA 80-G-53855; page 143 NA 306-NT-1391-7; page 144 NA 208 COM 482; page 145 NA 208-COM-1084; page 146 NA 044-PA-1748; page 149 NA 226-FPL-2665A; page 150 NA 111-SC-180476; page 151 IWM NYF9892; page 153 IWM K5287; page 154 NA 111-SC-179564; page 155 IWM E26634; page 159 (*top*) NA 127-CASA-71, (*bottom*) NA 127-119-64002; page 167 IWM A16486; page 170 NA 111-SC-203464, NA 111-SC-203461; page 174 NA 208-YE-2B-7; page 175 NA 111-SC-192258; page 179 IWM HU 55161; page 180 NA 111-SC-187704; page 181 IWM MH1984; page 182 IWM EA26941; page 185 NA 111-SC-194568; page 187 (*top*) NA 111-SC-193903, (*bottom*) NA 111-SC-194568-S; page 188 IWM HU 66477; page 189 NA 111-SC-193997; page 191 (*top*) IWM CL3407, (*bottom*) NA 111-SC197455; page 192 (*top*) NA 111-SC-222396, (*bottom*) NA 80G-239549; page 193 (*top*) NA 080-G-59493, (*bottom*) NA 127-N-72208; page 194 (*top*) NA 111-SC-212770, (*bottom*) NA 127-N-88073; page 196 NA 127-N-82619; page 197 NA 80G-238-322; page 199 (*top*) NA 26-G-3566, (*bottom*) NA 111-SC-40701; page 203 IWM MH4489; page 206 (*top*) NA 111-SC-198263, (*bottom*) NA 111-SC-201144; page 209 NA 260-MGG-1061-1; page 211 NA 111-SC-197660; page 212 IWM HU44874; page 213 NA 111-SC-197661; page 217 NA 111-SC-260486; page 220 NA 208-YE-182; page 221 NA 111-SC-2323989; page 224 NA 111-SC-210796; page 225 (*top*) NA 111-SC-337154, (*bottom*) IWM 50252; page 226 (*top*) NA 080-G-59525, (*bottom*) NA 111-SC-211907; page 227 NASM 2000-4554; page 228 NA 026-G-4098; page 229 NA 80-G-413988; page 230 IWM NYF 70679; page 231 (*top*) NA 080-G-32317, (*bottom*) NA 080-G-328610; page 232 (*top left*) NA 080-G-346694, (*top right*) NA 127-N-126599, (*bottom*) NA 111-SC-211476; page 234 IWM HU44924; page 235 IWM C5635; page 236 (*top*) NA 208-YE-193, (*bottom*) NA 111-SC-204516; page 237 NA 111-SC-231809; page 238 (*top*) IWM 68178, (*bottom*) NA 111-SC-206292; page 239 (*top*) NA 111-SC-206681, (*bottom*) NA 208-PU-154F-5; page 240 NA 208-AA-342BB-1; page 241 IWM BU 9192; page 243 NA 111-SC-208807; page 244 NA 208-LU-13H-5; page 245 (*left*) NA 208-N-43888, (*top right*) NA 080-G-490444, (*bottom right*) NA 111-SC-210644; page 246 (*top*) NA 111-SC-210626, (*bottom*) NA 080-G-348366; page 247 (*top*) NA 111-SC-210208, (*bottom*) NA 079-AR-508Q; page 249 (*top*) NA 111-SC-204480, (*bottom*) NA 238-NT-612.

FRANK E. VANDIVER, President Emeritus of Texas A&M University and former Acting President of Rice University and of the American University of Cairo, is currently director of the Mosher Institute for Defense Studies at Texas A&M. His previous books include *Mighty Stonewall, Their Tattered Flags: The Epic of the Confederacy, Black Jack: The Life and Times of John J. Pershing*, and *Blood Brothers: A Short History of the Civil War*. He lives in College Station, Texas.